The Presidencies of
ZACHARY TAYLOR
&
MILLARD FILLMORE

AMERICAN PRESIDENCY SERIES

Clifford S. Griffin and Donald R. McCoy, Founding Editors
Homer E. Socolofsky, General Editor

George Washington, Forrest McDonald
John Adams, Ralph Adams Brown
Thomas Jefferson, Forrest McDonald
James Madison, Robert Allen Rutland
James Monroe, Noble E. Cunningham, Jr.
John Quincy Adams, Mary W. M. Hargreaves
Andrew Jackson, Donald B. Cole
Martin Van Buren, Major L. Wilson
William Henry Harrison & John Tyler, Norma Lois Peterson
James K. Polk, Paul H. Bergeron
Zachary Taylor & Millard Fillmore, Elbert B. Smith
Franklin Pierce, Larry Gara
James Buchanan, Elbert B. Smith
Abraham Lincoln, Phillip Shaw Paludan
Andrew Johnson, Albert Castel
Rutherford B. Hayes, Ari Hoogenboom
James A. Garfield & Chester A. Arthur, Justus D. Doenecke
Grover Cleveland, Richard E. Welch, Jr.
Benjamin Harrison, Homer B. Socolofsky & Allan B. Spetter
William McKinley, Lewis L. Gould
Theodore Roosevelt, Lewis L. Gould
William Howard Taft, Paolo E. Coletta
Woodrow Wilson, Kendrick A. Clements
Warren G. Harding, Eugene P. Trani & David L. Wilson
Calvin Coolidge, Robert H. Ferrell
Herbert C. Hoover, Martin L. Fausold
Harry S. Truman, Donald R. McCoy
Dwight D. Eisenhower, Chester J. Pach, Jr., & Elmo Richardson
John F. Kennedy, James N. Giglio
Lyndon B. Johnson, Vaughn Davis Bornet
Richard Nixon, Melvin Small
Gerald R. Ford, John Robert Greene
James Earl Carter, Jr., Burton I. Kaufman
George Bush, John Robert Greene

The Presidencies of
ZACHARY TAYLOR
&
MILLARD FILLMORE

Elbert B. Smith

UNIVERSITY PRESS OF KANSAS

Published by the University Press of Kansas (Lawrence,
Kansas 66049), which was organized by the Kansas
Board of Regents and is operated and funded by Emporia
State University, Fort Hays State University,
Kansas State University, Pittsburg State University, the
University of Kansas, and Wichita State University

Library of Congress Cataloging-in-Publication Data

Smith, Elbert B.
The presidencies of Zachary Taylor & Millard Fillmore.
(American presidency series)
Bibliography: p.
Includes index.
1. United States—Politics and government—1849–1853.
2. Taylor, Zachary, 1784–1850. 3. Fillmore, Millard,
1800–1874. I. Title. II. Title: Presidencies of
Zachary Taylor and Millard Fillmore.
E421.S65   1988   973.6   88-5722
ISBN 0-7006-0362-X (alk. paper)

British Library Cataloguing in Publication data is available.

Printed in the United States of America
10 9 8 7 6 5 4

The paper used in this publication meets the
minimum requirements of the American National
Standard for Permanence of Paper for
Printed Library Materials Z39.48–1984.

To the memory of Nikolai Sivachev who,
like the peacemakers of 1850,
dreamed of reconciliation and peaceful change

CONTENTS

FOREWORD

The aim of the American Presidency Series is to present historians and the general reading public with interesting, scholarly assessments of the various presidential administrations. These interpretive surveys are intended to cover the broad ground between biographies, specialized monographs, and journalistic accounts. As such, each will be a comprehensive, synthetic work which will draw upon the best in pertinent secondary literature, yet leave room for the author's own analysis and interpretation.

Volumes in the series will present the data essential to understanding the administration under consideration. Particularly, each book will treat the then current problems facing the United States and its people and how the president and his associates felt about, thought about, and worked to cope with these problems. Attention will be given to how the office developed and operated during the president's tenure. Equally important will be consideration of the vital relationships between the president, his staff, the executive officers, Congress, foreign representatives, the judiciary, state officials, the public, political parties, the press, and influential private citizens. The series will also be concerned with how this unique American institution—the presidency—was viewed by the presidents, and with what results.

All this will be set, insofar as possible, in the context not only of contemporary politics but also of economics, international relations, law, morals, public administration, religion, and thought. Such a broad approach is necessary to understanding, for a presidential administration is more than the elected and appointed officers composing it, since its work so often reflects the major problems, anxieties, and glories of the nation. In short, the authors in this series will strive to recount and evaluate the record of each administration and to identify its distinctiveness and relationships to the past, its own time, and the future.

The General Editors

ACKNOWLEDGMENTS

While writing this book I have incurred many debts. I am grateful to earlier biographers and other historians from whose work I have profited; librarians who provided, borrowed, and loaned for me; copy editor Virginia Seaver, for reasons every author will know; colleague George Callcott, who was a devil's advocate and listened until his ears grew weary; Mark Stegmaier and Carolyn Hoffman for valuable suggestions; the University of Maryland for an ideal environment and working conditions conducive to professional achievement; Emory Evans and Richard Price for generosity in administering the university's clerical services; Richard Farrell for optimum teaching schedules; an uncomplaining office staff that saved me much labor; this includes Margaret Burkett, June Charney, Abid Qureshi, Pat Honey, and especially Patricia Linton, who spent many long hours on the word-processor, and Darlene King, who added the final touches; and my wife Jean, who tolerates much and still makes every day a joy.

1

★ ★ ★ ★ ★

PROGRESS AND PARADOX

The United States in 1848 was a nation of many paradoxes. The prevailing mood of those who expressed themselves publicly was one of exuberant pride and optimism, but for many these feelings were tempered by bad consciences, hurt pride, and angry resentments. The war with Mexico had been tragic enough for its casualties and their families, but the number was relatively small, and they were soon forgotten by the fortunate survivors. Zachary Taylor and Winfield Scott had won spectacular victories and had joined the pantheon of American heroes, and Scott had declared that Robert E. Lee was the greatest soldier of his lifetime. Ulysses S. Grant's performance was less spectacular but equally brave, and Jefferson Davis had served his father-in-law, Taylor, with sufficient ability and dedication to end their long estrangement. American marines would never be allowed to forget "the halls of Montezuma." More important, an envoy named Nicholas P. Trist had ignored the fact that President James K. Polk had discharged him several weeks earlier and had negotiated a peace treaty that added a vast new territory to the United States. Texas and California—the land of giants and the golden paradise—as well as the future states of Arizona, New Mexico, and Utah had been firmly attached, although in 1858, President James Buchanan would have to send an army to convince the Utah Mormons of the blessings they would enjoy as bona fide Americans. Furthermore, President Polk had reached a fair compromise with the British that gave the United States a clear title to what are now Oregon and Washington. The new empire would include the magnificent harbors of San Diego, Los Angeles, San Francisco, Portland, and Puget Sound. Senator Thomas Hart Benton of Missouri had prophesied in 1825 that transcontinental railroads and the course of nature would eventually link New York with India and China, and many others were now beginning to share what had once seemed a foolish pipe dream. Some had seriously advocated the annexation of Mexico itself, but Southerners eager to acquire Texas for slavery had developed second thoughts about incorporating a land where a dark-skinned majority had already abolished the institution. Equally important, these rich prizes had been taken with a minimal financial cost, and the nation's economy was booming. Soon the world would learn about the golden stones at Sutter's Fort in California, and a new burst of technological progress was already under way.[1]

Nowhere was there any danger of filling up all the empty spaces, even though the population was growing almost as fast as the nation's area. The United States had expanded from 1,753,588 square miles in 1840 to 2,944,337 square miles in 1850—an increase of almost 68 percent. The ebullient population, meanwhile, had leapt from 17,069,453 to 23,191,876 during the same period—an increase of almost 36 percent.

Everywhere one looked, great fortunes were being made without the governmental assistance that business had once hoped for. With Southerners leading the way, government-supported banks and protective tariffs on necessities had been eliminated, but they no longer seemed necessary. Pre–Civil War statistics are sketchy, but they tell a remarkable story. The production of Pennsylvania anthracite coal jumped from 1,129,000 short tons in 1840 to 4,172,000 tons in 1850. By 1860 the figure would be 10,984,000 tons. Corresponding figures for bituminous coal were 1,345,000; 4,029,000; and 9,057,000. Pig-iron foundries turned out 287,000 short tons in 1840; 563,000 in 1850; and 821,000 in 1860. The burgeoning network of telegraph wires and other industrial uses drove the copper output from 112 short tons in 1845 to 728 in 1850 and 8,064 by 1860. Thanks to California, the production of the gold necessary to support the bank notes of a private banking system increased from 24,000 ounces in 1840 to 2,419,000 ounces in 1850. Excluding home manufactures and the products of the independent hand trades, the value of manufactured products, less the value of materials consumed in production, rose from $240 million in 1839 to $310 million in 1845 and $450 million in 1849. The corresponding figures for agriculture were $710 million in 1839, $690 million in 1845, and $830 million in 1849. Cotton was by far the most valuable crop and the nation's largest export, bringing in $64 million from overseas in 1840, $72 million in 1850, and $270 million in 1860. America's total exports of goods and services, including transportation and travel, increased from $160,000 in 1840 to $166 million in 1850 and $438 million in 1860, but during the same years the imports for consumption grew even faster, from $134 million to $210 million and then $438 million. Small wonder that the prophets of Manifest Destiny had a strong following.[2]

Much of this spectacular growth had been possible because of the never-ending efforts by Americans to create better tools and machines. Despite the achievements of brilliant scientific thinkers like Joseph Henry, Benjamin Silliman, Asa Gray, and Benjamin Pierce, and despite the generous £100,000 bequest of the Englishman James Smithson for "the increase and diffusion of knowledge among men," the United States still lagged behind Europe in scientific study and research. In the development of new technology, however, the brash young nation was unsurpassed. Between 1840 and 1850, budding American inventors applied for 13,297 patents and received 6,033. Only a relative few of the inventions were successful, but they changed the lives of a great many people.[3]

By 1850, numerous men had patented various methods for cultivating and harvesting grain, but the two most successful were John Deere and Cyrus H. McCormick. The early Southerners who had migrated to the Old Northwest had often ignored the fertile prairies because of a belief that soil barren of trees would not grow crops and because of the inability of their crude plows to cut through the thickly rooted grass. In 1837, however, Deere and Maj. Leonard Andrus developed a steel plow capable of slicing through the prairie turf, and in 1847 Deere opened his factory at Moline, Illinois. In 1834, meanwhile, McCormick had patented a successful reaper, and in 1847 he had established in Chicago the company destined to become International Harvester. Northeasterners and immigrants who were not prejudiced against treeless plains quickly plowed them up and harvested a rich reward. Other factors were partially responsible, but corn production grew from 378 million bushels in 1839 to 592 million in 1849 and 839 million by 1859. Cotton, however, remained a labor-intensive crop, with Eli Whitney's gin for removing the seeds being the only major new technology until the invention of a planter in 1875. Weather was a prime factor in the success or failure of cotton in any given year, but the 1849 crop of 2,469,000 bales was the highest to date in Southern history.[4]

Transportation and communications facilities were growing even faster. The Baltimore and Ohio Company had opened the first thirteen miles of railroad track in 1830, and a line from Charleston to Hamburg, South Carolina, soon followed. By 1840 the rails covered 2,818 miles, and by 1850 they had been stretched to 9,021 miles. This figure would double by 1855 and reach 30,626 miles by 1860. By 1848 Chicago was already on its way toward becoming America's largest railroad center, and Stephen A. Douglas had begun to dream of an Illinois Central road that might help solve the sectional conflict by linking Chicago with Mobile, Alabama. The speed and the carrying capacity of the railroads were also increasing, and the first sleeping cars for passengers had appeared in 1837. The touch of luxury exemplified by the first Pullman car would be introduced in 1859. Already could be seen the faint outlines of a political struggle over whether the first railroad to California would begin in Chicago, St. Louis, Memphis, or New Orleans.[5]

Americans had always been fortunate in the location of their ocean harbors and navigable streams and had done much to link them up with great canals. For several years, large paddle-wheel steamers had already been plying the major rivers, and in 1847 the United States government subsidized the first two transatlantic paddle-engine steamers for service between New York and Bremen, Germany, via Southampton, England. Three years later a second steamer line of two similar ships was established to connect New York and Le Havre, France, and others soon followed. Working in London before emigrating to the United States in 1839, the Swedish captain John Ericsson had patented and demonstrated the advantages of the screw propeller in 1836. The British took the early lead in using this concept on ocean-going ships and in building their hulls with iron instead of wood. Americans, however, would soon follow this trend, and during the 1840s and the 1850s they still had the great Yankee clippers, the fastest large sailing vessels ever built. American commerce had become important in virtually every part of the world, with Great Britain being by far the nation's most important trading partner. In the years 1840 to 1850, American shipyards produced 12,714 documented merchant ships totaling 1,958,262 tons, and new ships totaling 456,997 tons were driven by steam and motors. Many of these, of course, were relatively small, but in 1850, American ships totaling 1,440,000 tons were engaged in overseas trade.[6]

Building upon the earlier discoveries of numerous Europeans as well as upon those of Benjamin Franklin and Joseph Henry, Samuel F. B. Morse in 1844 had connected Washington and Baltimore with the first experimental telegraph line. "What hath God wrought?" was Ezra Cornell's first message on the magic wire, and soon editors and politicians were gathered around a receiver in Washington, eagerly waiting to learn what had been wrought by the Democratic party's 1844 presidential nominating convention. The railroad tracks provided a natural right of way for telegraph poles and wires, and the new miracle of instant long-distance communication quickly grew like a spider web. By 1850 most of the major cities in the United States were linked, and a telegram from New York to Chicago cost only $1.55. The nearby city of Philadelphia could be reached for only twenty-five cents.[7]

Similarly, the replacement of stagecoaches by the railroads brought a revolution in postal communication. In 1848, with branches and stations excluded, there were 16,159 post offices, but the number climbed steadily to 24,410 in 1855 and to 28,488 by 1860.[8] Among other effects were the added opportunities and headaches incurred by the politicians with influence in selecting the postmasters and the postal clerks. Also, the telegraph and the faster mail service added an aura of authenticity to the news reports and editorials of local newspapers without in any way guaranteeing their accuracy and logic or reducing the personal stake of the editors in disseminating support for their own favorite viewpoints and politicians.

Jacksonian democracy, with its egalitarian emphasis, had both reflected and helped to create ambivalent attitudes toward education. In 1850 a majority of adult Americans had enjoyed very little formal schooling, and they were prone to idealize the self-made man who had risen from humble beginnings to achieve either wealth or high military or political status, or both. Daniel Webster, in his never-ending quest for the presidency, often reminded audiences that while he had not been fortunate enough to live in a log cabin, his older brother had enjoyed that distinction, and he himself had missed it by only a few short years. Andrew Jackson had brilliantly played the role of masterful leader endowed with intuitive talents unencumbered by schoolbook learning. The Whigs had briefly sought to offset the Jackson image with the redoubtable Tennessee backwoodsman Davy Crockett, and in 1840 they had elected William Henry Harrison president with a "log cabin and hard-cider campaign" quite unrelated to Harrison's actual experience and life style. Both Zachary Taylor and Abraham Lincoln would profit greatly from the same stereotype. Taylor had never been poor, but his years on the frontier and his disdain for pomp and circumstance fit the image very well.[9]

Still, most Americans recognized the advantages of education as a practical instrument in the never-ending competition for greater wealth and status. They wanted it for their children, although those who could afford private schools angrily objected to the idea of paying taxes to educate the children of the less fortunate. In colonial New England the church-dominated local governments had insisted that each community provide schools, and in 1850 a great many elementary schools and most of the colleges in America were still church-sponsored. In some states, public schools existed for the poor, but because of the stigma attached and because the children were often needed at home, most poor families would not send their children to them.

Inevitably, however, the rhetoric of Jacksonian democracy inspired the ideal of free, universal, secular education for everyone except Indians, blacks, and possibly women, depending upon the state. Zealots like James G. Carter, Horace Mann, Henry Barnard, Calvin Wiley, Charles Mercer, and Ninian Edwards, to name only a few, wanted tax support for free and equal schools, state control of the systems, and complete freedom from religious sectarianism. Although they faced strong opposition from taxpayers and from various church groups, by 1850 their goals had been achieved in several Northern states, and the issue was being debated in others. In 1850, 59 percent of all white males and 53 percent of all white females between the ages of five and nineteen were enrolled in a school of some sort. The percentages were probably much higher in the North, but in both sections, large numbers of children attended school for only part of the year and did not advance to a very high level.[10]

While most of the nearly two hundred institutions that called themselves colleges and universities in 1850 were either church-sponsored or endowed by wealthy donors, or both, the movement toward secular and public state universities had also made great progress. Certain narrow religious interests successfully opposed the creation of state universities in seven Northern states before the Civil War, but another twenty states could boast of their institutions— some of them fledglings and some of long standing, with a corresponding variety as to quality and size. Among the slaveholding states, only Texas, Arkansas, and Louisiana could not claim a state college or university, and these three would soon correct the deficiency.[11]

Expanded educational opportunities were supplemented by faster and cheaper methods of printing, which multiplied the newspapers, magazines, and books available to a voracious readership. Foreign visitors often commented that everyone in America seemed to be reading something. The technical machinery for producing an informed electorate was present, but the accuracy of the information rested too often upon the prejudices of the dispensers. Virtually every newspaper or magazine, as well as some of the fiction and poetry, supported a cause, a political party, or a particular politician and slanted its news or opinions accordingly. Particularly important were the Washington newspapers, which sent out a stream of news stories and editorials to be copied or paraphrased by editors of similar persuasion. Washington papers like the virulently Democratic *Union* and the more staid Whig *National Intelligencer* sent out the truth to the faithful and then reprinted local editorials from everywhere to show mass support for their own principles. Papers from the larger cities like New York, Boston, Philadelphia, and nearby Baltimore also had reporters in Washington, as did the smaller but sometimes locally even-more-influential Southern cities like Charleston, Atlanta, New Orleans, and Montgomery.[12]

Under different circumstances the advances in technology and education and the rapidly growing wealth and equality of opportunity in both sections might have produced intellectual, philosophical, religious, and political movements capable of welding the nation into a patriotic unit that could not be challenged. In fact, however, the institution of slavery had created a force that inevitably pushed the editors, orators, philosophers, novelists, poets, and religious leaders of each section in opposite directions.

Northern opinion makers in general had responded to the social evils that accompanied the early stages of industrialism by launching reform movements designed to shape American life according to the ideals of the Declaration of Independence and the social teachings of Christianity. Most of them voted Whig, but they were thoroughly in tune with the egalitarian doctrines preached, if not always practiced, by the Jacksonian Democrats. Better wages, fewer working hours, better working conditions, care for the poverty-stricken, support for the very young and the aged, women's rights, world peace, protection of seamen from harsh captains and the repeal of cruel maritime laws, efforts to provide Christian recreation for sailors to save them from the saloons and brothels, better treatment for animals, and the elimination or restriction of tobacco and alcohol were some of the goals supported by new philosophical and religious ideas that claimed God as an ally for the reformers. Virtually all the great names in Northern literature, theology, and philosophy were involved in one way or another.[13]

Inevitably the Northern reform spirit also turned to harsh criticisms of Southern slavery and the organization of movements dedicated to its end. By 1850 the abolitionists constituted a noisy, easily identified group that was attempting to win converts with journals, pamphlets, sermons, and speeches. Most abolitionists were not troubled by any feelings of responsibility for helping solve any Southern problems that an abrupt abolition might cause. Also, even those who recognized the magnitude and complexity of the issue were handicapped by Northern racial and ethnic prejudices that kept most Northerners quite unwilling to tamper with slavery where it already existed. They could attack slavery with harsh words, but they could not approach their fellow Southerners as representatives of a Northern majority willing to cooperate and share whatever social and economic problems the end of slavery might create. They represented only a small minority of the total Northern population, but their very existence was considered an insult by proud Southerners.[14]

During and immediately after the American Revolution, the South had had its own antislavery movements and discussions, featuring the objections of men like George Washington, St. George Tucker, Thomas Jefferson, and John Randolph. However, after the horrible race war between the Haitians and the French in the late 1790s, Denmark Vesey's rebellion in South Carolina (whether real or imagined) in 1822, Nat Turner's massacre of fifty-five whites in 1831, and the new Northern antislavery movements in the 1830s, no Southerner dared suggest openly that slavery was anything but a humane institution, supported by the Christian Bible and dedicated to the welfare of the slaves. A Southerner wishing to be published or heard and remain in the South could either ignore slavery or defend it. Ignoring it was difficult, and a well-argued defense was the surest road to popularity and influence. A few, like the Grimké sisters of Charleston and the Alabama planter James G. Birney, emigrated northward to become eloquent abolitionists, but few were willing to make this sacrifice. In the border slave state of Kentucky, the fighting politician Cassius M. Clay could attack slavery and offer to take on all comers with fists, teeth, or guns, but he was a rare phenomenon. Perhaps unfortunately, also, Southern intellectuals could not decry abolition without rejecting the accompanying social, economic, philosophical, and religious radicalism that supported it. In turn, the technological and industrial progress that had spawned the radicalism had to be abjured also. By 1850 Southerners everywhere were insisting that slavery was a positive good—a system providing the South with a stable and serene way of life infinitely superior to the chaotic struggles between rich and poor occurring in the North.[15]

The division was especially important among the churches, where people were taught what they must do or not do to inherit eternal life. In a world of frequent illnesses and death relatively unimpeded by primitive medical care, the churches offered a hope of reunion with loved ones in paradise for the faithful and a threat of dire punishment for the unredeemed and the sinful. Churches also served as gathering places for people of similar religious views who needed one another's company and support. The Roman Catholic Church was rapidly expanding to meet the needs of Irish, German, and other newcomers, but the country in general was overwhelmingly Protestant. Often persecuted during colonial days and still being attacked by nativist groups in the 1840s and 1850s, the Catholic Church sought to keep a low profile and to avoid taking sides in the slavery quarrel. The many shades of Protestantism, however, took a very different course.

In many Northern areas, particularly in New England and in areas settled by former New Englanders, new religious ideas went hand in hand with the reform movements. In churches both new and old, religious leaders stressed the command of the Christian gospel that to be saved the Christian must help and serve the less fortunate. Calvinist, Presbyterian, Congregationalist, and Dutch Reform churches had always taught that those chosen for salvation had a duty to help God make the world better. A new generation of Northern Methodists, Baptists, Campbellites, Christian Perfectionists, and Unitarians, among others, now preached in one form or another the doctrine that salvation could best be attained through service to others. Simultaneously, the older Calvinist pessimism about the natural depravity of man gave way to a belief held by many that human progress was limited only by man's refusal to make the proper efforts to achieve the millennium. This new belief in the natural divinity and the potential perfectibility of man reached its most eloquent expression in the philosophy of Transcendentalism, popularized widely in the hundreds of lectures delivered throughout the North by Ralph Waldo Emerson.[16]

The Southern clergy, however, were compelled to remain orthodox and to condemn or ignore the dangerous radicalism of their Northern brethren. Drawing much of their financial support from the planters, the Southern Protestant churches emphasized salvation through faith and the avoidance of the traditional sins of the flesh. They might advocate more humane treatment for slaves, but none questioned the righteousness of the institution. Indeed, numerous Southern theologians discovered that the slaves were descended from Ham, whose progeny for all time had been condemned to a life of servitude because of his disrespectful conduct toward his father, Noah. Other Southern theologians wrote highly detailed treatises on the moral superiority of slavery over a Northern free-labor system that encouraged most of the sins known to man.[17]

By giving divine approval to slavery if practiced in a humane fashion, the Southern churches may have contributed to the paternalism and the kind treatment practiced by a great many slaveholders. Also, many of the slaves themselves learned the rudiments of a religion that promised a better life in the hereafter. If the Christianity imposed upon slaves made them less likely to rebel or make trouble, and thereby helped to strengthen the institution, it probably made life far more endurable for a significant number of individual slaves.

Most important, however, the Southern churches helped to ease the consciences of slaveholders and enable them to deny to themselves and to each other that slavery was either immoral or unchristian. The opposite viewpoint of Northerners drawing their opinions from the same God and the same Bible was a galling experience. As a result, the nationally organized Methodists in 1844 and Baptists in 1845 split into Northern and Southern churches. The Presbyterians were already somewhat fragmented by other issues, but their major group would also later divide by section in 1861.[18]

We should remember, however, that the abolition of slavery where it already existed was never a popular doctrine among most Northerners. Most of the Northern clergy went no further than their membership and held back from advocating any specific action against slavery. When, however, the argument shifted from slavery per se to the question of extending the institution into new territories, it was a different matter. Northern clergymen, like the members of their flocks, could be rabid free-soilers without the slightest wish to see a horde of Southern slaves released to emigrate northward.

Also, despite the confused Southern tendency to identify free-soilism with abolition, the South had a significant number of leaders who felt that the abolitionist threat was being exaggerated out of all proportion by politicians hoping to win votes by stirring up needless fears. This group included the retiring president James K. Polk, the soon-to-be president Zachary Taylor, the often-frustrated presidential candidate Henry Clay, and senators like John Bell of Tennessee, John J. Crittenden of Kentucky, Sam Houston of Texas, and Thomas Hart Benton of Missouri. They were well aware of the many legal discriminations against free blacks in the Northern states as well as the growing enmity of Northern workers toward the two and a quarter million Americans who had come from other countries like Ireland and Germany. To these politicians the idea of any serious Northern action against slavery seemed preposterous. They also considered the demands of their fellow slaveholders for equal rights in faraway regions with existing antislavery populations to be equally foolish. They shared the basic view of the northern Transcendentalists that mankind's potential for progress was limitless, and they saw the American union as the guiding star leading the world in the proper direction. Each in his own way would do battle with anyone who would place needless obstacles in the path of this glorious destiny.

2

★ ★ ★ ★ ★

THE PRICE OF CONQUEST

The slaveholding president James K. Polk had not wished a second term, but an observer aware only of Polk's achievements and the economic state of the Union would have expected the Democratic party to be the overwhelming choice of the voters in 1848. Such, however, was not the case. The riches so easily obtained had left large factions of the electorate with badly bruised consciences and deep animosities related to their own specific and more local aspirations. In 1836 the abolitionists had attacked the revolution by which Texas won its independence from Mexico as a proslavery conspiracy. Leaders in all sections had denied this, but John C. Calhoun of South Carolina had proudly declared that the extension of slavery was an adequate reason for both the recognition and the annexation of Texas. Becoming secretary of state in 1844, Calhoun had explained in a public letter to the British government that he was annexing Texas for the sole purpose of perpetuating and extending the blessings of slavery, which he enumerated. Calhoun's letter appeared to validate the earlier charges of the abolitionists and was largely responsible for the defeat of the annexation treaty by the United States Senate. The question of immediate annexation split the Democratic party, denied former president Martin Van Buren the presidential nomination, and left an eloquent and powerful group of Jacksonian Democrats angrily licking their wounds. The Democrat Polk won the election, but a great many Northern Democrats were far from mollified, and some were further alienated by his

13

patronage policies, which ignored many of Jackson's closest former associates.

A congressional joint resolution had enabled President John Tyler and Secretary Calhoun to complete the annexation of Texas with its own enormously exaggerated, self-defined boundaries, but Polk had accepted their action and had provoked the Mexican War to validate the Texas claims. To many Northerners, both Democrats and Whigs, the Mexican War was an unjust and felonious attack by a powerful giant against a weak and helpless neighbor and was fought entirely for the expansion of slavery and the "Slave Power." The resolution admitting Texas to the Union authorized the state's division into five states, and the possibility of ten additional slave-state senators remained a nightmare to many who had not yet realized the pride most Texans took in the vast size of their state. The legislature of Massachusetts had resolved that

> such a war of conquest, so hateful in its objects, so wanton, unjust, and unconstitutional in its origin and character, must be regarded as a war against freedom, against humanity, against justice, against the Union, against the Constitution, and against the Free States; and that a regard for the true interests and the highest honor of the country, not less than the impulses of Christian duty, should arouse all good citizens to join in efforts to arrest this gigantic crime, by withholding supplies, or other voluntary contributions, for its further prosecution.[1]

Senator Thomas Corwin spoke for the Northwest of Ohio, Indiana, Illinois, Michigan, and Wisconsin and received widespread praise when he denounced the war as one in which the Mexicans should greet the Yankee invaders with "bloody hands" and "hospitable graves." Northwesterners also believed that the Democratic presidential platform of 1844 had promised them all of the Oregon territory up to the southern boundary of Alaska, and when Polk had compromised at forty-nine degrees, their cry of "Fifty-four forty or fight" had been loud and clear. They did not get fifty-four forty, but they did fight—for Texas, the great southwestern territories, and ostensibly the extension of slavery. When Polk vetoed a bill to improve the western rivers and harbors after western members of Congress had supported his successful efforts for a lower tariff and an independent Treasury, the anger of northwesterners at the South boiled over. The "slavocracy" was responsible for their frustrated ambitions, and their sons dying in Mexico were being sacrificed for an ignoble cause.

Naturally enough, all of this quickly became a quarrel over whether slavery would be permitted in the new territories. Texas was already a slave state, but Congress would decide the fate of the other areas. No slavery in any new territories, said Congressman David Wilmot of Pennsylvania in a proposed legislative amendment that became known as the Wilmot Proviso. Equality of rights in all territories, answered John C. Calhoun, or the American Union could not survive.

Ironically, the first practical application of Calhoun's demand came in 1848 in a fierce debate over whether or not the far-northern territory of Oregon should be granted territorial government with an antislavery provision in its constitution. Senator Henry S. Foote of Mississippi assured Senator John P. Hale of New Hampshire that in Mississippi, Hale would be hanged from the highest tree. Hale replied that in New Hampshire, Foote would be accorded all the courtesies due a United States senator. In vain did slaveholders Sam Houston and Thomas Hart Benton plead for reason by stressing the impossibility of slavery in Oregon.

At one point, Benton tried to strangle Senator Francis P. Butler of South Carolina. At another, Senator Simon Cameron of Pennsylvania and Foote rolled down the Senate aisle in a less than friendly embrace. Calhoun, however, delivered the most revealing oration during an all-night debate that ended when the Senate, by the margin of the votes cast by Benton and Houston, admitted Oregon without slavery.

The admission of Oregon with an antislavery provision, said Calhoun, would

> convert all the southern population into slaves; and he would never consent to entail that disgrace on his posterity. . . . The separation of the North and the South is completed. The South has now a most solemn obligation to perform—to herself—to the Constitution—to the Union. . . . She is bound to fulfill her obligations as she may best understand them. This is not a question of territorial government, but a question involving the continuance of the Union.[2]

Calhoun's insistence upon an essentially irrational debate over slavery in Oregon, after the inhabitants in that faraway northern region had ratified the forces of nature by barring the institution, would typify the extreme Southern position until 1861. No one in the Congress had ever suggested even the taxation of slavery, and those Americans who advocated the abolition of slavery where it already existed were a tiny minority. Severe restrictions against free blacks existed in virtually every Northern state, and Northern industrial workers everywhere feared the possibility of a flood of black immigrants if slavery should be abolished. As late as 1860 Abraham Lincoln was still expressing the hope that slavery might die of its own weaknesses within a hundred years. The unsuitability of slavery in places like New Mexico and Arizona, to say nothing of the future northern-plains and mountain states, was obvious to most thinking people. Simultaneously, the first settlers to arrive in such areas, including California, were almost certain to be people who opposed slavery for a variety of reasons usually devoid of moral or humanitarian connotations. Indeed, the Free Soil party that nominated Martin Van Buren for president in 1848 was thoroughly permeated with racial fears and prejudices. Slavery, of course, also violated the Protestant work ethic, the principles taught by the founder of Christianity, and the Declaration of Independence, and these noble reasons were more likely to be cited than the fact that people everywhere who hoped to go west did not want either slavery or free blacks in their midst. Southerners were always ready to argue that their slaves were treated better than were the Northern free blacks, but they were rarely willing to accept the implications of this as it related to the abolition movement.

Why, then, did Southerners choose to make impossible demands that could only stir up the wrath of Northerners who were otherwise ready and willing to leave Southerners and their "peculiar institution" alone? Many historians have struggled with this question but have come up with differing answers. A cogent viewpoint that began with the abolitionist Frederick Douglass in 1884 and has continued with various others in recent times still appears extremely plausible. Southern planters were accustomed to deference from both slaves and white inferiors. Like most Americans, Southern planters identified material success and status with superior virtue. They were usually religious, and their efforts to justify slavery with biblical evidence was clearly designed to convince themselves rather than others. They glorified freedom and were inordinately proud of the fact that a Southerner, Thomas Jefferson, had penned the Declaration of Independence. July 4 was as much a sacred holiday for Southerners as it was anywhere in the North. The planters were not accustomed to criticism, and contemporary mores dictated a violent response to criticism when it occurred. Almost any uncomplimentary statement could be construed as an attack upon one's honor, and one's honor could properly only be defended on the dueling ground. The earlier antislavery movement during and immediately after the Revolution had attacked the institution but had rarely involved any reproach to the slaveholder. Southerners had willingly accepted the antislavery restrictions of the Northwest Ordinance of 1787 and the Missouri Compromise of 1820 because no moral condemnation had been involved. The new abolitionism of the 1830s, however, was a different matter. William Lloyd Garrison and his followers did not hesitate to denounce the slaveholders as sinners in the eyes of God and man and as totally undeserving of anything but contempt and scorn from all righteous people. Theodore Dwight Weld was less vitriolic, but the condescension that marked the more forgiving attitude of his Christian approach was equally difficult for proud Southerners to swallow. The fact that only a relative handful of Northerners openly supported the abolitionists was quite irrelevant. The abolitionists published and circulated their views to all who would read them, and no one read them with greater interest and anger than did a great many Southerners.[3]

There had been many slave revolts before Nat Turner's bloody uprising in Virginia in 1831, but Southerners now blamed Turner's massacre upon the writings of the abolitionists, just as their descendants would later blame the modern civil-rights movement on Northern outsiders. This, of course, also roused the fears of the three-fourths of the Southern whites who owned no slaves but were terrified by the exaggerated warnings of the planters as to what abolition would bring.

In short, the moral and religious condemnations, and the threat to their self-esteem involved in the abolition movement as it existed by 1848, had created a new Southern state of mind. The overwhelming majority of Northerners remained willing to grant slavery the same tolerance it had always enjoyed, but for the Southerner this was no longer enough. He must have moral approval in the form of equal rights in the territories, and conversely any denial of those rights was an unacceptable insult to his honor. Thus, while no Southerner, including Calhoun, had the slightest intention of taking slaves to Oregon, the denial of the right to do so would "convert the southern population into slaves," and Calhoun "would never consent to entail that disgrace on his posterity."

In response, Northerners both east and west, already angry at the South because of the war and other policies, were quite unprepared to grant this approval, even when their racial prejudices and fears differed little from those of their Southern brethren. Also, of course, most Northerners were less aware than the Southerners of the difficulties involved in taking slavery to the Southwest. And whatever their indifference to the sorrows of the Southern slave, most Northerners did not wish to see either a blighting economic system or a horde of black workers in western territories that they or their children might someday wish to occupy.

The Americans of 1848 were by all accounts an aggressive, competitive, acquisitive, and quarrelsome breed. Whether they were fighting Indians, battling each other over land claims, turning isolated frontiers into farms and villages, developing railroads, building factories and cities, inventing new machinery and sources of power, exploring the nation's still uncharted wildernesses, defending or attacking slavery, or electing their public servants and leaders, Americans rarely doubted the righteousness of their own views or the inherent and willful selfishness or wickedness of their competitors and opponents.

The founding fathers, however, had recognized mankind's worst traits and had provided a political system that enabled people at every level of government to settle their more significant disagreements through a process of debate and compromise. In 1848 it was still working remarkably well. The nation had become far more democratic than the fathers had expected, and most white males were now authorized to help select the debaters and compromisers. This, however, had significantly lowered the intellectual quality of the politicians' appeals for votes. Elections, whether local, state, or federal, often ended with charges and countercharges of fraud and deception, and the physical threats and violence that often accompanied the open balloting was for a century the primary excuse for denying women the vote. Simultaneously, the spoils system whereby members of the winning party got most if not all of the constantly growing number of federal jobs at every level tended to muddy the waters of controversy still further.

Still, however, the electoral process had elevated genuinely dedicated political giants like Henry Clay, John C. Calhoun, Daniel Webster, John Quincy Adams, and Thomas Hart Benton, as well as the earlier heroes who had launched it. Historians still disagree on the abilities, motives, and statesmanship of Andrew Jackson, but he was the focal point for a nationwide burst of democratic rhetoric that later helped Abraham Lincoln persuade young Northerners everywhere to fight and die for the American Union.

The coming of Jacksonian democracy, with its exuberant emphasis on equality of opportunity for everyone except slaves, free blacks, Indians, and women, was not entirely an unmixed blessing. Aspiring politicians quickly realized that emotion-inspiring issues reducible to simplistic statements and slogans were extremely effective in getting otherwise indifferent voters to the polls. The primary opinion makers were the newspaper editors, most of them committed to a political party or to one politician within a party, and the lack of any kind of national media left local readers a prey to whatever the local editors wanted them to know or think. Fortunately, a great many newspapers did print verbatim the proceedings in Congress, and this exposed the more thoughtful readers to more than one viewpoint or opinion, but often the best of the speeches opposed by the editor were omitted.

No issue lent itself to the emotional style of politics more vividly than did slavery, and few if any other political systems could have made the issue of slavery more difficult to solve peacefully. Future generations of Americans would vent their more competitive aggressions and channel their love of excitement through collegiate and professional sports on a national scale, through the extraordinary adventures and drama of motion pictures, and, finally, through the constant vicarious violence of television. For the American of 1848, however, politics filled most of this need. The fortunes of one's political party or favorite candidate often transcended issues, and when the success of one's faction or favorite was intertwined with the pride, fear, religious feeling, genuine humanitarianism, and mutual self-righteousness inspired by the slavery quarrel, realities were all too often lost in a sea of angry words.

Issues involving selfish interests, however embellished with the trappings of principle, can usually be compromised or settled peacefully by reasonable people. Questions of moral right and wrong, however, are a different matter. Persons of strong principle cannot compromise such questions without sacrificing their personal integrity. Religious people make moral compromises at the risk of losing their souls and feeling a threat to their hopes for paradise. As long as slavery was confined to its existing borders, most Northerners felt no responsibility for it, and indeed, many could take satisfaction in its retention of black Americans who might otherwise come north and compete for their jobs. The extension of slavery into new territories or even the nugatory right to take slaves to a place like Oregon, however, stirred the consciences of many of those entirely ready to tolerate slavery in its existing habitat.

In 1848 the quarrel over the extension of slavery, while serious enough among the politicians, had not yet permeated the thinking and the emotions of most ordinary Americans. Northerners angry about the war and Polk's domestic policies might be determined to keep slavery out of the new territories, but most of them did not yet see a genuine Southern threat to turn the West into a slavery empire. Southerners could resent the effort to exclude slavery from territories they had fought so hard to attain, but not many were ready yet to identify free-soilism with a danger to slavery where it already existed. John Brown's raid would not occur for another eleven years. Thus the election of 1848 could still be a contest between the ambitious members of two genuinely national political parties, although the free-soil bolt from the Democrats was both a sectional aberration and an intraparty clash of conflicting personalities.

The South of 1848 still enjoyed a vigorous two-party system, and its Whig leaders could see both national unity and a presidential victory in the nomination of the Mexican War hero known as Old Rough and Ready. Zachary Taylor owned a Louisiana plantation and 145 slaves. Surely he could carry the South as one of its own who would protect the rights of slavery. Illustrating the attractions of a potential victory as opposed to principle, Northern leaders like the openly antislavery governor William H. Seward of New York were equally enthusiastic about Taylor. The young congressman from Illinois, Abraham Lincoln, had long worshipped at the shrine of the Whig party's most deserving candidate, Henry Clay, but the rail-splitter, like Seward, was ready to renounce his former allegiance and go for success with the general. The nomination of Taylor, Lincoln wrote, would enable the Whigs to blame the Democrats for starting the unpopular war and simultaneously claim the credit for its highly successful results. Others, like Clay's long-time close friend and supporter John J. Crittenden of Kentucky, fell quickly into line. In New York, the shrewdest operator in the Whig party, editor Thurlow Weed, was among the first to recognize Taylor's virtues. Weed's long-range dream was to see his friend Seward in the White House, but building a unified Whig party with the Whig general in the White House would do for the present.

The fact that Taylor was totally devoid of political experience and, indeed, had never even voted in a presidential election was irrelevant. American voters have often equated ignorance with innocence and innocence with political virtue. Taylor was the hero of four great battles in which he had been outnumbered, and except for owning slaves, he could not be linked with a single controversial issue. In 1850 Seward would declare that God's law against slavery outranked its protection by the United States Constitution, but in 1848 he was eager to elect a violator of the divine precept to his country's most powerful office. The Whigs' only presidential victory in their history had come in 1840, when the party had eschewed principle and nominated the ancient general William H. Harrison. Why not let history repeat itself and worry about the issues later?

The Democrats, who held their convention first, had no counterpart to Taylor. Polk had tried to create one by asking Congress to create the new rank of lieutenant general for Democratic senator Thomas Hart Benton. When this failed, Polk appointed Benton to major general and privately expressed a willingness to substitute Benton for his four major generals in the field. Benton had been eager to accept the overall strategic command, but when Congress denied Polk this option, Benton declined. He would not go to Mexico "just to wear a bunch of feathers in his hat."[4] Polk had already alienated most of the Democrats who had been closest to Andrew Jackson, and Benton's failure to achieve a president-making military career completed the estrangement of many of them from the Democratic party. Democratic general William O. Butler, a former congressman from Kentucky, had fought with distinction, but unlike Taylor and Scott, his name had not become a household word. Butler was much better qualified by political experience than his fellow native Kentuckian Taylor, but he would have to settle for the Democratic vice-presidential nomination.

Ultimately, the Democrats nominated for president the former Michigan territorial governor and United States senator Lewis Cass, on a platform condemning any federal interference with slavery. Cass had publicly advocated "popular sovereignty"—allowing the inhabitants of any territory to decide the slavery question for themselves when they created their territorial government. Southern followers of Calhoun, led by William L. Yancey of Alabama, denounced this doctrine as a betrayal of the South, and when the convention rejected their demand that slavery be protected in all territories, Yancey bolted the convention. Only one other delegate joined him, but Southerners everywhere, whether Whig or Democrat, were soon being bombarded with powerful attacks upon Cass and his principle.

Simultaneously, at the Democratic convention, two delegations appeared from New York, where the party was badly split into "Barnburners" and "Hunkers" by economic issues and personal feuds as well as by the Wilmot Proviso. The convention tried to side-step the slavery issue by seating both delegations and giving each delegate half a vote. The angry Barnburners withdrew to Utica, New York, where they nominated former president Martin Van Buren for president. A few weeks later they reconvened in Buffalo with a sizable contingent of "conscience Whigs," who would not support the slaveholding Taylor, and formed the Free Soil party. In a shouting, roaring, and singing convention, they renominated Van Buren, with Charles Francis Adams as his running mate. The Van Buren and Adams families had been bitter enemies for decades, but they were now firmly united on a platform of "Free soil, free speech, free labor, and free men!" Their platform called for "opposition to the aggressions of the slave power," along with a tariff, a frugal government, river and harbor improvements, and free homesteads for actual settlers. Their leaders included quality men like William Cullen Bryant, Francis P. Blair, Preston King, Samuel J. Tilden, Charles Sumner, and Salmon P. Chase.[5]

Despite Taylor's immense availability, his nomination did not come easily. Henry Clay was still the idol of most rank-and-file Whigs, and he was again eager to run. He deserved the nomination, but his earlier defeats in 1832 and 1844 counted heavily among those thirsting for victory. The Taylor advocates also had the difficult problem of getting support from the "conscience," or antislavery, Whigs. Taylor himself had carefully avoided making any public comments on the Wilmot Proviso. This enabled the Southerners to argue that he was safe, while his Northern adherents could insist that the general would not support the extension of slavery. Daniel Webster, for one, insisted that he trusted Taylor more than he did Van Buren on this question, even though Van Buren was the Free Soil candidate. Thurlow Weed shrewdly argued that Van Buren and the Barnburners hated Clay and would withdraw and support Cass if Clay should be nominated but that the nomination of Taylor would encourage the Free-Soilers to stay in the race and take votes from the Democrats. Also, the so-called cotton Whigs, like Abbott Lawrence and other industrialists, were for Taylor. A Whig victory could bring the economic policies they had been denied so long, and their own fortunes depended heavily upon trade with the Southern planters, whose slave-grown cotton fed their textile mills.

On the first ballot at the Whig convention, Taylor received 111 votes, to 97 for Clay, 43 for Scott, and 22 for Webster. During the next two ballots the Clay and Scott followers considered a combination, but the Webster delegates thwarted them by going for Taylor on the fourth ballot. Webster's managers later said they knew Webster could not win and felt that Taylor would be more likely than Clay to give him a top spot in a new administration.

The nomination was bitterly opposed by the conscience Whigs, as well as by those loyal to Clay. Faced with a rebellious convention, Weed and Seward hoped to make peace by nominating a New Englander for vice-president. Their choice was the wealthy industrialist Abbott Lawrence, but they were circumvented by the unexpected action of John Collier, an ambitious politician from Binghamton, New York. Delivering a long and eloquent speech on how much all Whigs everywhere owed Henry Clay and his followers, Collier nominated Millard Fillmore, a former New York congressman from Buffalo, for vice-president as a peace offering to Clay and his partisans. Collier very much exaggerated Fillmore's connections with Clay, but the speech had the desired effect. Conscience Whigs, who knew that Fillmore had consistently supported the Wilmot Proviso, joined with Clay's friends to defeat Abbott Lawrence and his promoter, Thurlow Weed. Fillmore was quickly nominated, to the chagrin of Weed, who had always professed friendship for Fillmore but had kept a wary eye on him as a potential threat to both Weed's own control of the New York patronage and the presidential ambitions of William H. Seward. Collier, in turn, had been thwarted and deceived by Weed on several earlier occasions and enjoyed both a moment of revenge and the elimination of Fillmore as a rival to himself in the upcoming choice of a United States senator. Ironically, Weed later deceived Fillmore into supporting the successful election of Seward to the seat that Collier coveted.

In the subsequent election, Taylor almost snatched defeat from the jaws of victory by publicly accepting the nomination of a small convention of Calhoun Democrats in Charleston, South Carolina. This undoubtedly drove some Whig voters to Van Buren, but it probably strengthened Taylor in the South, where the Democrats mounted a vicious attack on Fillmore. In the end, illogicality again triumphed as enough Southern Democrats switched to Taylor and enough Northern Whigs ignored the candidate's ties with slavery to elect him by a close margin. Van Buren, who had been pro-Southern on virtually every slavery issue during his own vice-presidency and presidency, took enough votes away from Cass to give New York and consequently the election to Taylor. During the election campaign, Fillmore remained discreetly silent on the question of slavery but indicated clearly that he was no opponent of slavery where it already existed.[6]

3

★ ★ ★ ★ ★

OLD ROUGH AND READY

Zachary Taylor would have attracted very little attention in a crowd. He was short and heavy, with a muscular body and a face that no one would have called handsome—a large head, mouth, and nose; coarse but thinning hair; and a weather-beaten complexion. He was a man with rough edges left by a lifetime of frontier military service. Unlike the dashing Gen. Winfield Scott, who decorated his six-foot-five-inch frame with immaculate and gaudy uniforms, Taylor cared nothing for formality, pomp, or circumstance and often wore old and mismatched uniforms without enough insignia to be recognized. To the soldiers, Scott was Old Fuss and Feathers, while Taylor was Old Rough and Ready.[1]

Despite superficial appearances, however, Taylor was by birth an authentic American aristocrat. His ancestors had settled in Virginia in the 1640s and had procreated a highly respected clan. His great-grandfather James Taylor was also James Madison's great-grandfather. James Taylor was also a favorite exploring companion of Virginia's governor Alexander Spottswood, belonged to the elite Knights of the Golden Horseshoe, and accumulated vast lands throughout the Virginia piedmont. Zachary Taylor's grandmother was Elizabeth Lee, a granddaughter of Richard Lee, whose other descendants included Richard Henry Lee, Light-Horse Harry Lee, and Robert E. Lee. Also through Elizabeth Lee, Taylor was descended directly from the Plymouth Pilgrim leaders William Brewster and

Isaac Allerton. And finally, his mother, Elizabeth Dabney Strother, also came from a distinguished Virginia family.

During the American Revolution, Richard Taylor, Zachary's father, had risen from lieutenant to lieutenant colonel, and Virginia had rewarded him with six thousand acres of western land. Richard's first two sons, Hancock and William, were born during the Revolutionary War. The third, Zachary, arrived in 1784 and was followed by three more brothers and three sisters. Zachary was born in Virginia, but his father had already gone to the Kentucky territory to stake out a plantation near the small town of Louisville.

In Kentucky, Richard Taylor earned both a great reputation as an Indian fighter and much respect as a public servant. In turn he was justice of the peace, collector of the port of Louisville, and delegate to Kentucky's State Constitutional Convention. He later served several terms in the state legislature. Four times he was a presidential elector—for his cousin James Madison in 1812, for James Monroe in 1816 and 1820, and for Henry Clay in 1824. He apparently weathered the great economic depression of 1819 without serious damage and was on the conservative side of the bitter Kentucky political quarrels over soft-money relief for debtors and over the New-Court-versus-Old-Court contest. Neither he nor his son Zachary joined the rush to elect Andrew Jackson in 1828.

Little is known about Zachary Taylor's boyhood, but growing up on a frontier with eight brothers and sisters probably contributed to his mental and physical toughness and a quick temper when confronted with insult or ingratitude. His formal schooling was limited, but he probably received considerable instruction at home. Both his parents were well educated. His mother had been taught by tutors imported from Europe, but managing a household of nine children may have restricted the time she had available for teaching, although the mere survival of all the children indicated that she was an unusual woman. Contrary to a popular stereotype of him, Zachary Taylor would later write clear, concise letters, usually marked by proper grammatical construction and only a few misspelled words. Indeed, in this regard, he was at least equal to the average American college student of today. His handwriting was not graceful, but it was more legible than that of many of his high-ranking contemporaries.

Zachary Taylor was no intellectual, but he always demonstrated a tremendous presence of mind in dangerous crises, a capacity for quick and usually correct military decisions, and a calm fearlessness in the face of physical danger. He also possessed another highly valued American trait not shared by either the great soldier-president

Andrew Jackson or some of Taylor's own illustrious Virginia kins-
men: he could manage his own private finances efficiently and effectively.

His father gave him a small plantation, which Zachary sold for
a fair price. From this beginning, he married both happily and well,
selected his financial agents and plantation managers wisely, avoided
excessive speculation, and accumulated a sizable fortune despite the
modest dimensions of his army pay. He lost $20,000 by signing
security notes for friends both before and during the great panic of
1819–20, but he refused to accept the help of the relief laws or an
inflated paper currency. He paid his debts in specie, ultimately recovered from the debacle, and finally left an estate valued at $140,000.
His latest biographer has estimated this fortune at $1.3 million in
1983 terms.

An important feature of Taylor's entire life was the continuous
ownership of slaves. His father owned seven slaves in 1790, but the
number had grown to twenty-six by 1800 and thirty-seven by 1810.
Zachary himself bought and inherited slaves, and he bought plantations with slaves included, until by 1848 the number was 145. By all
accounts, he was an enlightened and humane master. He never sold
a slave. He selected his overseers wisely and carefully, and one in
particular enjoyed a tenure of many years. In all of his letters, Taylor
referred to the slaves as servants. They were always well fed, well
clothed, and well housed, and he was affectionate in his personal
relations with them. Lady Emmeline C. E. Stuart-Wortley, an English-
woman who visited Taylor's river plantation in Mississippi, later
wrote a glowing account of Taylor's arrival by boat. The excited
slaves gathered to greet him and shake his hand, and she was astonished by the informality and the lack of servility. On at least one
occasion, Taylor instructed his overseer to "distribute . . . five hundred dollars . . . among the servants at Christmas . . . in such a
way as you think they deserve by their good conduct." Most of
Taylor's papers were destroyed when a Union army sacked his Louisiana plantation during the Civil War, and it is entirely possible
that the evidence of equal generosity in other years was lost. Taylor
provided no manumissions in his will, but he wrote: "I wish the
servants only moderately worked and kindly treated, which I hope
my children will have attended to."[2]

Taylor clearly represented the slaveholder at his best, and he
practiced slavery in conformity with the image that Southern leaders everywhere sought to project. Perhaps this explains his lack of
sensitivity to Northern criticisms of the institution. Taylor would

later become genuinely fond of the antislavery senator William H. Seward, and he would always defend the rights of those who denounced slavery and opposed its expansion. Feeling no guilt about his own role in the slavery system, Taylor felt no compulsion either to defend or to expand it, and he showed little if any personal animosity toward its critics.

Until the age of twenty-three, Taylor remained at home, assisting his father on the plantation. In 1807, however, when war with Britain seemed imminent, he enlisted as a first lieutenant of infantry. Whatever his formal education, he was considered qualified by family connections and background for an immediate commission, and two years later he was promoted to captain. In 1809 he survived a terrible ten-month period in New Orleans, when fatigue, mosquitoes, and disease killed 686 of a total garrison of 2,000.

In 1810 Taylor married Margaret Mackall Smith, the daughter of a rich planter. Margaret ultimately produced six children and spent some forty years working to keep him happy, either from a distance or at a long succession of isolated and usually dangerous frontier posts. During periods of separation he was a faithful correspondent, and all available evidence indicates a strong mutual devotion. His letters reveal a constant concern about her frail health and his unhappiness during their periods of separation.

Taylor's family status may have brought his first commission, but his rise thereafter rested upon instinctive military talent and devotion to duty. In 1811 he was highly commended by Gen. William Henry Harrison for having converted a chaotic situation at Fort Knox, Indiana, into a state of order and efficiency. A year later, Taylor was commanding Fort Harrison in Indiana, when a superior force of Indians led by Tecumseh set fire to the fort and threatened the lives of all present, including a number of women and children. Taylor and his men were all ill with fever, but he whipped them into action. By removing the roof that connected the burning blockhouse to other blockhouses, they limited the space through which the Indians might enter to about twenty feet, and under heavy gunfire from the Indians, they worked all night to fill the gap with a strong row of pickets. The fort was saved, and Taylor received widespread publicity and a promotion to brevet major. In 1814 in Missouri he fought with distinction against both the British and Indians.

When the war ended, Taylor was ready to resign in anger because others who had fought less had advanced faster. Between 1808 and 1814, Winfield Scott had advanced from captain to brigadier general, and Taylor's competitive feelings toward the new general would last a lifetime. Taylor was promoted to major and then reduced to captain when the army itself shrank from fifty thousand to ten thousand men. He resigned and returned to Kentucky but abandoned his corn and tobacco fields a year later when he was again offered the rank of major. For the next few years he built roads and forts on various frontiers, and in 1819 he was promoted to lieutenant colonel, at a time when numerous other officers were being demoted or discharged. In 1820 Mrs. Taylor survived a serious illness, but his two youngest children died. In 1823 he bought a small plantation with twenty-three slaves a few miles north of Baton Rouge, Louisiana.

From 1828 to 1837 Taylor commanded various forts in the upper-Mississippi region of present-day Minnesota, Wisconsin, Iowa, and Illinois. He played an important role in the vicious Black Hawk Indian War, which destroyed the power of the Indians in the region. A cholera epidemic killed more soldiers than the Indians did, but Taylor's forts suffered less than most because they were invariably clean and well managed. Taylor believed that the war could have been avoided if the initial "disgraceful" attack by the United States Army had not occurred. After the Black Hawk War, keeping settlers out of the regions that had been assigned to the Indians was a major problem, particularly after lead mines were discovered. Taylor asked the secretary of war to give all commanders the standing authority to "burn and destroy the establishments of all squatters together with every description of property and to remove them, and all other whites who may attempt to tresspass, encroach or enter upon the Indian Territory."[3]

During 1834–36 Taylor built and staffed a school for Winnebago Indians and complained almost constantly because the War Department ignored his suggestions for the improvement of Indian relations and refused to send the necessary funds to meet existing treaty commitments. Taylor was a man of strong opinions and never hesitated to express them unvarnished to anyone. In 1821, he denounced his cousin James Madison as "perfectly callous & unacquainted with the noble feelings of a soldier," while the late Treasury Secretary Alexander J. Dallas was "a lawyer grown grey in iniquity & chicanery . . . better calculated for the associate of a Robespierre than the minister of a free, enlightened, & great republic."[4]

The self-confidence that enabled Taylor to respect and occasionally like both Indians and antislavery critics was also reflected by his informal style of military leadership. A common minor punishment in the frontier army was "wooling," a somewhat humorous act in which the commanding officer would shake an offender by the ears. On one occasion, Taylor started to wool a stalwart young German recruit who knew nothing about the practice. The private promptly knocked his commander flat. Taylor's subordinates wanted to shoot the man on the spot, but Taylor's ego was not injured, and he had no fears that the incident would undermine his military discipline. Showing both fairness and common sense, Taylor decreed, "Let that man alone, he will make a good soldier."[5] The story was spread far and wide, and it contributed to his immense popularity among common soldiers. Taylor rarely if ever concerned himself with pomp and protocol, but in crucial battles his men invariably stood firm, even when the numerical odds were overwhelming.

In 1832 Taylor was very upset when his eighteen-year-old daughter, Knox, fell in love with a handsome Mississippi lieutenant named Jefferson Davis. Taylor objected to Davis because of some unspecified report that Taylor had heard and because he did not want his daughter to endure the hardships and dangers of a soldier's wife. At one point, Davis considered a duel challenge to Taylor, but he was dissuaded by the officer whom Davis asked to be his second. Taylor thought the problem was solved when Davis was transferred to a post several hundred miles away, but love only grew from the absence. Two years later, Taylor finally gave his reluctant consent, if not his approval. The eager Knox traveled to Kentucky to marry Davis at the home of her aunt. Her mother prepared her trousseau, and her father provided "a liberal supply of money." The triumph of romance, however, was soon followed by tragedy. A few weeks later, at the Davis plantation in Mississippi, the bride and groom both contracted malaria, and Knox died.[6] Davis and Taylor were not fully reconciled until Davis performed heroically under Taylor's command during the Mexican War. With all forgiven, the two men remained close friends until Taylor's death.

Like several others, Taylor took his turn in the army's futile effort to capture and transport some fifteen hundred Florida Seminole Indians to the west.[7] Over a ten-year period, more than one hundred thousand American soldiers took part in this fruitless exercise before the effort was abandoned. Generals Edmund P. Gaines, Winfield Scott, and Thomas Jesup all failed. Taylor first served under Jesup and defeated a large group of Indians in one of the few direct confrontations of the war. His preference, however, was to seek a negotiated peace. Promoted to brevet brigadier general, Taylor took full command in 1838 and stirred up a hornets' nest in Congress by accepting and trying to use thirty-three bloodhounds acquired from Cuba by the Florida government. The dogs, which had been trained to track African slaves, had no interest whatever in Indians, although for many weeks, several thousand soldiers followed the dogs back and forth through the Florida swamps before this fact became apparent. In Congress, numerous public memorials as well as members condemned the use of dogs as a cruel atrocity, while Senator Benton echoed Taylor's public assurances that the purpose of the dogs was "to find the Indians, not to worry them." When a report came that the dogs wore muzzles, others protested this waste of dog power. In the House, John Quincy Adams called upon the secretary of war to report on the martial history of bloodhounds and to state whether or not they would be eligible for military pensions.[8] Like his predecessors, Taylor did not find and defeat the Indians, but he did exhibit again his flair for leadership and efficient organization, his independence of thought, and his readiness to accept full responsibility for his decisions and actions.

A major factor in the Seminole War was the presence of large numbers of escaped slaves among the Indians. Another was the judicious use of money and favors to get Indians from other tribes as well as a few Seminoles to serve as guides in the pursuit of their fellow Indians. In his letters and reports, Taylor was meticulous in trying to keep his promises. He assured his guides that he would use his "influence to have any slaves who may have intermarried with the Indian Negroes purchased on reasonable terms & made free if they could raise the funds necessary." He was particularly concerned about "an old Negro named Romeo" and asked General Jesup to buy Romeo with the understanding that the guide Abraham would pay for him. Taylor later thanked Jesup for arranging the purchase. In no uncertain terms, Taylor informed the War Department that he would not seize blacks who belonged to the Seminoles and that he would not return any runaway slaves to alleged owners unless they could prove their claims. James C. Watson of Georgia paid the Creek Indians $15,000 for their claims to slaves they had captured, but Taylor and Jesup refused to honor the claims. Through Taylor's and Jesup's efforts, between three hundred and four hundred blacks ultimately accompanied the Seminoles to their new home in Arkansas.[9] During the presidential campaign of 1848, Taylor's fair dealings with the blacks in Florida were cited as evidence that he would not advocate the extension of slavery.

After quarreling with Florida civilians because he would not employ their militia, Taylor at his own request was relieved in May

1840. The settlers, he wrote in his final report, should learn to take care of themselves and should stop depending upon the federal government for protection from only a relatively few Indians. He later described Florida as a "miserable country . . . where an officer who has any regard for honesty, truth, or humanity, has but little to gain, and everything to lose."[10]

For six months the general enjoyed a well-earned leave, while struggling to pay off several thousand dollars in debts that he had incurred by signing the security notes of friends who had died with their notes unpaid. He also found time to take his family on a very pleasant northern tour with visits in Washington, Philadelphia, Boston, Niagara Falls, and western Pennsylvania. In Boston, he decided to send his thirteen-year-old son Richard to a tutor for preparation to enter Harvard. During this period also, the elderly Ohio general, William Henry Harrison, was nominated by the Whigs and elected president. Harrison's opponents had discovered that the candidate in his youth had joined an abolition society, but the slaveholding Taylor thought Harrison's election would be America's salvation from the Jacksonian Democrats.

If a man's breadth of vision can be measured at least in part by his ambitions for his children, Zachary Taylor was more enlightened than most. His daughters received the best private schooling available. Taylor did not want his only son, Richard, to be a soldier any more than he had wanted his daughter to marry one. He urged the young man to seek a "literary education" and ultimately sent him to Paris and Edinburgh for two years. Returning to earn a degree from Yale instead of Harvard, Richard Taylor emerged fluent in French, reasonably competent in Spanish, and an incessant reader of history and the classics. Eventually, Richard Taylor became a competent manager of his father's plantations and other business interests, and during the Civil War he served as a very capable Confederate lieutenant general. All of the children adored their father.[11]

In June 1841 Taylor assumed command of the Second Military Department, which was headquartered at Fort Smith in western Arkansas, and he immediately continued his reputation for making independent judgments. He denounced the ongoing construction of the massive fort there as a monument to folly and financial waste in a place where there was no danger of an Indian attack. He demonstrated great skill in keeping the peace among the Cherokees, Creeks, and Seminoles transported there by the government and in protecting the more recent emigrant Chickasaws and Choctaws from the warlike prairie tribes and from Texas raiding parties. He stubbornly overcame the War Department's resistance to building Fort Washita in a highly strategic location in present-day Oklahoma, and he got permission to abandon Fort Wayne because it was occupying some of the best lands of the Cherokees and interfering with the farms of the half-breeds. The angry white settlers and traders near Fort Wayne filled the air with dire warnings about their vulnerability to Indian massacres and worse, and the new nation of Texas was equally loud in its demands for greater protection. To Taylor this was all nonsense created entirely by white greed. The strongest tribes, he wrote, were the Cherokees, Choctaws, and Creeks, and anyone who had "visited these people in their new homes" knew that they had "completely laid aside their warlike habits" and were "assiduously cultivating the arts of peace."[12] In every way, Taylor dealt honestly, humanely, and intelligently with the Indians. He was a professional soldier always ready to fight when ordered to do so, but he was also remarkably free from rancor or personal animosities toward his military foes.

Indeed, Taylor often appeared to respect and even like his assigned enemies more than he did his American colleagues and superiors. His professional judgments often clashed with popular viewpoints as well as with what he considered the abysmal ignorance of several presidents and secretaries of war, but he compromised his own opinions only when ordered to do so. Also, he often reached conclusions that were seemingly unaffected by what would have appeared to be his own best personal interests. When the Ohioan president William Henry Harrison died in early 1841 and was replaced by the slaveholding Virginian vice-president John Tyler, Taylor considered the change a national catastrophe. Taylor owned several dozen slaves, but he rejected as nonsense Calhoun's argument that Texas must be annexed to preserve and perpetuate slavery. As part of his military duty, Taylor ultimately helped create a Texas much larger than the one he had initially defended, but at a time when Henry Clay, Martin Van Buren, and Thomas Hart Benton, among others, were opposing only the immediate annexation of Texas, Taylor was against it with no qualifications for the future. He wrote from Mexico in 1847:

> I was opposed to the annexation of Texas, believing as I did that the manner in which it was done, was at variance with the Constitution, & which no one now living will see the effects . . . which is to result from this which grown out of it on the institutions of our great & hitherto prosperous country; but I will not make

33

myself unhappy at what I cannot prevent; nor give up the Constitution or abandon it because a rent has been made in it, but will stick by & repair it, & nurse it as long as it will hang together.[13]

Ultimately, during John Tyler's last few days in office, Congress passed a joint resolution annexing Texas, and President James K. Polk took office with the annexation of Texas an accomplished fact. The new secretary of state, James Buchanan, immediately promised Texas three thousand men, should they be necessary. On 12 January 1846 General Taylor was ordered to the river that marked the southern line claimed by Texas. The Rio Grande was more than one hundred miles south of the previous longstanding boundary of the former Mexican province of Texas, but Taylor, quite properly in line with his orders, ignored Mexican threats and encamped across the river from Matamoros, Mexico. He assured the Mexican commander there that his advance was not an act of aggression, but no Mexican could have viewed it otherwise. After a few scattered encounters, the Mexicans ordered Taylor to retreat to the Nueces River, and he countered by blockading the river and stopping all supplies bound for Matamoros. On 24 April a large Mexican force killed sixty-three American dragoons north of the river, and the war had begun.

President Polk had spent a full Saturday preparing a request for war based upon the rejection of John Slidell's mission, the Mexican failure to honor debts to United States citizens, and the continuing threats to Texas. The news from Matamoros enabled Polk to spend the following day changing his message to a call for the defense of United States borders, but the project left him with a bad conscience because he had worked on Sunday.[14]

With the issue of war settled, Zachary Taylor became the consummate soldier. He promptly informed Washington that "if the enemy oppose my march, in whatever force, I shall fight him." A nation at least momentarily fired with patriotism responded proudly, and Taylor was suddenly a national hero before he had fired a shot. At Palo Alto, in Texas, his forces were outnumbered almost three to one, but he won a smashing victory by virtue of superior artillery and well-disciplined infantry. The American losses were nine killed and forty-five wounded, while more than two hundred Mexicans fell dead and four hundred were wounded. Taylor pursued, and the much bloodier battle of Resaca de la Palma was an even more one-sided victory. In both cases, the United States troops were inspired by Taylor's reckless disregard for his own safety. The public had been warned by the presses that his little army was in a desperate situation, and the victories made the general appear overnight as a military genius. Congress and several states passed resolutions of praise, and the Louisiana legislature appropriated $500 to buy him a new sword. When Congress authorized a medal, no portrait or any other likeness of him was available.[15]

On 13 May, however, the day war was declared, President Polk appointed Gen. Winfield Scott to be the overall commander in the field. Polk expected Scott to proceed immediately, but the general announced that he would spend the summer in Washington, raising troops and organizing supplies. Scott was disrespectful toward both Polk and Secretary of War William L. Marcy, and Polk's natural suspicions of a Whig general with presidential ambitions magnified the impact of the general's tactlessness. Polk decided to relieve Scott, and Taylor's victories made him the obvious choice. Taylor was nominated major general by brevet and was given the overall command.

Taylor received the news without enthusiasm but with his usual dedication to duty. Planning to advance against Monterrey by going up the Rio Grande and the San Juan River, Taylor waited impatiently for weeks for needed boats, wagons, and horseshoes and ultimately became involved in an angry quarrel with his old friend Q.M. Gen. Thomas Jesup. Meanwhile, Taylor was swamped with militia and three-month volunteer reinforcements who were difficult to discipline and were soon being charged with robbing, stealing, and killing in the city of Matamoros. The scrupulous Taylor had begun his invasion with an order that his troops respect the "rights of all persons . . . in the peaceful pursuit of their respective avocations . . . on both banks of the Rio Grande." No person "under any pretext whatsoever" was to interfere with the "civil rights or religious privileges" of the people. He would not even use private homes for hospital purposes without the consent of their owners, and he meticulously tried to keep life in the conquered areas in its preinvasion status. After the battle of Matamoros, Taylor had his surgeons attend the enemy wounded, and he personally contributed several hundred dollars for their support.[16]

Taylor's most recent biographer has faulted the general for not having used reserve troops to pursue and crush the Mexican armies after his victories and has suggested that Taylor lacked "the killer instinct" necessary to be a great general. This judgment is probably correct, but Taylor's alternatives were less simple immediately after a bloody battle on unfamiliar terrain in 1846 than they appear 140 years later. During the American Civil War, several generals would follow their killer instincts and launch frontal assaults that had catastrophic results for their own troops.[17]

Ultimately, Taylor got part of his army to Monterrey, but only after herculean efforts and despite the deaths of thousands from disease. Taylor has also been criticized for not having taken the proper sanitary measures necessary to avoid or minimize the presence of dysentery. Ignorance, however, should not be confused with negligence. Poor judgment may have been a factor, but unfortunately, germs had not yet been discovered, and no tourist guides were available to warn many thousands of hot, thirsty troops not to drink the water.[18]

With ten thousand troops and most of his heavy artillery left behind, Taylor attacked Monterrey with only six thousand men. The battle, which involved hand-to-hand fighting through the streets, was fierce and bloody. The Mexican commander finally offered to surrender the town in exchange for a promise that for eight weeks Taylor would not advance beyond the mountains behind which the Mexicans were to retire. The armistice could be negated by either government. To save lives, Taylor immediately accepted and explained to various high-placed friends that the Mexicans had assured him that their government was preparing to accept a United States peace offer. He would not have soldiers killed for nothing, and a further storming of the city would have endangered the lives of women and children. Also, it would take him eight weeks to prepare for any further advance anyhow. The Mexicans, Taylor insisted, had surrendered a city fortified by nature as well as by an armed force much larger and better armed with artillery than were the United States attackers.

Several weeks later in Washington, President Polk finally got the news from Monterrey and was furious. Secretary Marcy wrote a stinging rebuke, ordering Taylor to terminate the armistice at once. Later, when Congress officially thanked Taylor for his brilliant victory, Polk's followers in the House added the amendment, "Provided that nothing herein contained shall be construed into an approbation of the terms of the capitulation of Monterrey." The Senate, however, defeated the amendment after an angry debate. General Taylor, who had never cast a presidential vote, had suddenly become a national political issue, and Polk had begun to worry more about Taylor than about Scott as a future Whig president. Polk would have recalled Taylor had it not been for Taylor's high public standing, and Scott now stood ready to be forgiven for past transgressions.[19]

The harsh criticism from officials safe in Washington instead of praise for his heroic efforts convinced the angry Taylor that Polk and Scott had joined hands in a conspiracy against him. Ultimately, General Scott was selected to head an invasion at Vera Cruz, and Taylor angrily complained that he must now face twenty thousand enemy troops with less than a thousand regulars and a volunteer force but pledged that "however much I may feel personally mortified and outraged by the course pursued . . . , I will carry out in good faith, while I remain in Mexico, the views of the government, though I may be sacrificed in the effort." Privately, he was convinced that Scott and Polk were determined to destroy his career only because he had been mentioned for the presidency. In November 1847, after hearing a false report that Polk had died, Taylor wrote that "while I regret to hear of the death of anyone, I would as soon have heard of his death if true, as that of any other individual in the whole Union, even though it should have the effect of producing great changes in measures as well as men, so far as the management of national affairs is concerned; as they may be bettered & cannot possibly be worsted."[20]

Taylor's immediate reaction to the gutting of his army was to consider resigning, but he realized that nothing would please his enemies more. He now had only six thousand troops, and all except two squadrons of cavalry and part of his artillery were inexperienced volunteers, but he would fight nonetheless. Informed that strong enemy forces were advancing against him, he said to the correspondent of the *New York Tribune*, "Let them come; damned if they don't go back a good deal faster than they came." Ignoring Scott's orders to fall back to a more defensible position at Monterrey, he marched boldly against Gen. Antonio López de Santa Anna, who was approaching with some twenty thousand men. Near a hacienda known as Buena Vista, Taylor shrewdly took advantage of the mountain terrain and flamboyantly rejected Santa Anna's demand for unconditional surrender within the hour. Two days later the Mexicans retreated after numerous efforts to break the United States lines had been repulsed with heavy losses. The advantageous terrain, his superior horse-drawn light artillery, and the heroic efforts of subordinates like William T. Sherman, Braxton Bragg, Jefferson Davis, and John Wool were essential elements in the victory. By all accounts, however, the catalyzing agent that kept company after company in place under withering fire and against heavy frontal charges was the presence of Taylor himself as he moved fearlessly from one position to another, encouraging and demanding a maximum effort from his men. His losses were 267 killed, 456 wounded, and 23 missing. Of the casualties, 69 were officers. Lt.-Col. Henry Clay, Jr., was killed, while Col. Jefferson Davis was painfully wounded.[21]

President Polk blamed Taylor for an unnecessary battle and heavy loss of life. Taylor argued that he had "saved the honor of the country & our glorious flag from trailing in the dust." Responsibility for the bloodshed, he insisted, belonged to Polk, Marcy, and Scott for having left him with an army small enough to invite the attack. Two months earlier, Taylor had written Gen. Edmund P. Gaines a private letter harshly criticizing the administration and discussing the pending Vera Cruz invasion. Taylor had instructed Gaines to burn the letter, but Gaines, himself angry at the administration, gave it to the press in January. Polk felt that Taylor and Gaines should be tried for giving aid and comfort to the enemy, but his cabinet reduced the penalty against Taylor to another letter of strong censure from Secretary Marcy.[22]

Taylor replied that he had written nothing he would not repeat, that his views were shared by many responsible statesmen, and that his letter had given the Mexicans no information they did not already have. He would continue to serve the public, and he would look for his reward to the "consciousness of pure motives, and to the final verdict of impartial history."[23] Taylor's friends in Congress printed ten thousand copies of his letter. After Buena Vista, criticism from the administration served only to advance Taylor toward the presidential nomination. He had defeated an overwhelmingly superior enemy, and for the public that was enough. The expansionists could credit him with a major share of their success, while the Northern Whig leadership could be reminded that he had personally opposed both the annexation of Texas and the acquisition of the extra territory taken during the war.

For nine months after Buena Vista, Taylor sat peacefully with troops in northern Mexico while General Scott fought his way to Mexico City. Taylor was not idle, however, because alienation from the administration only enhanced his political appeal. In December 1847 a group of young Whig congressmen led by Alexander H. Stephens of Georgia and including Robert Toombs of Georgia; William B. Preston, Thomas S. Flournoy, and John S. Pendleton of Virginia; Henry A. Hilliard of Alabama; Truman Smith of Connecticut; and Abraham Lincoln of Illinois, organized a Taylor-for-President Club. Actually, they were joining a bandwagon that was already rolling. State legislatures; party meetings, mostly Whig but occasionally Democratic; important editors and private citizens; and well-known politicians took turns endorsing Taylor for the presidency. Democratic efforts to discredit him had little effect, although he was infuriated when Senator Lewis Cass attacked him for the Gaines letter. Taylor would dare "Cass & the whole concern to show . . . one word that is untrue in the letter to Gen'l Gaines."[24]

Taylor's answers to the presidential overtures indicated both political naïveté and clear-cut, intelligent views on some important questions. They help to explain some important positions he later took as president. He confessed over and over that he had had no time for politics and that he lacked experience. He did not like political parties as such, he would spend no money, and if he were to be elected president, "it must be by the spontaneous move of the people, & not by any agency of mine . . . as I am not at all anxious for the office under any circumstances, & will be the president of all the people if at all, & not of a party." Still, however, his election "would be the most signal rebuke ever ministered to a party under similar circumstances."[25]

In June 1847, Taylor opposed taking any more territory than the area already conquered, and he feared that a continuation of the war might result in annexing more. It was clear to him that slavery had already been abolished by Mexico and could never be revived in any Mexican territory to be annexed. "So far as slavery is concerned," he wrote Jefferson Davis, "we of the South must throw ourselves on the Constitution & defend our rights under it to the last, & when arguments will no longer suffice we will appeal to the sword, if necessary to do so. I will be the last to yield an inch." He was not really interested in the presidency, and he cared far more about Davis's recovering from his wound and "in the termination of this war, so that the volunteers who are suffering so much from disease, would get to their homes." He had not voted in 1844, but he would have voted for Clay if he had had the opportunity.[26]

In July, also, Taylor wrote that he would prefer others if any of them could be elected. He doubted his own qualifications, but he would serve if the people called. He would not, however, "give any pledges to what I will do in certain contingencies, other than to support the constitution as near as practicable, as was construed by our first chief magistrate." If Clay, Crittenden, John McLean, or John M. Clayton could be elected, Taylor would retire, but he would "undergo political martyrdom rather than see Gen'l Scott or Cass elected." He would prefer even the Democrats Silas Wright or Martin Van Buren over either Scott or Cass.[27]

A few weeks later, Taylor commented to Davis further that many of the subjects dividing the parties had already been settled for many years to come, "if not by the act of limitation at least by common consent; yet many rabid politicians on both sides hold on to the whole of them with greatest tenacity, and enter on their discussion when generally acknowledged to be dead, with the same warmth and zeal as if the existence of the union depended on their doing so." Reminding Davis of Taylor's own great financial stake in slavery, Taylor added that while he would "respect the opinions and feelings of the non-slaveholding states on that subject and be careful not to do any act which would interfere with legal rights as regards the same," he would be "equally careful that no encroachments were made on the rights of the citizens of the slaveholding states as regards that description of property, or in fact anything else; let justice be done to and in every part of the country, North, East, South, and West, in accordance with the provision of the Constitution, which seems to me to be the proper and only course to pursue." Slavery, he wrote, had become the most dangerous question in American history because "the intemperate zeal of the fanatics of the North, and the intemperate zeal of a few politicians of the South" would "no longer admit of a proper and calm discussion, neither in the pulpit or Congress, in the newspapers or in primary assemblies of the people."[28]

In October 1847 Taylor was certain that the Wilmot Proviso against slavery in any of the conquered territory would "shake the Senate to its center," but he hoped that a compromise would allay the violent passions on each side and "have the effect of perpetuating instead of wrecking or shortening the Union." He also would "not be surprised if Mr. Calhoun & his friends take such a course as will enduce the non slave holding states to unite on [someone] from said states for the presidency, if so, it settles the question, they having the majority." He had long doubted that there would ever again be a president from a slave state, "much less a slave holder."[29]

In late September 1847 he wrote a well-publicized letter that threatened his nomination but probably strengthened his vote-getting appeal among the general public. He had always favored the policies of the Whig party, he wrote, but he would not "accept a nomination exclusively from either of the great parties that divide the country." This would make him "the slave of a party instead of the chief magistrate of the nation" if he should be elected. He had always believed in the principles of Jefferson, but he had never voted. If he had voted in 1844, he would have voted for Henry Clay. As for the issues, the United States Bank was dead, and would not be revived in his time. The "tariff . . . only for revenue; internal improvements, which will go on in spite of presidential vetoes; & the Wilmot proviso, which was brought into Congress to array the South against the [North] must, or ought to be left to Congress." The president should have nothing to do with making laws. He must approve or veto them, but when they were passed over his veto, he must see that they were executed.[30]

As late as February 1848 Taylor announced that he would feel bound to decline a nomination "by Whig or Democratic convention, State or National, exclusively on party grounds." He must remain free of all pledges and independent of all parties. In the same letter he denied that he would withdraw from the national campaign if the Whig party were to nominate Henry Clay.[31]

Taylor's insistence upon being a national rather than a party candidate was shrewd politics for the national election, but it might have cost him the nomination had it not been for the timely intervention of Crittenden, Logan Hunton, James Love, Balie Peyton, and other supporters. To become the candidate and the president of all the people he first had to be nominated by the Whigs, since his often-expressed and well-known antipathy to the Democrats made a selection from that quarter impossible. After persuading Taylor that this was so, they sent a letter over his signature to his financial manager and brother-in-law John Allison, in which Taylor declared flatly that he was "a Whig, but not an ultra Whig." Even in this letter, however, Taylor insisted that he would be a president independent of party. The letter also repeated a Whiggish approach to the presidency that Taylor had already expressed privately. He would veto only those measures that were clearly unconstitutional, and he would make no effort to control the Congress on questions of domestic policy such as the tariff, currency, and internal improvements.[32]

Despite his ownership of slaves and his numerous statements that alienated large segments of the Whig party, Taylor was nominated on the fourth ballot. Several days later he first learned of his nomination when the river steamer en route from Memphis to New Orleans stopped at his plantation long enough for the shouting passengers to give him the word. In turn, the Whig leadership waited for weeks for his official letter of acceptance because his refusal to pay the postage on the many letters that had poured in had caused his official notification to be sent back to the dead-letter office. While waiting for it to be retrieved, he decided that the convention was "one of the purest, most talented & patriotic body of men . . . ever met together in this or any country for a similar object, to designate who was to rule over them." If elected, however, he would serve "more from a sense of duty than from inclination."[33]

In late August, Taylor publicly accepted the nomination of a small group of South Carolina Democrats and thereby created an immediate crisis that had to be solved by another letter to Captain Allison. The general's vice-presidential running mate, Millard Fillmore, strongly advised Taylor to do this because Weed and Seward had actually threatened to have the New York Whig convention nominate a third candidate. Taylor's biographer Holman Hamilton believed that Taylor wrote the letter himself; K. Jack Bauer thinks it was a joint effort of Taylor and Alexander C. Bullitt; and Fillmore's biographer Robert Rayback credits it simply to Taylor's advisers. Regardless, it was a strong letter that made no apologies but did reiterate the candidate's devotion to Whig principles. The South Carolina Democratic nomination was a compliment, and "it should not be expected that I would repulse them with insult. I shall not modify my views to entice them to my side; I shall not reject their aid when they join my friends voluntarily."[34]

When the final vote was tabulated, his victory over Cass, Polk, and Scott was complete and his satisfaction total: My election, he wrote,

> has no doubt astonished those in power, who resorted to every measure to break me down as far as they could do so, when in a foreign country in front of the enemy, & to destroy me by the vilest slanders of the most principled demagogues this or any other nation ever was cursed with, who have pursued me like bloodhounds up to the present moment, & who will continue to do so, as long as their employers or masters will it, notwithstanding the signal rebuke they have met with from a majority of the free and independent voters of the country; the maxim is a correct one that the sovereign people when left to thems(elves) rarely err, & the recent election proves that even when every effort is resorted to on the part of their rulers to mislead & deceive them, they are capable of judging for themselves & showing their servants who they placed in high places that they are capable of judging for themselves & deciding who shall rule over them.[35]

In his view, democracy, the people, and Zachary Taylor had been vindicated.

4

★ ★ ★ ★ ★

THE ACHIEVER

Just as Zachary Taylor's rough exterior belied his aristocratic heritage, the immaculate grooming, impeccable dress, and polished manners of Millard Fillmore concealed a background of severe poverty. Taylor's abilities had carried him far beyond the family connections that had been responsible for his first commission, but Fillmore was entirely a self-made man. His father, Nathaniel Fillmore, left the stony soils and arctic climate of Vermont in 1799 to buy a public tract in Cayuga County, New York, where Millard, the eldest child, was born a year later. The new farm was also cursed with soil unsuitable for the crops being planted, and Nathaniel actually lost but little when a defective title forced him to abandon it. He moved to Sempronius, New York, and spent the next several years as a hard-working but poor tenant farmer. The newly rented 130 acre tract was not much better than the farm that Nathaniel had lost, and Millard grew up semiliterate, physically powerful, and thoroughly accustomed to backbreaking labor. His father did not even permit such diversions as hunting and fishing.[1]

Fortunately, Millard's ambition to escape the land coincided with his father's determination to keep his sons from becoming farmers. At the age of fourteen, the boy was apprenticed to a cloth dresser, but he soon returned home because of harsh treatment. Shortly afterward he was again apprenticed, this time to a textile mill. He was painfully aware of his ignorance, and he worked constantly to improve the minimal reading skills he had acquired during a few scattered months of schooling. He carried a dictionary everywhere he went, and when some neighbors organized a lending library, he read every book available.

During a period of unemployment because of a slack season at the mill, Fillmore enrolled at the nearby Academy of Good Hope, where he met Abigail Powers, a minister's daughter who encouraged his ambitions and shared his dreams. Then Nathaniel Fillmore moved again, this time to become the tenant of a local Quaker judge, Walter Wood, who recognized Millard's talents and persuaded him to study law. Wood employed Fillmore as a clerk in his law office and lent him money for subsistence during the long period of legal apprenticeship. The young man also taught school and saved enough money to buy the remaining time of his apprenticeship at the mill. Fillmore continued to study law in Wood's office until a dispute caused him to leave. Nathaniel also again grew restive and moved to Aurora, near the rising town of Buffalo. In Buffalo, Millard Fillmore got another teaching job and again became a law clerk. Finally admitted to the bar at the age of twenty-four, he opened an office in East Aurora and married Abigail two years later.

The young lawyer studied and read constantly, and he was soon admitted to practice before the state supreme court, as his reputation rapidly grew. He was by all accounts an excellent lawyer who represented his clients with both talent and diligence. He was a slow and deliberate speaker rather than an exciting orator, but his arguments were cogent and his grammar was correct.

Unlike Zachary Taylor, Fillmore was strikingly handsome. He was tall and dignified and always dressed meticulously in the latest fashion. Like the young Abraham Lincoln, he was driven by a burning ambition to escape from all traces of his humble beginnings. Fillmore's life style was not pretentious, but he and Abigail and their two children lived comfortably as one of Buffalo's leading families. They were charter members of Buffalo's first Unitarian society. Fillmore helped form the Buffalo High School Association, which opened in 1828, and he served as a vice-president of the Lyceum, which conducted lectures, debates, and scientific experiments and maintained a reading room. When the Young Men's Association replaced the Lyceum in 1837, he gave it time, money, and a great many books. From 1842 until his death he was honorary chancellor of the newly created University of Buffalo.

Buffalo was a growing city superbly located at the end of the Erie Canal between Lakes Erie and Ontario. It was therefore only natural that Fillmore should support the National Republicans of John Quincy Adams and the American System of tariffs, National Bank, and internal improvements proposed by Henry Clay. When the Albany editor and politician Thurlow Weed shrewdly strengthened the National Republicans by combining them with the Anti-Masons, Fillmore joined the effort and was elected to the New York State Assembly in 1828, even though the Jacksonian Democrats swept most of the state. Gradually he became the recognized leader of the Whig party in western New York. He was almost perfect in the role: a kind, gentle, and generous husband and father; an orthodox Unitarian; a citizen immersed in his community's efforts at self-improvement; and an ardent and effective advocate of the best interests of his constituents.

In the assembly, Fillmore worked to abolish imprisonment for debt, as well as the religious oath for courtroom witnesses. In Buffalo, meanwhile, his legal career was enormously successful. He promoted turnpike companies, ferries, banks, school charters, and dams. He helped create a fire department that had special wells and reservoirs as well as fire engines. He helped get the Erie Canal's terminal facilities greatly enlarged. In 1832 he was elected to Congress, and Daniel Webster arranged for him to practice law before the Supreme Court. Fillmore took a neutral position on the United States Bank because he disliked both Nicholas Biddle and the opponents of the bank. In 1834 he was busy getting the former Anti-Masons, the National Republicans, and the Whigs combined into the new Whig party, and he therefore refused to run for reelection. Two years later, however, he was again elected to Congress, where he served three terms, 1837–42. During the third term he was runner-up in the voting for Speaker and became chairman of the powerful Ways and Means Committee. In this capacity, he did a masterly job of steering the tariff of 1842 through the House. He won the plaudits of all Whigs everywhere, but again he decided against seeking reelection.

Meanwhile, in New York, William H. Seward had been defeated for reelection to the governorship, and jealousies between the Seward-Weed faction of Whigs in Albany and the group led by Fillmore in Buffalo were becoming more pronounced. In 1844 Fillmore was the Whig candidate for governor, but he was defeated by the Democrat Silas Wright. During the campaign, Fillmore made numerous speeches against the annexation of Texas. He ran well ahead of Clay's presidential effort, but he lost by a small margin. The Liberty party effort that gave the state to Polk probably also injured Fillmore. Also, more and more new immigrants from abroad were pouring into New York, and they usually voted Democratic.

For the next four years, Fillmore vociferously attacked Polk's domestic policies as well as the Mexican War. In his view, the interests of the North were being sacrificed for a wild and wicked scheme of conquest to add another vast slave territory. The South was running the country to the detriment of Northern businessmen. In July 1847, four thousand angry delegates attended a convention in Chicago to protest loudly their failure to get federal appropriations for improvements of rivers and harbors. Fillmore attended, and a month later he was a leader when a Buffalo meeting echoed that of Chicago.

In 1847 Fillmore was elected state comptroller by the largest plurality ever won by a Whig over a Democrat in New York State. Again he went to Albany, where he served both his state and his city extremely well. He got the Erie Canal basin enlarged, and he framed the outline of a new banking code. He designed a state currency system that congressional Republicans would later adopt in the National Banking Act of 1861. Paper money in New York would now be backed by New York State and federal bonds, instead of by commercial paper. With an impeccable reputation, many friends, and virtually no enemies except for jealous rivals within his own party, Fillmore went to the Whig convention of 1848. His nomination for vice-president surprised him as much as it did Thurlow Weed.

Fillmore played an indispensable role in the 1848 election campaign. The Whig leaders, remembering the tactics that had won in 1840, wrote no platform at all but let Taylor and Fillmore develop their principles as the campaign progressed. The Democrats charged, quite correctly, that the Whigs were proslavery in the South and antislavery in the North. The Southern Democrats attacked Fillmore viciously with charges that he was an abolitionist bent on stopping the interstate slave trade. Fillmore denied this. He stayed clear of the territorial slavery question, but he did inform a group of Southerners that while he thought slavery was an evil, it was a subject that the national government should have nothing to do with. The question, he said, rested entirely with the individual states.

Fillmore's greatest contribution, however, was in the North, where anger among Whigs still simmered over the nomination of the slaveholding Taylor. When Fillmore insisted that the general had no wish to extend slavery, he was speaking the truth, but this was difficult to prove, and Taylor's acceptance of the South Carolina Democratic nomination created a genuine crisis. Weed called for a mass meeting of New York Whigs, who were expected to demand a new state convention to nominate another candidate and desert Taylor. Fillmore, however, went to Weed and angrily insisted that the meeting be canceled. After hours of fierce argument, Fillmore persuaded Weed to adjourn the meeting for two days, during which time they could advise Taylor to publish the second letter to Captain Allison. This letter effectively explained Taylor's position in terms that satisfied most Northern Whigs. This action probably saved the victory for Taylor, because any division of the Whig ranks by a fourth candidate would have given New York and the election to Lewis Cass.[2]

The bare facts of Fillmore's political career in New York only scratch the surface of the intelligence, character, determination, and hard work that it had required. New York politics was a labyrinth of conflicting ambitions, personal feuds, genuine disagreements over policy, and constantly shifting alliances within each major party. The Democratic party's division between Hunkers and Barnburners had created the Free-Soilers and the third-party candidacy of Martin Van Buren. The Whigs were split by equal rivalry between the friends and enemies of Thurlow Weed for control of jobs and honors, between the conflicting interests of the rural and urban areas, and by the competition between the eastern and western parts of the state for all manner of public appropriations.

In Albany, editor Thurlow Weed played the game for the personal satisfactions created by the wielding of power as well as for financial advantages. At an early date he had decided to make his close friend and confidant William Henry Seward president of the United States. Seward was brilliant in his own way, but as a presidential candidate he was handicapped by his short height and unprepossessing appearance, not to mention his habit of making wild statements without having previously assessed their consequences. Fillmore would have been a better star for Weed's ambitions, but he was in fact much too conscientious for Weed's taste. Indeed, Fillmore's election to the vice-presidency was a serious blow to Weed's long-range plans. Fillmore's emergence as vice-president was a tribute to his record and talents, as well as something of a vindication of the American political system. Like Zachary Taylor, Fillmore had attained a sweet triumph over those who wished him ill, but for Weed and Seward the game was just beginning.[3]

5

★ ★ ★ ★ ★

THE ADMINISTRATION

Zachary Taylor had faced Indian, British, and Mexican arrows, bullets, and artillery unscathed, but he was less fortunate on his way to the White House. At Madison, Indiana, a trunk fell on him and inflicted painful injuries to his arm and side. At Cincinnati, Ohio, the crowd pushed him into a boat guard and severely bruised his left hand. He caught a bad cold, which was not alleviated by delays when his steamboat on the Ohio River first ran aground and then was delayed by ice jams. He did, however, enjoy the huge crowds, bonfires, cannon salutes, and fireworks that greeted him along the route.

Because 4 March fell on a Sunday, the inauguration was postponed until Monday, and this furnished historians and others with a trivial question for a meaningless argument. David Atchison, president *pro tempore* of the Senate, would later claim that he had been president for a day, but if any important decision had been required, Taylor could have taken the oath of office at any time during the period.

March 5 was a cold, windy, gloomy day, and the personal relations between the two men in the open carriage leading the long procession did nothing to improve the atmosphere. Taylor had once been cheered by the heartwarming rumor that Polk was dead. Polk, upon learning of Taylor's election, had written that "without political information and without experience in civil life," Taylor was "wholly unqualified for the station. . . . Having no opinions or judgment of his own upon any one political subject, foreign or domestic, he will be compelled to rely upon the designing men of the Federal party who will cluster around him, and will be made to reverse . . . the whole policy of my administration. . . . The country will be the loser by his election, and on this account it is an event which I shall deeply regret."[1]

Polk, of course, had posed a vital question. Taylor had indeed been elected to the nation's most powerful office with no previous experience or training, and the election of presidents on the basis of fame and personal image unrelated to political philosophy or policy is a continuing problem for American democracy. On the other hand, some of America's most ineffectual presidents have been men of great political experience, and on rare occasions an amateur has demonstrated remarkable natural skills. Neither George Washington nor Abraham Lincoln, after all, had enjoyed any significant political experience, and Woodrow Wilson's previous time in office had been minimal. The presidency, in fact, is an office so totally different from any other and offers the opportunities for so many different styles of leadership that the performance of any given president-elect is often difficult to predict.

Zachary Taylor was accustomed to making hard decisions and standing by them. He was highly intelligent and was better informed on various important issues than a great many people, including James K. Polk, realized. Indeed, on the most important issue of all—the extension of slavery and the incorporation of the new territories into the United States—Taylor and Polk were in full agreement. Both were large slaveholders tied firmly by self-interest, custom, and belief to the preservation of slavery. Both thought the Wilmot Proviso was unnecessary and dangerous. Both were certain that slavery had no place in the new territories and considered Calhoun's position to be as foolish and dangerous as that of Wilmot. Both wanted California to be admitted to statehood as soon as possible. Polk was not committed to immediate statehood for New Mexico, but he fully expected it to become a free territory, and Taylor would accept a free New Mexico territory as long as it was protected from the ambitions of Texas.

As for any reversal of Polk's favorite domestic policies, such as the lowered tariff and the independent Treasury, the Democratic party, dominated by the South, would still outnumber the Whigs by 35 to 25 in the Senate and by 112 to 109 in the House. Polk's gloom over the elevation of the despised Taylor was understandable but not really justified. Polk later recorded in his diary that Taylor had casually remarked that because California and Oregon were so far away, it would be better if they were to become independent states and never join the Union at all.[2] Polk considered this an example of appalling ignorance, but Taylor was clearly stating a preference for what might have been, rather than a policy for the present or the future. Taylor knew that California and Oregon were already part of the United States and that Oregon already had a territorial government. He had already been accused of unduly trying to influence Congress in favor of a temporary civil government for California. He had objected personally to Polk's conquests when they were made, and perhaps he was taking a final opportunity to irritate the president he had hated for so long. Also, amid the loud cheering and shouting that surrounded the open carriage during the trip down Pennsylvania Avenue, Polk may not have understood what Taylor was saying anyhow. The retiring president wished to hear foolish remarks and recorded one that was certainly never made as a serious proposition.

The new president's Inaugural Address was brief and, in Polk's view, badly delivered. In it, Taylor avoided specifics but stated principles the old general clearly took seriously. He knew he faced "fearful responsibilities," but he would be assisted by men well known for "talents, integrity, and purity of character." His guide would be the Constitution, and for its interpretation he would look to the decisions of the judiciary and to the example of the earlier presidents who had shared in its formation. He would abstain from entangling alliances, he would cultivate friendly relations with other nations, and he would exhaust "every resort of honorable diplomacy before appealing to arms." As "far as it is possible to be informed," he would make "honesty, capacity, and fidelity indispensable prerequisites to the bestowal of office." He would recommend to Congress measures to encourage and protect agriculture, commerce, and manufactures, and this would include the improvement of rivers and harbors. He would work for a speedy extinguishment of the national debt and the utmost economy in all public expenditures. He would look to Congress "to adopt such measures of conciliation as may harmonize conflicting interests and tend to perpetuate that Union which should be the paramount object of our hopes and affections."[3]

Snow was falling as the Taylors and Fillmore made their way to glittering all-night inauguration balls at Carusi's Saloon, Jackson Hall (built by the Democrat Francis P. Blair with money collected from bets on the election of Polk), and City Hall, where the man-

agers included Abraham Lincoln and Robert E. Lee. Fillmore's exhil-
aration was dampened somewhat by Abigail's absence in Albany,
but it was still a moment of triumph. At four A.M., Lincoln could
not resurrect his hat from the general pileup of outer garments, and
he went home without it. For a brief moment, the storm clouds of
sectional anger seemed to be forgotten, but they would soon reap-
pear. First, however, certain games of political control for self-serving
ends had to be played for their own sake. New officeholders at
every level had to be appointed, and a multitude of disappointed
aspirants had to be appeased. The task would not be easy.

Alexander H. Stephens had predicted that because Taylor had
"been elected by the people without the aid of schemers and intrigu-
ers and without any pledge save to serve the country faithfully, having no friends to reward and no enemies to punish," he would face a
"bitter hostility by a set of leeches who look upon the public offices
as nothing but spoils for political hacks to revel on."[4] The prophecy
was soon justified. In selecting members of a cabinet and other advisers, Taylor was severely handicapped by the fact that he knew so
few politicians personally. The able and dedicated Unionist John J.
Crittenden was Taylor's first choice for whatever cabinet post Crittenden would take, but the Kentuckian steadfastly resisted the pleas
of numerous friends as well as Taylor. Crittenden had been harshly
criticized for abandoning his old friend Henry Clay for selfish reasons, and he had never forgotten the "corrupt bargain" charge made
in 1825 when Clay supported John Quincy Adams against Andrew
Jackson and then became secretary of state. To maintain his long-
standing reputation for unselfish honesty, Crittenden almost had to
decline any offer from Taylor. Also, Crittenden had just been elected
governor of Kentucky and quite properly felt that he had an obligation to serve. Taylor was much hurt by his friend's refusal, and
though Crittenden offered advice from time to time through mutual
friends, Taylor often ignored it.

Senator John M. Clayton of Delaware had made two powerful
speeches defending and praising Taylor when the Polk administration had condemned Taylor's disobedience of orders that had produced the battle and victory of Buena Vista. Taylor remembered,
and as a leading Whig senator, Clayton was a logical choice for
secretary of state. In turn, Clayton was able to advise Taylor on his
other cabinet choices, and indeed, each new appointee became an
adviser in the choice of further appointments.

The results were mixed. Taylor's cabinet can be criticized harshly
if the historian evaluates them by reading the speeches and editori-

als of their enemies. But so can that of Abraham Lincoln and any other president who serves during troubled times. Taylor announced that he wanted a geographical balance, and this he achieved. Clayton, an enormous man of some six feet five inches and two hundred and forty pounds, was a distinguished lawyer and senator, and in the primary role of his office—conducting foreign affairs—he did very well indeed. In the Senate he had authored a sensible compromise designed to save face for both sides during the angry and senseless debate over slavery in Oregon, but the House had rejected his effort. He was still ambitious to be a mediator between North and South, but his talents were occasionally diluted by excessive drinking, and no moderate on the question of extending slavery could avoid the barbs of either the more extreme Southerners or the Northern advocates of the Wilmot Proviso. He was suspect in the South because he had once voted for the Wilmot Proviso. Clayton's drinking was probably increased by personal tragedies, including the recent deaths of a much-loved wife and favorite son. Clayton was often criticized for inefficiency, absent-mindedness, and a lack of organization in his department. On the other hand, he achieved a great deal of work with only two assistants, William Hunter and George P. Fisher. No one denied that Clayton worked long hours in trying to keep up with his many responsibilities, and excessive drinking on only one or two occasions would have been enough to generate the reputation that dogged him.[5]

Secretary of the Treasury William M. Meredith was a successful Pennsylvania lawyer. At least some observers noted his bulky frame, hunched shoulders, and black hair and were reminded of a bulldog. He had long represented the iron and manufacturing interests of Pennsylvania, and he felt that the lowered tariff written by his predecessor, Robert J. Walker, and passed in 1846 was both an insult and a serious blow to his state's best interests. Meredith was ready to promote higher tariffs, but he soon found the task impossible. His extremely personable wife quickly made friends with the president and his family, and Taylor soon came to look upon Meredith with great affection.[6]

The new Department of the Interior went to Thomas Ewing of Ohio, a distinguished lawyer and senator from Ohio. Ewing was a large and powerful man with a huge belly and a completely bald head. His wife, Maria, was a devout Catholic who reared their two daughters and four sons in the faith. The Ewings also were foster parents to the young William T. Sherman, who ultimately married one of their daughters. As the supervisor of patents, pensions, public lands, and Indian affairs, Ewing dispensed a considerable number of jobs, and he believed strongly that wherever possible, Democratic officeholders should be replaced by Whigs. He soon gained a reputation as the administration's hatchet man, but he ran his department efficiently.[7]

Georgia's former governor George W. Crawford, a successful lawyer and a member of a distinguished family, was appointed secretary of war at the request of the Georgia congressmen Robert Toombs and Alexander H. Stephens. Suave and handsome in his immaculate and well-styled clothes, Crawford would prove to be the weak link in the cabinet. He had been for several years the attorney for a claimant in a financial case against the government that dated back to 1773. He mentioned this to Taylor but did not specify the amount of the potential personal reward involved. Taylor, as well as his Georgia friends, assured Crawford that no significant conflict of interest existed. Although no legal wrongdoing was ever proved, the claim would later damage the reputations of Crawford, Meredith, and Attorney General Reverdy Johnson, but Taylor could not have foreseen this in early 1849.[8]

The new secretary of the navy was a red-haired Virginia aristocrat, William Ballard Preston. He was sometimes embarrassingly ignorant of naval affairs, but he shared Taylor's devotion to the American Union. Preston believed ardently that the slavery-extension problem could be and should be settled on terms that would be acceptable to the North, and in Congress he had recently advocated the immediate admission of California to statehood. Like Crawford, he was strongly recommended by Stephens and Toombs. Intensely loyal to Taylor, Preston would soon be branded as a Southern man with Northern principles.[9]

Postmaster General Jacob Collamer was a stern-visaged son of Vermont. He had been a judge and had served six years in Congress. Democrats described him as dull, plodding, and narrow-minded. Whigs thought him highly perceptive and very able. The postal service was growing rapidly, but Collamer would do little to change the basic organizational structure. Perhaps most important, he had control of some seventeen thousand postmasterships, and he was ready to make changes. He would later become a Republican senator, and in 1861 he would draft the bill approving Lincoln's efforts to suppress the Southern secession with military force.[10]

And finally, Attorney General Reverdy Johnson of Maryland was a wealthy lawyer with a brilliant legal reputation. There was no Department of Justice, and the attorney general would have to write his own briefs and argue cases before the Supreme Court in person. Johnson had been blinded in one eye when a bullet had ricocheted from a target while he was coaching a friend who had been challenged to a duel. The vision in Johnson's remaining eye had also declined, and some charged that he argued from instinct rather than from erudition or reading evidence. He would later defend Andrew Johnson in his impeachment trial and serve with great success as minister to Great Britain.[11]

True to his promises, Taylor had chosen three cabinet members from important slaveholding states, three representing both the Northeast and the Northwest, and one from tiny Delaware, which was nominally a slave state but was not involved emotionally in the slavery quarrel. Historians have noted critically that Taylor did not offer a cabinet post to either Clay or Webster, whose illustrious careers had spanned more than thirty years. Certainly either or both would have given the administration some much-needed prestige. Clay, however, had been Taylor's chief rival for the nomination and had refused a direct request to endorse Taylor's candidacy. "I entertain with you," Clay wrote, "the strongest apprehension from the election of General Cass, but I do not see enough of hope and confidence in that of General Taylor to stimulate my exertions and excite my zeal." He would gladly recommend Fillmore, however, as "able, indefatigable, industrious, and patriotic," a man of "rare merits." Taylor's advisers considered Clay's dominating personality a serious problem. Alexander H. Stephens begged Crittenden to join the cabinet to defend Taylor against Clay's "reckless spirit of Ruling or Ruining."[12] Except for the thirty-day president, William Henry Harrison, who had appointed Webster as secretary of state, no president since John Quincy Adams had elevated an intraparty rival of greater reputation than himself. The American public may have erred by not making Clay president in 1840 or 1844, but Zachary Taylor was not obligated to correct this mistake. Webster had given Taylor a critical nudge toward the nomination, but Taylor owed him no real debt either. Also, both Clay and Webster had been elected to the Senate, where presumably their influence might prove more valuable to the Whig party than it would be in Taylor's cabinet.

Such questions as how often the cabinet met as a group and how their recommendations and advice were transmitted to Taylor are difficult to answer. The Taylors enjoyed dispensing hospitality, and the cabinet members and their wives probably came often to dinners and receptions. As a military commander, Taylor was not accustomed to take votes on important decisions, although he was always open to advice. He clearly spent much time with Clayton in dealing with various foreign-policy problems, and the secretaries of war and the navy probably took part in the discussions related to Britain and Nicaragua. Taylor must have consulted Ewing and Crawford on Indian problems. In September 1849 Taylor assured Jefferson Davis that total harmony prevailed among his ministers, that none had tried to influence him unduly, that any who might have done so would have been sternly rebuked, and that he was pleased because none of them was trying to become the next president. Collamer, he wrote, was "too stiff & blunt" to make many friends, but he was "honest . . . and will administer faithfully . . . the laws."[13] Taylor apparently developed a close personal friendship with Meredith, whose involvement with the later Crawford scandal obviously caused Taylor much pain. Taylor's approach to the problem of slavery, California, and the territories was clearly stated before his election, and it never wavered. He selected only men who agreed with it, but he would have remained firm if they had changed their minds. Only Crawford ultimately came to feel that the president's zeal for protecting New Mexico went too far, and Taylor did not hesitate to overrule his secretary on the issue. Also, he took a stronger position than that recommended by Clayton on an important foreign-policy question. One can only speculate, but Taylor apparently allowed his secretaries to run their departments with minimal interference and accepted their advice only when it coincided with his own views. Even on patronage questions he was rarely out of touch. On 14 July 1840 Collamer apologized to Crittenden because he had not been able to appoint the governor's choice for postmaster of Louisville. Taylor had preferred someone else, and Collamer complained, "I am but a subaltern, and obey, but it seems that in so doing I must lose all the personal attachment and respect of those whose respect I value."[14]

Perhaps the only certain generalization to be made about Taylor's cabinet choices is the fact that contemporary judgments of their character and abilities cannot be trusted. If they had all been angels straight from heaven, the criticisms by Democratic editors and politicians would have been just as harsh. If they had been totally incompetent, their few defenders would have praised them with equal eloquence. The cabinet members were seriously handicapped by the fact that every federal job was desired by several members of their own party, and their choices ultimately split the Whigs themselves into winning and losing factions. How deeply this cut into the thinking of the general public cannot be measured, but every disappointed

office seeker or discharged officeholder, whether Whig or Democrat, had relatives and friends. In early 1849 William H. Seward
commented that everyone in America seemed to be going either to
California to find gold or to Washington in search of an appointment. And because the hero of Buena Vista was still immensely
popular with the general electorate, the cabinet members bore the
brunt of the assault. They had their defenders, but the language of
invective is best utilized by attackers. Francis P. Blair, who had
edited the Democratic party's *Globe* throughout the Jackson, Van
Buren, and Tyler administrations, had honed the art of colorful but
reasonably polite insult to a fine art.[15] His successor, Thomas Ritchie,
editor of the *Union*, eschewed all courtesy as well as Blair's wit and
humor; he attacked with a blunderbuss. Almost from the first day
of Taylor's presidency, the *Union* pictured him as a senile fool with
no principles other than those imposed upon him by a knavish,
scheming, unscrupulous cabinet composed of corrupt traitors. Taylor's
own editors, Alexander C. Bullitt and, later, Allan A. Hall at the
Republic, and his equally devoted defenders, Joseph Gales and William W. Seaton at the *National Intelligencer*, wrote thoughtful and
well-argued editorials, but they were never a match for Ritchie, even
in their influence upon future historians.

Like every president since John Quincy Adams, Taylor allowed
his friends to establish a newspaper authorized to speak for the president and dedicated to convincing the public that his views and policies were above reproach and that his opponents were unscrupulous
knaves or worse. Albert T. Burnley, formerly of Frankfort, Kentucky, was a close personal friend of John J. Crittenden's. Burnley
had gone to Texas and had been at the Alamo a week before its fall.
Later, Sam Houston and the Texas Republic had sent Burnley on
delicate missions to Britain and France. By 1848 he was a wealthy
businessman in New Orleans and a go-between for Crittenden and
Taylor before the latter's nomination. In 1849 Burnley was ready to
come to Washington and be the publisher of the *Republic*. To do the
actual editing and to write the editorials, Alexander Bullitt of New
Orleans and John O. Sargent of Boston were selected. Bullitt had
been a coeditor of the New Orleans *Picayune* and had written one
of Taylor's public letters during the election campaign. Sargent had
written for the *Boston Atlas* and the *New York Courier and
Enquirer*.[16]

During the Jackson and Van Buren administrations, the
Democratic party editor Francis P. Blair had been a major dispenser
of patronage. Taylor, however, quite properly left this task to the

cabinet members responsible for the performances of the appointees. The most active dispensers of federal jobs were Interior Secretary Thomas Ewing and Postmaster General Jacob Collamer, both Northerners, while in selecting ministers, consuls, and other diplomats, Clayton also showed an independence unappreciated by the *Republic's* publisher and editors. Burnley was away most of the time, and Bullitt in effect ran the paper. Bullitt was not only disgruntled at the cabinet over patronage matters; he also felt strongly that the information he needed in order to serve as the oracle for other Whig papers throughout the country was being denied by the secretaries. The fact that the hated William H. Seward was close to the cabinet, and particularly to the Virginian William Ballard Preston, was even more galling. Long before the policy differences between the president and Henry Clay, the *Republic's* editors had developed a bitter personal hatred for most members of the cabinet.[17]

As early as 3 July 1849, only four months after the inauguration, Crittenden was urging his friend Orlando Brown to "try and break down the barrier that seems to divide Bullitt from the administration. . . . Tell Bullitt that his paper is still too much on the *defensive*. He does not show forth old Zach enough, his plainness, his integrity, his patriotism, and that therein lies the hostility of old Ritchie and that whole breed of politicians." Three weeks later, Crittenden instructed Brown to tell Bullitt that he had finally got the paper up to "the right *temperature*; he must keep it as hot as a furnace till the Union is purged in 'liquid fire' . . . the rage of Ritchie & Co. must be attributed to its natural cause—their exclusion from the domination and spoils they have so long indulged in." Crittenden was still worried about the distrust of the cabinet being expressed by Bullitt, Sargent, and Burnley and was anxious to see them "all cured of this *disorder*."[18]

The patronage problem for the president of a party that had been starved for appointments for twenty years was well-nigh unsolvable. Taylor was responsible, even if he played no direct role, for thousands of federal jobs ranging down to who would deliver the local mail or clean the government buildings. The Whig party was divided between North and South and between Whig factions in each section and state, and the many patronage questions involving individual competitions could only exacerbate the differences. The party's only previous presidential administration had been a political catastrophe when President Harrison died and was succeeded by the former states' rights Virginia Democrat John Tyler. The Whig party had excommunicated Tyler because of his vetoes, and Tyler, who was considered a renegade by both parties, had either left Democrats in place or had replaced them with men equally anathema to loyal Whigs. In short, Whig party workers held virtually none of the federal jobs in 1849, and they were panting for the many opportunities they had anticipated for so many years. As the most populous state, New York was especially important. The dispenser of the patronage there would control the state's political machinery and enjoy much influence in other states.

By temperament and conviction, Millard Fillmore was in complete harmony with Taylor's cabinet, but editor Thurlow Weed in Albany, New York, was determined to make the vice-president an outsider in the Taylor administration. On the surface, Weed was affectionate and cooperative toward Fillmore, but behind the scenes Weed plotted to destroy the man he considered a barrier to the future presidential ambitions of Seward. John Collier had nominated Fillmore for vice-president, but with a plea for party harmony, Weed was able to persuade Fillmore to support Seward instead of Collier for the United States Senate. Once elected, Seward rushed to Washington to begin an effort to eliminate Fillmore's influence in the distribution of the New York patronage.

Few American leaders have equaled William H. Seward in talent for ingratiating himself with others, regardless of disagreements on principle or policy. He would later thrive in the Lincoln administration even after his various secret efforts to give Fort Sumter to the South without bloodshed. In early 1849 Seward went to Baltimore to try a patent suit. He had met the president-elect's brother Col. Joseph Taylor at the Whig convention and had made a very pleasant impression on the colonel's wife. In Baltimore, Seward quickly renewed this relationship and proved equally charming to Zachary Taylor's son-in-law and daughter, Dr. and Mrs. Robert C. Wood. Before the inauguration, Seward impressed Zachary Taylor favorably by supporting a senatorial resolution approving statehood for California, and he quickly became a highly regarded personal friend at the White House. Taylor had never condemned those who argued against slavery as long as no action was involved, and Seward's reputation for antislavery sentiments had no apparent effect upon a very pleasant personal relationship. The new senator was equally effective in developing friendships within the cabinet and was reportedly very close to the Virginian William Ballard Preston.[19]

Apparently, Seward gave complete lip service to the goals of the president and his administration. Taylor and his cabinet members were united in their hopes that the slavery quarrel could be muted, that Southern and Northern Whigs could be reunited to promote the original economic goals of the Whig party, and that they could win the White House again in 1852. The Southern cabinet members agreed with their Northern colleagues that previous Mexican laws and customs, including Indian peonage, as well as geography and climate, had already made slavery a dead issue in the former Mexican territories. These Southern members wanted to get California and New Mexico into the Union as states as soon as possible in order to end the Southern agitation against restricting slavery in the territories. Not even John C. Calhoun had ever questioned the right of a state to make its own decision in such matters. Their purpose, as well as Taylor's, was to give the North the substance of the Wilmot Proviso without making the South swallow it as a formally enacted principle. Only North-South unity could make possible another Whig presidential victory in 1852, and the cabinet considered Southern territorial demands to be an unnecessary and dangerous goad to otherwise quiescent Northern feelings about slavery. Secretary of War Crawford, however, apparently did believe that the disputed claim of Texas to most of New Mexico should be honored in exchange for a free California.[20]

This was not a secure administration armed with a popular mandate. The combined vote of Cass and Van Buren had exceeded that of Taylor by almost 160,000 votes. Taylor had carried eight slave states and seven free states, while Cass had carried seven slave states and eight free states. The large states of New York, Massachusetts, and Pennsylvania had given Taylor the electoral majority, but the Free Soil party had also run well in a great many Northern states, had elected nine congressmen to the House, and had even beaten Cass in Massachusetts. The Democrats had won a three-vote edge in the House and a ten-vote margin in the Senate. The Southerners predominated among the Democrats. The Southerners in Taylor's cabinet had to assume that a great many Northern Whigs might be compelled to insist upon the Wilmot Proviso, if only to prove their independence of the slaveholder in the White House. Naturally enough, the cabinet looked for Northern allies wherever they could be found. Popular wisdom held that Thurlow Weed controlled most of New York's Whig representatives, and Weed's protégé Seward stood ready to be cultivated. In all likelihood, Clayton and Preston thought they were wooing Seward at the same time that he was wooing them. Whether such an arrangement was formalized or whether it just evolved day by day, Seward apparently received the patronage for the entire state of New York in exchange for his and

Weed's support for Taylor's moderate solution to the territorial problems. It is also possible, however, that in the face of an overwhelming and time-consuming problem, allowing Seward to manage New York was simply the line of least resistance.

Assuming the sincerity of Seward's often-expressed antislavery views, the arrangement cost him nothing because he had every reason to believe the areas would reject slavery anyhow. Seward also won Taylor's personal regard by writing a strong defense of Taylor's efforts as president-elect on the final night of the preceding session of Congress. Taylor had personally urged a temporary civil government for California, and critics had charged that this was a violation of his campaign pledge not to try to influence the deliberations of Congress. In his increasingly warm and intimate conversations with Taylor and the cabinet, Seward probably also reminded them of Fillmore's earlier open support for the Wilmot Proviso and his statement to a Southern delegation that he considered slavery an evil. For these and perhaps other reasons impossible to determine, Fillmore, who had done so much to ensure Taylor's victory, suddenly found himself isolated and thoroughly humiliated by his own administration.

Pressured by office seekers and still following earlier agreements that he had made with Weed and Seward, Vice-President Fillmore submitted his own list of job recommendations to Seward, who insisted upon more time to consider the appointments. In return for their preconvention support, Taylor gave his New York City friends the privilege of naming the all-powerful revenue collector for the port of New York. This group happily nominated former governor John Young, who as a congressman had been one of the few Whigs to support openly the Mexican War. Young was anathema to Weed, however; so Seward persuaded Secretary of the Treasury Meredith to block the appointment. The New York City group's second choice, Hugh Maxwell, was not a Weed follower either, but because he was less objectionable than Young, they allowed the choice to stand. Then Fillmore and Seward agreed to meet at Clayton's office to present a nominee for marshal who would be agreeable to both of them. After Clayton postponed the meeting, however, Seward sent Clayton the name of his own choice, which he falsely claimed was from Fillmore as well. As a result, a Weed crony was appointed without Fillmore's knowledge. When this precipitated an open quarrel, Weed himself came to Washington and proposed a solution. The New York patronage should be denied to both Seward and Fillmore and given to Governor Hamilton Fish. Fish, of course, was actually a spokesman for Weed. Collectorships, postmasterships, and other federal appointments, both high and low, went to men who had always opposed Fillmore or who were now ready to do so in exchange for preferment. The ultimate humiliation came when Fillmore's candidate for collector of the port in his own home city of Buffalo was rejected in favor of a Weed-supported hack. "We could put up a cow against a Fillmore nominee and defeat him," chortled the *Buffalo Express*. All over New York State, the professional politicians decided that their self-interest lay with Weed and acted accordingly.[21]

Meanwhile, however, Southern moderates like Alexander Stephens and Robert Toombs from Georgia began to suspect that the president might support the Wilmot Proviso. They believed that Seward had cast a spell over the president. In fact, long before he had even met Seward, Taylor had concluded that the new acquisitions from Mexico would be and should be free.

Taylor was a slaveholder, but he had always supported the right of nonslaveholders to oppose the expansion of slavery. He believed that nature and previous laws and customs had already settled the issue of slavery in the new territories, and he saw no merit in rousing Northern animosities against slavery when nothing could be gained. This view was identical to that held by both Thomas Hart Benton and Sam Houston, but it is doubtful that either Benton or Houston had influenced Taylor. However, Taylor's longstanding dislike for Benton and, indeed, for almost all Jacksonian Democrats, had abated considerably in 1848 when Taylor had learned that Benton at a social gathering had said that if given the overall command, he would put all military operations under the control of Taylor.[22]

Historians often consider a president weak if they disagree with his policies, and William H. Seward and Zachary Taylor's cabinet have at times been credited with undue influence over the allegedly ignorant old general. True, they did manage his patronage policies, but this happens with all presidents. No president can know the qualifications of all candidates for appointment in every state, and devising the means for efficiently and accurately selecting qualified employees is quite properly the duty of the cabinet officers, who, after all, are primarily heads of the executive departments. Even though various contemporary Southerners believed that Seward was the evil genius behind some of Taylor's convictions, it is far more likely that Seward acquired influence by supporting policies already determined by Taylor and his cabinet. The Free-Soil senator Salmon P. Chase, among others, was certain of this.[23] Long before he had been elected president, Taylor had stated the basic convictions from which he did not deviate during his brief term in office. If he and most of his cabinet were a harmonious group on important policies, it was because they agreed on what should be done and not because strong advisers had captured the mind of a weak and ignorant president. Indeed, on the subject of Texas and New Mexico, Taylor's belligerence went far beyond that of his advisers. No one had to let Taylor be Taylor; no one could have kept Taylor from being Taylor. He was neither weak nor modest, and *no* had always been one of his favorite words.

Taylor probably looked upon his friendship with Seward as a symbol of the tolerance and harmony between North and South that he was trying to establish. His acceptance of Seward's openly expressed antislavery views was admirable, but allowing Seward to assume the appearance of an influential adviser was a serious political mistake. Antislavery remarks were an insult to Southern honor, and Southern gentlemen were more likely to challenge those who made them to duels than to invite them into their homes as frequent guests. Whether or not Seward exercised any significant influence on policy, the mere fact that he was welcome at the White House at all was enough to send Southerners into fits of rage. Treating the ubiquitous New Yorker with proper courtesy while holding him at arm's length would not have been easy, but in retrospect, someone should have suggested it. The most obvious candidate for advising the president on this matter was John J. Crittenden, who had a well-deserved reputation for sensitivity and tact as well as political judgment, but while the Kentucky governor kept himself informed, this possibility apparently escaped his notice. Instead, the complaints that Taylor received against Seward came in the form of vicious and often grossly exaggerated attacks by Democrats from both sections and by Southern Whigs, and the old general reacted by defending both his own judgment and his new friend's character. Unfortunately, to be effective a political leader must occasionally choose or reject friendships on the basis of political expediency rather than personal taste. A shrewder or more experienced politician might have kept Seward marching in the band without appearing to give him the baton, but the combination of Seward's aggressiveness and Taylor's capacity for easy friendship with anyone who offered support and loyalty created what was probably a very incorrect impression among suspicious and sensitive Southerners.

Actually, of course, Taylor's problems with the executive patronage went far beyond the struggle between Seward and Fillmore. During the campaign, Taylor had said that he would be the president of all the people rather than the leader of only one party. He soon discovered, however, that he had been referring to national issues rather than to the dispensation of jobs. Andrew Jackson and Martin Van Buren had built a powerful Democratic party organization through the so-called spoils system, but the process had required more than one presidential term. Except for the brief thirty days of William Henry Harrison's presidency, the Democratic party had held the White House since 1829. The Southern states' rights Democrat Tyler had been elected vice-president by the Whigs, but as president he had returned to earlier Jacksonian economic principles and had carried on a bitter warfare with those who had elected him. By 1849 the civil service had grown to some 18,000, with third- and fourth-class postmasters composing the great majority. Most desirable were the 929 presidential appointments that required the advice and consent of the Senate. The applicants for these positions were likely to have at least some political influence in their home areas, and some were very influential indeed. Men from every part of the nation wanted to be cabinet and subcabinet officers, judges, diplomats and consuls, district attorneys, marshals, port collectors and port naval officers, Land Office and Indian Affairs commissioners, territorial judges and secretaries, first- and second-class postmasters, and occupiers of various other miscellaneous posts. Many of these officers also had large staffs selected by themselves rather than by the president. Occasionally a genius at wielding the appointing power to his or his party's advantage has appeared in American politics, but most congressmen, senators, presidents, and other party leaders have found the system a thankless burden.[24] The later civil-service laws designed to protect most nonpresidential appointees would be passed with strong bipartisan support.

The spoils system obviously worked much better for incumbents seeking to stay in power than it did for those trying to use it for breaking new ground. Every new appointment gained the loyal support of the appointee, his family, and his friends. As often as not, it also created even stronger enmities among the supporters of the several candidates who did not get the job, and the closer the competition and the more difficult the selection, the greater the hostility incurred. Loyal Whigs had been thirsting for the spoils of office for twenty years, but no matter how many efficient or otherwise worthy Democratic incumbents the Taylor administration might dismiss and make angry, a far greater collection of disappointed and angry Whigs would be the inevitable result. Many Democrats had voted for Taylor, and they would charge that he had basely betrayed his promise to be the president of all the people. Factional rivalries within the Whig party existed in virtually every state, and this was compounded further by the North-South split within each party on the question of slavery extension. There were Southern Whigs who, like Taylor, would accept a free California and a free New Mexico as long as the federal government refrained from influencing the decision. There were Northerners who were determined to support the Wilmot Proviso almost as a penance for what they considered to be the nation's sinful war that had added the territories. In the heat of controversy, men would change their minds more than once. The president's friends of today would become his enemies tomorrow, and vice versa. Taylor has been criticized for not having used the patronage to strengthen his own policies. A great many appointments had to be made, however, before the president would have a chance even to know who his supporters and opponents were. Michael F. Holt has cited contemporary critics as evidence that Taylor did in fact try to broaden the base of the Whig party by awarding offices to Democrats and to Nativists.[25] This may have been true, but very few Democratic spokesmen thought so at the time. Led by the *Washington Union,* the *Richmond* (Va.) *Enquirer,* and the *Charleston* (S.C.) *Mercury,* the Democratic presses almost immediately mounted a constant drumfire against Taylor for having betrayed his pledge to be the president of all the people.

It was a time-wasting and physically wearying process for a president and cabinet with more important things to do. On 11 July 1849 Secretary of State Clayton complained to Crittenden that he had not had a day's rest for nearly five months: "If I am *kind* in manner to some men, they take occasion to construe *that* into a *promise of office.* The President says that it has now come to such a pass that if he does not *kick* a man downstairs he goes away and declares he *promised him* an office." Clayton also added: "If you will come here and take my office I will give it to you with pleasure, and with a *proviso* to stand by you all my life. . . . The honor of *serving* the man I now *serve* is the only reward I can offer you. That is indeed *an honor.* I have never met with a man who more justly deserved the respect and devotion of his friends and of all good men." Small wonder that Seward's modest offer to shoulder this burden for the enormous number of appointments to be made in New York did not fall upon deaf ears.

Clayton and others persuaded Taylor to make overtures to certain people whose support he needed. Henry Clay's son, Webster's brother-in-law and son, Crittenden's son, Truman Smith's nephew, John Collier's brother, Benton's son-in-law, and the son of the *National Intelligencer's* editor, William Seaton—all received important appointments. Interior Secretary Ewing's nineteen-year-old son became an assistant secretary to Taylor with the onerous responsibility for signing land patents. In general, however, the Taylor administration did a rather remarkable job of dividing the plums among the regional areas and among the factions of the Whig party, with New York being the one notable exception. Even in New York, Taylor ignored both Weed and Fillmore in his selection of a port collector. Of 17,180 governmental employees in 1849, 3,400 were removed and 2,800 resigned. The Whigs, who had previously held virtually none of the 929 presidential appointments, received 540 of these prizes, while the Democratic leaders and presses screamed to high heaven about the injustice of it all.[26]

Among the deserving Whigs who came away empty handed was Abraham Lincoln, who had wanted to be commissioner of the general Land Office but had waited too long to make his wishes known. The Democrat Nathaniel Hawthorne was distraught over the loss of his job as customs surveyor at Salem, Massachusetts, but the enforced idleness gave him both the incentive and the time to write *The Scarlet Letter* and other masterpieces.

In short, President Zachary Taylor was certain to be severely maligned by a great many contemporaries, regardless of his policies or his capacity for leadership. Already poised for the attack, Thomas Ritchie led a host of Democratic editors in making vicious denunciations designed to regain the hearts of Democrats who had voted for the Whig hero and to sow angry divisions among the Whigs themselves.

During most of his presidency, Taylor bore insults and condemnations with both equanimity and angry defiance. He had often been a center of controversy during his long military career, and he took the presence of enemies for granted. Indeed, like Andrew Jackson, he seemed almost to enjoy quarrels over principle. He had never been reluctant to make up his own mind and to stand firm against overwhelming pressures, and this trait did not desert him in the White House.

Taylor's inner strength was probably enhanced greatly by his happy family relationships and personal friendships. By all accounts he and Mrs. Taylor enjoyed a lifelong love affair, and his sons-in-law William W. W. Bliss and Dr. Robert C. Wood were like his own sons. Bliss, a brilliant young army officer with a genius for languages, had been the general's chief aide for several years and had only recently married Taylor's daughter Mary Elizabeth. Called "Perfect Bliss" by the family, he served as the president's private secretary, while Mary Elizabeth substituted for her frail mother as the president's official hostess. Wood, a physician married to Taylor's older daughter, Ann, lived in Baltimore. The Woods had four children, and the younger ones were frequently at the White House. The doctor himself had long been the recipient of Taylor's most intimate and informative letters, and the president was delighted to have him nearby. Taylor's younger brother also lived in nearby Baltimore, which made the family circle almost complete. Taylor's son Dick had recently graduated from Yale and was now managing the family plantation in Louisiana. Other relatives and friends were also ready to visit their famous kinsman, and the Taylor hospitality followed the usual Southern pattern of making visitors welcome to stay for long periods. While Mrs. Taylor's delicate health and personal inclinations dictated that Mary Elizabeth be the official hostess at the steady round of formal White House dinners and other entertainments, Mrs. Taylor was the unquestioned head of the private household and spent many pleasant hours with her children and grandchildren. After so many years of periodic separations, Taylor now enjoyed a comfortable home surrounded by those he loved most. He could also look out a window and see his favorite war-horse, Old Whitey, grazing with equal contentment on the White House lawn. Unquestionably, this happy situation lessened the impact of the constant criticisms and pressures he endured.

William H. Seward was not the only friend whose views on slavery and other vital matters did not interfere with Taylor's personal feelings. Varina Davis, the second wife of the Mississippi senator, long remembered how the Taylors had treated her like their long-lost daughter and Jefferson Davis like the son-in-law he had briefly been. The private conversations of Taylor and Davis were not recorded, but by late 1849 their differences with regard to slavery in the new territories were wide and deep. On 11 September 1849, after assuring Davis that he and not the cabinet was in full control of the administration, Taylor added: "I wish you to pursue that course . . . which your good sense, interest," and "honor . . . prompt you to do. . . . Even if not in accordance with my views . . . it will not interrupt our personal intercourse, or my esteem & friendship for you."[27]

Washington was still just a country town with enormously wide streets that alternated between mud and dust, but after his years on the military frontiers, Taylor found it a fascinating metropolis. He loved to don comfortable old clothes and walk through the streets among the shops and open air markets that littered Pennsylvania Avenue and other thoroughfares. No president had yet been assassinated, although an attempt had been made against Jackson, and the idea of needing any personal protection probably never crossed the old soldier's mind. His popular image as a man of genuinely democratic instincts and feelings had done much to put him in the White House. It was a well-deserved reputation earned honestly without the aid of public-relations experts.

6

★ ★ ★ ★ ★

THE STATESMAN

The greatest challenge of Zachary Taylor's brief presidency was the slavery quarrel and its threat to the Union, but even in the 1850s an American president could rarely spend a day giving his undivided attention to a single problem or crisis. There were always letters to be read, job applicants to be met, applications to be reviewed, bills to be signed or vetoed, cabinet officers to be consulted on a myriad of major and minor issues, Indian affairs to be settled, and foreign nations to be propitiated, cajoled, or defied. There were frequent social affairs involving senators and congressmen of both parties as well as foreign dignitaries. Taylor was a gregarious person who enjoyed the ceremonial duties of his office, and he was always intimately involved with the affairs of his family and friends.

At one point in the sectional debates, Taylor prevented a duel between Jefferson Davis and Congressman William H. Bissell of Illinois. Bissell, who had been at Buena Vista also, dared to disparage the exploits of the proud Davis during the battle. When Bissell refused to retract the statements, Davis sent a challenge that was promptly accepted. Taylor, however, announced that both men had performed admirably, that each was referring to a different phase of the battle, and that no cause for disagreement existed. With unusual tact, the old man managed to make it sound as though both men were being entirely truthful and that neither had insulted the other. Neither could fight without appearing to dispute the veracity of his former commander, and honor was therefore saved all around with no one injured or killed.[1] Taylor probably also argued persuasively with Davis on a more personal level. Those intrigued by "what might have beens" may speculate as to whether the Confederacy might have done better with a different president if a fatal duel had ensued.

In dealing with Indians, Taylor had always tried to be both realistic and fair. In July 1849, wild rumors spread that the Florida Seminoles were again killing whites. Florida officials wanted the president to call out volunteers and carry on a full-scale Indian war. The Indian nation, not just a few outlaws, was the enemy, wrote Bvt. Maj. Gen. David E. Twiggs from Florida. His proof: the Seminoles had purchased 120 rifles since 1842 and had supplied themselves with everything needed for war.

Zachary Taylor had been down this road before. He sent Twiggs additional troops, but refused to call up the Florida militia. A further investigation revealed that five young Seminoles led by an outlaw had killed three whites. Capt. John C. Casey, disagreeing with Twiggs, conferred with Indian emissaries, who assured him that the Seminole nation wanted only peace. Ultimately, Chief Billy Bowlegs met with Twiggs and agreed to hand over the culprits. Two escaped, but three were delivered, and the crisis passed without another Seminole War.[2]

Similar situations occurred in the Southwest. On 25 August 1849 Henry L. Kinney wrote the president from Texas that more than two hundred people had been killed, $40,000 had been stolen, and women had been carried into captivity. Later, however, he could list only thirty-nine people killed, wounded, or captured in the Corpus Christi area. On the other hand, the ranking general, George M. Brooke, reported that no Indian depredations had occurred at all. Taylor and War Secretary Crawford authorized Brooke to enlist the Texas Rangers if the Indians made trouble. In mid August, Brooke did this, and all Indian depredations, both real and imagined, suddenly stopped in the Corpus Christi area.

Further west, in the Laredo region, the Navajos and Comanches made trouble, but again the issues were settled with minimal bloodshed. In New Mexico, Col. John Washington, a hero of the Mexican War, led 320 troops in a successful battle against the Navajos, who signed a peace treaty binding upon their entire tribe. In every case the actual battles were held to a minimum, the Indians were given every chance to make a face-saving peace, and hostilities were stopped when the Indians agreed to do so. The *Washington Union* charged that Taylor had started two Indian wars, but in fact, Taylor's sense of justice and his policy of trying to keep the peace even at the risk of infuriating the local citizenry probably prevented Indian wars of a far more serious nature.[3]

Taylor had dealt with Indians all his life, but the leaders and representatives of foreign nations were a new experience. He had always kept abreast of developments abroad, however, and he was really no less qualified to exercise successful diplomacy than several of his predecessors had been. He would treat European nations with the same resolute honesty, good sense, and moderation he had always displayed toward both Mexicans and Indians.

Like Andrew Jackson, Taylor was forced into a trivial argument with France, and like Jackson, he won the argument by taking a firm stand. A Frenchman named Alexis Port had an involved claim of a thousand dollars rising out of the auction of confiscated Mexican tobacco during the Mexican War. The French minister, Guillaume Tell Lavalée Poussin, engaged in an angry name-calling contest with Secretary of State Clayton, but the matter was dropped when Taylor supported Clayton and threatened to make a vigorous protest to Poussin's government. Shortly afterward, an American ship commanded by E. W. Carpender rescued the French barque *Eugénie* from a reef off the coast of Mexico. Carpender considered the case one of salvage under international law and announced that he would keep the *Eugénie* until the proper expenses and rewards should be paid. Poussin demanded that the ship be released, but Clayton answered by sending the Frenchman a copy of Carpender's report. Again, strong language was exchanged, and Taylor had Clayton instruct Richard Rush, the American minister to Paris, to protest Poussin's conduct and let the French make the next move. The French foreign minister, Alexis de Tocqueville, the author of three highly perceptive but not uncritical volumes on American democracy, agreed unofficially to replace Poussin. Later, however, Tocqueville told Rush that Clayton had also used undiplomatic language and had seemed to infer that Poussin would be retained. When this news reached Washington, Clayton wrote Tocqueville directly that the president was dissatisfied and that the United States had dismissed Poussin. In France, meanwhile, Tocqueville had already appointed a successor to Poussin and considered the matter of the ships closed, but Clayton's note wounded French dignity and reopened the controversy. Tocqueville demanded to know whether Poussin's dismissal was caused by a misunderstanding or by "an intention to wound the French Government?" Clayton was ready to call it a misunderstanding and end the matter, but the president was adamant. The United States, Taylor insisted, expected "functionaries of other

Governments" to comply with the usages of "civilized nations" and would decline correspondence with any minister guilty of "intentional discourtesy." Newspapers on both sides suggested the possibility of war, but fortunately Louis Napoleon—currently president but soon to become emperor of France—recognized his need for American friendship and was aware of his enemies on the Continent. In early November he assured the new American minister, William C. Rives, of his high regard for the United States, and Taylor complimented the French in his annual message. Thus ended two teapot tempests with the United States having its way on all counts.[4]

Taylor was equally firm and forthright in his dealings with Portugal, which for years had been neglecting to pay certain damages stemming from an incident in the War of 1812 and a later controversy in 1828. During the war the British had been able to capture the American ship *General Armstrong* because the Portuguese had allowed the British to seize American ships in Portuguese waters. In 1828 the Portuguese had confiscated money from the American ship *Shepherd* on the pretext that the captain had taken the money illegally from Portuguese soil. Portuguese courts had exonerated the captain, but the money had never been returned. Zachary Taylor believed that nations as well as individuals should pay their just debts, and his newly appointed chargé in Lisbon, Henry Clay's son James, was eager to cooperate. Secretary of State Clayton wrote Clay that the president was determined to collect the money but hoped that he would not have to break diplomatic relations. It would be Portugal's fault if the United States should have to use "ulterior measures to enforce its demands," and the deadline for a reply on the oldest claim was October 1849.

Portugal's foreign minister, Conde Do Trojal, answered before the deadline. He rejected the *General Armstrong* claim outright but promised to study the others. In his annual message to Congress, Taylor announced that Portugal's refusal "to do justice" had "assumed a character so grave" that it would require a special message. He never sent the special message, but in March 1850, when the compromise debates were boiling, he ordered James Clay to deliver a final ultimatum in Lisbon. If Portugal would not give assurances that the claims would be paid, Clay should demand his passports and leave. Trojal offered to pay one of the minor claims and to allow a third party to arbitrate the *Armstrong* case, but Clay refused. In June, Trojal finally offered to submit all claims to arbitration. Unfortunately, Clay could not communicate with Washington overnight, and he had no authority to accept this eminently reasonable solution. Even when Trojal offered to pay everything but the *Armstrong* claim, Clay had no alternative but to demand his passports. When Taylor died, the controversy was at its peak, but the ensuing favorable settlement by President Fillmore owed much to Taylor's earlier firmness.[5]

Taylor's decisiveness toward Portugal was matched in his dealings with the newly formed German Confederation headed by Prussia. In 1848 during an armistice in the war between the Confederation and Denmark, the Germans, who had virtually no navy, looked to the United States for both officers and ships. The Polk administration sent a commodore to Prussia to consult with the Germans, and it authorized the Brooklyn Navy Yard to convert the merchant steamer *United States*, recently bought by the Germans, into a warship. When a renewal of the war seemed imminent, Polk declined to make American officers available for service in the German navy, but work on the *United States* was almost finished when Taylor took office. The Danish chargé protested that continued work on the ship would violate American neutrality. Taylor immediately ordered all United States naval officers to abstain from participating or advising in the conversion of the ship, and he canceled any further work on it. Clayton informed the German minister that the United States Neutrality Act of 1818 required the "forcible detention" of any ship that might be expected to make war on a friendly nation. Fines and imprisonment would be imposed upon anyone violating the law, and the ship could be forfeited. Speaking for Germany's Iron Chancellor, Otto von Bismarck, the German chargé, Baron von Roenne, protested vigorously, but Taylor and Clayton won the argument. In May the ship was allowed to sail, but only after the Germans gave a bond to be forfeited if they used the ship against Denmark. Shortly afterward, the war ended, and the question of collecting the bond never occurred. Taylor, however, had upheld the laws of neutrality.[6]

The spirit of Manifest Destiny that had sent the United States into Mexico and had inspired the cry of "Fifty-four forty or fight!" when Polk was settling the Oregon boundary with the British had not yet completely subsided despite the sectional complications it had caused. In the House, Long John Wentworth of Illinois had prophesied that the Speaker would one day recognize the members from Mexico, Canada, and Patagonia; and perhaps Mexico and Canada were fortunate that the slavery quarrel was absorbing so much of their powerful neighbor's ebullient energies. The enthusiasm for all of Mexico had abated in the South when the full implications of new free states inhabited by dark-skinned American citizens had been recognized, but a great many northwesterners as well as anti-British Irishmen in the Northeast still had designs on Canada. The United States and Great Britain would ultimately become partners in two world wars and a massive alliance system, but in 1849 a great many Americans still remembered the burning of the White House and the "rockets' red glare" in Baltimore Harbor. For them, monarchist Britain was a treacherous imperial enemy ready to wound the still-young American democracy in any way possible, and the spirit that had launched unsuccessful invasions of Canada between 1812 and 1814 was far from dead.

In 1849 a substantial and noisy Canadian faction advocated annexation to the United States. Some members were Tories, angry over British reforms that had increased the influence of the liberals and the French Canadians, while many of the French still resented British control regardless of any concessions. A Montreal mob actually stoned the carriage of the governor general and set fire to the Parliament buildings. A painful economic depression was widely blamed upon Britain's free-trade policy adopted during the Polk administration in exchange for the lowering of United States duties on British manufactures in the Walker Tariff of 1846. Canadians now had to compete with United States farmers in selling grain to Britain, while certain United States duties still deprived the Canadians of equal opportunities in United States markets. To some, annexation to the United States seemed to be a logical solution to this problem. The movement climaxed in October 1849 when more than a thousand Canadians signed an "Annexation Manifesto," listing their economic grievances and calling for "a friendly and peaceful separation" from Britain and a "union upon equitable terms" with the United States. The annexationists, however, were very much in the minority. A far stronger antiannexationist movement immediately appeared, and even William Lyon McKenzie, who had led the Canadian revolt against Britain in 1837, declared his aversion to "American democracy as it presented itself in the form of political corruption, crass materialism and human slavery."

The Canadian discontent, however, triggered a strong movement for annexation in various American newspapers, and this in turn created fears in Britain that filibustering from the United States might provoke an actual Canadian revolt. The Taylor administration might have feigned indifference and followed a policy of "wait and see," but this was not the president's style. When the British chargé d'affaires, John F. Crampton, officially inquired about the administration's attitude toward such matters, Secretary Clayton answered promptly. The president was determined to enforce the neutrality laws and would not hesitate to send General Scott and American troops to prevent any American violence against Canada. The threat had always been more noise than action, but the British were greatly reassured. Crampton informed his government that Taylor was "remarkable for the fearless and determined manner in which he follows up a course when he has . . . made up his mind that it is his duty to pursue it. . . . Should circumstances . . . render such a precaution necessary, there have been few Presidents of the United States whose personal influence would give greater effect to a measure of that sort than would that of General Taylor."[7]

Taylor's prestige with the English was probably also enhanced by his offer made through Clayton to help the British find their lost arctic explorer Sir John Franklin. The government first asked private whaling vessels to join the search, and then, in response to appeals from Mrs. Franklin and others, Taylor asked Congress to appropriate funds for an expedition. This the lawmakers declined to do, but in May 1850 the wealthy merchant Henry Grinnell offered to provide two ships if the United States government would man and supply them. This was done. Unfortunately, all efforts to find the doughty explorer failed, but Taylor's sympathetic efforts did not go unnoticed.[8]

The favorable British evaluation of his character probably helped Taylor considerably when he had to cope with British efforts to gain and hold a significant permanent base in Central America. Various American leaders had long advocated the construction of a Central American or Mexican canal as soon as possible. The least time-consuming existing route to California involved sailing to Nicaragua or Panama, traveling overland to the Pacific, and then taking another ship for the remainder of the journey. Enterprising transportation companies had already established facilities that enabled individuals to do this in varying degrees of comfort, but cargo ships and the naval vessels designed to protect America's new windows on the Pacific had a long, tedious, and often dangerous journey. Storms were frequent, and for sailing ships, the passage through the Strait of Magellan, at the southern tip of South America, was particularly hazardous. A canal could shorten the journey by as much as nine thousand miles and two to three months. Obviously, also, those who could raise the necessary capital and build such a canal as a private venture would achieve untold wealth. The actual construction of a canal would eventually require the vast resources of the United States government and would not be completed until 1914. No one knew this in 1849, however, and any efforts by a foreign nation to interfere with this noble dream had to be taken very seriously indeed.

The Nicaraguan route encompassing Lake Nicaragua and the San Juan River was obviously the most feasible route. Unfortunately, however, the heritage of Spanish colonial rule had left Central America in a state of economic, social, and political chaos. Attempts to create stable democratic institutions were terribly handicapped by extremes of wealth and poverty and the unwillingness of the fortunate few to share anything with the illiterate masses. The absence of any substantial middle class exacerbated the technological backwardness, the racial conflicts, the struggle over the wealth and the temporal power of the Catholic church, and the conflicts among ambitious and unscrupulous politicians ready to exploit every situation for their own ends. After winning their independence, Guatemala, El Salvador, Honduras, Nicaragua, and Costa Rica in 1823–24 had become the United Provinces of Central America. By 1839, however, the union had disintegrated into five separate nations torn by conflicts among themselves and by struggles for power within each. Various dictators and would-be dictators, usually calling themselves either Liberals or Conservatives, kept the new nations in an uproar.[9]

The region offered more potential wealth in crops, fruits, and gold than was immediately obvious, and entrepreneurs from both Britain and the United States found their way there at an early date. In 1856 a Tennesseean named William Walker would actually invade Nicaragua and make himself president for a time. The British had stretched Canada to the Pacific and were also much interested in trade with the west-coast nations of South America. Also, the Suez Canal route to the Far East was still a distant dream. The British, therefore, were also vitally interested in the possibility of a Nicaraguan canal, and they were much more experienced than Americans in the art of policing the conduct of their adventurous citizens, protecting them from capricious local governments, and then expanding this protection into political control.

San Juan, the primitive little town at the Caribbean end of the proposed waterway, was considered part of Nicaragua by the Nicaraguans and by the United States, but the area was actually inhabited by the Mosquito Indians, who were beyond any control by Nicaragua and recognized no allegiance to it. The Mosquitos were a hybrid group descended from the original Indians, runaway black slaves, and white adventurers. Through close relations with British Jamaica, they had avoided Spanish control, and a number of British traders had lived among them for many years. The Indians were few in number and would have posed no threat to either Nicaraguan or United States interests, but Great Britain, from its tiny colony of British Honduras, had recognized the Mosquitos as an independent nation under British protection and had given San Juan the new name of Greytown. In 1845 the British had endowed an Indian teenager with the name George Augustus Frederick and had crowned him king of the Mosquitos. Contemporary Americans aware of these events were certain that this action was a plot against the United States, but most modern historians have accepted the British claim that the move was designed to protect the Indians against unscrupulous British traders. Certain Englishmen, however, did believe that the area should be joined to the existing British Honduras, and in 1848 a British consul general, backed by warships, took possession of San Juan, pulled down Nicaragua's flag, substituted a newly designed Mosquito banner, and announced that he would rule henceforth as the representative of "His Mosquito Majesty." President Polk sent a Kentucky lawyer, Elijah Hise, to investigate.

On 16 March 1849 the newly inaugurated President Taylor and Secretary Clayton received a long dispatch from Hise reporting that Nicaragua, El Salvador, and Honduras had protested the British aggression, which was clearly designed to give Britain control of both ends of any projected canal.

A month later, Taylor and Clayton appointed E. George Squier, a twenty-seven-year-old scholar interested primarily in archaeology, to replace Hise. This young man, who was highly intelligent but had had no experience as either a traveler or a diplomat, was instructed to conclude treaties with Nicaragua, Costa Rica, and Honduras and to negotiate a contract for the Atlantic and Pacific Ship-Canal Company to dredge and operate a canal under United States protection. The treaty with Nicaragua was to secure for all American citizens a free transit between the oceans on the same terms enjoyed by all Nicaraguans. Because of the conflicting claims related to San Juan, the United States would not guarantee the independence of the country through which the canal might pass, and Squier was to avoid getting the United States involved in entangling alliances or unnecessary controversies. The United States asked only for an equal right of passage for all nations and would join Nicaragua in protecting the company designated to dig the canal.

The slowness of communications and travel caused numerous complications. The well-known historian George Bancroft, who had been appointed by Polk, was still the United States minister in London. Clayton instructed Bancroft to inform the British that their claim to San Juan on behalf of His Mosquito Majesty had no reasonable foundation and would not be allowed to threaten American rights or interests. Bancroft should first protest orally, but if this failed to get results, he should send a formal written complaint to Lord Palmerston, the British foreign secretary. Palmerston, however, found numerous excuses to avoid meeting with Bancroft. Polk's envoy, Hise, meanwhile, unaware that he had been recalled, exceeded his original instructions and signed a treaty pledging United States protection for Nicaragua against Britain in exchange for a right of way for the projected canal. He reported to Clayton that there had been no time to wait because the British were planning to seize all of Nicaragua's ports. Taylor, already enmeshed in the sectional quarrel, now had to worry about Hise's unauthorized pledge that if necessary, the United States would force the British to give up San Juan.[10]

In August 1849 Bancroft finally got his long-awaited interview with Palmerston. Nicaragua's envoy had already pleaded in vain for the restoration of San Juan, and Bancroft asked point-blank if Britain intended to annex it. No, said Palmerston. The British commissioners were holding it only temporarily. Bancroft argued that the Mosquito Kingdom did not exist; that even if it did, its jurisdiction did not include the San Juan River; and that in any case the British had no right to establish a protectorate. Palmerston, however, was not ready to restore the port and insisted that his own policy was best calculated to produce a canal that would benefit both nations.

Taylor and Clayton, meanwhile, were concerned that Hise's treaty would make Bancroft's efforts appear to be a deception. Bancroft had been recalled, but his replacement, Abbott Lawrence, was not yet ready to sail. William C. Rives, however, was en route to his assignment in Paris, and Clayton therefore directed him to stop in London to clarify the United States position. The meeting between Palmerston and Rives was friendly, but they disagreed on the matter of the Mosquito title. Palmerston assured Rives that Britain would work for peace between Nicaragua and the Indians and then would aim at international agreements to protect the future canal and guarantee its benefits equally to all nations.

By then, Squier had reached Nicaragua and soon reported that Nicaragua had granted the Atlantic and Pacific Company a ninety-seven-year contract and had agreed to a treaty that would recognize Nicaraguan sovereignty, under United States protection, over the canal route and would guarantee its neutrality. Both the treaty and the contract were waiting for ratification by the Nicaraguan legislature. Clayton immediately sent the treaty and further instructions to Lawrence, who had finally arrived in London. Britain, he wrote, could not use such an insidious scheme to control the San Juan port and river, but the canal might be kept free from obstruction by the Mosquitos if Britain would sign a treaty with the United States guaranteeing the independence of Nicaragua, Honduras, and Costa Rica; upholding the Mosquitos' right to pursue their chosen occupations within limits; extinguishing the Mosquitos' title to territory necessary for the construction of the canal; and requiring compensation by Nicaragua to the Indians for the land they would give up. Lawrence was to show Palmerston a copy of Squier's treaty and argue for "a great highway, dedicated to the equal advantage of all." Taylor would not support the Hise treaty or the Squier treaty if satisfactory agreements with Britain could be reached. Otherwise, however, he would ask the Senate to approve one of the treaties, both of which bound the United States to protect the interests of Nicaragua. Lawrence could promise that Nicaragua would pay the Indians a "proper annuity." The United States was "ready for any alternative." The president would never allow Britain to enjoy any "exclusive possession" within Nicaragua, but if the British would accept the United States offers, both nations would achieve a result more "to the glory of each . . . than the most successful war in which either could engage."[11]

Lawrence presented the American terms and asked for a British statement in writing with regard to occupation, colonization, and the neutrality of any future canal. Did Britain intend to occupy or colonize any part of Central America, and would Britain join in guaranteeing the neutrality of a canal, railway, or other communication?

Palmerston's answer was surprisingly conciliatory. Britain did not intend to colonize or occupy any part of Central America, and it would try to obtain the consent of the Indians to arrangements that would make San Juan applicable to the purposes of a canal. Britain was pleased to learn that the United States had no ulterior purposes and was ready to enter "a mutual agreement."

This amity, however, was short-lived. Palmerston soon expressed the further opinion that Squier's treaty was an unprovoked aggressive United States act designed to compel Britain to surrender San

Juan to Nicaragua. Britain would not abandon its protectorate. Palmerston then left London for business elsewhere, while Lawrence suffered from a prolonged illness. The negotiations stopped, but the action did not. British sailors, under orders from the consul representing the Mosquitos, seized Tigre Island at the Pacific end of the proposed canal. Tigre Island was clearly Honduran soil, and the British excused this action by citing the financial indebtedness of Honduras to Britain. Squier, however, had already persuaded Honduras to cede Tigre Island to the United States for eighteen months, and this meant a direct confrontation between the two great powers over the tiny properties of people who would have much preferred the absence of both. Britain now had physical possession of both ends of the canal route that had been granted by Nicaragua to an American company.

With Sir Henry Bulwer en route to Washington as the new British minister, John F. Crampton, who was temporarily in charge of the British legation, met with Taylor and Clayton in September. Taylor "waived all ceremony" and joined fully in the conversations. He had nothing but friendly feelings, but he concurred wholeheartedly with the presentation made by Clayton. The United States, said Clayton, would abandon the Hise treaty unless forced to honor it to "counteract the exclusive claim of some other country." The alleged Mosquito title to part of the canal route was such a claim, and the United States could not accept it. The disputed area should be ceded to Nicaragua for a suitable indemnity, and the Indians should be removed to another section without any damage to their interests. Americans, said Clayton, saw the Hise treaty as an effort to defeat a British monopoly on the canal route. Both nations should abandon any claim to Nicaragua and should agree to share the use of any future canal. Otherwise, the United States would have to support the Hise treaty in self-defense. Taylor, reported Crampton to Palmerston, concurred but made plain his hope that any misunderstanding or collision could be avoided by "frankness and fairdealing."

In early 1850, with Taylor already intensely preoccupied with the sectional crisis and a cabinet scandal, Sir Henry Bulwer arrived from London to renew the Nicaraguan controversy. A lesser president might have been tempted to trumpet the international quarrel with Britain as a force for national unity. Seward, in 1861, would strongly urge Lincoln to take a similar course. Taylor, however, kept the quarrel as low-key as possible.

Bulwer was something of a British Henry Clay—a great story-teller, a clever and witty writer, a lover of roulette and gambling in general, a shrewd diplomat, and immensely popular wherever he went. By 3 February 1850, Bulwer and Clayton had produced a tentative agreement for Taylor and Palmerston to consider. Neither country would occupy or colonize Nicaragua, Costa Rica, the Mosquito Coast, or any other part of Central America. Neither would seek to gain or hold advantages that would not be offered to the other. Should an Anglo-American war ever occur, neither would capture the other's ships in the canal, and those who would be employed in building the canal would be protected from detention, confiscation, or violence. Free ports would be established at each end of the canal, and the governments claiming jurisdiction would help build it. Britain and the United States would guarantee the canal's neutrality and would secure capital investments for its construction. Every nation, state, or people could contribute to the plan, and any other approved transisthmian construction would also receive protection and encouragement.

The agreement ignored the British Mosquito protectorate, as both men tried to avoid an insoluble disagreement. Bulwer was determined not to yield the protectorate, while Clayton felt that the language of the agreement in effect denied the Mosquito claims, even if the British would not do so explicitly. With regard to the British seizure of Tigre Island, Bulwer stated that Britain was not seeking any colonies; the occupation was only temporary to settle a lien on unpaid debts. He insisted, however, that while British protection for the Mosquitos was not directed against the United States, any American support for Nicaragua against the Mosquitos would be an act of hostility toward Britain.

Zachary Taylor was unmoved by niceties of language. As reported by Clayton to Bulwer, the president had decided that the United States could not abandon its alliance with Nicaragua unless Britain gave up the Mosquito protectorate. The principle that Indian titles could be extinguished at will came from English precedents and applied to the Mosquitos as much as to the Indians of the United States. Fewer than five hundred Indians were involved in the controversy, and sensible nations should not waste lives and treasure over them. Britain had seized the one indispensable outlet for a future canal, while the United States had gone to the rightful authority, Nicaragua, for permission to dig. Nicaragua had given permission only to the United States, but the latter was ready to give all nations "equal advantages with ourselves." Taylor believed, furthermore, that the United States was making a greater sacrifice than was Britain because even though no Central American country would refuse to join the United States if given the opportunity, we would agree not to occupy any of them if the British would abandon their alliance with the Mosquitos. And finally, said Clayton, the president had instructed him to say that "if you . . . interfere to assist the Mosquitos, we . . . shall interpose in behalf of Nicaragua."[12]

On 19 March, Taylor asked the Senate to approve Squier's treaty by which the United States would protect Nicaragua in return for the canal route already controlled at each end by the British. The British claim to San Juan, wrote Taylor, was without foundation, and he would ratify the treaty if the Senate would agree.

Bulwer, meanwhile, had received Palmerston's approval for the agreement that Taylor had rejected, but he had no authority to go further. When Taylor sent the Squier treaty to the Senate, however, Bulwer offered another solution. He and Clayton should sign a convention without a formal rejection of the protectorate but with an assurance by Bulwer that Britain would not use the arrangement to do the things disclaimed in the earlier letter to Lawrence. Clayton reminded Bulwer that in this letter the British had disavowed any purpose of occupying or colonizing any part of Central America, had claimed no dominion in the Mosquito territory, and had agreed not to settle or fortify adjacent territory. The president, he added, had instructed him to declare that nothing in any treaty should be interpreted as an admission of any right or title for the Mosquito king to any part of Central America. With this understanding, said Clayton, he would sign the convention.

In reply, Bulwer protested the Squier treaty. Clayton answered that Taylor had read the proposal carefully and had found "not a syllable in it inconsistent" with his support for Nicaragua. The president believed that if he refused to recognize the Nicaraguan title to the disputed territory, he would break faith and forfeit "the right acquired by the Nicaragua treaty & the contract to cut the Canal." If Bulwer insisted that the United States deny Nicaragua's title, the negotiation might as well be abandoned. Both of the conflicting positions, Clayton pleaded, were mere shadows, and a substantial goal should not "be abandoned for the sake of shadows." "Rely on it," he closed, "I send you the Prest's ultimatum."[13]

Bulwer remained both adamant and unhappy. He now informed Clayton that he had been led to believe they could settle the canal question without bickering over Nicaragua and the Mosquitos, but

Taylor's attitude might be considered "cause for an increase in our Naval Armaments." It was one thing merely to state an opposition to the Mosquito claim, but something quite different to offer ultimatums that might justify the expansion of the British navy. However, a settlement might still be possible if the United States, instead of recognizing a Nicaraguan claim, would merely state "that you will do your utmost to obtain" a settlement of differences between Britain and Nicaragua. Also, Bulwer warned, the United States would get no British capital for building the canal if it recognized Nicaragua's title over land that Britain thought belonged to the Mosquitos.

No further notes were exchanged, and no conversations were recorded, but on 19 April 1850 Clayton and Bulwer signed a treaty, which Taylor promptly submitted to the Senate. According to the treaty, neither government would obtain or maintain "exclusive control" over the canal or "erect or maintain . . . fortifications commanding the same . . . or occupy, or fortify, or colonize, or assume or exercise any dominion over Nicaragua, Costa Rica, the Mosquito coast, or any part of Central America, or make use of any protection which either affords or may afford, or any alliance which either has or may have to or with any State or people for the purpose of erecting or maintaining any such fortifications, or of occupying, fortifying, or colonizing Nicaragua, Costa Rica, the Mosquito coast, or any part of Central America, or of assuming or exercising dominion over the same." Neither one would "take advantage of any intimacy, or use any alliance, connection, or influence that either may possess, with any State or Government through whose territory the canal may pass, for the purpose of acquiring or holding, directly or indirectly, for the citizens or subjects of the one any rights or advantages in regard to commerce or navigation through the said canal which shall not be offered on the same terms to the citizens or subjects of the other."[14]

His purpose, announced Taylor when submitting the treaty, was "to establish a commercial alliance with all great maritime states" and to protect a canal through Nicaragua. He had found Britain "in possession of nearly half of Central America, as the ally and protector of the Mosquito King." He had tried to secure a canal route for the United States while seeking to maintain the independence of the Central American republics, but if the Senate confirmed both this treaty and the Squier treaty, certain amendments might be necessary.[15]

Taylor's senatorial opponents on the sectional issues found the treaty hard to swallow, while Democratic newspapers denounced it far and wide. Clayton, however, had carefully taken numerous senators into his confidence during the negotiations, and the Senate as a whole rose to its best potential by debating the subject largely on its own merits. A combination of both parties approved the pact by a vote of 42 to 11.

The wording of the treaty clearly negatived the British Mosquito protectorate, and after several weeks of delay, the British Foreign Office instructed Bulwer to deny that the agreements applied "to her majesty's settlement at Honduras or its dependencies." Five days later, Clayton agreed in writing that the treaty did not include British Honduras, but he would not affirm or deny the British title either there or in the alleged dependencies. The treaty was not changed, but Bulwer and Clayton exchanged controversial further opinions. Bulwer's note dated 4 July interpreted Clayton's refusal either to confirm or to deny the British titles as a recognition that the British title would remain what it had been before the treaty. Clayton, however, claimed that he had refused to accept Bulwer's declaration. On 5 July, Taylor, from his deathbed, proclaimed the treaty. The agreements had been worded in such a way that each government could interpret them to its own advantage. The only alternative would have been war or a severe loss of national face and prestige.

During the later Pierce administration, Stephen A. Douglas and others would launch a furious attack on the treaty because of its alleged generosity toward Britain. The first section, they charged, would keep the United States from building the canal, and the remainder was a violation of the Monroe Doctrine. In 1853, Clayton was back in the Senate, and he defended himself and Taylor by reminding the critics that most of them had voted for the treaty. The British contributed to the debate by claiming that the Bay Islands were dependencies of British Honduras Belize (British Honduras) and that the Mosquito protectorate remained valid. Clayton denied these allegations, while Bulwer insisted that his final note had been part of the treaty. A search turned up Bulwer's note in the archives, but it had not been endorsed by Clayton or by any other American, and it might well have been put there by someone else. After several more years of potential crisis, the British finally decided that their access to Southern cotton and United States markets was more important than a war to defend the Mosquitos. In 1858 they formally acquiesced in the American interpretation of the treaty and began to withdraw from the disputed area. Certainly the treaty was an important foundation for the continuing American demands which the British finally accepted. By 1900 the United States was again eager to dig a canal and persuaded the British in the Hay-Pauncefote Treaties of 1900 and 1901 to modify the Clayton-Bulwer Treaty to give the United States the sole right to build and control a canal. The provisions that it should be open to all nations on reasonable and equitable terms, however, were reincorporated in the new treaty. In retrospect, Taylor's stubborn stand against the claims of powerful Britain in 1849–50 helped to check British expansion in Central America, protected American interests as well as the independence of the area, and accomplished these objectives without generating a war crisis. The later attacks on the treaty were produced by partisan politics and not by any reasonable analysis of the treaty's impact on the situation in 1849–50.[16]

Another event holding Zachary Taylor's attention when he was not worrying about the salvation of New Mexico was the Hungarian revolution of 1848. When Lajos Kossuth led a group of Hungarian liberals and nationalists in protests against Austrian domination, Austria granted the Magyars an independent Hungarian ministry and abolished various feudal practices. The Austrian government, however, did not fully honor its agreements, and Kossuth responded with an open revolt in partnership with a small army of Poles equally determined to win their independence from the Hapsburgs. After several bloody battles, the Hungarians in April 1849 formally declared their independence and appointed Kossuth as governor.

Overnight, Kossuth became an American hero, and President Taylor was eager to offer Kossuth's government formal recognition— but only after making certain that Kossuth was likely to win. In June, Taylor ordered A. Dudley Mann, a Virginian attached to the United States legation in Paris, to proceed to Hungary and determine the actual status of Kossuth's regime. Mann reached Vienna on 12 July 1849, only to learn that the Russians had intervened to help Austria and that the rebels had been crushed with severe losses. In August, Kossuth's army surrendered, and in September he fled to Turkey. Recognition by the United States was now impossible, but Taylor was on record as having favored it if Kossuth had had any real chance at all. As might have been expected, various opponents in Congress and in the newspapers attacked the president for not having recognized Kossuth's government before it was defeated.

In his annual message of December 1849, Taylor informed the Congress that while he had scrupulously avoided any interference in the conflict between Austria and Hungary, he had been "in accordance with the general sentiment of the American people" and had been prepared, "upon the . . . establishment by her of a permanent government, to be the first to welcome independent Hungary into the family of Nations." He had sent an agent "with power to declare our willingness promptly to recognize her independence in the event of her ability to sustain it." Russia had extinguished the hopes of the Hungarians, but American feelings had been "strongly enlisted in the cause, and by the sufferings of a brave people, who had made a gallant, though unsuccessful, effort to be free." In January 1850 Taylor cordially welcomed a visiting delegation of Hungarian refugees, and assured them that "the oppressed of every land will here find the same protection that we ourselves enjoy. Here your rights, and liberties, and religion will be respected and maintained." In March, when the sectional quarrel was spewing fire and brimstone in the Congress, the Senate asked Taylor for a copy of his instructions to Mann.[17]

The Austrian government, already irritated by the criticisms inherent in Taylor's message to Congress, was further upset when Mann's instructions were revealed. Also, a speech by Lewis Cass demanding the suspension of diplomatic relations with Austria did not help. The Austrian government protested formally that the Mann mission was an unjustified interference in the internal affairs of Austria. Various Democratic members of Congress dubbed the Whigs the Austrian Party and continued their efforts to foment a controversy, but in December 1850 Daniel Webster, who had succeeded Clayton, eloquently defended Taylor's policy and the right of the United States to take an active interest in the struggles of European peoples for freedom. An active interest and an actual involvement were two different matters, however, and Taylor handled the issue with both good judgment and political skill. His successor would find Kossuth an even greater problem.

Given the vigor of Taylor's dealings with the British, a significant number of his fellow slaveholders probably expected him to continue United States efforts to acquire Cuba. Southerners, including Calhoun, Jefferson Davis, and the editor James D. B. De Bow, had long dreamed of liberating Cuba from Spain and adding new territory for slavery. President Polk's secretary of state, James Buchanan, a Pennsylvanian tied to the South by powerful bonds of personal friendship, was certain that "we must have Cuba. . . . We shall acquire it by a coup d'etat at some propitious moment, which . . . may not be far distant."[18] Polk had offered to negotiate a sale of the island to the United States, but the Spanish had replied that they would prefer to see it sunk in the ocean. The movement for annexing Cuba was encouraged further by Cuban students and exiles who spread the word that the people would revolt against Spain if encouraged to do so by the United States. Cubans in New York organized a junta to raise money and publicize their goals. Cuban citizens sent some $30,000 from Havana. Various American newspapers cooperated with attacks on Spanish institutions and further paeans to Manifest Destiny.

The practical result was the organization of a filibustering expedition by one Narciso López, a dynamic and charismatic former governor of a Cuban province. The glorification of democratic and patriotic principles by López may have been conditioned by his heavy losses in mining, planting, and gambling, but his enthusiasm was contagious for those eager to see the fertile fields of Cuba, which were already being cultivated by slaves, beneath the United States flag. López, in turn, offered the command of his great adventure to Jefferson Davis and Robert E. Lee, both of whom refused. He then decided to be his own commander in chief. Col. G. W. White, a Mexican War veteran, gathered recruits, while López bought steamers and helped White with magnanimous promises to anyone who would volunteer.

Just as an alleged British threat had encouraged the annexation of Texas and the annexation of California, similar rumors concerning "Perfidious Albion" and the Spanish were circulated by Americans yearning for Cuba. On 2 August 1849, however, Taylor and Clayton cut through any haze surrounding this possibility by informing the Spanish that any cession of Cuba to Britain would be an "instant signal for war." The warning, of course, was entirely unnecessary. In turn, Taylor took an equally dim view of López and White. Having been informed that White and some eight hundred volunteers were ready to sail for Cuba from the New Orleans area in late August 1849, Clayton ordered the district attorney in New Orleans to enforce the law, and he sent similar instructions to New York. He also advised the Spanish minister, who was vacationing on Long Island, that his presence was required in Washington. Secretary of War Preston ordered Commodore Foxhall A. Parker to proceed to the mouth of the Mississippi River and use force if necessary to prevent any hostile military effort against any territory or dominions with which the United States was at peace. Taylor, meanwhile, stated his case publicly: it was his duty to prevent aggression against friendly nations. Americans who violated their country's "laws and treaty obligations" would be subject to heavy penalties, as stipulated by acts of Congress. They could expect no protection from the United

States, "no matter to what extremities they may be reduced." Whenever possible, governmental officers would arrest every offender. Southern expansionists of both parties, as well as numerous Northern Democrats, were furious, but Taylor was not just speaking for the record. White and his men on Round Island were blockaded and denied supplies, while the government also seized two ships in New York. The vicious abuse showered upon Taylor only made him more determined to uphold the neutrality law of 1818.

During the ensuing months, López designed a subterfuge to evade the United States neutrality laws. He would sail first to a neutral region, which was not illegal, and then launch his actual Cuban invasion from there. Again he received powerful aid from prominent Southerners. The editor of the *New Orleans Delta* provided weapons from stores furnished by Southern states. Officially bound for Panama, López's fleet of one steamer and two sailing ships rendezvoused off the island of Contoy, near Yucatan, on 14 May 1850. Forty-nine men deserted before the expedition left, and the Spanish captured both sailing vessels with fifty-two other men. Aboard the steamer *Creole*, López reached Cardenas, a small Cuban port eighty miles east of Havana, on 19 May. The local garrison of forty soldiers surrendered, but the popular uprising that López had expected to support his projected revolution did not occur. As Spanish reinforcements approached, López put his supplies back on the *Creole* and assigned a rear guard of Kentuckians to cover the retreat. The Kentuckians killed some thirty or forty Spaniards before everyone departed during the night. The *Creole* then ran aground, and López had to jettison her provisions, weapons, and ammunition to get the vessel afloat. With some seventy Americans killed or wounded, she managed to escape a Spanish ship and return to Key West.

Taylor acted without hesitation. He ordered the district attorney in New Orleans to prosecute the leaders to the limit. The district attorney, Logan Hunton, may have cooperated with the vessel's escape from New Orleans in the first place, and whatever the strength of his prosecution, any convictions by a Louisiana jury were impossible. With the leaders being lionized and a new drink named in honor of López, the primary organizer, the former senator John Henderson, was acquitted by three different juries. Taylor, however, had done his best, and this strengthened his efforts considerably when he intervened on behalf of the Americans whom the Spanish had captured. The prisoners had been seized before they got anywhere near Cuba, and Taylor and Clayton argued that the "intention to commit a crime did not constitute a crime" and that Spain had no right to arrest the violators of a United States law in neutral waters. A Spanish court found forty-nine of the men not guilty, and the other three were freed a few months later. By promising the Spanish that the United States would help them keep their possession of Cuba, Taylor had upheld both domestic and international law, had kept the peace with Spain, and had saved the lives of fifty-two foolish young Americans.[19]

In all of these relatively successful dealings with foreign nations, the question naturally arises of whether the bulk of the credit should go to Taylor or to Clayton. The answer must be that Taylor selected Clayton in the first place, approved and took full responsibility for every policy, clearly played an important role in the formulation of some of the policies, and actually took a stronger stand than Clayton did when dealing with the British and Nicaragua. Because Taylor bore the brunt of the incessant attacks by opposing politicians and newspapers on each of his policies, it is only fair that he should receive much credit for his firmness, good sense, decisiveness, clarity of expression, and patriotism. In each case, it is difficult to imagine an alternative policy that would have served American interests better.

7

★ ★ ★ ★ ★

THE CRISIS

In 1849 the United States was facing problems far more serious than Thurlow Weed's vendetta against Millard Fillmore. In January, John C. Calhoun led the Southern members of Congress into a supposedly secret caucus. Slaveholders Thomas Hart Benton and Sam Houston were not invited, but Houston attended anyhow and tried to keep the affair within moderate channels. After long and bitter wrangling among the Southerners and after a final session that lasted all night, Calhoun's "Address of the Southern Delegates in Congress to their Constituents" was approved by a vote of forty-eight to forty-one. Even though only one-third of the Southern members of Congress had signed it, the "Address" drew nationwide attention. Calhoun argued that every policy affecting slavery from the Northwest Ordinance of 1789 and the Missouri Compromise of 1820 to the recent admission of Oregon as a free territory had been an aggression against the South. Unless all such tyranny could be stopped, slavery would be abolished in the South, a horrible race conflict would follow, and the result of the bloody shambles would be a South ruled by the blacks serving as masters over the whites. Any further encroachments would justify secession.[1] Calhoun conveniently ignored the recent annexation of the vast slave area of Texas with its legal right to subdivide into five slave states and the recent election that had placed a rich slaveholding planter in the White House as the immediate successor to his fellow slaveholding presidents Tyler and Polk. Indeed, of all the previously elected presidents since 1789, only John

Adams and John Quincy Adams could not be classified as Southern or pro-Southern presidents in their attitudes toward the constitutional rights of slaveholders.

Echoing Calhoun, the Virginia legislature authorized the governor to call an extra session to consider retaliation if the Wilmot Proviso should pass. In South Carolina a state convention approved the "Southern Address" and concurred in the Virginia resolutions. Florida, North Carolina, and Mississippi took similar actions, and meetings or conventions in Alabama, Mississippi, Tennessee, and Georgia expressed strong approval. Many editors mirrored as well as helped develop such sentiments.

Only two Southern Whigs supported Calhoun's "Address," however, and Whig newspapers tried to cool the atmosphere. To Robert Toombs the action was "based not on the conviction that Gen'l T. can *not* settle our sectional difficulties, but that he *can* do it. They do not wish it settled." The *Richmond* (Va.) *Times* avowed that nine-tenths of the Southern people distrusted Calhoun's judgment, and the *Savannah* (Ga.) *Republican* stated in no uncertain terms that it would stand by the Union. Democrat Howell Cobb, who owned a thousand slaves, refused to sign the "Address." Writing to his wife, he referred to Calhoun as "an old reprobate" and added: "If it would please our Heavenly Father to take Calhoun and Benton *home*, I should look upon it as a national blessing." His Whig fellow Georgian Robert Toombs assured Crittenden that "we have completely foiled Calhoun in his miserable attempt to form a Southern party." Leading Southern Whigs like Robert Toombs, Alexander H. Stephens, and John M. Clayton, as well as Democrats like Thomas Hart Benton and both Thomas J. Rusk and Sam Houston from Texas publicly expressed vehement opposition.[2]

Benton, Calhoun's most bitter personal enemy, spent the summer of 1849 campaigning for reelection throughout Missouri on a platform of total opposition to both Calhoun and the Missouri legislature, which had ordered him to support Calhoun's position. The United States, said Benton in a well-publicized speech, owed a "great example to a struggling and agonized world." The supporters of liberty in ancient empires were looking to America for support, but what did they see? They saw

> wrangling and strife, and bitter denunciations, and threats of disunion. They see a quarrel about slavery! to them a strange and incomprehensible cause of quarrel. . . . They see us almost in a state of disorganization—legislation paralyzed—insult violence out-

rage on the floors of Congress. . . . Once called the model republic by our friends, we are now so called in derision by our foes;
and the slavery discussion and dissensions quoted as the proofs of
the impracticable form of government which we have adopted. . . .
Our ancestors . . . left us the admiration, and the envy of the
friends of freedom throughout the world. And are we, their posterity, in the second generation, to spoil this rich inheritance—
mar this noble work—discredit this great example—and throw
the weight of the republic against the friends of freedom throughout the world[?][3]

The smoldering embers of Northern bitterness against the Mexican War were quickly fanned again into flame by the Southern
demands and by Calhoun's "Address." Newspapers like Horace
Greeley's *New York Tribune*, Samuel Bowles's *Springfield* (Mass.)
Republican, Thurlow Weed's *Albany* (N.Y.) *Evening Journal*, James
Watson Webb's *New York Courier and Enquirer*, William Cullen
Bryant's *New York Evening Post*, and a long list of western papers
took up the cry. In their view the South had dictated the annexation
of the vast area of Texas and the unjust Mexican War and had just
elected another slaveholding president. It had also blocked economic
legislation dear to numerous Northern hearts and pocketbooks. And
now the Southerners were demanding that slavery be imposed upon
the previously free territories of California and New Mexico. Some
Northerners argued that the aggressions of the Slave Power must be
stopped, even at the price of disunion.[4]

Other Southern publicists, meanwhile, took up the message of
Calhoun's "Address" with multiplied zeal. The *Southern Quarterly
Review* had been a failure, but under the new editorship of William
Gilmore Simms and with an emotional cause to promote, the magazine suddenly became a financial success. Its columns were filled
with defenses of slavery and calls for secession if the South should
be denied its territorial rights. Able writers like Beverley D. Tucker,
Augustus B. Longstreet, and George Fitzhugh found the new opportunities for agitation both exciting and profitable. They charged correctly that various Northern state governments were restricting and
preventing Southern efforts to recover runaway slaves, although they
grossly exaggerated the number of escapees. They also insisted that
the Northerners were planning to abolish slavery in the District of
Columbia and thereby create a federal haven for the fugitives. Worst
of all, however, they wrote, was the insulting and dishonoring effort
to exclude slavery from the new territories, even though the South

had contributed twice as many volunteers to the war effort as had the North.[5]

In the midst of the excitement, the new president was far from idle. In April he sent Thomas Butler King, a slaveholding congressman from Georgia, to California with instructions to promote the organization of a state government that could request immediate admission to the Union. King and his small entourage of army officers were not to influence Californians in either direction with regard to slavery, but Taylor was certain that the resulting state constitution would exclude slavery. This would enable California to skip the territorial stage. The quarrel over slavery extension applied only to territories, and no Southerner, without contradicting his own doctrine of states' rights, could object to any action on slavery taken by a state.

In July, Taylor proclaimed a national day of fasting and prayer against a serious cholera epidemic. On 9 August he began an extended tour of several cities in Maryland, Pennsylvania, and New York. Everywhere he was greeted by large and enthusiastic crowds. Many Southerners had long dreamed of making Cuba another slave state, and filibustering expeditions for this purpose always enlisted numerous young Southern volunteers. At Harrisburg, however, Taylor denounced the most recent such effort. Americans, he warned, would be subject to arrest and heavy penalties if they broke United States laws against attacking friendly nations. In Pittsburgh, the Louisiana planter advocated a protective tariff, and at Mercer, Pennsylvania, he addressed the question of the hour: "The people of the North need have no further apprehension of the extension of slavery," and the Free Soil party was no longer either necessary or desirable. Taylor, of course, was referring to the limits imposed by nature, but to many Southerners the statement implied that the Whig party had become the barrier to slavery extension. The speech may have been prompted by the close congressional campaigns going on in both Pennsylvania and Ohio. In any case it mirrored Taylor's long-held beliefs and did not indicate any sudden conversion to the Wilmot Proviso.[6]

At Meadville, Pennsylvania, the president became seriously ill, but after three days he had recovered sufficiently to visit Niagara Falls. There he could hardly walk, and his doctors insisted that he cancel all formal appearances and proceed directly to Washington via Albany and New York City. Both Southerners and New Yorkers noted the prominence of Sewardites and the absence of Fillmore's friends in the president's entourage. The trip left his Southern supporters very uneasy, while his enemies were warning that he would sign the Wilmot Proviso if it should pass.

Meanwhile, as senators and congressmen around the country were putting their personal affairs in order and preparing for their long and arduous journeys to Washington for the upcoming session, the legislature of Mississippi, at Calhoun's urging, issued a call for a Southern convention to meet in Nashville on 1 June 1850. The Carolinian obviously believed that by June the country would be badly divided by the issues facing the incoming Congress, and he hoped that the machinery for a successful movement toward independence would already be in place.

When Congress met in December 1849 for the long session of 1850, the bitter sectional quarrels provided a dramatic setting for the aging political heroes of the past thirty years to deliver magnificent farewell performances. One editor, contemplating the meeting of Clay, Webster, Calhoun, and Benton once more in the Senate, found his mind "wrapt in admiration of the times when the esquires of that body were worthy the steel of a templar, and every knight was terrible 'like an army with banners.' There were giants in those days, and these were greatest where all were great."[7]

Much has been written about the godlike Daniel Webster; the grim, emaciated, and dying Calhoun; and the gaunt, fast-weakening but still brilliant and charming Henry Clay in their last great efforts. In the actual struggle, however, others played equally dynamic roles. The debates between Benton and Clay reveal much about the real nature of the arguments. Stephen A. Douglas, the energetic "Little Giant" from Illinois, actually wrote the bills that ultimately became the compromise, and James Pearce of Maryland was equally important. At one point the Texas senators, Houston and Rusk, may have held the balance between compromise and civil war. Jefferson Davis and William H. Seward spoke against compromise for opposite reasons. For sheer volume of oratory and effectiveness in shaping the course, if not the final result, of the debates, the real hub of the conflict may have been Henry S. Foote of Mississippi. The vital roles played by Taylor and Fillmore have often been both misunderstood and underestimated.

The major issues were clear-cut, although some were illogical. In March 1848 gold had been discovered in far-off California, and by December 1849 the region had more than enough greedy, hardworking, often angry, and occasionally heavy-drinking citizens to qualify for statehood. No territorial government had yet been provided, and lynch law and vigilante committees were the only visible opponents of the widespread crimes, both petty and serious, that always marked a gold rush. Government lands and resources were being stolen, and individual property claims, often tenuous at best, usually had to be defended by superior force. The territory desperately needed law and order. Benton and others had already promised their support for a new state, and when Congressman Thomas Butler King arrived with presidential instructions to midwife California into statehood, the people of California did not hesitate. They promptly organized a convention, approved a state constitution that prohibited slavery, and elected a state government as well as two senators and a congressional representative. Both senators, one of them Benton's son-in-law John C. Frémont, as well as the congressman, the governor, and the lieutenant governor, were all from slaveholding states. The majority of the population were Southerners, and no legal action beyond the existing Mexican laws had previously been taken to bar slavery. Indeed, a handful of slaves had been taken there without incident, but most of the people, including Southerners, did not want the institution. Slavery was not a practicable system for the area, and the Californians were merely recognizing this fact in their constitution. Only the acceptance by Congress of this constitution and the admission of its representative and senators to the Congress stood between California and immediate statehood. No congressional action on slavery was necessary or justified, and the Wilmot Proviso was not involved at all. The right of states to control their own domestic institutions, particularly slavery, had been for decades a vital part of Southern holy writ, and Zachary Taylor had violated no Southern principles by suggesting it.

The simplest stratagem for avoiding a conflict would have been for California to delay its action against slavery until the day after its admission to the Union. Southerners might threaten secession over an antislave provision the day before California's admission but would have no grounds for protest at all on the day after. The practical result was the same, but to Calhoun and his followers, barring slavery before admission was an insult and a denial of fundamental Southern rights. Barring slavery the day after admission, however, would have been the exercise of a power that the Southern doctrine of states' rights had always glorified. In a public letter more than a year earlier, Thomas Hart Benton had urged the people of both California and New Mexico to practice "total abstinence from the agitation of the [slavery] question" until they reached statehood and could settle it as they pleased.[8] In retrospect, President Taylor should have offered the same advice.

Realistic Southerners like Henry S. Foote knew that the admission of a free California was inevitable, but they had the votes to delay the process. If the president, the unionist Whigs, and most Northerners wanted California quickly, they could pay for it by concessions elsewhere. The price that Foote and other Southerners ultimately set for the admission of California grew out of a far more concrete and much more dangerous issue. As in California, the Mexicans had long since abolished slavery in New Mexico. Getting New Mexico to become a separate slave territory would be impossible, but converting most of New Mexico into part of the existing slave state of Texas offered solid possibilities. In 1836 Texas had ambitiously and irresponsibly defined its boundaries to include some 60 percent of present-day New Mexico, but the latter remained, by its own choice, under Mexican rule until the arrival of Gen. Stephen W. Kearny and the United States troops in 1846. In June 1841 Texas had sent an expedition of three hundred men, including two commissioners, to Santa Fe to attempt the opening of free trade with Texas. All were captured and imprisoned for several years, and two were shot, thus adding the vindication of martyrs to the already existing economic and political motivations for Texas to annex New Mexico. In 1843 a Texas army of two hundred men, dispatched to stop traders en route to Santa Fe, defeated a New Mexican army led by Governor Manuel Armijo, but the governor and his army retreated to Santa Fe while United States troops, acting as an escort for a Missouri caravan, captured and disarmed the angry Texans. When Texas was annexed in 1845, its leaders insisted that Santa Fe was part of Texas, but when General Kearny conquered the area, he issued a proclamation claiming the territory, with its original boundaries, for the United States and promising in effect that the area would eventually become an equal state in the American Union. This was obviously a pledge that New Mexico would not become part of Texas. When the Texas leaders protested, President Polk and Secretary of State Buchanan assured them that the military government was only temporary, but Polk later declared that the question should be settled by Congress. In March 1848 the Texas government announced the creation of Santa Fe County and a judicial district that included the disputed area of present-day New Mexico and the only part of the territory that had any white population. When Texas appointed a district judge for the area, however, the Santa Fe press recommended that he bring along an army strong enough to escort him home without a coat of tar and feathers. Texas responded with a call for mobilization and various proclamations that Texas law would be upheld. On 31 December 1849 Texas announced that Santa Fe County would be reduced in size, that three additional counties would be formed, and that the changes would be enacted by force if necessary.[9]

In addition to the problems of international and domestic law was the question of whether most of New Mexico would be part of the slave state of Texas or retain its status as the antislave territory of New Mexico, although slavery was in no way the cause of the original dispute. The New Mexicans did not wish to be swallowed up by a former enemy whose capital was 800 miles distant. Santa Fe leaders of both Mexican and United States origin were quite naturally jealous of their own political positions, and the people were ready to follow them. The territory began arming and organizing to defend itself and appealed to the federal government for military protection. If the unreasonable determination of Texas to subjugate the area should provoke a clash with the United States government, and if other Southern states should support their Texas sister, a civil war might well begin in 1850.

To the slaveholding general in the White House, the Texas threat to New Mexico was just another example of greed and lawlessness, and the slavery issue was just a smoke screen. He had always kept his and his country's commitments to defeated enemies, whether Indians or Mexicans, and the territorial and political integrity of New Mexico had been part of the agreement by which New Mexico had surrendered peacefully. This was a principle he would not compromise regardless of the cost.

And finally, there was the enormous territory far beyond present-day Utah that was claimed by the Mormons and their dictatorial governor Brigham Young. If the slavery quarrel had not existed, the question of polygamy in Utah might have caused equal noise though far less danger. As it was, the proper incorporation of Utah would have to wait for a brief lull in the slavery conflict several years later, but in 1850 its territory had to be reduced to a manageable limit. Fortunately, its boundaries were north of the Missouri Compromise line of 36° 30', and Southerners who were demanding equal rights for slavery among the Spanish-speaking New Mexicans apparently considered the exotic religious culture of the Mormons to be beyond redemption.

As congressmen and senators gathered in their homes and board-inghouses to plan strategy and reinforce one another's fears, pride, beliefs, emotional attachments, and competitive instincts, other issues helped solidify their positions on California and New Mexico. Several Northern states had passed laws designed to hinder the efforts of Southerners to recapture fugitive slaves, and the Supreme Court, in the case of *Prigg* v. *Pennsylvania*, had decreed that the primary responsibility for such efforts rested with the federal government. Regardless of the humane intentions reflected in the state laws, they were clearly in conflict with the federal constitution and with earlier national laws on the subject. The number of escapees was far less than was generally supposed, and most fugitives were being recaptured without incident, but every exception was an insult to the South and a moral condemnation of the institution and those who practiced it. Ironically, the border states, from which escape was most feasible and from which most escapees fled, were relatively quiet on the subject. The deep Southern states, however, from which a successful escape was almost impossible, apparently felt the symbolic implications of the problem most keenly and behaved as though they were suffering critical losses of slave manpower.[10] Southern leaders wanted the Northern liberty laws repealed or declared unconstitutional, and if federal laws providing coercive machinery for returning the fugitives overrode the prevailing sentiment in the Northern states, so much for their own favorite doctrine of states' rights.

A corresponding grievance voiced by antislavery forces was the existence of a large slave market within earshot of the Capitol. During the late 1830s and the early 1840s, abolitionists had flooded Congress with petitions asking for the abolition of slavery in the District of Columbia, the one place in the United States with institutions unprotected by states' rights. Year after year the petitions had been tabled by overwhelming majorities. Eliminating the slave trade in the District, however, was much more feasible, and the abolitionist effort in the District had therefore been reduced to a less ambitious project. The abolitionists would fulfill a moral obligation and perhaps establish a valuable precedent by abolishing the slave trade in the District. Eliminating the District slave markets would have little practical effect because the more hospitable soil of Virginia was just across the Potomac, but Southerners considered the movement a dangerous step toward something more far-reaching as well as an implied sectional insult.

In the Senate, the tone of the upcoming debates was indicated immediately when someone suggested that the famous Irish priest Father Theobald Mathew be invited to visit the Senate chamber. The good father had been imported to preach temperance to Irish workers in New England. William H. Seward, however, supported the suggestion with a speech praising the priest for having once written an article criticizing slavery. The invitation was approved only after an angry debate that found the Mississippi senators on opposite sides. Jefferson Davis angrily opposed the motion, while his colleague, Henry S. Foote, just as warmly supported it. Davis's father-in-law at the White House ignored the argument and honored Father Mathew with a White House banquet.[11]

Zachary Taylor's annual message to Congress delivered on Christmas Eve 1849 was apparently written in collaboration with his cabinet, but it expressed his personal views very clearly. It listed some impressive achievements, offered some sensible recommendations, and made an eloquent appeal for a rational approach to the issue of slavery and the territories. After congratulating his fellow citizens on the prosperity and stability of the country, he reviewed America's relations with Britain, France, Germany, and Portugal and repeated his determination to check United States filibustering against Cuba. He defended his policy of expressing full sympathy to the Hungarian rebels without granting any formal recognition because the Russians had joined with the Austrians to quell the uprising. The Senate, he announced, would soon receive treaties of amity and commerce with the nations of Central America, and there was reason to hope that a canal could be built across Nicaragua by private interests under the protection of the United States. Should it "be construed under the common protection of all nations, for equal benefits to all, it would be neither just nor expedient that any great maritime state should command the communication. The territory through which the canal may be opened ought to be freed from the claims of any foreign power." He did not mention Britain and the Mosquitos, but his meaning was clear. Likewise, he added, the Sandwich Islands (Hawaii) should be assisted in their efforts to remain independent.

As for domestic policy, the Congress should establish a bureau of agriculture to "elevate the social condition of the agriculturist, to increase his prosperity, and to extend his means of usefulness to his country, by multiplying his sources of information." The existing tariff rates should be revised "to place home labor at last on a sure and permanent footing" and to augment the national revenues. A branch mint should be established in California, and after a geological and mineralogical exploration, its mineral lands should be "divided into small lots suitable for mining and be disposed of by sale or lease, so as to give our citizens an opportunity of procuring a permanent right of property on the soil." Congress should seriously consider reducing the cost of postage to five cents for every letter regardless of the distance involved.

Sandwiched among less important matters were Taylor's recommendations on the burning question of the hour. The people of California, he wrote, were qualified by every reasonable standard for immediate statehood, and they had written a constitution "impelled by the necessities of their political condition." When they applied for statehood, it should be granted. New Mexico, he added, would probably follow suit in the near future. Before the admission of California and New Mexico, the people of each one would have "instituted for themselves a republican form of government, 'laying its foundation in such principles and organizing its powers in such form as to them shall seem most likely to effect their safety and happiness.' " Both should receive favorable consideration, and to maintain "the harmony and tranquility so dear to all," Congress should "abstain from the introduction of those exciting topics which have hitherto produced painful apprehensions in the public mind. . . . I repeat the solemn warning of the first and most illustrious of my predecessors against furnishing 'any ground for characterizing parties by geographical discriminations.' "

After this strong recommendation, the president added a highly significant statement of his Whiggish views toward the veto power: it was "an extreme measure, to be resorted to only in extraordinary cases, as where it may become necessary to defend the executive against the encroachments of the legislative power or to prevent hasty and inconsiderate or unconstitutional legislation."

And finally, the message closed with an eloquent appeal to national spirit and a statement of Taylor's own intentions that could not be misinterpreted:

> But attachment to the Union . . . should be habitually fostered in every American heart. For more than half a century, during which kingdoms and empires have fallen, this Union has stood unshaken. The patriots who formed it have long since descended into the grave; yet still it remains, the proudest monument to their memory and the object of affection and admiration with everyone worthy to bear the American name. . . . Upon its preservation must depend our own happiness and that of countless generations to come. Whatever dangers may threaten it, I shall stand by it and maintain it in its integrity to the full extent of the obligations imposed and the powers conferred upon me by the Constitution.[12]

Partisan Democrats represented by the *Daily Union*, as well as various Southerners in both parties, immediately dubbed Taylor's suggestions the "no action plan," but the term was not justified. The president's policy did not impose slavery on people who did not want it in areas where it could not have thrived anyhow, and it did not insult the Southerners with a federal prohibition against their cherished institution. Taylor advocated early statehood for California and New Mexico to prevent a congressional debate over territorial slavery and the Wilmot Proviso, but this was hardly a "no action" plan. It was an appeal by a slaveholding president to his fellow slaveholders to face reality and avoid stirring up unnecessary animosities against themselves in a struggle already settled by geography, climate, existing law and customs, and the will of a large population already in California and New Mexico.

The message has also been criticized on the grounds that it contained no eloquent appeal that might have stirred the patriotic emotions of angry partisans and did not announce some dynamic program to rally the support of his own followers. Without resorting to hindsight, however, it is difficult to imagine how Taylor could have made the situation more harmonious even if he had sacrificed his own basic principles. Congress was quite prepared to quarrel over fugitive-slave laws and the District of Columbia slave trade without receiving any suggestions from the president. With the most important issues he dealt wisely, and his appeals to George Washington and the founding fathers and his eulogy to the heritage they had bequeathed to Americans and the world were dramatic even in an age when people often confused flamboyance with eloquence.

The Christmas season provided a temporary lull in the arguments. Exemplifying the character and blessings of American democracy, a huge crowd gathered at the White House for a "levee" on New Year's Day. No one was turned away, and the leaders of both parties and both sections mingled freely with each other and with several hundred other people of every rank and degree. Unfortunately, reported a newspaper, "Several gentlemen lost their pocketbooks, containing small sums of money; and . . . a valuable gold watch was taken from the belt of a lady—the ring connecting the watch with the chain having been cut with some sharp instrument, the loss not noticed by her until leaving the mansion."[13]

The momentary good will soon disappeared. The *Union*, echoed by other Southern papers and leaders, charged that the two slaveholders Taylor and King had conspired to create a free California and had thereby endorsed and promoted the Wilmot Proviso. Taylor's "do nothing policy" had suddenly become a policy of doing entirely too much. Each house of Congress in turn sent the president a formal request for more information.

Taylor replied to each house with the same letter. Upon entering office, he wrote, he had found California being ruled by the military commandant, and with no legislative authority to do otherwise, he had left the situation unchanged. However, to enable Congress to act "with as full knowledge and as little difficulty as possible," he had sent Thomas Butler King with messages to California along with certain other officers to both California and New Mexico. He had strongly recommended that the citizens of both areas form state governments and apply to Congress for admission to the Union, but he had not authorized "any Government agent or officer to interfere with or exercise any influence or control over the election of delegates or over any convention in making or modifying their domestic institutions or any of the provisions of their proposed constitution." Instead he had specifically directed that "all measures of domestic policy adopted by the people of California must originate solely with themselves . . . without the interference of the executive." He had recommended early statehood for the two areas because of "an earnest desire to afford to the wisdom and patriotism of Congress the opportunity of avoiding occasions of bitter and angry dissensions among the people of the United States." As long as they remained territories governed by Congress, the issue of slavery would be argued. Admission as self-governing states, however, would "remove all occasion for the unnecessary agitation of the public mind." Also, if New Mexico could become a state, the Supreme Court would have jurisdiction over the boundary dispute with Texas. Otherwise, Congress would have to settle the issue. Meanwhile, the "property, lives, liberties, and religion of the people of New Mexico" were being better protected by the United States military than they ever had been before the treaty of cession.[14]

Even if Congress should impose conditions on the admission of California contrary to the will of its citizens, Taylor added, they could change their constitution at any time after admission, and the American public would support them. "To assert that they are a conquered people and must as a State submit to the will of their conquerors . . . will meet with no cordial response among American freemen. Great numbers of them are native citizens of the United States, not inferior to the rest of our countrymen in intelligence and patriotism, and no language of menace to restrain them in the exercise of an undoubted right . . . guaranteed to them by the treaty of cession itself, shall ever be uttered by me or encouraged and sustained by persons acting under my authority." Likewise, the people would faithfully execute the laws.[15]

Zachary Taylor had often denounced the Wilmot Proviso as unnecessary and deliberately inflammatory, but he was entirely ready to promote self-determination in New Mexico and California. He considered the Proviso irrelevant to the realities of the situation, and he did not expect it to pass. He had harshly criticized Andrew Jackson's domineering administration, however, and had often said he would veto no measure unless it was clearly unconstitutional. The principle of the Wilmot Proviso had been overwhelmingly approved by the South in the Northwest Ordinance of 1787 and the Missouri Compromise of 1820, for which Calhoun himself had voted. A pledge to veto the Proviso would have contradicted Taylor's often-expressed views of presidential power.

Thus, on 23 February, when Taylor's early promoters Stephens and Toombs came to the White House and demanded that he drop his request for the admission of California, they met a firm refusal. Questioned further, the president assured them that he would approve any constitutional measure passed by Congress and would faithfully execute the laws. As the two Georgians stormed out of the room, they passed Senator Hannibal Hamlin of Maine, who had been waiting to see Taylor on another matter.

Hamlin found the president angrily pacing the floor and later remembered that "with an expletive which I will not repeat here, he said, with an emphasis that I shall never forget, that if they attempted to carry out their schemes while he was president they should be dealt with by law as they deserved and executed." Thurlow Weed entered a few minutes later and was warned by the departing Hamlin that the old man was in an angry mood. Weed later recalled that Taylor had said he had told Stephens and Toombs that "if it became necessary, in executing the laws, he would take command of the army itself, and . . . if they were taken in rebellion against the Union, he would hang them with less reluctance than he had hung deserters and spies in Mexico." Weed remembered further that Taylor had said that he had once assured Jefferson Davis that the South should "act promptly, boldly, and decisively, with arms in their hand" if Northern aggressions should become unbearable. Now, however, he was convinced that the demands of the Southern radicals were "intolerant and revolutionary." In his story, Weed also included Thomas L. Clingman of North Carolina as having been with Toombs and Stephens.[16]

Twenty-five years later, Weed's publication of the story brought angry denials from Stephens, Toombs, and Clingman. Clingman avowed that he had never been there at all. Toombs admitted that he and Stephens had had more than one spirited conversation with Taylor, but they both insisted that he had never used any such language. Called upon by Weed for corroboration, Hamlin remembered the event clearly, but with certain variations. He did not remember that Clingman was present, but in Hamlin's version, Taylor had indeed threatened to execute any future secessionists. Hamlin, however, did not quote Taylor as having made the threats directly to the Southerners. Of the five narrators, Weed alone had a reputation for stretching the truth. The most likely version is that of Hamlin. Taylor probably did tell both Hamlin and Weed that he would hang any future traitors, but at this early stage of the controversy he probably did not threaten his former friends directly. At any rate, the Southern congressmen and senators had no doubt as to the slaveholding president's devotion to the Union.[17]

A week later, Congressman Horace Mann of Massachusetts, after dining with Taylor, reported that the president was certain that he could blockade the Southern ports and crush any secession attempt without bloodshed. If this idea seems foolish in the light of the later Civil War, it should be remembered that the widespread public support for secession in 1861 would have been far more difficult to muster in 1850 with a slaveholding planter in the White House.

While the Senate was wrangling over specific issues as various leaders introduced bills in line with their own sectional viewpoints, the House became entangled in the process of electing a Speaker. The presiding officer of the Senate was Vice-President Fillmore, but the corresponding office in the House was elective, and the chosen person exercised great power in the selection of important committees. Election was by majority vote. The Democrats held a three-member margin over the Whigs, but the ten Free-Soilers could tip the balance either way. The leading candidate in the beginning was the forty-year-old Robert C. Winthrop, who represented the conservative Boston Whigs. A combination of Northern and Southern Whigs had elected him Speaker in 1847, and he had performed with fairness and ability. The Georgians Toombs and Stephens had no logical reason to oppose Winthrop, but in a show of independence from the Whig caucus, which they refused to attend, they influenced enough Southerners to prevent Winthrop's quick nomination. Of the sixty-nine Northern Whigs, only Winthrop had a chance to win enough votes in both sections. The Democratic leader was Howell Cobb of Georgia. Only thirty-four years old, Cobb was fat, jolly, good-humored, and personally very popular. He had been an effective minority leader during the previous session of Congress, and at this point he was still a Unionist. He was one of the four Southern Democrats who had refused to sign Calhoun's January 1849 "Address."

Cobb received the most votes on the first ballot and on the last, but after three weeks of bitter wrangling and sixty ballots, no one had yet received a majority. The Free-Soilers were adamantly opposed to both Winthrop and Cobb, and no one else could command enough votes even with Free Soil support. On the first ballot, Cobb received 103 votes of the 113 necessary for a majority, as a handful of Southerners took reprisal for his opposition to Calhoun's "Address." Winthrop received 97. After eight ballots, Cobb still led Winthrop by 99 to 98. A proposal by Andrew Johnson to settle the issue by a plurality vote failed. On the twentieth ballot, Winthrop had 102 votes, and he held this number for ten more ballots while Cobb slipped to only five votes. Then most of the Southerners suddenly turned to William J. Brown of Indiana, and with further support from five Free-Soilers, he reached 112 votes. An explanation for this unlikely combination was in order, and a rumor quickly spread that Brown had promised choice committee assignments to the Free-Soilers in a letter to David Wilmot himself. George Ashmun of Massachusetts, a Winthrop supporter, asked Thomas H. Bayly of Virginia directly if Brown had made any such pledges to a member of the Free Soil party. He had heard rumors that this was so. As the members listened intently in a chamber that for once was quiet, Bayly answered that "common rumor" was "a common liar." Bayly then turned to Brown himself and asked if any such correspondence had taken place. Brown shook his head no. A few minutes later, however, an angry but somewhat chastened Bayly spoke again. He had been mistaken: correspondence between Brown and Wilmot showed that Brown had indeed made the promises in return for Free Soil support. The South had almost been betrayed by whatever assurances they had also received from Brown's friends.[18]

Two days later, William Duer of New York called Democrat Richard K. Meade of Virginia a disunionist. "It is false," Meade declaimed. "You are a liar, sir," answered Duer. The two men rushed at each other, but fortunately they were quickly separated by colleagues. After several more days of arguing, quarreling, jockeying, and wheeling and dealing, in which the sections tended to become more and more polarized, Winthrop rose again to 95 votes on the fifty-second ballot, but fell back to only 13 votes by the fifty-ninth. Cobb had only 2. At this point the weary members finally agreed that if no one got a majority after three more efforts, the candidate with a plurality would be the Speaker. On the sixty-third ballot, Cobb, the owner of more than a thousand slaves, was chosen with 102 votes to 99 for Winthrop.[19]

The result was a victory for moderation, but the debates engendered by the Free-Soilers caused many Northern members to react strongly against what they considered unnecessary Southern intransigence. The Whigs could probably have won the speakership if they had received all-out support for Winthrop from their Southern members. Winthrop had never supported the Wilmot Proviso, and his rejection seemed quite unreasonable. Similarly, the deceptive move by Brown alienated numerous Southerners. Stephens and Toombs had opposed Calhoun's "Southern Address" and had been willing to accept a free California if Southern honor could be preserved by the abandonment of the proviso in dealing with New Mexico. They had previously displayed no personal enmity toward the principle's advocates, but now they decided that any denial of equal rights in the territories was an unacceptable insult. Toombs responded to the "discreditable trick" of Brown and the Free-Soilers by avowing that "before this House and the Country, and the presence of the living God, . . . if . . . you seek to drive us from the territories of California and New Mexico . . . and to abolish slavery in this District, thereby attempting to fix a national degradation upon half the States of this Confederacy, *I am for disunion*; and if my physical courage be equal to the maintenance of my convictions of right and duty, I will devote all I am and all I have on earth to its consummation."[20]

The sectional debates in the House usually paralleled those in the Senate, but the initiatives for compromise and the most important battles over philosophy and policy in 1850 came in the Senate, where the slaveholding and the nonslaveholding states were divided evenly at thirty each. Jesse Bright of Indiana, however, owned slaves in Kentucky, while several border slave-state senators like Benton and Clay held no brief for the extension of slavery. The only two avowed abolitionists were John P. Hale of New Hampshire and Salmon P. Chase of Ohio, although William H. Seward often aroused more Southern antipathy than did both of them combined. Hale was witty and rarely if ever showed any personal ill-will toward the Southerners. Chase was pompous, self-righteous, and humorless. Seward, whose true feelings and idealistic rhetoric often seemed contradictory, was a painful splinter under Southern fingernails. The mere fact that Seward was welcome at the White House was enough to make some angry Southerners feel betrayed by President Taylor. Eighteen of thirty-two Senate Democrats lived in slave states, as did twelve of the twenty-five Whigs. Two-thirds of the Northern Democrats were from the Old Northwest, and many of them, like Bright, had strong personal ties with the South. Southern strength among the Democrats, who controlled the Senate, was immediately apparent when Hale, Chase, and Seward received no committee assignments at all.[21]

On 16 January, Thomas Hart Benton and Henry S. Foote introduced contradictory bills for dealing with Texas and New Mexico. Benton would reduce Texas to one state of 150,000 square miles that would eventually be divided into two slave states of equal size in return for a payment of $15 million. Each of the two new slave states would be larger than any existing state, the territorial integrity of New Mexico would be preserved, and $15 million would be a generous recompense for territory that had never been part of Texas anyway. The bill, argued Benton, would stop the dangerous conflict between Texas and New Mexico, would relieve Texas from the anomaly of free soil between her limits in the area north of 36° 30', and would give the South two additional senators.[22]

Benton had never owned any Texas bonds, but he was certain that Texas would not surrender its claim without compensation, and he took the Texas military threat seriously. He and Sam Houston had served together in the War of 1812 and had been friends for many years. They shared a common disdain for Calhoun or for anyone else who might threaten the Union. Among slaveholders, they alone had stood for the admission of a free Oregon Territory in 1848, and in 1854 they would again be allies against the repeal of the Missouri Compromise. Benton was probably the most dedicated defender of New Mexican territorial rights in the Senate, but he and Houston remained friendly. There is no evidence that they discussed the issue privately, but it is difficult to imagine that they did not. Benton did not recognize any validity whatever in the Texas claims, but he argued throughout that a generous financial settlement would be a proper and safe solution.

Foote's bill would return California to territorial status and validate the claims of Texas to all of the populated area of New Mexico. Before introducing his bill, Foote launched a vicious personal attack upon Benton that would continue throughout much of the session. Considering the slaveholding Benton a formidable opponent, the Southern faction represented by Foote had apparently assigned Foote to taunt Benton into some rash action, and Foote clearly relished the task. Foote was a bald, homely little game rooster who combined a sharp intellect with a nervous and pugnacious temperament. He had already fought four duels that indicated more courage than marksmanship. He had been shot down in each of the first three but had managed to wound his opponent in the last. During the previous year he had promised Senator John Hale the honor of being hanged to the highest tree if the latter should ever visit Mississippi. On the final night of the 1848 session, Foote and Senator Simon Cameron of Pennsylvania had grappled and rolled down the Senate aisle. The writer Sarah J. Lippincott described Foote as "a most restless statesman, . . . afflicted with a sort of patriotic form of the dance St. Vitus. . . . How he ever stood still long enough to be shot at, is a mystery to me; and how any man could look into such a funny face and fire is another." Ironically, Foote was actually closer to Benton than he was to Calhoun on the overall question of saving the Union, and he would later write a book in which he blamed the Civil War on Southern extremism. Ultimately, Southerners would call him the Southern Vallandigham, after the famous Union traitor. In 1848 he had praised Benton publicly as a "statesman superior to Edmund Burke," but in 1850 Foote entered the lists as Calhoun's defender against Benton and attacked the Missourian almost daily with personal insults normally excluded from congressional debates by both rules and custom.[23] As president of the Senate, Vice-President Fillmore agonized over the extent of his power and duty to call Foote to order, but did not risk turning Foote's invective toward himself as often as he should have.

At sixty-eight, Benton was twenty-two years older than Foote but was physically much larger and stronger. Benton, who had long since been dubbed "Old Bullion" because of his support for hard money, had once routed an armed assailant with rocks, had exchanged pistol shots with Andrew Jackson at a distance of five feet, and had killed an opponent in a formal nine-foot duel. The latter affair had left him full of remorse and determined never to duel again. He had ignored all subsequent challenges, including one in 1848 delivered by Henry Foote on behalf of Andrew Pickens Butler of South Carolina.

In 1844 Benton had opposed the initial move to annex Texas because of its inflated illegal boundaries and its involvement with the slavery argument, and he had played an instrumental role in the bloodless conquest of New Mexico, where he had several personal friends. Also, one of California's prospective new senators was his son-in-law John C. Frémont. Aside from these personal considerations, however, Benton had always believed and argued that slavery could not be expanded, that slavery where it existed was in no danger, and that unnecessary controversies over rights that could not be exercised should be avoided. When the Missouri legislature had ordered Benton to support Calhoun's position on slavery extension, Benton had openly defied the instructions and had stumped the entire state of Missouri. In speech after speech his opponents were needlessly endangering the American Union, "man's last best hope on earth." By splitting the Democratic party on the issue, he had guaranteed his own defeat for reelection by a Whig candidate, but he had one final role to play in the Senate.[24]

Like Taylor, Benton was a slaveholder, and his views were identical to those of the president. In 1850 Benton was ready to ignore party distinctions and become Taylor's chief spokesman in the Senate. Whether any written communications ever passed between the president and the senator is problematic. Benton's papers were destroyed when his house burned in 1855, and Union troops performed the same historical disservice on most of Taylor's letters when they destroyed his Louisiana plantation during the Civil War. Taylor, however, was a very convivial president who invited numerous people for occasional dinners and receptions at the White House. In all likelihood, he and Benton had opportunities to strengthen each other's convictions—or perhaps draw comfort from each other, because the convictions of both were already set in concrete.

A rather shadowy force working for compromise of the Texas–New Mexico conflict was the public debt of Texas that remained from the former republic's tenure as an independent nation. When Texas became a state in 1845, its custom houses were replaced by those of the United States. Almost immediately, various leaders and creditors began to argue that because Texas could no longer collect customs revenues to pay its debts, the United States should assume this obligation. The total amount was approximately $10 million, and half of this consisted of bonds purchased by various speculators at very large discounts. Some of these bondholders had been influential in getting Texas annexed in the first place, and they and others were eager to see Congress pass legislation that would commit the United States government to redeeming their securities at par, or at least close to that figure. Both Clay and Webster stood very close to some of the larger bondholders, although each had vigorously opposed the annexation of Texas in 1844–45. In contrast, Senator Benjamin Tappan of Ohio, a large Texas bondholder whose brothers Arthur and Lewis were militant abolitionists, had upset both family and friends by voting for the annexation. While Henry Foote and other Southerners were doing everything possible to get Texas rewarded with New Mexican territory rather than money, James Hamilton, the former South Carolina congressman and future senator and governor, was working in every possible way to get the appropriation. When Calhoun hobbled to his seat to have his final speech read in the Senate, he was supported on Hamilton's arm. On 11 February 1850 Hamilton sponsored a bondholders' meeting at the National Hotel to consider "matters of essential importance to their interests." Henry Clay's close friend Gen. Leslie Combs of Kentucky traveled throughout the East to stir up support for the compromise. Combs ultimately received $96,393 for Texas bonds that Sam Houston estimated had cost Combs not more than $15,000. Apparently, the largest bondholders of all were the Washington bankers William W. Corcoran and George W. Riggs, Jr. The two entertained numerous congressmen and senators with lavish parties, and the House sergeant at arms often loaned money on Corcoran's behalf to lawmakers who found themselves short of funds. The efforts of the bondholders and their lobbyists were obvious to everyone and may have affected Zachary Taylor's personal attitudes towards some of the compromisers. On the other hand, those struggling to create a trough and put their snouts into it were probably a very important force for sectional peace in 1850.[25]

With almost all constructive work in both houses of Congress at a standstill over contradictory bills and extreme demands on both sides, Henry Clay, who had guided both the Missouri Compromise of 1820 and the compromise tariff of 1833 through the Congress, stepped forward once more to play the role of fire extinguisher. On the night of 21 January he walked through cold and stormy weather to enlist a promise of support from Daniel Webster, and eight days later, Clay presented a series of resolutions designed to end the quarreling. Under Clay's plan, California would be admitted as a state without any congressional action on slavery, and New Mexico and Deseret (Utah) would be given territorial status on the same basis. Texas would relinquish part of its claim to New Mexico in exchange for federal assumption of the Texas public debt. The slave trade would be abolished in the District of Columbia, but slavery would be allowed there as long as it existed in Maryland or until Maryland and the District would be willing to accept a fully compensated emancipation. And finally, Congress would enact a new and effective fugitive-slave law and would recognize the principle that Congress had no jurisdiction over the domestic slave trade.[26]

The debates over Clay's propositions began immediately and went through various phases. First came the generalized statements of support or opposition. Clay, Calhoun, Webster, Jefferson Davis, Seward, and others spoke in turn. For several weeks, President Taylor offered no opinions, but on 13 February he presented California's new constitution, without elaboration but obviously hoping that it would immediately be submitted to a vote. Again he was widely condemned for doing nothing. The Democratic *Union* had already charged that Taylor and Seward were deliberately stirring up the "anti-slavery excitement of the North" to produce a Southern "attempt to secede from the Union, in order to give General Taylor and the cabinet an opportunity to run up the Union flag, call its party the Union party, and thus rescue itself from inevitable defeat and prostration, which must be its fate, if it cannot be saved by some such desperate and dangerous experiment." The *Union* also denounced Clay's propositions as a blow at the South in disguise, and various Southerners, including Foote and Jefferson Davis, attacked them. The Texans immediately insisted upon the validity of the Texas claims to New Mexico.[27]

On 4 March, before an overflow crowd on the floor and in the galleries, John C. Calhoun, wrapped in flannels, tottered into the Senate chamber and announced that Senator Mason would read Calhoun's speech. It was to be not only his final justification for secession but also a rejection of any possible compromise. Calhoun had already told Henry S. Foote and others that the time for compromise was past and that he would hold any Southern man dishonored who would attempt such a thing. According to Foote, the "Southern Address" and the Nashville convention were Calhoun's steps toward "termination of a political union which had positively become hateful to him." With the Nashville convention, wrote Foote, Calhoun hoped to defeat any efforts at compromise and "enable the South to set up a new government, under a constitution which he repeatedly avowed he had prepared for her, and in which the perpetuation of African slavery would be a leading and fundamental feature."[28]

The great threat to the Union, Mason read, lay in a deep-seated unrest and fear within the Southern states, whose people were convinced that consistently with honor and safety, they could no longer remain in the Union. The South was being outstripped in population and political power. The admission of the present territories and the exclusion of the South from the areas taken from Mexico would bring the balance to forty Northern senators against only twenty-four from the South. This inequality, Calhoun had written, was due entirely to three classes of federal legislation: measures like the Northwest Ordinance of 1787, the Missouri Compromise, and the recent Oregon bill, all of which had barred Southerners from the areas involved; monetary and financial policies that had caused wealth to flow from the South to the North and had prevented immigration to the South; and those measures and precedents that had changed the government from a federated republic into a consolidated democracy. Only the adoption of measures guaranteed to give the South security could save the Union. Invoking the illustrious name of the great Southerner and slaveholder George Washington would not do it. Washington had led the colonies to separation and independence when the union with Britain had become a threat. Neither Clay's plan nor the administration's scheme to admit California without a specific application of the Wilmot Proviso could satisfy the South. Southerners were already barred from California by the threat of liberation for their slaves. The North, Calhoun concluded, could save the Union only by conceding to the South an equal right in all territories, by enforcing the fugitive-slave laws, by ceasing all agitation for abolition, and by passing a constitutional amendment that would guarantee the South the power to protect itself. California would be the test question, and the alternatives were clear. If the North could not accept Calhoun's demands, "let the States we both represent agree to separate and part in peace. If you are unwilling we should part in peace, tell us so, and we shall know what to do, when you reduce the question to submission or resistance."[29]

Calhoun's views were not shared by all slaveholders, and conspicuous among his opponents had been the slaveholding presidents Polk and Taylor. Both had considered Calhoun's views the dangerous ravings of a frustrated politician, who, having failed in his burning ambition to reach the presidency, had turned against the Union for selfish and personal reasons. Whatever Calhoun's motives, his final statements are highly relevant to any evaluation of Zachary Taylor. The late David M. Potter wrote that hindsight is a handicap to the historian because he enjoys a view of final outcomes and results that is denied the decision makers. This is, of course, true when the historian looks for motives, but hindsight is a very valuable tool if it proves that one set of ideas and policies was clearly superior to another.

If a deep-seated unrest and fear existed in the South, Calhoun's continuous sounding of the tocsin was in large part responsible, but the threats and injustices that Calhoun described as the basis for Southern fears and discontent and, thus, as the motivation for his own conduct did not really exist in 1850. He assumed first that the

Northwest and the Northeast would always act as a unit against the South and that the presence or absence of slavery would always determine the interests of the new southwestern area. Party lines had always crossed those of section, and the South had always more than held its own in combination with scattered support in the other sections on most issues, including the recent acquisition of Texas. Common agrarian interests would always provide a basis for affinity between the South and the Northwest unless other controversies should intervene. Even the Carolinian's statistics were inaccurate: there were thirty slave-state senators instead of twenty-four. Four years later, both houses of Congress would vote to repeal the Missouri Compromise restriction against slavery in the western territories north of 36° 30'. In 1857 the Supreme Court would rule that no territory anywhere could ban slavery, and later in the same year, a majority of eight in the Senate would vote to make Kansas a slave state in the face of clear evidence that the overwhelming majority of the Kansas inhabitants opposed any such action.

Calhoun assumed further that all Southerners were slaveholders, and he argued, in effect, that except for antislavery restrictions, enough slaveholders would have emigrated into the Ohio Valley, Iowa, and Oregon to make these regions proslavery in their political affiliation. Three-fourths of the Southern white population had no connection with slavery, and the unsuitability of those regions for slavery had long been accepted by Southerners themselves. Indeed, Calhoun himself had voted for the Missouri Compromise in 1820. Nonslaveholding Southerners had emigrated freely into these nonslave areas. The governor, the congressman, both prospective senators, and the secretary of state of California were all from slaveholding states, and Senator William M. Gwin, in particular, had been a lifelong follower of Calhoun; nevertheless, California had voted resoundingly against slavery.

With regard to pro-Northern financial policies, Calhoun was on equally soft ground. Protective tariffs had been gradually reduced to a very moderate level between 1833 and 1842 and had been virtually eliminated in 1846. They would be lowered even further in 1857. Calhoun himself had supported the United States Bank against Andrew Jackson but had changed sides under Martin Van Buren. Regardless, Jackson had destroyed the Bank forever, and Polk's Independent Treasury system had been passed with overwhelming Southern support. In stressing these measures as a reason for the relative decline of the Southern population, Calhoun was completely ignoring the institution of slavery as a deterrent to foreign and

Northern immigration. The center of wealth had shifted from the agrarian South to the industrial North, but this was essentially the result of science, invention, and the South's rejection of any economic and technological innovations that might threaten slavery.

Calhoun's charge that the government had changed from a federal republic to a consolidated democracy in which the minority had no redress if overruled by the interests of the majority was a provocative analysis. It ignored the Bill of Rights, however, which defended every minority's right to oppose governmental policies and seek converts to its point of view. His corollary assumption that this alleged preponderance of Northern strength would eventually force the South to choose between secession and the abolition of slavery was not supported by any existing realities. Congress had a long and consistent record of noninterference with slavery, and this principle would be reechoed by Abraham Lincoln in 1861. A constitutional amendment opposed by thirteen of the fifteen former slaveholding states would be impossible even today. There was little likelihood that the representatives of an extremely property-conscious society would ever have enacted an unconstitutional law destroying Southern slave property and then would have voted the arms and men necessary to fight any Southern resistance. Even in the midst of the anger and hatreds engendered by the Civil War, Abraham Lincoln felt compelled to justify his Emancipation Proclamation on the grounds of military necessity because the racial prejudice and fears that kept the nonslaveholding white Southerners supporting slavery were just as prevalent in every Northern state. Technological pressures and the libertarian ideals magnified by two world wars would probably have ended slavery at some future date, but the choice of time and method would have remained in Southern hands if the South had not triggered the Civil War. Abolition at the hands of the North became a threat to the South only when it was united with a determination to save the American Union. And finally, Calhoun's insistence that the South might secede in peace or successfully defend its independence requires no comment.[30]

In 1850 a great many slaveholders like Zachary Taylor, Thomas Hart Benton, Henry Clay, and Sam Houston recognized the flimsiness of Calhoun's accusations. One editor estimated that no more than nine senators and forty representatives would support Calhoun's sentiments. When friends asked Benton why he did not reply, he answered, "When I was at the bar, I never interrupted the adversary counsel while he was proving up my case for me."[31]

Three days after Calhoun's speech, the majestic Daniel Webster took the floor with an equally large audience on hand. His role as a nationalist had been cast in the great nullification debates of 1833, but he now spoke with a new tolerance and generosity toward his Southern opponents. He spoke, "not as a Massachusetts man, nor as a Northern man, but as an American." The extremists on both sides, he said, were mistaken, because right and wrong could not be calculated with mathematical precision. The issues must be settled by mutual charity and concessions. In language bordering on arrogance for its self-confidence, Webster, in different words, echoed Calhoun's view that the American future lay with the free states, but he pleaded with his fellow Northerners to be gracious and avoid unnecessary insults to the South. Slavery was clearly impossible in California and New Mexico, and the Wilmot Proviso was unnecessary. He would abandon it as a needless indignity to the South. Also, Webster added, Southerners were entirely justified in their demands for a stronger federal fugitive-slave law, and he would willingly support any such legislation. Having proffered the olive branch, Webster denounced the secessionists, including Calhoun, "who, I deeply regret, is prevented by serious illness from being in his seat today."

"The Senator from South Carolina is in his seat," answered a sepulchral voice. Webster smiled and spoke directly to Calhoun. Peaceful secession was an impossibility, and the upcoming Nashville convention was both dangerous and unnecessary. The very thought of "hatching secession over Andrew Jackson's bones" was ridiculous.

Webster sat down amid loud applause while Calhoun rose to his feet. "I cannot agree," he quavered, "that this Union cannot be dissolved. Am I to understand . . . that no degree of oppression, no outrage, no broken faith can produce the destruction of this Union? . . . The Union *can* be broken." Webster answered that the Union could be broken, but that such a calamity would be a revolution.[32]

Webster's support for a compromise that included a fugitive-slave act and did not support the Wilmot Proviso inspired curses and charges of betrayal among his former idolaters in New England, but there was at least one immediate compensation. Later in the day, the great banker William W. Corcoran sent Webster two notes canceling $5,000 that Webster owed and added a letter of congratulations with a check for $1,000.[33] There is no evidence that Webster had expected anything for supporting a settlement that would earn

Corcoran a great deal of money in appreciated Texas bonds, but the godlike Daniel did not return the gift. It is entirely possible also that Corcoran might have rewarded Webster even if Corcoran and his bank had not possessed any Texas bonds. Corcoran sympathized deeply with the South and later spent most of the Civil War period in Europe, and in 1850 Webster's stance on the Wilmot Proviso and the fugitive-slave problem was clearly an effort to soothe Southern feelings. Unlike Webster, Benton had been denouncing the bondholders since 1844 and would continue to do so, but in 1850 he was just as ready as Corcoran and Webster to buy sectional peace with an award to Texas.

At this point, no serious conflict between Clay's proposals and the recommendations of President Taylor had yet been emphasized by anyone, and Ritchie and other Democratic editors were still denouncing both the president and the senator. Webster had told Robert Winthrop that he actually preferred Taylor's plan and saw no important differences between the proposals of the president and those of Clay. Taylor, said Webster, wanted New Mexico admitted as a state after it had made its own decision on slavery, while Clay wanted New Mexico to be admitted as a territory with a future right to decide the slavery question for itself. On 8 March, the day after his speech, Webster told Winthrop that he had intended to compliment Taylor but had not had the time. Webster intended to do so in a later speech. He had "omitted a tribute he would gladly have paid to the President's patriotic policy . . . which it was his purpose to advocate in the Senate." If it came to a vote, he would support the president's plan.[34]

A few weeks later, on 31 March, Calhoun died, his tortured mind busy to the last with a final ultimatum to offer as the only alternative to secession. On a few scraps of paper, he left a plan whereby the Constitution would be amended to provide two presidents, one from the North and one from the South, with no law to become effective unless signed by both. In fact, of course, the incumbent president and both of his predecessors were slaveholders. The next president, Fillmore, would be less a friend of Southern extremism than many historians have thought, but Pierce and Buchanan, who would follow Fillmore into the White House, would zealously support the most ardent Southern demands. Of the twelve presidents who had served as of 1850, eight had been slaveholders. Harrison had lived only a month, and Van Buren had supported the South in every controversial situation. The slaveholding states, in fact, had consistently dominated the presidency and would continue to do so until the divisive actions of Southern extremists would accomplish the election of Lincoln in 1860. Calhoun assumed without question that any Southern president would share Calhoun's own views of the South's best interests, but this was by no means true. More likely, however, he knew the plan would be rejected and hoped that this would be regarded in the South as just another example of Northern tyranny.

For a brief moment, Calhoun was a force for unity. He was accorded a magnificent funeral. In the Senate, Clay, Webster, and others delivered brilliant eulogies, but Benton was as silent as Calhoun had been after the death of John Quincy Adams. Webster urged his colleague to show magnanimity and speak, but Benton answered, "He is not dead. There may be no vitality in his body, but there is in his doctrines. . . . My people cannot distinguish between a man and his principles; between a traitor and treason. They cannot eulogize the one and denounce the other." Few were openly as vocal as Benton, but privately a good many people felt no regret. South Carolina's future governor Benjamin F. Perry believed that Calhoun's death was fortunate for the country and his own fame, while its former senator William C. Preston called Calhoun's death "the interposition of God to save the country."[35]

Meanwhile, the senators and the people in the galleries had heard numerous other significant orations. To Jefferson Davis, Clay's proposals were no compromise at all because they gave the South nothing. Davis demanded that the Missouri Compromise line of 36° 30' be extended to the Pacific Ocean with the South having the right to take slavery to any territory, including California, south of the line. Even this would be a Southern concession, he said, and anything less would be an intolerable aggression. Like Calhoun, Davis spoke as though all Southerners were slaveholders and insisted that if the South could be debarred from the common domain of all the states, the Union would soon reach the condition predicted by Calhoun "when, without an amendment of the constitution, the rights of the minority will be held at the mercy of the majority." Davis offered no specific amendment, but he insisted that one was necessary in order to protect the South. Calhoun was then still alive, and Davis may well have been in his confidence with regard to the presidential amendment proposal that later died with Calhoun. Like Calhoun, Davis insisted that all agitation against slavery must cease. Ten years later, Abraham Lincoln would deny that the Republican party had any actions or plans against slavery, and he would make a significant point: "But we do let them alone—have never disturbed them—so that, after all, it is what we say, which dissatisfies them. They will continue to accuse us of doing until we cease saying." Certainly, strong evidence to support Lincoln's view was present in the 1850 demands of Calhoun and Davis that *all words as well as actions* against slavery must stop. Slavery, said Davis, required no apology. It had rescued the slave from barbarous Africa and had given him civilization, economic security, and the Christian Bible. It would be a very good thing for California. Happily, the demands of Davis for slavery in areas where it had already been rejected by the existing population were not shared by most Southerners in 1850, but Davis would be heard from again.[36]

Northerners like Seward, Salmon P. Chase, and John Hale opposed the compromise proposals as vehemently as Davis had. Seward spoke eloquently for this group when he assailed all legislative compromises as "radically wrong and essentially vicious, involving the surrender of the exercise of judgment and conscience." Slavery, declaimed Seward on 11 March, was a sin against God's law, a "higher law" than the United States Constitution. Objecting to all compromises, Seward attacked this one in particular. It would exchange human freedom in other areas for "liberty, gold, and power on the Pacific coast." Seward struck boldly at the South's most sacred principle. The Constitution, he said, did not really recognize property in slaves at all, because in both the three-fifths clause and the statement regarding the return of fugitives from labor, the Constitution used the word "persons." Indeed, he continued, slavery should not even be allowed to dominate the slave states because in all of them the slaveholders were only a small minority of the total population. Slavery was "only a temporary, accidental, partial, and incongruous" institution, while freedom was "a perpetual, organic, universal in harmony with the Constitution." The founding fathers had permitted slavery only because it already existed, and slave-state leaders themselves had established freedom throughout the Northwest Territory. None of them would have voted to establish slavery anywhere. Britain, France, and Mexico had abolished it, and the rest of Europe was following their lead. Slavery was incompatible with all the world's best ideals and must never be established again anywhere.[37]

Seward had spoken the words that lacerated Southern feelings most—a harsh, self-righteous disapproval backed by world opinion and based upon ideals shared by the South, and an unwillingness to grant the slaveholders even a shred of moral defense. In fact, Seward was entirely tolerant toward slavery where it already existed, but

Southerners found his bland assumption of moral superiority well-nigh unendurable. Various abolition and religious presses praised Seward's effort, but the president and most newspapers of both parties denounced it angrily. Senator Willie Mangum of North Carolina rushed to the White House to protest and reportedly found Taylor "so excited that he stuttered." At the president's orders, Alexander Bullitt in the *Republic* denounced the speech as "a law-breaking, Constitution defying, disunion doctrine" against "Whig teaching as understood and practised everywhere." Other Whig papers followed suit, and Southern Whigs, as well as Fillmore supporters in New York, rejoiced that Seward had obviously destroyed his influence at the White House. If personal friendship and influence were synonymous, however, their happiness was premature. Within a week, Taylor's anger had subsided, and Seward and he were personally back on good terms. Among other overtures, Seward presented Taylor with a silver currycomb for Old Whitey. Seward's enemies derided his sycophancy, while Taylor probably found the act amusing. Henry S. Foote threatened to currycomb Seward, but the New Yorker responded by inviting Foote to a sumptuous dinner at his residence. Foote accepted, and while the two men came no closer to agreement on any issues, they established a very civil personal relationship.[38] Illustrating the principle that heretics are usually hated far more than infidels, Foote continued to insult and harass the slaveholding Benton at every possible opportunity.

In the House, meanwhile, the exchanges were equally vitriolic. The brilliant Georgia triumvirate of Toombs, Stephens, and Cobb used clever parliamentary tactics to delay a vote on California, while the dynamic young senator from Illinois, Stephen A. Douglas, worked behind the scenes to find a compromise formula they would support if it was passed by the Senate.

At the White House, Zachary Taylor wrestled with the British over Central America, argued with the French, checked the Cuban filibusters, rejected efforts by others to start and prolong Indian wars, and watched the proceedings in Congress. He did not fully understand why the Southerners were rejecting his efforts to spare them the humiliation of the Wilmot Proviso by allowing California and New Mexico to become states with self-determination on the slavery issue, but he was certain that his policy was best for both sections and the country in general. He was not opposed to compromises in general or to any of Clay's proposals in particular. He was determined, however, to defend New Mexico against the demands of

Texas, and he was ready to crush any attempts at disunion by force if necessary.

In late February the president got another opportunity to state a basic principle. When he was invited to dedicate the cornerstone of a new monument to George Washington in Richmond, Virginia, he attracted huge crowds and made an excellent impression. Early on one of the mornings there, he rose in time to engage in his favorite habit of strolling through the marketplace. At Fredericksburg, en route home, he added a serious note to his usual expressions of gratitude for Virginia's hospitality: "As to the Constitution and the Union, I have taken an oath to support the one and I cannot do so without preserving the other, unless I commit perjury, which I certainly don't intend to do. We must cherish the Constitution to the last . . . we must fall back upon Washington's farewell advice, and . . . preserve the Union at all hazards." The speech was widely circulated and was predictably damned by his enemies and praised by his friends. It also won the approval of many who had not yet formed strong opinions about their president.[39]

The old general had a tough skin, but he bitterly resented the vicious name-calling being directed against himself and his cabinet. On 18 April 1850, Orlando Brown, the commissioner of Indian Affairs who served as liaison between the president and John J. Crittenden, spent several hours with Taylor. The president, he reported, spoke as a proud, brave, and deeply injured man could speak of "unmerited wrong and unprovoked persecution." Taylor, however, was "unconquerable. . . . He exclaimed that he always kept his flag flying in front of his tent and would never strike it." He had declined to express his views on slavery and the territorial questions until it became necessary, and he knew that his plan for solving them had "met with great favor everywhere." The Democrats, however, knew that "it would greatly enhance the fame of the administration," and this was why they were encouraging Clay and attacking the president's policies.

Brown added, quite correctly, that the Democrats had carried out "a systematic and unscrupulous attack on the President," while Clay and Webster, instead of supporting the Whig party and the president, were trying to reweave "the broken web of their own political fortunes." The Democrats, with "hypocritical cunning," were stimulating Clay and Webster to assault the administration—making each man believe he could be elected president in 1852. The cabinet members, wrote Brown, were working with ability and fidelity, but they lacked the qualities that could make an administration popular. Trying to gain "a great reputation as a *working cabinet*, they secluded themselves too much." This left them open to charges that they were offensive and impolite.[40]

Brown probably oversimplified the motives of both Clay and Webster. No one, however, can read the *Washington Daily Union* or follow the congressional debates without recognizing a vigorous effort by the Democrats to split the Whigs into warring factions. Until 8 May, however, Taylor's relations with Clay remained harmonious though not warm. The real break between the neophyte president and the ancient veteran senator would come only after Henry S. Foote and others had reshaped Clay's compromise proposals into a single bill.

Taylor had never hesitated to put his opinions into action. Convinced that the Southern complaints about the abolitionist threat were groundless, he authorized his son to buy him another plantation less subject to flooding by the Mississippi River. By early June 1850 Richard had acquired "a plantation and a number of servants." The total investment was $115,000, and Taylor anticipated that "85 or 90 good hands" would produce an annual profit of $20,000.[41] Obviously, he saw no real threat whatsoever in Seward's radicalism and therefore felt no urge to break off their personal friendship and deny Old Whitey a silver currycomb. Indeed, Seward may have assured Taylor that the speech was strictly for home consumption and was designed only to keep Northern antislavery Whigs loyal to their party. No evidence supports this, but Seward's overall career invites the speculation.

8

★ ★ ★ ★ ★

AN UNDESERVED ALBATROSS:
THE GALPHIN DILEMMA

Until April 1850, most observers were much impressed with Zachary Taylor's appearance. The sectional debates and the constant attacks upon his cabinet had not disturbed his sense of moral rectitude. He was certain that the omnibus bill could not be passed, and he felt that Clay and the Democrats were subjecting his own solution to dangerous delays. If necessary, however, he would defend New Mexico against the avarice of Texas, and he would preserve the Union against any attempts at secession. If either or both should require military action, he had no doubts about his own capacity as a military commander. Similarly, he was not moved by the incessant attacks upon his cabinet, particularly when they were equaled by the attacks upon himself. He knew that the wild accusations had a specific purpose—a Democratic presidential victory in 1852—and he did not doubt that presidential ambitions were also motivating Clay and Webster in their support of the omnibus idea. He was certain that his secretaries were doing as well as anyone could, and he had total faith in their loyalty and integrity.

In April, however, came revelations that shook him to the core. The ancient Galphin claim that Secretary Crawford had pushed so diligently before joining the cabinet had been approved without debate by the Senate and the House in 1848. The Polk administration had paid the principal of $43,518 but not the interest, which was now five times the principal. When another attorney asked for the interest, Treasury Secretary Meredith referred the request to the comptroller, who first advised against paying it but later changed his mind and recommended the payment of the interest that had accrued since 1838, the year when the claim had first been pressed against the federal government. Meredith then asked for a ruling by Attorney General Reverdy Johnson, who advised that the interest should be paid for the entire seventy-three years since the incident had occurred. As a result, Meredith paid out $191,352.89, thus bringing the total payment to nearly $235,000. As the Galphins' original counsel and agent for sixteen years, Secretary of War Crawford had already received half the principal and would now receive half the interest. In 1850 this was an enormous sum—approximately $1 million in 1980 dollars, with no income tax to be levied.

The Galphin claim was in fact a very complex issue.[1] In 1773 the British government, in exchange for grants of Indian land, had accepted the responsibility for paying extensive debts owed by Indians to fur traders. When the American Revolution occurred, however, only those traders loyal to the crown were actually paid, and Galphin was therefore penalized for becoming a Revolutionary patriot. Indeed, the 1850 investigating committee concluded that Galphin's "great influence with the Indians caused them to resist the importunities of England and [they] refrained from taking part in the war. He was especially and peculiarly the means of averting, to a great extent from Georgia and Carolina the cruelties and atrocities of Indian warfare."[2] During and after the Revolution, the state of Georgia took over the lands, and its legislature later enacted a provision for payment to claimants like Galphin who could prove that they had been "friends of America." Ultimately, however, Georgia ceded the area to the United States. On numerous occasions, first Galphin and then his descendants had proved his status beyond a doubt, but the state of Georgia had decided that because Galphin's original claim had been against Great Britain, the federal government should pay it. In 1832 the federal government finally opened the way for a successful prosecution of the claim when the Congress passed an act for the payment of Virginia's Revolutionary claims. The original act of the Georgia legislature had called for the payment of 6 percent interest. Regardless of appearances, when the Congress agreed that the United States should pay the original claim, there was no legal or constitutional reason for Meredith or Johnson to refuse to pay the interest, although they could probably have exercised the arbitrary power to scale it down. The Congress had not intended to make George Crawford a rich man, but however undeserved such a result may have been and however fraudulent it might look, the settlement was entirely legal.

Johnson had given the decision much thought, and his closely reasoned opinion was quite lengthy. The act of 1848, he wrote, not only authorized but practically required the payment of the interest accrued since 1776. The treaty of 1773 had charged the lands themselves with the payment of the principal and the interest on the debt, and this charge remained an encumbrance on the lands regardless of their disposition. Galphin had struggled to take the territory from British rule and subject it to the sovereignty of Georgia. When Georgia had ceded the lands to the United States in 1802, the latter was bound "in law and honor" to execute the provisions of the treaty of 1773. This principle had already been followed in the Virginia cases that the United States had assumed by an act of July 1832. The justice of the claim was indisputable, and when the Congress voted in 1848 to pay the principal, it was also bound to pay the interest—as it had already done in the Virginia cases. And finally, Johnson concluded: "A government never presents itself in a more commanding and elevated condition than when it answers fully to all just demands. . . . It is under a conviction that this will not be done in the present instance by anything short of the entire payment and from a full conviction that the law of 1848 authorizes and calls for payment, that I have come to the conclusion here stated."[3]

Despite the legality and justice of the claim for Galphin's descendants, however, Crawford's acceptance of such a huge reward from his fellow cabinet colleagues while serving as secretary of war could easily be portrayed as a corrupt betrayal of the public trust by all three men. Displaced and partisan Democrats, as well as disgruntled Whigs who had failed to gain a place at the public trough for themselves or their friends, now had glaring evidence of the perfidy and corruption they had already been denouncing. The reputation of the administration and the fate of its most cherished policies were certain to be affected, but Crawford, supported by his fellow Georgians Stephens and Toombs, was unmoved. A proper political solution, which might have vindicated all three secretaries and the administration, would have been for Crawford to return his share to the government after deducting a sizable fee based upon his actual time and effort devoted to the cause. No one ever blamed the Galphin heirs, but Crawford's reward seemed to go beyond the bounds of honest greed. The wealth, however, was more important to Crawford than either his good name or the administration he served. He believed that he had done nothing wrong, and he would keep the money. To his credit, he himself demanded a congressional investigation, which would probably have occurred anyhow.

Taylor's reputation for simple honesty had been a major obstacle to the Democratic party's hopes for unseating him in 1852, but now his administration could be accused of raiding the Treasury. Almost everyone, whether Democrat or Whig, who had ever opposed the president for any reason at all attacked the officers involved and the president without mercy. Meredith and Johnson pleaded ignorance of Crawford's stake in the result because another attorney had actually reopened the issue. Clearly, however, they could not have been unaware of Crawford's role as the Galphin attorney in 1838 and 1848. Crawford insisted that before accepting his appointment to the cabinet, he had told the president about the case but had assured him that it had nothing to do with the War Department. Taylor, said Crawford, had answered that taking the office would not affect Crawford's "preexisting individual rights." Obviously, Taylor had not really understood the full scope of the problem. According to Thomas Ewing later, the other cabinet members urged Taylor to drop Crawford, but Taylor refused until the facts could be developed more fully. The important decisions had been made by Johnson and Meredith, and no evidence was ever presented to indicate that either profited in any way from the settlement.[4]

The scandal was totally unrelated to the slavery debates, but it affected them nonetheless. Crawford, in fact, was the only cabinet member who differed with Taylor's position on New Mexico. Stephens and Toombs, who were attacking Taylor in the House, had persuaded Taylor to appoint Crawford in the first place. Toombs had sponsored various Galphin memorials, and Stephens had delivered the check for the principal to Crawford. Remaining consistent, they defended the claim. Ironically, Seward, the nominal friend of the administration, declared that the administration should rid itself of Crawford and Johnson, and preferably also Meredith, while some Southerners believed it was all a Northern plot to eliminate Crawford because he was the South's only ally in the cabinet. With excellent reasons for discharging the one cabinet member who questioned his policies, Taylor refused to take action until all the evidence had been heard. If Crawford had no right to the money, then Meredith and Johnson were equally at fault, and the condemnation and disgrace of three men he had admired and trusted was not an action to be taken lightly.[5]

Responding to Crawford's demand, a House committee composed of five Democrats and four Whigs reported several resolutions that triggered speeches by more than twenty members. This debate coincided with the compromise debates, and the position of the House members on the slavery issues usually paralleled their arguments on the Galphin matter. The full House ultimately passed resolutions declaring that Polk's treasury secretary, Robert J. Walker, had acted properly in paying the original claim but that Meredith had paid an unjustified interest claim without proper authority. The committee also recommended the enactment of laws against what the cabinet members had done and thereby indicated clearly that no existing laws had been broken. The Congress should pass laws forbidding any governmental officer to pay any interest unless directed to do so by law and forbidding any cabinet officer from deciding on any claim in which another member of the same cabinet might be interested. After many weeks of well-publicized criminal accusations, threats of censure against the president as well as the cabinet, and amendments implying corrupt activities by the cabinet, the House in its final report agreed that Meredith and Johnson had been ignorant of Crawford's involvement in the case and censured no one, not even Crawford. According to the Congress, the sin was horrendous, but the sinners were innocent.[6]

Amid the sound and fury, the *National Intelligencer* printed the full details of the case and reached a verdict of innocent. The administration's own editors, Bullitt and Sargent, however, agreed with the critics. Already hating those involved, Bullitt felt personally that the mere fact of a cabinet minister's having served as a claims agent "needed only to be stated to be condemned."[7]

The opposition presses spread their accusations far and wide, but they may have influenced future historians more than they did their contemporaries. Writing in 1965, Samuel Eliot Morison concluded that Taylor, "like certain other military presidents, . . . trusted too many rascals . . . this Galphin claim affair . . . smelled worse than anything of the sort prior to the Credit Mobilier scandals in the administration of the next soldier president, U. S. Grant."[8] On the other hand, Johnson, who made the key decision, continued with his distinguished law career and later served as a United States senator and as an ambassador to Great Britain. Meredith later served six years as attorney general of Pennsylvania. Crawford withdrew from politics until 1861, when he served as chairman of Georgia's secession convention.

Zachary Taylor was facing British intransigence in Nicaragua and the sectional crisis at home with flag flying, but the Galphin scandal was a different matter. Honesty was an article of religious faith for Taylor—he had once refused the help of state relief laws in Kentucky when security notes that he had signed for defaulting friends had left him heavily in debt. He could not overlook the possibility of collusion between Johnson and Meredith for the benefit of Crawford. Also, however, loyalty to subordinates and friends and the ability to give and receive deep affection were ingrained parts of Taylor's character. During the months of unjustified partisan attacks, he and the cabinet had become embattled comrades in arms. If Johnson and Meredith were telling the truth and if neither had been aware of Crawford's stake in the Galphin settlement, they were innocent of any wrongdoing. As the administration's chief legal officer, Johnson had rendered an opinion, and Meredith had acted upon it. None of the three had broken any existing law, although the result for Crawford was difficult to justify. A more experienced politician concerned only with his hopes for reelection might have discharged all three immediately and thereby enhanced his already well-known reputation for bold and decisive action. For once, however, Taylor's ability to simplify problems and act quickly was absent in the face of a moral problem filled with doubt and uncertainty and involving his personal relations with men he had liked and trusted. If Crawford had not been a cabinet officer, the affair would probably have attracted minimal attention. Would the payment have been made if Crawford had remained only a Georgia lawyer? Taylor could not deny that he had assured Crawford that his existing private concerns would not be sacrificed if he joined the cabinet. Were Taylor's friends blameless victims of political partisanship, or were their protestations of innocence false? As the House investigation dragged on through May and June, various friends commented on the president's dejected and haggard appearance, while others, like Alexander Bullitt, raged privately and publicly at the undeserved suffering that Taylor's cabinet was causing.[9] As Taylor faced more important problems without flinching, the inner conflict between his personal feelings and his sense of duty, complicated by indecision as to where his duty toward the cabinet actually lay, grew ever more intense. According to Thurlow Weed, Taylor slowly reached the agonizing decision that Seward was right, that the cabinet must go.[10] Whether or not Weed remembered correctly, the Galphin affair was undoubtedly a terrible burden for a president with Taylor's personal predilections.

9

★ ★ ★ ★ ★

THE OMNIBUS BILL

Throughout April and May, the Congress grappled with the task of organizing Clay's compromise proposals. Southern moderates, represented by Henry S. Foote, had reconciled themselves to a compromise that would admit a free California, but they were determined to exact the highest possible price at the expense of New Mexico. The plan was simple. They would combine California, the Texas–New Mexico dispute, and the slavery question in both New Mexico and Utah into a single bill. A free California would be the price that the South would have to pay for amendments favorable to Texas and an insurance policy for the passage of the strongest possible fugitive-slave act. In the words of South Carolina's senator Andrew Pickens Butler,

> The great object to be obtained was this . . . there were three vessels at sea—one of them (California) was strong enough to carry the other and weaker vessels into port, if connected with her. California was a large and safe ship, and the other smaller boats in danger were to be attached to her, and she would carry them all safely into port.[1]

This particular trade-off of California for the Texas claim to New Mexico had been considered as early as January 1849, when William B. Preston, then a congressman, had introduced a bill to create a state of California with an eastern boundary within fifteen to twenty miles of the Rio Grande and grant everything east of this line to Texas. This proposal had led Robert Toombs to write that California could not "be a slave country; we have only the point of honor to save; this will save it, and rescue the country from all danger of agitation." Toombs, Stephens, and Cobb had apparently had this in mind when they were busy foiling "Calhoun in his miserable attempt to form a Southern party."[2]

President Taylor and numerous members of Congress were heartily in favor of a peaceful compromise but believed that the object could be achieved far more quickly by dealing with each of Clay's propositions separately on its own merits. On 13 February, when Taylor submitted the California constitution, Benton lauded Clay's efforts and proposed that California be referred to a select committee to be chaired by Clay. Foote immediately protested that he had a similar motion ready, whereby a committee of fifteen would be appointed by ballot and would have the authority to deal with all of the controversial questions. He did not wish the questions to be divided.

On the following day, both Douglas and Clay advocated the separation of California from the other pending questions. Clay did not think it right "to embrace in a single motion the question of the admission of California and all the other subjects . . . the subject, for example, of the establishment of a boundary line for Texas, and the proposition to compensate Texas for the surrender of territory." He did not want California subjected to "all the delay, the uncertainty, the procrastination" that a combination would bring.[3]

Clay's argument triggered a savage attack by Foote. Clay, said Foote, had been posing as a friend of compromise but had now turned traitor. The reason, according to Foote, lay in recent conversations that Clay had had with his former enemy Benton, who was betraying the South for the interests of his son-in-law, the newly elected senator from California, John C. Frémont.

Denying that he had ever advocated a combination of the various subjects, Clay angrily defended himself against the charge of inconsistency. When Foote repeated his accusation of treachery against the South, Clay sternly replied that he knew no South, no North, no East, no West: "My allegiance is to this Union and to my state; but if any gentlemen suppose they can exact from me an acknowledgement of allegiance to any ideal or future contemplated confederacy of the South, I here declare that I owe no allegiance to it; nor will I, for one, come under any such allegiance if I can avoid it."[4]

Foote closed the exchange by accusing Clay of giving his adversaries

> all the *trump cards* in the pack, and depriving his partners and himself of the privilege both of holding *honor* and of *winning the odd tricks of legislation.* He is doing more than this even; he generously gives his adversaries *two bullets and a bragger with the age superadded,* whilst he rashly stakes his all upon the imaginary potency of a mere *broken hand!*[5]

Foote's "bragger with the age superadded" was obviously Benton, and on the following day, Andrew Pickens Butler continued the effort to drive a wedge between Clay and Benton by denouncing Clay's effort to separate the measures. On 20 February, Senator Jeremiah Clemens of Alabama taunted Clay unmercifully. Clemens had read

> that a time was coming when the lion and lamb should lie down together, but I did not expect to witness anything approaching that happy state in my day. All incredulity, however, is now at an end, and I am prepared to believe in any miracle, and treat with grave consideration any prophecy. When Thomas H. Benton and Henry Clay, "the great expunger" and "the great embodiment" are found holding sweet converse with each other, forgetting the animosities of thirty years, and lovingly pulling side by side in the same team, there can be nothing so wild and fanciful as to defy belief.[6]

Such a miracle, he concluded, could spell only danger for the South.

Clay and Benton had been bitter political enemies for many years, and Benton's successful effort to get expunged from the Senate record a Clay-sponsored resolution censuring Andrew Jackson had been one of the greatest humiliations of Clay's life. Foote and Butler had hit Clay in a soft spot. Hotly denying that he had had any advance notice of Benton's motion to make him head of a select committee, Clay insisted that Benton's crossing the chamber to speak to him had not been related to the subject, although he would gladly address his worst enemy as friend if it would conciliate the Union. Again Clay urged the admission of California as a separate measure.

Foote answered with his heaviest barrage. Benton, he said, was using Clay to further Benton's own nefarious schemes of treachery to the South. Benton's motion for a select committee headed by

Clay was part of a bargain by which Clay was to help smuggle California into the Union with no compensation for the South. Clay's speech on the compromise resolutions, charged Foote, had more in it to mortify and wound Southern sensibilities than even the speeches of professed abolitionists, "not excepting even the far-famed Garrison, and Phillips, and Douglass."[7]

Clay again defended himself against Foote's accusations, but his words lacked the angry defiance of earlier occasions. Soon he would shift to Foote's position and support a combination bill. Foote and other Southerners apparently convinced Clay that cooperation with Benton was destroying Clay's usefulness as a moderating influence upon the South. Foote and his Southern supporters were determined to have a combination bill, and no alternative could satisfy them. Although he had agreed several times with President Taylor and Benton that the parts of his compromise should be considered separately, Clay now cast his lot with Foote as the best chance for success.

Foote had not only enlisted most of the Southerners behind his strategy; he also carried the influence of Thomas Ritchie and the Democratic party's newspaper, the *Daily Union*. Foote arranged a meeting between Clay and Ritchie, and when Clay agreed to support the move for a select committee of thirteen to organize the compromise issues into a single, or omnibus, bill, the *Union* changed overnight from an attitude of harsh criticism to one of lavish praise for both Clay and the compromise.

No evidence supports the charge, but the Virginia fire-eaters Henry A. Wise and Edmund Ruffin, as well as the more moderate R. M. T. Hunter, were convinced that Clay had bought Ritchie's support. The Congress had given Ritchie its printing contract, but the costs had been higher than expected, and Ritchie wanted Congress to pay additional money. The three Virginians believed that Clay's support for this was Ritchie's payoff; Ruffin estimated the price at $100,000.[8]

If, indeed, Thomas Ritchie's financial problems influenced his support for Clay and a combination bill, the policy was entirely consistent with much of what the paper had been saying all along. The *Union*, after all, was the Democratic party's official organ, and destroying Zachary Taylor's reputation in time for the next election was its primary political duty. A considerable number of Democrats in both North and South had voted for the general, and they must not be allowed to make this mistake again. Taylor had said that he would be president of all the people, but according to the *Union*,

the general had "shown himself to be the most proscriptive and bitter federal President since the days of John Adams the first. . . .
[Taylor] has not only recklessly repudiated the promises and pledges
which he has made to the American people, but he has sinned against
the virtues of gratitude and patriotism."9 Ritchie himself was a prod-
uct of the Jacksonian spoils system, but a Whig president who dared
to follow the Jacksonian example had to be a criminal or worse.
Also, of course, how could the *Union* serve the cause of the Democratic party better than by promoting and maintaining a quarrel
between the Whig president and the leading Whig senator? And
finally, Ritchie's intensity may have been enhanced by his formal
expulsion from the floor of the Whig-dominated Senate during the
previous session.

The *Union* had greeted Taylor's annual message with the charge
that he had "criminally withheld his sentiments from the public"
and was continuing a "policy of criminal concealment." The president, said the *Union*, was guilty of a "voluntary refusal to recommend any scheme of compromise, and his actions in California were
those of a king by Divine right." When the formerly Democratic
New York Evening Post supported Taylor on California, the *Union*
announced that editor William Cullen Bryant had changed from "a
tolerable poet, inditing indifferent verses, a few of which may per-
chance be remembered a decade of years," into "a malevolent and
embittered fanatic." Bryant had followed a rather consistent course
from espousing the libertarian rhetoric of Jacksonian democracy to
supporting Van Buren and the Free-Soilers in 1848. His verses would
be remembered long after both his and Ritchie's editorials would be
forgotten. Over and over, the *Union* insisted that Fillmore was an
abolitionist and that the cabinet members, including the slaveholders, were Free-Soilers dominated by Seward.10

The *Union* did have some problems with attacking Taylor's policy of federal nonintervention with regard to slavery, because this
had also been the platform of Lewis Cass, the Democratic presidential candidate in 1848. First, the editor accused Taylor of having
stolen the principle from Cass. Then Ritchie announced that Cass
and Taylor agreed on freedom of choice for the people in the territories prior to their admission into the Union, but he insisted that
there was a difference. General Cass was *"in favor of providing governments for their security and protection in the intermediate
period,"* but Taylor was *"for leaving them without any government
or protection or security at all."*11 This, of course, was nonsense,
because both California and New Mexico were under the protection

of sizable contingents of troops, and the Utah Mormons would have preferred going their own way without any connection to the United States at all. The only territory being threatened was New Mexico, and from beginning to end, the *Union* argued for the full claims of Texas against New Mexico. Also, no one worked harder than Thomas Ritchie to portray the boundary dispute as a national crisis and to build up popular Southern support for the rights of Texas against both New Mexico and the federal government.

The *Union* had greeted Clay's initial proposals with skepticism and disapproval. There was "nothing of the true spirit of compromise in his speech or resolutions." On 7 February 1850, under the heading "Mr. Clay's Pretended Compromise," the *Union* charged that Clay had insulted the South by suggesting that slavery could not go to the territories because of natural barriers. The fact that Clay was trying to solve the various problems all at once, however, met with the *Union*'s approval from the day of Clay's first efforts. Henry Foote's exertions and speeches were uniformly praised, and Ritchie was clearly a partner in the plan to unite the territorial slavery question and the boundary dispute with California as the best hope to get results favorable to the South. Most historians have concluded that Ritchie was persuaded by means fair or foul to support Clay and the omnibus, but the evidence can be easily interpreted to argue instead that Clay capitulated to Foote and Ritchie. By early April the *Union* was contrasting the "conciliatory and patriotic spirit displayed by the venerable and illustrious statesman of Kentucky" with that of the "weak, feeble, and imbecile President and cabinet."[12]

The *Union* had an equally vitriolic echo in Richmond, Virginia, where Ritchie's two sons, William and Thomas, Jr., were editing the *Richmond Enquirer*. Thomas, Jr., had killed his rival editor J. H. Pleasants in a duel. Pleasants had been disabled by the first shot, but Ritchie had continued to vindicate his honor by shooting Pleasants a total of eight times. The *Enquirer* attacked its enemies, both real and alleged, without mercy or fear. Like the *Union*, it began by denouncing Clay's compromise resolutions as a total surrender to the North, "humiliating . . . to his own State, and the entire slaveholding interest in America," but wheeled into line after the measures had been combined into one bill.[13]

The *Charleston* (S.C.) *Mercury*, on the other hand, remained consistent by opposing every form of the compromise from beginning to end. According to the *Mercury*, the combined bill should be defeated because statehood for California was unconstitutional, the dismemberment of Texas was unlawful federal tyranny, noninterference in New Mexico was another form of the Wilmot Proviso, and the fugitive-slave bill was an invasion of states' rights.[14]

Taylor's biographers and others have attributed the ensuing conflict between Zachary Taylor and Clay at least in part to personal differences—Clay's dominating personality and angry disappointment at losing the presidential nomination; Taylor's jealousy of Clay's eminence and resentment because the Kentuckian had not supported Taylor's solution to the slavery quarrel. As a primary explanation, however, this view is probably unfair to both men. If personal enmities played any serious role at all, the awakened memories of Clay's many fierce battles with Benton may have been more significant than any animosity Clay might have felt for Taylor. Throughout the Jackson and Van Buren administrations, Clay and Benton had angrily debated almost every national question with both sarcasm and wit, and on the biggest issue of Clay's career—the United States Bank—Benton had won hands down. Men are often motivated by feelings they do not even recognize, and a chance to have a final go at each other may have influenced both Clay and Benton. Clay's support was essential to get the measures combined into a single bill, but his first step in that direction was taken with great reluctance.

On 12 March, Henry S. Foote moved the reference of a set of compromise resolutions to a select committee of thirteen with instructions to report a single bill settling all outstanding sectional issues. This launched a bitter six-week battle in the Senate with numerous other senators as well as President Taylor expressing strong opposition to the whole idea. Up to this point, there had really been no serious conflict between Clay and the president, but this effort found Taylor in full agreement with Benton. The Whig president and the Democratic senator were entirely consistent. The committee was sponsored by Foote and Ritchie, and its avowed purpose was to frame an omnibus bill that would unite the leading measures. Ritchie had denounced the president almost daily since his inauguration. Foote, in bills, speeches, and resolutions, had advocated the return of California to territorial status and its division at 36° 30′, and the *Union* had described Taylor's efforts to make California a state as "criminal conduct." Both the senator and the editor had repeatedly argued for the full claims of Texas against New Mexico. The plan to unite the two issues had to have a purpose of some sort, and both Taylor and Benton feared the worst.

For a time, Webster also agreed that the committee was both unwise and unnecessary. He praised Benton for trying to keep California separated from the other issues, and on 4 April, in a sharp exchange with Foote, Webster urged that the various questions be considered one at a time, beginning with California. Like Clay, however, Webster surrendered to Foote and pointed out to Benton that measures could be added or subtracted by amendment. The committee issue, said Webster, was not important.

Benton's answer anticipated the views of numerous future historians. The committee, insisted Benton, would go into session as a compromise committee, and if its efforts were unsatisfactory, any attackers would have to bear the odium before the nation of being obstructors of compromise. The feeling had been spread throughout the country that the committee would alleviate the country's wounds, and anyone later opposing that "healing nostrum" would become known as a man of dissension.[15] Benton, of course, was thinking of himself, but his prophecy would be even more applicable to the future reputation of Zachary Taylor.

Stephen A. Douglas also believed that Foote's proposal was inexpedient. Douglas moved that the resolution be tabled, but this motion was defeated by 28 to 26. Of the 28 votes favoring the establishment of the committee, 23 were from the South, and Benton was the only Southerner to vote with Douglas. The Little Giant repeatedly warned that the compromise measures could never pass unless treated separately, and he declined a place on the committee because "he did not believe that the Omnibus Bill had any conceivable chance of success and he wished to keep in a position to save something from the wreck."[16] Douglas, however, unlike Benton and Taylor, had no personal emotional stake in the territorial integrity of New Mexico, and he therefore steered clear of the ensuing debates.

On 8 April, Benton spoke for both himself and the president in a speech that was in part an answer to the dead Calhoun. The plan, he charged, was to "logroll" California into or out of the Union, depending upon the fate of the angry, distracting "rollers" to be attached. He would support most of the suggested measures separately, but they should not be combined. California, having settled the slavery question for itself, had no connection with the inflammatory Wilmot Proviso. He would support the admission of California without any mention of slavery, but he would not mix it with the Proviso controversy. He would also vote government for the territories without any mention of slavery, but Texas was a separate matter. A new state must be carved from her side, her boundaries must be reduced, her dispute with New Mexico must be settled, and her surplus territory must be ceded to the United States. These were tremendous issues that should be settled on their own merits. California and Texas were incompatible subjects of equal dignity, but coupling the two would enable Texas to control the admission of the new state of California. Texas had several great problems to solve, but the inability to settle any one of them would veto the admission of California.

He would willingly support a new fugitive-slave law, Benton continued, but California had nothing to do with the subject and should not be tied to it. Laxity in enforcing this law was the only point at which the Northern states had "given just cause of complaint to slaveholding sisters." The slave states, he insisted, were agitated without cause by the efforts of a mere handful of abolitionists. The refusal of Congress to touch slavery in the states for the past sixty years should satisfy the slaveholder, but if not, "let him go to the market—that quick and truthful reporter of all danger to property; and he will quickly, from the price that is offered to him, find that nobody is afraid of abolition but himself." The Constitution was the "binding compromise." It had "been faithfully kept by every Congress from 1789 to 1850," and the South's complaints of aggressions, encroachments, and oppressions were not justified. Congress had the undisputed power to oppress slavery by taxing slavery, but no Northern member had ever hinted at such an action. Slave property was worth more than a billion dollars, and no other government in the world had left such a mass of wealth untaxed. Obviously, the Congress had no disposition to "commit flagrant violations of the Constitution, to harass or destroy slave property." Instead, in 1836, Congress had extended slavery a hundred miles north of the compromise line by adding the Platte territory to Missouri and, in 1845, had added the immense slave area of Texas.

Benton had only praise for Clay's efforts to restore "peace and harmony to a distracted country. . . . The Senator's . . . frank, manly, noble speech delivered on this floor had done much to quiet the public mind—far more than any hugger-mugger work" any committee could accomplish. The preservation of the Union, however, did not lie

> in a committee room, nor in this Chamber, nor in the hands of politicians; but in the hearts of the people, . . . who know that they . . . are enjoying, more blessings under this Union than ever fell to the lot of men upon earth; and who are determined that their children shall have the same right to the blessings of civil and religious liberty, and the same chance for the wealth and

honors of the country which they themselves had. There is where the salvation of the Union lies, and not in the contrivances of politicians, or the incubations of committees.[17]

Benton was entirely justified in fearing that the dismemberment of New Mexico was the major question at stake. From a practical standpoint, a Texas victory over New Mexico was the only possible chance for slavery to make a gain in the territories, and the Southern bloc of senators supporting the omnibus committee clearly realized this. The combination of the issues into a single bill was a skillful Southern tactical move, executed primarily by Henry S. Foote, with the Texas senators caught in an emotional trap between their devotion to the Union and their duty to promote the interests of Texas.

Throughout the debates, Foote did everything possible to provoke Benton into either an unpremeditated physical attack or a duel. After weeks of patience, Benton on 26 March appealed to the chair against such tactics and denounced Foote's insults as both false and cowardly. Foote answered with an open challenge. The stains on Benton's character, he said, "might well relieve any man of honor from the obligation to recognize him as a fitting antagonist." He would not denounce Benton "as a *coward*," but if Benton wished to "*patch up* his reputation for courage, now greatly on the wane," he could do so by making known such a desire. At present, said Foote, Benton was "shielded by his age, his open disavowal of the obligatory force of the laws of honor, and his senatorial privileges."[18]

On 17 April, Benton's patience gave out. As Foote began a tirade, Benton rose and lumbered toward Foote, who pointed a five-chambered pistol at Benton and retreated down the aisle toward the vice-president's desk. Senator Henry Dodge of Wisconsin momentarily halted Benton until the old man saw the pistol. Breaking loose, Benton, with his coat thrown open, again advanced toward Foote and shouted: "I have no pistols! Let him fire: Stand out of the way! Let the assassin fire!" As pandemonium swept the chamber, colleagues disarmed Foote and led Benton back to his seat.[19]

Foote later explained that he had carried the pistol because of his small size and a fear that he might be assaulted. He had assumed that Benton was also armed. A committee of investigation ultimately absolved Foote of any intent to assassinate Benton but admitted that Foote had, "without any sufficient provocation, indulged in personalities . . . of the most offensive character, such as were calculated to rouse the fiercest resentment in the human bosom. These were suffered by Mr. Benton for a long time with great forbearance."[20] Although Foote went unpunished, the adverse publicity and, perhaps, a reconsideration of the dangers involved put a damper on his tongue. Henceforth, all exchanges between the two were relatively civil. Benton's only revenge would be literary. When Foote announced that he would write a little book in which Benton would play a large part, Benton replied that he would write a very large book in which Foote would not appear at all. Each kept his promise.

Whatever Foote's purpose, the affair damaged his reputation and hurt the Southern cause. Many Northern papers agreed with an article in the *Pittsburgh Mercury* headlined "ASSASSIN FOOTE," and the episode would be recalled six years later when Preston Brooks attacked Senator Charles Sumner. If the Southerners really wanted the concessions they professed to crave, brandishing a pistol on the floor of the Senate was not conducive to their success. The affair was also duly noted at the White House, and various newspapers had already pointed out the incongruity of the lifelong Democrat Benton's leading the Whig forces of President Taylor, while the founder of the Whig party, Henry Clay, had become the darling of the Southern Democrats and the *Daily Union*.

On 8 May the controversial committee, with Clay as chairman, reported a series of bills. Most important was the first, which combined the issues of California, the territories, and the Texas boundary: California should be admitted without any mention of slavery by the Congress; the territories should receive territorial governments expressly forbidden to legislate on the subject of slavery; Texas, for an unspecified payment, would accept as its boundary a line running from twenty miles north of El Paso northeastward to the junction of the Red River with the hundredth meridian. The latter provision, though far less than Texas was demanding, would still have given Texas the southeastern corner of present-day New Mexico, an area roughly equal to the state of Maryland. The proposition did leave New Mexico most of its existing cities and towns, but it could be further amended for the benefit of Texas as long as it remained in the same bill with the admission of California. The remaining propositions for a more stringent fugitive-slave law, the abolition of the slave trade in the District of Columbia, and rules for the partition of Texas were kept separate, but their chances for passage clearly depended upon the fate of the omnibus bill dealing with the more vital questions. The fugitive-slave bill provided stringent federal machinery for the recovery of escapees and severe penalties for any Northerners caught giving them aid or comfort. It did, however, require the slaveholder to provide a written record documenting the identity of the slave and the facts of the escape, and it provided a jury trial for the fugitive in the state from which he allegedly had fled. Although the latter provision meant little, it did comply with the federal Constitution's requirement of a jury trial in cases involving more than twenty dollars. Unfortunately, this provision would later be removed by amendment. Meanwhile, the *Charleston Mercury* and other Southern papers denounced the proposal as an infringement of every state's right to retain exclusive control of the relation of master and slave.[21]

Under Clay's guidance, the committee had done reasonably well. Nonetheless, the omnibus bill never had a chance for approval without significant amendments, even though many observers believed that it could have been passed quickly if broken into its component parts. Five members of the committee immediately made speeches explaining their differences with the majority, and the report touched off an explosion of anger among radical Southerners and the Texans.

On 5 May, Douglas proposed another test vote to determine the Senate's preference between an omnibus bill and dealing with the three measures separately. His motion to table the bill and take up California was defeated by a vote of 28 to 24, with 8 Northern and 20 Southern votes keeping the omnibus bill alive. A group of Southerners had created and would accept no change in the omnibus principle, but neither they nor the Northern extremists would support the bill unless it could be amended to suit themselves.[22]

From this point until 7 June the Senate battled furiously over amendments, with Jefferson Davis and William H. Seward leading their respective groups against any compromise at all. Various amendments to bar slavery in the territories, protect it in the territories, give the territorial governments authority to protect it, or formally bar any laws on the subject—all were voted down. On 5 June, Benton offered an amendment to abolish Indian peonage in the new territories, but the South crushed it by a vote of 32 to 20 and thereby voted to retain what had often been cited as an insurmountable barrier to African slavery.[23]

On 14 May, Alexander C. Bullitt and John O. Sargent, the editors of the administration newspaper, the *Republic*, resigned because of angry quarrels with the cabinet and perhaps because they had decided to support their long-time idol Henry Clay instead of the president. Their replacement, Allan A. Hall, a Tennessee Whig with twenty years of newspaper experience, indicated that the paper would continue to support Taylor's plan as the best hope for a compromise. Hall had been serving as assistant secretary of the treasury.[24]

Just as Benton had predicted, a great many people, including Clay, defined opposition to the omnibus bill as opposition to compromise in general. On 21 May, Clay for the first time made open war against the administration. The country, he said, was threatened by five gaping wounds, but the president's plan would heal only one of them while leaving the other four "to bleed more profusely than ever." Taylor's plan, he charged, would not establish any civil government for New Mexico and Utah, had failed to fix the boundaries of New Mexico, and had left the people there exposed to a threatened invasion by Texas. The plan ignored the fugitive-slave problem and offered no solution to the burning slave-trade question in the District of Columbia. It would please only the Northern extremists while provoking and insulting the South. The Southern leaders would go home to face angry editors, legislators, and voters. When Congress reconvened for the next session, Clay predicted, the four unsettled questions would still be malignant tumors.[25]

Despite warnings from Crittenden and others that he should avoid the appearance of opposition to compromise, Taylor allowed Hall to publish a five-column editorial in the *Republic*, which attacked Clay as vainglorious, dictatorial, and unfair. If the denunciation misjudged Clay's motives, the charge of unfairness was justified. Taylor had not only asked the Congress to admit California. He was also working diligently for the rights of the people of New Mexico and trying to uphold the pledges of the United States made to New Mexico at the time of the annexation. He had also stated many times that the people of New Mexico should decide the question of slavery for themselves. The fugitive-slave question and the abolition of the slave trade in the District were matters for Congress to settle, and as Hall and the *Republic* pointed out, Taylor had expressed no opposition to any act dealing with them and was no impediment to the healing of any of Clay's five wounds.[26] The inhabitants of California, New Mexico, and Utah had indicated clearly that they did not want slavery. Utah was safe, but Taylor had every reason to believe that the omnibus-bill process, whether Clay fully realized it or not, was an effort to impose slavery on part or all of New Mexico east of the Rio Grande by annexing it to Texas.

Too many historians, including Taylor's biographers Brainerd Dyer, Holman Hamilton, and K. Jack Bauer as well as Fillmore's biographer Robert Rayback, have accepted the view that President

Taylor was the chief obstacle to a successful compromise. Both Hamilton and Rayback argued that if the measures had not been combined into a single omnibus, Taylor would have signed the admission of California but would have vetoed some of the other provisions. In fact, however, they cite no real evidence that Taylor would have rejected any part of the compromise that was actually passed.[27] Taylor's objections were directed entirely against a combining of issues that could not pass as one bill because too many Southerners were determined to strip New Mexico of its chief towns and cities and because too many Northerners felt that the omnibus was already overly generous to Texas and/or wanted a formal restriction against slavery in New Mexico. Neither group composed a majority, but their combined strength against the omnibus for opposite reasons made its passage impossible. Meanwhile, the longer the debates continued, the greater the personal rancor grew and the more inflexible the arguments became, as the debaters reacted to each other with increasingly sharp resentments.

Historians K. Jack Bauer and Michael F. Holt seem to agree with Robert Toombs that Taylor deliberately abandoned his Southern political ties in favor of an alliance with the Northern Unionists. Supposedly, this would have guaranteed Taylor's renomination in 1852 and, according to Holt's provocative analysis, reflected the disappearance of most of the traditional economic conflicts that had given each major party its basic identity. This may be true, but Taylor's position and actions can also be explained with equal logic in simpler terms that do not include either a conscious effort to reshape the political party structure or a decision to favor the North. Taylor had never concerned himself with party politics, and he saw himself as the president he had vowed in 1847 to be—the leader of all the people of every party and every section. He had indeed regarded the tariff and banks as dead issues and had written that he would defend the freedom of Northerners to criticize slavery. He had also, however, denounced the extremists on both sides, expressed hope for a satisfactory compromise, and promised that his sword would defend the South against any real threat to slavery. He believed that his policies were best for the South as well as for the North and that they were more likely to produce a lasting compromise. In his view, at worst the omnibus bill was a threat to the independence of New Mexico, and at best it was prolonging the struggle, making a settlement ever more difficult, and increasing the danger of a military conflict between Texas and New Mexico. Acted upon one at a time, the different parts of the compromise—including statehood for California and a viable New Mexico with self-determination on the question of slavery—could be passed in an acceptable form, and this would end the crisis.[28]

In 1850 the strongest newspaper voice supporting both the traditional Whig party and the compromise was probably the venerable *National Intelligencer*. It had been the organ of the Federalists, the National Republicans, and the Whigs since 1809; and its years of devotion to the interests of Clay and Webster were apparently the reason why President Taylor established the *Republic* instead of allowing the usual Whig voice to speak directly for his administration. Throughout the debates the *Intelligencer*'s editors, Joseph Gales and William Seaton, produced eloquent editorials supporting the compromise and the Union and filled their columns with editorials from dozens of western and Southern papers expressing the same sentiments. The paper was read by Whigs and Democrats alike, and more than any other source it kept the members of Congress aware of the sentiment for compromise and the Union in their own districts and states. Likewise, the paper's own editorials were sent far and wide for other editors to reprint or use for information and inspiration. From beginning to end, however, the *Intelligencer* preferred Taylor's plan of action to the omnibus bill, and it printed dozens of editorials from other papers expressing the same views.

On 23 January 1850, after Taylor's message asking for California statehood and suggesting that New Mexico should follow suit, the *Intelligencer* opined that "if there ever was a Document entitled to the praise of honesty, frankness, and devotion to the welfare of the Republic, it is the Message . . . by the PRESIDENT on Monday." In several issues the paper defended Taylor against the charge that he had sent Thomas Butler King to create a California without slavery. The decision of California against slavery had not been influenced in any way by Taylor, and the *Intelligencer* quoted several Southern papers to the effect that Calhoun's own view of states' rights supported California's right to do as it pleased. When Taylor at Fredericksburg, Virginia, in late February said that he must defend the Union or commit perjury and that he had no intention of committing perjury, the *Intelligencer*'s columns rang with praise. After Calhoun's final address on 10 March, the paper ridiculed his basic premises and pointed out that the South had controlled the White House and the federal government for forty-eight of its sixty years.[29]

The *Intelligencer* defended with equal ardor the traditional Whig attitude toward the presidency and pointed out the inconsistency of those Whigs who were blaming Taylor for not being in effect another

Andrew Jackson. Taylor, said the *Intelligencer*, had taken office against "the Executive influence, Executive patronage, Executive dictation, and the Executive veto." Under Jackson these elements had "resolved the Government into the one-man power and almost annihilated the Legislature." Congress under the Democrats had "ceased to be what it was intended to be under the Constitution, the independent and only legitimate organ for the expression of the public will." To correct this great evil had been a major reason for electing General Taylor. As for the alleged quarrel between Taylor's cabinet and the Whigs in Congress, the *Intelligencer* insisted that it was entirely over the question of patronage—whether Democratic officeholders should be proscribed indiscriminately or be replaced on an individual basis when vacancies occurred.[30]

Most importantly, above all other matters, the *Intelligencer* wanted a compromise of the sectional issues and considered Zachary Taylor an ally rather than a barrier to compromise. After the omnibus had been reported out of committee, the *Intelligencer* was perfectly willing to accept it but saw no significant contradictions between it and the goals of Taylor: "Preferring the plan recommended by the President to Congress . . . as well considered, constitutional, and just—and offering fewer difficulties to be overcome than any other that is likely to succeed—we should yet hail with satisfaction the adoption of any plan which would do justice to the political claims of California, and at the same time restore to the minds of the People of this country the quiet that has been unhappily disturbed." The fate of the country, said the *Intelligencer*, did not depend upon the choice of a plan or method, and the paper was not "advocating with undue vehemence any one in preference to another."[31]

On 24 June the *Intelligencer* supported Taylor by quoting from James K. Polk's final message. Polk had pointed out that no one could impose slavery on people who did not want it and no one could prevent it if the people did want it, and had added that it was "fortunate for the peace and harmony of the Union that this question is in its nature temporary; and can only continue for the brief period which will intervene before California and New Mexico may be admitted as States into the Union."[32]

The replacement of Bullitt and Sargent at the *Republic*, apparently at the insistence of Meredith, has often been cited as evidence that Taylor opposed the compromise. Their official reason for resigning was "personal differences . . . between ourselves and members of the Cabinet" that were "inconsistent with the relations in which we stand toward President TAYLOR and the WHIG party." They were withdrawing from a position in which they could no longer remain silent in their "view of certain controverted questions." The two, however, insisted that "our confidence in President TAYLOR is unimpaired and . . . the sentiment which has induced us to devote the volunteer services of years in his cause remains as ardent and as unalloyed as when we first took the field in his behalf. In his personal integrity—in his unselfish patriotism—in his nationality, neutrality, and elevated honor, we retain an undiminished confidence."[33]

On 6 May, before the resignation of the editors, the *Republic* warned that the *New York Courier and Enquirer* was trying to start a conflict between the administration and the Whigs in Congress. Bullitt and Sargent saw no reason for this: "We may claim for ourselves whatever merit belongs to a preference for, and a decided support of, the PRESIDENT's plan; and we do not now see any discrepancy between the *principle* of that platform and the propositions which have been foreshadowed, in advance of the report of the Committee of Thirteen as to produce the *estrangement* which it has been sought to foment between the Administration and the Whigs of Congress." There was "no necessary enmity to the PRESIDENT in the resolutions of Mr. Clay and Mr. Bell, the speeches of Mr. Webster, Mr. Berrien, Mr. Badger, and other distinguished Whigs." Also, however, the editors could not sympathize with the *Courier-Enquirer's* denunciations of these men for deserting the administration.

Only five days before their resignation, the *Republic's* editors announced that they still preferred Taylor's plan but would support anything that would bring peace. There was no real discrepancy between the president's plan and the omnibus, and a "*settlement*" was more important than "the *plan* of settlement." On 10 May they offered another column of high praise for Taylor's efforts to bring peace, and on the following day they again blamed the *New York Courier and Enquirer* for trying to foment trouble between Taylor and the Congress. On 13 May, the day before their resignations, they again praised Taylor's policies and efforts.[34]

According to Bullitt, the Galphin affair was the event most responsible for his resignation. "I despise the Cabinet," Bullitt wrote on 2 June." They are . . . ignorant, cold, contriving, selfish, and treacherous . . . monsters. . . . I held still until I saw an effort made to saddle the President with the Galphin affair. This was so . . . gratuitous an act that my disgust boiled over. That a Cabinet Minister should be a claim agent . . . needed only to be stated to be condemned." According to what Bullitt actually wrote, he was less disturbed by policy differences between Clay and Taylor than he was by his long-standing feud with the cabinet over patronage and other matters and by the revelations of the Galphin affair.[35]

The new editor, Allan A. Hall, also minimized the differences between the president and the senator until 21 May, when Clay, in his "five gaping wounds speech," accused Taylor of being interested only in California and indifferent to the other problems. The speech was accompanied by another vicious personal attack on Taylor by the *Union*, and the *Republic* answered both. The *Union*, wrote Hall, had falsely charged that Taylor was "opposed to 'the Compromise'— which means the Compromise in all its parts and provisions—and that he is 'against the settlement of the slavery question.' " Clay, he added, had been equally unfair and had completely misrepresented Taylor's plan. Taylor had recommended statehood for California and New Mexico, self-determination for both on the subject of slavery, and adjudication of the boundary dispute by the courts. Clay's charge that the president's failure to urge the passage of the fugitive-slave bill and the abolition of the slave trade in the District of Columbia meant that Taylor opposed either or both was equally false. Indeed, Hall insisted, Taylor had indicated no indifference or opposition to any solution yet offered for any of the five wounds. The president's plan was superior to the omnibus, and it had the same purpose. Unfortunately, however, Clay had left the "tranquil shades of Ashland . . . to lead and not to follow . . . to originate measures of compromise and pacification, not to adopt such as others might recommend."[36]

Naturally enough, partisan Democratic leaders, Clay himself on occasion, and, loudest of all, the *Union* continued to warn that if California were admitted alone, the president would veto other important parts of the compromise. Oddly enough, most historians have chosen to accept this intensely partisan view, while ignoring the denials of the *Intelligencer*, the *Republic*'s editors who resigned, the *Republic*'s editor who replaced them, and various members of Congress who were close to the president. Taylor said almost nothing publicly, but he had often denounced the veto as a tool of presidential tyranny. Those in the best position to know his views insisted that he had no objection to any part of Clay's compromise as long as New Mexico was protected from seizure by Texas. Both strong evidence and logic, therefore, indicate that Taylor would have approved every part of the compromise in the form it ultimately assumed when passed. The admission of California to immediate statehood was Taylor's own idea. His policy toward New Mexico was a means to an end rather than an end in itself. The final grant of self-determination on slavery to a viable New Mexican territory with its populated areas intact would certainly have satisfied him. He might have disliked the financial reward given Texas for ceding most of its New Mexican claim, but the measure was certainly constitutional, and a veto of it would have contradicted everything he had ever said about the veto principle. A slaveholder could not have objected seriously to a new fugitive-slave act, and nothing he ever said or did indicated any objection to moving the slave markets across the Potomac River into Virginia.

On 7 June the real core of the omnibus bill came to the front, and Clay's hopes for a quick settlement of the New Mexico boundary received its first jolt. Despite the Kentuckian's opposition, Jeremiah Clemens of Alabama introduced an amendment to give Texas the full extent of its claims, and various Southerners spoke in its favor. In opposition, Clay reminded the Senate that the Nueces River had once been considered the rightful boundary of Texas by almost all Whigs, and he warned that if successful, the amendment would lead to "blood and slaughter" in New Mexico. Buying the disputed territory from Texas, Clay insisted, did not create free territory because nonintervention with slavery was a vital part of the bill, and the committee bill was more than generous to Texas. Thomas Rusk delivered an impassioned speech supporting Clemens, but various Northerners demolished the validity of the Texas claim to the settled New Mexican areas. John Hale pointed out that only two days after Congress had approved the joint resolution annexing Texas, it had also passed another joint resolution dealing with foreign trade between the United States and New Mexico. Others emphasized the presence of a United States consul in Santa Fe, both before and after the annexation of Texas by the United States, and cited the agreements signed by Gen. Stephen W. Kearny with New Mexico when its leaders surrendered to the United States. The region had never been governed or controlled by Texas, and Kearny had promised in effect that New Mexico would eventually become a state equal to the other existing states. The later Treaty of Guadalupe Hidalgo had also ceded the area to the United States, and as one senator asked, if the area already belonged to the American state of Texas, why did the United States have to conquer it and then buy it? The Clemens amendment failed by 37 to 17, with 11 senators from slaveholding border states voting against it, and 17 Southerners, including Foote, supporting it.[37]

Further amendments by Foote, Douglas, Thomas G. Pratt of Maryland, and James Shields of Illinois followed. Foote's three amendments would run the southern boundary of New Mexico from the Rio Grande at the 34th parallel (some 120 miles north of the present-day boundary), reaffirm the validity of all Texas claims if the latter should reject the cash offer made by the bill, and retain the Missouri Compromise principle in all Texas areas that might be ceded. Pratt's amendment echoed Foote's Missouri Compromise principle but was worded to emphasize the perpetuation of slavery in the areas to be held by Texas. Douglas would run the boundary from a point sixty miles north of El Paso. Shields would run it from El Paso. Radical Southerners and the Texans would take nothing but the original claim. The debate now produced sharp controversies between Clay and Foote, who would not accept the solution recommended by the committee he had insisted upon creating.[38]

In all, during the month of June 1850, sixteen senators made twenty-eight attempts to amend the omnibus bill. Only six amendments passed, only four of which were important. The committee bill denied the territories the right to make any laws "in respect to African slavery." John Berrien of Georgia persuaded the Senate to change the wording to prevent the territory from "establishing or prohibiting African slavery." This would allow the territorial legislatures to protect slavery if it should be established by a judicial decision. Albert Yulee of Florida succeeded with an amendment specifying that the Constitution applied to a territory by its own force. This would be the basic principle of the Dred Scott decision seven years later. John Hale's successful amendment would give the Supreme Court the same appellate jurisdiction in the territories as in the states. Hale was an abolitionist and a Free-Soiler, and the South had usually controlled the Supreme Court, but Hale was apparently looking toward a more distant future. Pierre Soulé, the fiery Louisiana Frenchman, had less difficulty getting the Senate to pass an amendment stipulating that any future western state would be admitted regardless of whether or not it recognized slavery. This was a favorite Southern principle that would most likely help produce free states.[39]

In the House, meanwhile, the omnibus bill faced even greater difficulties. Between 8 May and 11 June, fifty-eight congressmen delivered hour-long speeches. Only thirteen agreed with the omnibus, although six favored most of it. Almost everyone could support at least one segment. Nineteen defended Taylor, while only three advocated the Wilmot Proviso. On 15 June, Samuel W. Inge of Alabama offered an amendment declaring simply that the people of the territories should have self-determination either for or against slavery. The amendment attracted support from both Northerners and Southerners, and Robert Toombs avowed that the South had always supported this principle. This, of course, was also what President Taylor had been recommending all along, and it was a proper face-saving position for Southerners who recognized the hopelessness of implanting slavery in California and New Mexico. Thaddeus Stevens of Pennsylvania, however, had already begun the career that would ultimately gain him the epithet "Scourge of the South." Stevens disliked Southerners as well as slavery on principle, and he would do nothing to help Southern moderates hold the line against Southern extremism. He announced that he would oppose the amendment because "he did not want to hold out the idea to the South, for he desired to deal frankly, even if offensively with them." He wanted all Southerners to understand that the vast majority of Northerners were determined that there should be no more slave states, "however much they might be inclined to lay the flattering unction to their souls now."[40]

Alexander H. Stephens answered Thaddeus Stevens and those who might agree with him:

> You are for the plan only so far as it suits your interest. You will let the people settle the question, provided they settle it your way, but if they do not, then you will reject their application to be admitted as states. Sir, I want this House purged upon this question. I want no equivocation, no evasion, no dodging, and no skulking. If you are for the President's plan, if you are in favor of leaving this question to the people, untrammeled, to decide for themselves, have the manliness to say so; and if you are not, don't show the pusillanimity of attempting by fraudulent practices to make people believe that you are when you are not.[41]

Unable to get a small handful of specific Northerners to make such a pledge, enough Southerners voted against the amendment to defeat it.

In the Senate on 10 June, Benton attacked the omnibus bill and defended the president. The five gaping wounds described by Clay, Benton said, were limited only by the number of fingers on his left hand. "When the fingers gave out, they gave out; and if there had been more fingers, there might have been more wounds." Never were the "business-doing and the working people" better off. The political distress, Benton insisted, was confined to the politicians. "Never were the political blessings of the country greater than at present: civil and religious liberty eminently enjoyed; life, liberty, and property; the North and South returning to the old belief that they were made for each other; and peace and plenty reigning throughout the land."[42]

If Benton's observations seem overly optimistic in the light of future events, there was much evidence to support them in June 1850. National prosperity was at a peak, and the Southern convention at Nashville had already failed. Procompromise letters and petitions with thousands of signatures were pouring into Washington. The overwhelming popular acceptance of the compromise plan in both North and South indicated clearly that the American people really did not wish to be disturbed. Clay, of course, was in large part responsible for much of the conciliatory feelings rising in all sections, but neither Taylor nor Benton would have denied this fact. They did not oppose the spirit or the measures of the compromise as long as New Mexico was protected, but they were certain that the omnibus procedure was both a threat to New Mexico and a barrier against any compromise at all.

The boundary dispute, Benton insisted, should be settled on the basis of actual possessions. The line in the omnibus bill took seventy thousand square miles away from New Mexico; this area included parts of the Pecos River valley that could probably support slavery, but the inhabitants did not want it and should not be afflicted with it. His own views on slavery, said Benton, had come from the teachings of the Virginia school of Tucker, Jefferson, and Randolph. These men "were not enthusiasts or fanatics: they were statesmen and philosophers." They knew that emancipation "was not a mere question between master and slave—not a question of property merely—but a question of white and black—between races; and what was to be the consequence to each race from a large emancipation." The "incurability of the evil" was the greatest objection to slavery extension. It was wrong to "inflict an evil which can be cured: how much more to inflict one that is incurable, and against the will of the people who are to endure it forever! . . . It seems to be above human wisdom. But there is a wisdom above human! and to that we must look. In the meantime, not extend the evil." Southern rights, said Benton, were embedded in the Constitution: "a right to hold slaves as property, a right to pursue and recover them as property, a right to it as a political element . . . by making five count three in the national representation." He would not bargain away such rights in any compromise. Opponents of the omnibus bill were being denounced as enemies of compromise, but the committee itself was torn by dissension, and the happy consummation of Clay's plans, like the mythical ancient wedding feast, had suddenly changed to a battle among the members.[43]

On 14 June, John Hale charged that the Texas bondholders were exercising a corrupting influence on the debates. Foote answered that the Wilmot Proviso was far more corrupt because it was highway robbery.[44] Foote also challenged Hale to name those who were being influenced by the bondholders. Hale could not do this, but he had the last word when he asked if Thomas Jefferson's Northwest Ordinance barring slavery north of the Ohio River had been highway robbery. This comparison was made frequently by the congressional Free-Soilers, and it does raise a significant question. Why was the principle that was supported so overwhelmingly by the South in Jefferson's Ordinance of 1787 and in the Missouri Compromise of 1820 so totally anathema to the South of 1850? These measures had created far more free territories and states than the areas that were being disputed in 1850. The antislavery movement in 1850, though much more strident and vocal, was no more dangerous to Southern slavery than it had been in 1787 or 1820. The abolitionists of the 1830s and 1840s, however, had denounced the Southerners as sinful, immoral, unchristian, undemocratic, and by implication, un-American. The formal denial of equal rights in territories that were quite unsuitable for slavery and that had already banished the institution had become a moral condemnation and a mortal insult to Southern honor that could not be accepted by proud men.

While the Congress was debating and quarreling, far away Texas was bringing the boundary conflict to a head. The Texas legislature had already sent Robert S. Neighbors to Santa Fe to organize the new Texas counties. The agent was treated with civility, but the New Mexican officials, the United States army commander, and the New Mexican people were demonstrably ready to resist Texas at all costs. As early as May 1848 the *Santa Fe Republican* had suggested that Texas "send with her civil officers for this country, a large force, in order that they may have a sufficient bodyguard to escort them back safe. . . . Texas should show some little sense, and drop this question, and not have it publicly announced that Texas' smartest men were tarred and feathered by attempting to fill the offices assigned them."[45] If anything, this sentiment was even more prevalent in 1850.

While Neighbors was struggling with his impossible task, President Taylor's agent, George McCall, arrived with orders for Col. John Munroe, the military commander, to encourage the people to seek statehood. Despite the protests of Neighbors, Munroe called a constitutional convention, and by 25 May 1850 an exuberant collection of delegates had created a new state constitution that barred slavery. Following the theory that the best defense is a good offense, the convention defined the state's eastern boundary as the 100th parallel, well within the ancient bounds of Texas and a full two degrees east of the line being urged by Benton.[46]

Neighbors returned to Austin with a detailed report of his failure. The governor, Peter H. Bell, had been elected on a platform of taking direct action against New Mexico, and the latest development sent the entire state into an uproar. Newspapers characterized the actions of Taylor and Munroe as an insult and an outrage against the rights and the dignity of the state. Throughout June, July, and August, at mass meetings all over the state, angry orators declaimed that Texas had entered the Union with a promise that its self-defined boundaries would be respected. Texas, they warned, would leave the Union just as willingly as it had joined it. Thus, the Senate debates on Texas began with the New Mexican constitution en route to Washington, Texas loudly threatening to march against Santa Fe, and the president ready to protect New Mexico with force if necessary.

Governor Bell now sent President Taylor an angry and disrespectful letter demanding an explanation and a disavowal of Colonel Munroe's efforts to make New Mexico into a new state. He also began writing letters to enlist the support of other Southern governors. As the news swept across the South, angry editorials filled the presses, volunteer military companies were organized for aid to Texas, and the governor of Mississippi made a formal offer of military assistance. Old Rough and Ready, however, was not one to be swayed by threats either in Washington or in Texas.

On 11 June the Senate passed a resolution asking the president whether he had ordered the military in Santa Fe "to hold possession against the authority of Texas, or in any way to embarrass or prevent the exercise of her jurisdiction over that country" and asking him to furnish copies of any correspondence between the War Department and the military in Santa Fe since the president's last report. On 17 June, Taylor replied. No such orders had been given. All correspondence was enclosed. He had previously pointed out that the boundary was disputed. Now he must report that "a certain Robert S. Neighbors, styling himself commissioner of the State of Texas," had gone to Santa Fe to organize counties under the authority of Texas. While the president had no power and no desire to interfere in the boundary dispute, he must "observe that the possession of the territory into which it appears that Mr. Neighbors has thus gone was actually acquired by the United States from Mexico, and has since been held by the United States, and, in my opinion, ought so to remain until the question of boundary shall have been determined by some competent authority."[47]

A few days later, Lt. Alfred M. Pleasanton was preparing to join his regiment in New Mexico and called upon the president. Taylor, the lieutenant later remembered, spoke bluntly. The troops in New Mexico would be reinforced and no armed force from Texas would be permitted into the territory. He should tell Colonel Munroe that "if he has not force enough out there to support him, . . . I will be with you myself. . . . I will be there before those people shall go into that country or have a foot of that territory. The whole business is infamous, and must be put down."[48]

Taylor's intentions were clear, and his message to Congress, predictably, was denounced by the Texans and numerous other Southerners. Jefferson Davis correctly pointed out that the issue was whether the territory would be governed by Mexican laws that outlawed slavery or by the proslavery laws of Texas. Davis charged that negating the Texas claim would rob the South.

On 29 June, Lewis Cass, Taylor's Democratic opponent in the recent election, offered an amendment to have the Committee on Military Affairs inquire into the expediency of prohibiting by law any officer of the army from exercising any civil power in the United States without authorization from Congress and of providing an adequate punishment for such an offense. The amendment was obviously aimed at the president and the military government of New Mexico, but Cass defended it as being necessary for the maintenance of civilian control over the military. He insisted that allowing Gen. Bennet Riley to summon the Californians into convention and allowing Colonel Munroe to do the same in New Mexico could be the first steps toward creating a military dictatorship. Cass had once been a stalwart adherent of Andrew Jackson's when Old Hickory was being denounced as a military despot by Henry Clay, but in 1850 he apparently had forgotten that the American president is both a civilian and a military commander, regardless of his previous military status. The old Jacksonian Sam Houston was more consistent. Despite his professed anger at the policies of Taylor and Colonel Munroe in New Mexico, Houston denounced the Cass amendment, which ultimately failed.[49]

On the other hand, Senator James Cooper of Pennsylvania, an omnibus supporter who considered the Wilmot Proviso unnecessary, had nothing but high praise for the president. Taylor, said Cooper, was "a firm, honest, consistent man," who had made no effort whatever to coerce the Congress to support his views. "He has offered no threats, and regards it as no crime that members of Congress disagree with him." Cooper cited an earlier letter from Taylor expressing fear that even the known opinions of the president might influence the Congress.[50]

On 3 July, Senator John Bell of Tennessee began a powerful three-day defense of the president and his policies. The California constitution, said Bell, would have been the same regardless of anything Taylor might have done, and Clay's five-gaping-wounds speech was entirely unfair because Congress would not have passed the omnibus bill even if Taylor had supported it. On 5 July, Bell challenged anyone to show evidence that Taylor had ever tried to use any influence against the compromise. In a rather ingenious argument, the Tennesseean insisted that Taylor's plan offered the South a better chance for slavery in New Mexico than did the omnibus bill. Slavery was being kept out of New Mexico by the present territorial laws inherited from Mexico, and the South's own principle of noninterference by the federal government would bar any pressure for their repeal. Indeed, the federal government had the power to keep slavery out of the territories and would do so. Once the area became a state, however, Congress would have no power over New Mexico, and Southerners might have at least a chance to persuade the new state to tolerate slavery. Thus, Taylor's policy of immediate statehood for New Mexico offered the South more than did the illusory effort to exchange California for the Texas claims to New Mexico. Henry Foote, however, was not convinced. If New Mexico became a state, he avowed, "the Union cannot continue to exist."[51]

The *Charleston Mercury* agreed that statehood for New Mexico would end the Union, but it condemned Clay, Webster, Foote, and even Ritchie alike for trying to promote any kind of compromise at all. Ritchie, "that old Palinurus," was "at last a false pilot" and "was running the ship upon the breakers of heresy and treason." The *Mercury* cited with approval the view of the *Columbus* (Ga.) *Times* that anyone who would trust the federal government to protect the South was "unworthy of the name of a Southerner, an American, or a patriot." Only a "knave . . . does not see that the time is here to strike a blow for Southern rights, or basely to surrender them."[52]

On 2 July the *Union* reported that Texas was preparing to march with twenty-five hundred men. The two hundred Texans already in New Mexico were expected to cooperate, and the United States officers obstructing Texas would probably be brought to trial. If the "adjustment bill" should be defeated, Texas would absorb New Mexico, and if the United States should interfere, the Southern states would "give her [Texas] all the aid she needs. The quarrel will afford a pretext for the disunionists of the South to commence the movement of dissolution."[53]

The *Union* thought this was an ample reason for the immediate passage of the omnibus bill, but the angry president felt otherwise. On 1 July the Toombs-Stephens Whigs appointed a committee of three to make another effort to change the old general's mind. Charles M. Conrad, Humphrey Marshall, and Toombs each called on him separately and got the same answer. He would not abandon New Mexico. On 3 July, Taylor was again equally emphatic with Toombs. Meanwhile, Secretary of War Crawford refused to sign an order to Munroe to resist any attempts of Texas "to exercise jurisdiction in New Mexico." Taylor calmly announced that he would sign the order himself.[54]

Despairing of any success in changing the president's mind, Alexander H. Stephens warned Secretary of the Navy Preston "that if troops were sent to Santa Fe, the President would be impeached." Who would impeach him, asked Preston? "I will if nobody else does," replied Stephens. Actually, however, at the beginning of July 1850 the president had never been stronger in Congress, particularly in the Senate. Every Northern Whig but two stood firmly for Taylor's policy of statehood with self-determination in regard to slavery for California and New Mexico, and several Democrats had begun to switch to his side. The impossibility of getting a majority to vote for contradictory measures in the same single package was finally becoming obvious.[55]

The American national holiday on 4 July 1850 was a fateful day for the United States, although much of it appeared to follow a predictable pattern of exuberant celebration marred by occasional accidents. In Washington, bands played, parades marched, orators spoke, and relatives and friends gathered for innumerable picnics. The *Intelligencer* reported that in the evening, "Professor Grant's Calcium Light, exhibited from the west front of the Capitol, shone forth with dazzling splendor, brilliantly illuminating the Avenue, from the Capitol gate to the grounds surrounding the President's House, more than a mile in extent." Meanwhile, two people had drowned in the Potomac, another had lost an arm by falling from a tree at a Sunday School picnic, and a child had been blinded by fireworks.[56]

At the White House, President Taylor began the day in a state of severe emotional distress and severe fatigue from sleeplessness. If Thurlow Weed can be believed, Taylor had finally made the painful decision to replace most of his cabinet. His schedule began with an early morning Sunday School recital, and either before or immediately afterward he ate several green apples. In the afternoon he had a ceremonial duty to perform at the newly commenced Washington Monument. The heat had been overpowering for weeks and had indeed probably added much to the emotional quality of the congressional debates. Many prominent people, including Clayton, Seward, Crawford, Bliss, and Joshua, were seriously ill from what some people suspected might be cholera. Washington's primitive water supply and sewage system were threats to everyone, and the rarity of epidemics was a tribute to the ruggedness of those who ruled America.

At the appointed hour, Taylor took a carriage to the monument, listened to Henry S. Foote deliver a long oration, and participated in a stone-laying ceremony under a blazing sun. Unpredictable as always, Foote delivered a stirring plea for understanding and harmony: "May sectional jealousy, fanatical rage, the accursed ambition for notoriety and power, the low appetite for place and its emoluments, and the spirit of political rivalry be banished forever from the council halls of the nation! Let justice, brotherly feeling, and true courtesy restrain the turbid current of angry and mischievous debate."[57]

President Taylor may have been impressed with the words, but he knew the orator. Beckoning Foote to his side, he asked, "Why will you not always speak in this way?"[58] Foote later insisted that the president sat in the shade during the oration and faced the sun only later. Probably suffering from a mild sunstroke, Taylor returned home and ate raw fruit, probably cherries, and, reportedly, various raw vegetables as well, which he washed down with large quantities of iced milk. Within hours, he was suffering from all the symptoms of acute gastroenteritis, and the medical science of 1850 only made it worse. To Taylor's doctors, it was "cholera morbus," and calomel (a mercury compound) and opium were the prescribed remedies. On 6 July he was strong enough to sign the Clayton-Bulwer Treaty with Britain and to write a letter, but for the next four days he steadily declined as the doctors continued to dose him with quinine and calomel.

While the president suffered, the House on 6 July, by a vote of 91 to 88, added to the Galphin resolutions an amendment censuring

Taylor for his "connection" with the claim. Toombs and Stephens had proposed Crawford, their fellow Georgian, for the cabinet in the first place, but both supported the censure. Two days later, the entire proposal failed.

On Tuesday, 9 July, crowds gathered outside the White House, where the news was alternately cheerful and dismaying. At 2:00 P.M., the president was sinking. At 3:00 P.M., he was barely alive. At 4:00 P.M., he had improved and was going to live. Bells rang and crowds cheered. Bleeding and blisters induced by the doctors had done no more good than the earlier massive doses of calomel and quinine. At 10:35 P.M., he died. His last words were: "The storm in passing had swept away the trunk. . . . I am about to die—I expect the summons soon—I have endeavored to discharge all my official duties faithfully—I regret nothing, but am sorry that I am about to leave my friends."[59]

The grief of his family and friends was heartrending. Three times the casket was opened to give Mrs. Taylor one more final look, and she would not allow embalming. The funeral was magnificent, with Clay, Cass, Berrien, Benton, and others serving as pallbearers. Taylor would have appreciated the selection. Dominating the army section of the procession was General Scott, his huge figure on horseback topped off by a "towering plume of yellow feathers." Taylor would probably have smiled at this apparition also. More than a hundred carriages followed the catafalque, drawn by eight white horses, to the temporary tomb where Taylor would rest until he could be taken back to Kentucky. Old Whitey, riderless, with his stirrups reversed, pawed the air and tossed his head "with a military air." More than one hundred thousand people lined the streets.[60]

For the moment at least, the lawmakers and the people of all sections of the country were united by a common sorrow. In Congress, laudatory speeches replaced the angry debates, and people everywhere remembered the old man's honesty and his years of unselfish national service. On 7 July the *Union* had demanded his impeachment "for usurping kingly powers and for trampling on the rights of a sovereign state." Three days later, with the president no longer a candidate for reelection, the *Union* eulogized

> the Hero, in all the majesty of the Patriot, whose name is associated with some of the most brilliant achievements in our annals, who has carried the fame of his country to the remotest nations, and whose reputation will never die. The name of the Hero of Palo Alto and Buena Vista will live as long as the name of the nation whose standard he so often bore to victory and to glory.[61]

The erratic Horace Greeley's *New York Tribune* had spent most of the year alternating between praise for Taylor's California policy and denunciation of his willingness to allow either the Congress or the courts to set the Texas boundary instead of firmly declaring the rightful boundary by executive fiat. On 10 July, Greeley announced that Taylor's immense popularity with the American people lay in

> the great goodness of his heart, the exceeding sincerity of his char-
> acter, in his transparent common sense, so broad and strong as to
> amount to wisdom, in a firmness that faced every danger and
> shunned no responsibility, and in a patriotism and sense of honor
> which threw an almost chivalrous halo over the sturdy elements
> of his nature. . . . A Southern man and a slaveholder, his mind
> was above the narrow prejudices of district and class and steadily
> aimed at the good of the nation as a whole.[62]

None of the great divisive issues had been settled, however, and the new president would have little time to ponder the fates that had suddenly made him the master of his recent humiliators. Consistent as always, the *Charleston Mercury* regretted only that Taylor "did not carry into his new position the qualities that made him imminent as a soldier. He had no natural aptitude for civil administration, no light of long experience to guide him, no love for the labors and the deep studies that form essential parts of the President's office, and no talent for the ruling of Cabinets." The editor would concede only that the president's plan should be blamed upon the cabinet: "His memory deserves not to be loaded with the responsibility of a measure that has done so much to make the sectional controversy irreconcilable." In short, Taylor had died a failure because he had not imposed slavery upon the territories taken from Mexico, and his Northern successor would inherit the same responsibility.[63]

10

★ ★ ★ ★ ★

THE NEW PRESIDENT

With the possible exception of Lyndon B. Johnson, Millard Fillmore may have been America's most unhappy vice-president. He and Abigail had never liked Washington and were always homesick for friends and the familiar surroundings of Buffalo. During his final term in Congress, he had finished second in the balloting for Speaker and had won universal praise for his work as chairman of the powerful Committee on Ways and Means. If he had so desired, Buffalo would have given him a lifetime career of distinction in the House, or his well-earned reputation in the House would probably have made him a senator with even greater opportunities for influence and fame. With no taste for either, he had twice resigned to return home at the end of a term in Congress. He had not sought the vice-presidential nomination, but he had worked much harder than Taylor had for the election of his party's presidential ticket. He had come to Washington ready to cooperate with Weed and Seward for the benefit of New York and eager to do whatever a vice-president could do to serve his country's best interests. Weed and Seward had deceived and humiliated Fillmore, however, and had left him politically weaker than he had been as comptroller of New York. He must have winced when the son of his old friend the wealthy New York merchant Hiram Ketchum had failed to get a presidential appointment to West Point. "It seems to me," wrote Ketchum, "that the Second officer of the Govt. might have this much power conceded to him, where he and the president were both elected by the same party." "Where Is

Fillmore?" asked the *Albany Express* on 16 May 1849. "The recent appointments in New York and Maryland answer this question in the most significant manner. He is nowhere." A particularly galling insult was his inability to obtain an appointment for his able Buffalo law partner, Nathan K. Hall.[1]

Assuming that four years in Washington would be their limit, the Fillmores were reluctant to buy a house, but renting quarters suitable to their station for a reasonable sum was not easy. For months, Fillmore lived at Willard's Hotel while various agents besieged him with offers and importunities. A lady broker, Mrs. Oliver Reed, was especially persistent. She was determined to please him with "new and elegant furniture of the latest style and the bedroom supplied with everything for your comfort." As she did for another client, she would charge him and Abigail each sixteen dollars per week, "your daughter the same when alone, and your son for the time with you at 10's a week." If Fillmore were to bring a carriage, she would supply "a stable at moderate rent, find the food at market prices and present the bills of such purchases at such times as you may wish." She would also provide a footman any time he or the ladies might need one "for a trifle and it may be no additional expense." She would furnish "dinners in the latest style, with all the rariest [sic] luxuries of the market." The house being promoted with the extras actually belonged to John Rives, editor of the *Congressional Globe*, who was planning to move to the country. Whatever Fillmore's feelings may have been on the matter, the offer collapsed when Mrs. Rives decided that she did not wish to leave the city. Robert Beale offered his house to Fillmore for $1,000 a year. It would include a good cow and "a good cook & dining room servant for 'moderate wages.' " The house had cost Beale $10,500, and he would take care of the house and furniture when Fillmore might be absent.[2]

Abigail, meanwhile, came for a time, but she returned home on 1 April 1850. Facing his empty hotel room, Fillmore was desolate. "How lonesome this room is in your absence," he wrote. "I can hardly bear to sit down—and Mr. Stanley and myself have been out making calls on the President and others all the evening. But you have scarcely been out of my mind since you left." With "no one to play backgammon with," he could only sit in despair. He had been busy, however, "investigating his power to call a senator to order." On 5 April he wrote her another long, informative, and affectionate letter. He had addressed the unruly Senate on the subject of the vice-president's power with regard to maintaining order, and his views had been well received and entered in the official journal. Two days later he was overjoyed by a letter from her, which he answered immediately. He had just called on Jefferson Davis, who was ill, and on Senator Dawson, who was crushed with grief at the sudden death of his wife. Thank God, he wrote, Abigail had arrived home safely.[3]

If Fillmore thought his lack of influence would lessen the expectations of ambitious American office seekers, he was much disappointed. Dozens of letters poured in each week throughout his terms as both vice-president and president, and he often answered them. Frequently, letters came from wives and mothers describing the plight of their hungry children as well as extolling the virtues of their husbands and/or sons. In July 1849 Fillmore sent condolences to Susanna Hamilton because her husband did not get the job at the customs house, but he complained that her accusations of deceit were unfair because he had done the best he could.[4]

From Steubenville, Ohio, F. A. Priest wrote the vice-president that he "was highly gratifyed upon the receat of your kind and sympathizing epistle, it breathed feelings of a tender hart, and mutch humility in as mutch as you condesended to write to [me] at all, I have tryed every honest way to save my little home, and I now feel that I must give it up, unless something extreordinary Should take place." John M. Morse, a nineteen-year-old schoolteacher hoping to become a lawyer, wanted Fillmore's advice on what to study. Morse had no "time to spend nor money in learning superfluities. Please give me advice as you would a son. I shall wait impatiently for an answer." George Cottingham wanted to be either a porter or a door-keeper at the White House. He was without funds and was afflicted by various ailments. Someone had assured him that the District of Columbia was an ideal place for good health, and he hoped the vice-president would get him the job necessary for his removal to Washington.[5]

The well-known Kentucky diplomat Charles S. Todd, who had served as minister to Russia during the Tyler administration, now wanted back the post from which he "was removed by Mr. Polk and where it is supposed I was quite acceptable." Fillmore judiciously answered that he was restricting his recommendations to people from his own state but that he was certain Todd's great reputation would carry more weight than any support from Fillmore himself.[6]

J. R. Jewett sent the vice-president a collection of newspaper clippings describing Jewett's invention of an electric voting machine guaranteed to save the Congress many hours being spent in roll-call voting. Unfortunately, Jewett was more than a century ahead of his time. Another letter introduced Dorothea L. Dix, who had come to Washington to plead for better treatment for the insane. This began a close friendship between Fillmore and Miss Dix that continued throughout his life.[7]

By law the regents of the newly created Smithsonian Institution included the vice-president, the chief justice of the Supreme Court, three senators, three representatives, and six private citizens. Always a promoter of education and higher learning, Fillmore took this responsibility very seriously, and he conferred often with the Smithsonian's secretary, Joseph Henry, on matters of budget and policy. This interest probably helped to forge a close friendship between Fillmore and Senator James Pearce of Maryland. For many years, Pearce was chairman of the committee for the Library of Congress, and Fillmore appointed him to the Smithsonian Board of Regents. Pearce was always a spirited champion of federal appropriations for scientific research, and Fillmore had been Buffalo's most ardent promoter of every kind of educational activity or institution. They were both strong supporters of Joseph Henry's efforts to expand the scope of the Smithsonian Institution's activities.[8]

Millard Fillmore was neither quarrelsome nor vindictive by nature, but his bland exterior and impeccable manners concealed a fighting spirit in its own way just as tough as that of Zachary Taylor. Fillmore had not risen from dire poverty to the nation's second-highest office without a driving ambition, enormous energy, and a shrewd eye for his own best interests. His months as vice-president were a humiliating experience, but he did not surrender. As he sat day after day on the dais facing the angry senators debating the compromise, his mind was often in New York where his closer friends were helping him organize groups of younger Whigs determined to challenge the control of Thurlow Weed. As early as 24 July 1849 Fillmore asked his supporters around the state to compile the names and addresses of "good" Whigs in each New York town. He preferred young, industrious, and ambitious men who would help win the next election and, coincidentally, would support the positions of Millard Fillmore. Dozens of responses poured in, and most agreed with the wisdom of one P. J. Wagner, who assured Fillmore that he would be careful to select "persons who are not just friends of Bill & Thurlow." In November 1849, just before the beginning of the dramatic congressional session, Fillmore went directly to Taylor and pointed out that the administration's appointments were destroying the vice-president's influence in New York. Fillmore had been a loyal supporter, but he felt badly mistreated. In the future would he be "treated as a friend or foe?" He also repeated this complaint and question to Treasury Secretary Meredith. Both Taylor and Meredith assured Fillmore that he would be given greater consideration in the future. Taylor always appreciated those with an open and direct approach, and having had no experience in state politics, he was probably not fully aware of the Weed-Seward vendetta against his vice-president. Fillmore also encouraged his friends to start a rival newspaper in Albany to "restrict, and tame Weed and his dependencies—harmonize and strengthen the party—protect our friends from proscription and slander, and weaken, if it does not destroy this arbitrary, and over-shadowing influence" in Albany. Fillmore's friend John T. Bush began raising the money and looking for a talented editor. At one point, Fillmore had Bush try to buy Weed's *Evening Journal*, but it was not for sale at any price.[9]

By March 1850 Bush had raised $10,000 and had launched the *New York State Register*. Most of the backers were New York Whig leaders and New York City merchants. Fillmore himself contributed $500. The new paper would advocate traditional Whig principles and oppose Weed, but it would not attack the administration in any way.[10]

Despite his own mistreatment, Fillmore sympathized with his chief's patronage problems and began his term in full agreement with Taylor's goals. In late July 1849 Fillmore wrote his friend Edward Everett, president of Harvard University, that since he "had no favors to bestow, either legislative or official," he had expected a time of leisure, but instead he was being overwhelmed by office seekers. The patronage system was making many enemies for the administration: "Every appointment creates an active bitter enemy in the person removed, renders inefficient the friend appointed, and paralyzes the energies or converts into active enemies all the disappointed candidates." Taylor, he added, was justly popular because of "the highest integrity and the most disinterested patriotism, but the great mass are inert, while the displaced office holder and the scheming politician are ever on the alert." Enemies everywhere, wrote Fillmore, were accusing Taylor of yielding too much power to his cabinet. This was creating an incorrect impression—"most unjustly—that he shrinks from responsibility; and that the patronage . . . is prostituted to promote the ambitious aspirations of some of those who wield it with his assent." Nonetheless, Fillmore hoped for the best. His own recommendations for his state and city had been ignored, and this "I think will relieve me from future importunity."

His own advice on policy was being neither sought nor followed. If Taylor approved the Wilmot Proviso, he would lose the South. If he rejected it, he would lose the North. "I see but one chance of escape, and that is for California and New Mexico to form constitutions for themselves prohibiting slavery, and then apply for admission as states. The South cannot object to this, and it may save their honor and the Whig administration."[11] Fillmore did not add that this was precisely the conviction being followed by the president and his cabinet.

Keeping order in the rambunctious Senate was also an ordeal for the conscientious vice-president because his authority and responsibilities as the body's president were not entirely clear. Fillmore researched the question carefully, and on 5 April he expressed his views to the Senate. The first Senate in 1789 had established rules authorizing members to call one another to order, with the added stipulation that anyone so challenged must sit down until the question should be decided by the presiding officer. No debate was permissible, but its president could ask the sense of the Senate. If the call to order was for improper language, the words should immediately be written down. In 1826 Vice-President John C. Calhoun had formally denied himself this authority, and in 1828 the Senate had changed the rules to allow a member to challenge any condemnatory ruling by its president. The initial power to call a member to order remained, however, and Fillmore announced that in his opinion the power imposed a duty upon the Speaker to exercise it. He hoped the senators would exercise proper decorum, but he would feel obligated to call anyone to order who did not.

Fillmore's brave words and common sense had an immediate but short-lived impact upon Henry Foote, who immediately expressed profound regret if he had said or done anything that the Senate "would consider as disrespectful to it in its corporate capacity."[12] Twelve days later the disgraceful encounter between Foote and Benton occurred, and several newspapers condemned Fillmore for not having prevented it. Actually, while Fillmore had had reason to call Foote to order on several earlier occasions, the events of 17 April suddenly erupted before any preventive action could have been taken. After this fracas, the continuing angry speeches were remarkably free from personal insults, and Fillmore handled his parliamentary duties with considerable skill. Foote was so immature and unpredictable that Fillmore may well have decided that calling him to order would be more likely to cause violence than to prevent it. Even before the Benton episode, Foote had been knocked flat on a

Washington street by Senator Solon Borland of Arkansas, but this had not improved Foote's manners. Foote would later cause the same kind of disruptions as a member of the Confederate Congress.

Throughout the months of crises, Taylor and his cabinet made no effort whatsoever to use Fillmore's talents as a legislative manager. Fillmore's biographer treats this as a serious error in judgment and a waste of talent, and perhaps it was.[13] Traditionally, however, vice-presidents did not usually participate in the legislative experience. Taylor had on several occasions expressed a determination to leave important matters to Congress, to avoid any presidential interference, and to veto only those measures he might consider flagrantly unconstitutional. Because Taylor himself did nothing beyond sending information and occasional requests to Congress, he was not likely to think of using his vice-president as a lobbyist or floor manager.

Fillmore had once been a vocal supporter of the Wilmot Proviso, but listening to Clay and Webster eloquently denounce it as a meaningless reenactment of the will of God had undoubtedly helped influence him to consider it unnecessary. The whole idea of a satisfactory compromise was clearly in tune with Fillmore's entire career. Also, his conflict with Seward in New York threw him into partnership with a great many New York City merchants whose profits were being seriously reduced by sharply curtailed orders from the South. Most merchandise from abroad and much of that from the interior cleared through New York City, and unusually heavy orders in 1849 had roused great expectations among those who imported and reshipped the goods, arranged and often financed the sales, and provided the transportation. In early 1850, however, Northern businessmen and bankers were being deluged with letters from the South, which threatened to stop trading because of the slavery quarrels in Washington. New York's commercial interests were not prepared to substitute Seward's higher law for their own material ambitions, and they were eager for a peaceful settlement with the South. Fillmore's friends soon found themselves allied with a rich and powerful pressure group ready to fight the influence of Seward and Weed. At one point, New Yorkers presented Congress with a procompromise petition bearing twenty-five thousand signatures, which Howell Cobb thought were more influential than the speeches of either Clay or Webster.[14]

The actions of the New York commercial leaders, both in 1850 and in 1860, provide a sharp contradiction to the later Marxist argument that Northern business capitalists promoted the Civil War to get rid of the restraining forces of Southern slavery and feudalism. In both crises, what passed for American big business worked hard to promote peace. In Lincoln's cabinet in 1861, Seward would forget his "higher law" and would try to prevent a war by making efforts to give Fort Sumter to the South without a struggle. In New York City, the businessmen's mayor, Fernando Wood, would threaten a secession by New York City if Lincoln should attack the South.

All of this made Fillmore a natural ally of Clay and Webster. Still, however, Fillmore had doubts about the propositions. By 18 June he feared that he might have to cast a tie-breaking vote, but he would wait to "see what shape it assumes before I determine to say yea or nay." By 1 July he was leaning toward voting for the omnibus bill should this become necessary. He informed the president that if he had to cast the deciding vote and if he should feel it his duty "to vote for it, as I might," it would not be "out of any hostility to him or his Administration, but the vote would be given, because I deemed it for the interests of the country."[15] In fact, of course, Fillmore still could not commit his vote one way or the other, because no one yet knew what the final version of the bill would be. Perhaps most important, by 8 July, when President Taylor succumbed to his illness and his doctors, Millard Fillmore had been compelled to listen to virtually every speech made in the Senate on every side of the burning issues. More than President Taylor, Fillmore knew the personalities of all involved and understood the emotions of pride and honor that often transcended practical considerations. He had always had a talent for getting things done, and now his frustrations caused by a role of idle contemplation were suddenly at an end. The slaveholding planter would now be replaced by the libertarian New Yorker, who was equally determined that slavery should not be expanded into territories where the local citizenry opposed it and who was equally devoted to the preservation of the American Union.

As the nation's presses of both parties and every section rang with eulogies for the fallen hero, the new president must have felt mixed emotions. Just as Taylor had been vindicated against his enemies by attaining the White House, Millard Fillmore had been suddenly transformed from a lowly outcast, seeking friends among the president's enemies, to president of the United States. He would now have full power over the favors and privileges most desired by those who had sought his political destruction. Like Taylor, Fillmore was a religious man. He did not sleep a moment on the night after Taylor's death, and his grief must have been mixed with a renewal of his faith in divine justice. At noon on 10 July, Fillmore took the oath of office in a simple ceremony before an overflow crowd in the House chamber. He made no speech, but in his later official communication, he described Taylor as "a great man."

Fillmore graciously suggested that Mrs. Taylor need not hurry to leave the White House, but Margaret Taylor had had enough of Washington. She left almost immediately, and the Fillmore family was soon settled into a house still uncomfortable in many ways but much improved by Taylor's numerous repairs. They did not complain.

Like Zachary Taylor, Millard Fillmore enjoyed the blessings of a loving and understanding wife and intelligent and cooperative children. Also, like Mrs. Taylor, Abigail Fillmore suffered from chronic illnesses and could not handle extensive social duties alone; but like Taylor's daughter, Mary Elizabeth, the teen-aged Mary Abigail Fillmore assumed the role of hostess with ability and grace. Like his predecessor, the new president sorely needed and always had the comfort of a loving family.

With Taylor gone and with the loud praise fading into silence, the Congress and the American people again turned their attention to the sectional crisis. First, however, came Fillmore's relatively mild revenge, which, fortunately, could be disguised by a political process acceptable to everyone. Taylor had been distraught over the problems of his cabinet. Fillmore had no such problem, because new presidents were expected to name their own department heads. Because he had been cast aside deliberately by Taylor's cabinet and Seward and inadvertently by Taylor himself, most observers expected Fillmore to throw his influence squarely behind the omnibus bill and use the full weight of his appointive powers.

These expectations, however, came true only in part. Fillmore selected men who had advocated compromise, but he did not favor those who had insisted upon the omnibus process. Ohio's Senator Thomas Corwin, who had bitterly opposed the Mexican War and had strongly advocated the Wilmot Proviso, became secretary of the treasury. The Southern Whigs wanted Toombs in the War Department, but Fillmore gave this scant consideration. Charles M. Conrad of Louisiana became secretary of war. Conrad had been one of the first to promote the presidential candidacy of Taylor and had been one of the three selected to ask Taylor not to interfere militarily in the Texas–New Mexico dispute. John J. Crittenden, whom Taylor had wanted so desperately, could now accept an appointment without the appearance of being rewarded for having deserted Clay. He became attorney general. William A. Graham of North Carolina assumed control of the Navy Department, while Alexander H. H. Stuart of Virginia became secretary of the interior. Stuart would later oppose Virginia's secession until Fort Sumter made it inevitable, and he would play a major role in getting Virginia restored to the Union with minimal reconstruction. The appointment of Fillmore's Buffalo law partner, Nathan K. Hall, to the patronage-dispensing post of postmaster general must have given Fillmore enormous satisfaction. Only a few days earlier, New York's governor Hamilton Fish had written the vice-president a highly patronizing letter explaining why Fish could not reappoint one of Fillmore's friends.[16] Fillmore would have been less than human if he had not relished the new tone in the governor's communications. And finally, as the new secretary of state, Daniel Webster brought both prestige and political support from almost every section but his own. Like Fillmore, Webster had been restored to political life by the death of Taylor. Webster's support for the compromise, and particularly for the new fugitive-slave bill, had brought him political excommunication in Massachusetts. In a popular poem, John Greenleaf Whittier had compared Webster to the fallen Lucifer, but the godlike Daniel now had a final chance to qualify for the presidency in 1852.

It was now Seward's turn to sulk in despair. He and Weed threatened fierce warfare in New York unless Fillmore avoided the influence of Clay and Webster. Fillmore's studied indifference left Seward convinced that he must now develop a new subject for agitation. "I shall endeavor," Seward wrote Weed, "to develop a new one on the admission of New Mexico."[17]

Southern extremists who had excoriated Taylor were no happier with Fillmore. Their presses were filled with dire warnings. Not only was the new president the tool of the compromisers, but he did not even have the restraint of Taylor's enormous self-interest in the preservation of slavery.

For entirely too long, historians have overemphasized the sharp break between the Taylor and the Fillmore administrations and have ignored the continuity. Fillmore has been considered more sympathetic and more acceptable to the Southerners than Taylor, but the new cabinet consisted of four Northerners and only three members from slave states instead of the previous Southern majority. The influence of Seward was gone, although whether Seward had used Taylor or Taylor had used Seward is arguable. The eminent historian Allan Nevins suggested that a civil war over New Mexico may have been averted by the death of Taylor. This is at least possible, but Fillmore did not revoke Taylor's order for the military defense of New Mexico should such become necessary. Instead, Fillmore ordered an additional 750 soldiers to New Mexico. General Scott notified Colonel Munroe that the troops were for additional protection against Indians and against "another and more painful contingency" that might develop.[18] Aside from the fact that Fillmore, unlike Taylor, did not threaten to lead the army in person, there was no discernible difference between Fillmore's Texas policy and that of Taylor. Various people had expressed the fear that Taylor might veto the compromise, which Fillmore presumably would not do. One argument for the omnibus bill was the alleged fear that if the bills were separated, Taylor would sign the bills he liked but veto the others. Taylor would certainly have vetoed any bill that gave Texas any territory actually occupied by people wishing to remain part of New Mexico. The charge by his enemies, however, that he would have vetoed any other part of the compromise was strongly denied by his friends and press supporters. At the time of Taylor's death, the omnibus bill was hopelessly mired in efforts to enact impossible amendments, and the Southern effort to swap California for most of New Mexico had failed. Regardless of who was president, alternative actions had to be considered, and the ultimate decisions would probably have been about the same if Taylor had lived. Fillmore's wielding of the patronage may have contributed to the majorities that some of the measures finally received in the House, but specific examples are difficult to find. Perhaps the most important change was the recasting of personal enmities once the polarization into friends and enemies of Zachary Taylor had ended. Great political decisions affecting the lives of millions of people are often determined by temperamental considerations of pride and honor quite irrelevant to the actual issues.

11

★ ★ ★ ★ ★

THE COMPROMISE

The great political struggle of 1850 in Washington was not the only story that excited Americans during the crucial months. For many weeks the usual newspaper litanies of calamities, shipwrecks, train accidents, assaults, robberies, and murders featured the killing in Boston of Harvard Professor George Parkman by his colleague Professor John W. Webster, whom Parkman was threatening with loss of tenure for his failure to pay a debt. Webster, a noted professor of chemistry, was ultimately hanged before what was reportedly the largest and most festive crowd ever assembled in Boston. These continuing accounts, with all the gory details, in the newspapers may have interested as many ordinary readers as did the seemingly endless congressional debates.

Another event attracting much attention was the triumphant American concert tour of the "Swedish Nightingale," Jenny Lind, who was brought to America by the great showman and sometimes charlatan Phineas T. Barnum. Glowing reviews of her performances were further enhanced by the announcement that she had donated her New York purse of ten thousand dollars to the city's numerous charities. When the singer finally appeared in Washington in December 1850, most of the city's notables attended. During the concert she introduced Henry Clay in the audience, and the old statesman was obviously delighted by the roar of applause. Even some of his long-time enemies were pleased. In keeping with its consistently dim view of all events to the north, the *Charleston Mercury* complained that "from the multitudinous braying of the jacks, a stranger from the moon might conclude there had never been another jenny on earth, though according to the best account there was good singing before the time of Agememnon, and the art has been spreading and perfecting ever since."[1]

Meanwhile, for three weeks after the death of Zachary Taylor, the debates on the omnibus bill ran their course. On 15 and 16 July, Clay and Benton enjoyed their last all-out confrontation. The writer Sarah J. Lippincott found Benton "the perfect embodiment of a great, inflexible, untiring will, the power of which one can only doubt when the eye is turned to the other side of the chamber, where sits his watchful, skillful, irresistible opponent, with the old fire of his wondrous intellect unquenched, and the strength of his Napoleonic will unbroken."[2] Obviously, the great Kentuckian had lost none of his legendary appeal to women. Benton was now ready to set the New Mexican boundary at 102° longitude west, which would have left the present cities of Lubbock and Amarillo just barely inside Texas. His argument was based upon a map that had been authenticated by the entire Texas delegation in Congress and by the Texas secretary of state, which showed that the occupied and settled limit of Texas was this line. The omnibus boundary, he insisted, would give Texas seventy thousand New Mexican citizens who owed no allegiance to Texas. It made the admission of California and the government for the territories dependent upon what Texas would accept rather than upon what Texas should have.[3]

The defeat of Benton's amendment was followed by still-another series of amendments from Foote. He would push the southern boundary of New Mexico one hundred miles north of the omnibus-bill line to the 34th parallel and would split California at the 35th parallel with the southern half to become a new territory named Colorado.[4] Despite Foote's erratic belligerence and ranting histrionics, he was probably his section's most realistic advocate. In sharp contrast to his colleague Jefferson Davis, Foote had always stood for gaining everything possible through accepted parliamentary maneuvering. Running on a Unionist platform, he would defeat Davis for governor of Mississippi in 1851.

On 9 July and 15 July, Andrew Pickens Butler of South Carolina delivered long and dramatic speeches against any compromise that might violate Southern honor. He admitted that slavery probably could not be expanded, but he denounced those who were insisting upon a Wilmot Proviso to prevent it. The Missouri Compromise, said Butler, had taken a vast territory away from the South, but he was nonetheless ready to accept the principle for the Southwest. It was "a principle of honor and right" that California should be divided at 36° 30'. "How," asked Butler, "can you expect us to continue in the Confederacy with the solemn advertisement that, in any acquisition hereafter to be made in Mexico or in the West Indian Islands, we may spill our blood, stand upon bloody fields, and bear our share of the expense of the contest, but that our competitors shall have the fruits of victory? What honorable man would consent to such conditions?"[5]

On 22 July, Henry Clay delivered his final great oration. Arguing eloquently that the net result of the compromise measures would be all that either North or South could hope for, he appealed to reason, unselfishness, human tolerance, understanding, and, finally, a sense of destiny. Individual man, he said, was but "a mere speck upon the surface of the immense universe—not a second in time compared to eternity." Should any individual oppose himself "to the onward march of a great nation, to subsist for ages and ages to come? . . . Forbid it God! Let us look at our country and our cause; elevate ourselves to the dignity of pure and disinterested patriots, wise and enlightened statesmen, and save our country from all impending dangers. What if, in the march of this nation to greatness and power, we should fall beneath the wheels that propel it forward? What are we—what is any man worth who is not ready and willing to sacrifice himself for the benefit of his country when it is necessary?" It was a noble appeal, but the wrangling was resumed almost before he had taken his seat.[6]

All pending amendments were swept aside on 24 July. Bradbury of Maine, a supporter of the omnibus bill, moved an amendment to allow the president to appoint two commissioners to meet with Texas commissioners to work out a boundary settlement. Debate on this amendment lasted for three days. Benton offered amendments to protect New Mexico: the proposed commission should have no power to establish a boundary unacceptable to New Mexico. Virginia's Senator Mason offered the same amendment in reverse with Texas to have a veto, but both amendments were defeated.[7]

At this point, the Texans fired their main batteries for the last time. Thomas Rusk offered an amendment awarding Texas the entire disputed area and defended it with a hair-raising speech of defiance against federal encroachment. Houston stopped whittling long enough to add his own impassioned plea. He insisted that the government's unconstitutional actions against Texas were serious grounds for complaint, and Texas expected "every State and every representative of every State . . . to vindicate her in the maintenance of her rights until they are fairly adjudicated." Houston's speech was more conciliatory than it sounded. A fair adjudication by the Supreme Court was exactly what Zachary Taylor had recommended all along. In retrospect, the Texans were apparently just leaving a final message for the record when they would face reelection. Rusk would remain a strong Unionist until his death in 1857. When Texas seceded in 1861, Houston resigned the governorship and refused to take an oath of allegiance to the Confederacy.

When Butler of South Carolina attacked Bradbury's plan for a commission, he met a veritable buzz saw in the form of Henry S. Foote, who was now determined that this plan should be the solution. Foote insulted Butler and openly declared his readiness to accept a duel challenge. Seward's amendment to admit New Mexico as a state and refer the dispute to the Supreme Court was defeated by a vote of 42 to 1. On 29 July, Dayton moved that a settlement be made by the Supreme Court, but the Texans objected. They would take neither a commission nor a court decision and continued to upbraid the government. The court-decision amendment lost by 39 to 18. Bradbury's commission idea met the same fate by a 28 to 28 tie, because there was no vice-president to cast a deciding vote. Foote, Bradbury, and Rusk joined forces to offer the commission idea again with a rider declaring the military movement toward statehood in New Mexico to be null and void. Benton attacked this as a slur against the memory of Zachary Taylor, and it was overwhelmed by a vote of 42 to 12. Benton, the Texans, and the ultra-Southerners voted together for a move to strike everything from the commission amendment except orders to the commissioners to establish the boundary, but a 29–to–29 tie vote also defeated this amendment.[8]

On the next day, Dawson of Georgia offered an amendment to make territorial government ineffective in New Mexico east of the Rio Grande during the period of a commission's labors. Benton protested with reason that all the fertile valleys, towns and people, and the capital of New Mexico were east of the river, and that a government for the remainder of the territory would be ridiculous. The Indians thus favored would be amazed. Clay supported the proposition, but Douglas insisted that Texas should be pledged not to seize the area. Dawson offered to modify his amendment to grant a government east of the river on 1 June 1851, if the area, meanwhile, had not been awarded to Texas. Rusk protested that this would give the territory to New Mexico if the matter remained unsettled.

Benton again denounced the bill as a sick man with a succession of doctors, each promising a cure, but each making the patient worse. All moves, said Benton, were aimed at the support of Texas, with the same amendments being offered over and over again. He commended the Texans, however, for their manly lack of hypocrisy. Their position was clear: "Give us what we demand, the whole of New Mexico, and California may come in; refuse us the whole of New Mexico or the price we demand, or California cannot come in." Houston, although he would remain one of Benton's closest personal friends, was stung by this and hotly denied that Texas was interested in either money or a new boundary. Texas, Houston insisted, wanted only the old boundary, and he and Rusk were interested only in preserving the harmony of the Union. He and Rusk now shifted to support the Dawson amendment restricting territorial government east of the river, and combined with the rejuvenated Bradbury commission plan, it carried by the tiny margin of two votes, 30 to 28. A commission would decide the boundary, but during the interim, New Mexico could not form a territorial government for the area east of the Rio Grande.

The Texas question was apparently settled, and supporters of the omnibus bill now hoped for its quick passage, although the *Union* was certain that it would fail. The bill might have passed in this form by a margin of one or two votes, but the effect could have been disastrous. The boundary would have still depended upon an agreement by Texas, and New Mexico, denied a territorial government, would undoubtedly have proceeded with its own plans for statehood. Texas had called for a special legislative session to meet on 12 August and was preparing to march. Each aggressive step taken by Texas made turning back more difficult. Further postponement could lead only to more explosive tensions and the greater likelihood of a military confrontation. An immediate settlement was desperately needed, but the omnibus bill as amended would not provide this even if it could pass, which was still by no means certain. Perhaps some found symbolic significance on 26 July, when word came that the ship *Elizabeth*, returning from the Mediterranean with a large statue of John C. Calhoun on board, had capsized and sunk during a storm off Long Island only a few hours from New York Harbor.

With Calhoun's European statue lost at sea, a live reincarnation in the form of Jefferson Davis began the proceedings of 31 July with a long and significant oration against the omnibus bill or any other compromise. Tall, handsome, dignified, and humorless, Davis occasionally appeared to operate in a world all his own. He announced that nonintervention by the federal government had become a doctrine "which held the hand of government powerless for the purpose of giving protection to constitutional rights throughout the United States." The principle would strip the states of every advantage for which the federal government had been formed. Davis apparently saw no inconsistency between the Southern devotion to states' rights and a requirement that the federal government protect slavery in areas where it was not wanted. He would not object, Davis continued, if the bill "prohibited the Territorial Legislature from establishing or prohibiting any species of property held in any of the states of this Union," but "confining the restriction to African slaves" was intolerable. "I claim that this species of property stands upon the same general basis with every other." He had offered an amendment to preserve the territorial legislature's right to pass laws protecting slave owners in their property and had accepted another amendment denying the legislature any power to either bar or establish slavery as long as the legislature was not forbidden to protect slave property. The principles had been rejected, and this made the bill intolerable. To the historian, forbidding a legislature to establish slavery while allowing it to pass laws protecting slave property seems quite inconsistent, but to Jefferson Davis, the one without the other was an insulting discrimination against the South. Repeating a favorite Calhoun principle, Davis attacked the political system of rule by a numerical majority and charged that the founding fathers had been replaced by "representatives of fanaticism and schemers for power, whose policy is at open war with the practice and principles of the Constitution their and our ancestors formed, and of which we now claim the protection." Perhaps most important, Davis was certain that there would be no conflict between federal troops and those of Texas because most Americans would never fight against the South. During the nullification crisis of 1833, he had been ready to tear up his commission rather than obey any orders to attack South Carolina, and he believed that most Northern soldiers and the Northern people still felt the same way. Davis was certain that if a civil war should come, the North would have to hire foreign mercenaries to do the fighting. The Union could "never be preserved by force," and threats of a civil war were "a phantom of politicians." In 1861 this illusion probably helped to influence his decision to attack Fort Sumter.[9]

At the White House, meanwhile, the new president agreed with the conclusion that Taylor, Benton, Douglas, and Webster had shared all along. An immediate solution was imperative, but no satisfactory compromise was possible as long as the bills were combined. Fillmore had offered Senator James Pearce of Maryland a cabinet post, which Pearce had refused, but the two men had remained close friends. Fillmore and Pearce conferred and may have designed the course that Pearce followed. Fillmore's biographer, Robert Rayback, concluded that the two men had a well-laid plan, but he offered no conclusive evidence.[10] On the other hand, the president and the senator were friends, they agreed on the issues, they often met, and Fillmore undoubtedly favored Pearce's action. The results, however, also involved considerable confusion, spontaneous anger, and reactions that no one could have predicted with certainty.

Since 1846, Pearce, a tall, dignified, and eloquent "gentleman of the old school," had consistently opposed the claims of Texas to any territory outside its original boundaries set by Mexico. He had supported the omnibus bill throughout, but as late as 20 July he had delivered a spirited defense of President Taylor. The Texas senators had cited Taylor's letters complaining about alleged atrocities committed by Texans as proof of the old general's unfair prejudices against Texas. Pearce reviewed all the earlier arguments against the Texas claim, denied that Taylor had been anything but objective, and added his own conviction that the atrocities had indeed taken place.[11]

On 31 July, after Jefferson Davis had finished his oration, Pearce announced that while he had supported the omnibus-bill committee's boundary for Texas, he could not accept the Dawson amendment. Newspapers everywhere, he said, were claiming that the amendment abandoned everything east of the Rio Grande to Texas, and "knowing how the slightest acquiescence, the least act of legislation, will be used to sustain the title of Texas," he could not sanction it. The amendment made the omnibus bill "cranky, lop-eared, crippled, deformed, and curtailed its fair proportions." He would therefore offer three amendments to strike out everything in the bill related to New Mexico, reinsert everything except the Dawson amendment, and replace Dawson's proposition with one of his own.[12]

The weary Henry Clay was stunned. With his voice breaking, he pleaded with Pearce to reconsider: "Light was beginning to break upon us—land was beginning to be in sight once more—and is it possible, upon slight and unimportant amendments . . . that we should now hazard the safety, the peace, if not the Union of the country."

The Dawson amendment could be amended without striking the entire proposition.[13]

Pearce denied that he was trying to destroy the bill. If the boundary dispute could be stricken, he would move immediately to reinsert it with a provision that the territorial government of New Mexico could not go into effect until 4 March 1851.

The Texas hero Thomas Rusk answered Pearce with the story of a duelist who, after his opponent's gun had misfired three times, threw down his own weapon. He was "willing to be shot at, but to be eternally snapped at was more than human nature could bear." Criticisms of Texas were the first thing he heard in the morning and the last thing at night. If New Mexico were to establish a territorial government while the commission was working on the boundary problem, that act itself would be a decision against the rights of Texas.[14]

James Shields of Illinois expressed sentiments probably shared by other colleagues. He had voted against the Dawson amendment, but had later voted for the Bradbury commission plan with the Dawson amendment attached. It was a vote he was "not prepared to defend here or elsewhere. . . . I am really gratified that my friend from Maryland has presented a mode by which I can redeem myself."[15]

Benton supported Pearce by comparing the bill to the strolling players of England who performed Hamlet with the part of Hamlet omitted because the ghost was sick. Challenging anyone to name a single town or village west of the Rio Grande, Old Bullion, amid considerable laughter, enumerated the tiny Indian settlements and pictured their astonishment when asked to form a territorial government. President Taylor, said Benton, had announced that he "would maintain possession of New Mexico until the question of title was decided by the competent authority. . . . Sir, in that message, [was] more sound sense—more knowledge of constitutional and municipal law—a juster view of what is due the United States, to New Mexico, and to Texas . . . than in all that has been delivered on this floor on the subject." And finally, Benton repeated his usual plea and prediction. "Untie these incongruous measures. Take up these measures one by one, and they will all be passed . . . by a majority, and the theory of our government will be satisfied."[16]

Whether or not these words influenced anyone, the Senate voted 33 to 22 for Pearce's amendment striking New Mexico from the bill. When Pearce then moved to reinstate the commission plan with a stipulation delaying the beginning of effective territorial government for New Mexico until 4 March 1851, Douglas offered an additional amendment to make territorial government for New Mexico dependent upon a report of the commissioners by 15 December 1850. This, he argued, would delay its effect until settlement of the boundary and keep the rights of both parties meanwhile unimpaired. This lost by a vote of 32 to 24. At this point, David Atchison, Benton's Missouri colleague and bitter enemy, moved to strike California from the bill. He argued that the Pearce amendment would establish a New Mexican government in Texas territory unless an agreement could be reached by April 1851, and he would rather vote for the Wilmot Proviso than for such a violation of the rights of Texas. Yulee of Florida, a Southern extremist throughout, dealt the fatal blow by moving to strike out everything related to Texas and New Mexico. If passed, this would separate Texas from the omnibus bill and thus break it up. If separated from California, the Texas claims would obviously lose what Butler had called the "great ship" that was trying to bring them into port. The Texans, however, had apparently had enough. Joining the opponents of the omnibus bill, they tipped the vote to 29 to 28 in favor of making their fight to annex New Mexico without California statehood being an asset to exchange for it. If the Texans had stood by the omnibus bill, the vote would have been 30 to 27 for keeping it intact. A few minutes later, the move to reinstate New Mexico into the bill also failed, and after three ballots, Atchison's efforts to strike out California also succeeded. Only Deseret (Utah) was left. In the words of one happy observer, the bill had "died of amendments and passed the Senate with no passenger in the Omnibus save the Utah travellers. The Mormons alone got thru' living—the Christians all jumped out."[17]

The final vote turned the chamber into a carnival of joy for those now convinced that the compromise could pass, as well as for those still opposed to any compromise at all. According to the *New York Express*, the abolitionist John Hale and Jefferson Davis were equally delighted, while Seward was dancing around like a little top. The Free-Soiler Salmon P. Chase was shaking hands with Pierre Soulé of Louisiana. They were "all in the clouds," wrote Benton, "triumphing over Clay, Webster, Cass, Foote, the omnibus, and the devil!" In contrast, Cass looked unhappy, Foote gave himself up to despair, and Clay sat "melancholy as Caius and Marius over the ruins of Carthage."[18]

Clearly, the excessive heat, as well as fatigue and confusion, influenced the events of 31 July. Nineteen Northerners joined with fourteen Southerners to pass Pearce's amendment striking everything related to New Mexico from the bill. Only five Whigs joined with Clay to vote against it. Yulee's successful effort to strike Texas garnered sixteen Northern and thirteen Southern votes, while twelve Northerners and sixteen Southerners voted against it. Ten Northerners and twenty-four Southerners voted to strike out California, although this clearly meant that California would soon be admitted as a state. Twenty Northerners and only five Southerners voted to keep California tied to Utah.[19] Actually, these votes only served to demonstrate how illogical the omnibus-bill technique had been from the beginning, and its collapse was a triumph for the late President Taylor as well as for the incumbent Millard Fillmore.

August 1 was a day of wild and angry recriminations. Clay announced that he was now willing to see the bills passed separately, but he denounced Pearce as a fomenter of disunion. Pearce answered in kind, and various other senators exchanged barbed insults. Clay made it clear, however, that even if Kentucky should raise the standard of disunion, he would "go against her."

Clay was disappointed, but he had acquitted himself well. His parliamentary method had failed, but his proposals were still on the table. If the six months of wrangling had enhanced some personal enmities, they had also made clear to all sides what could and what could not be accomplished. The profound hopes of the general public for a compromise had been roused almost everywhere, and most senators and congressmen had become too weary to keep up their aggressive demands in the face of public pressures for a settlement. Many acute observers had always believed that each measure could be settled with honor as soon as they could be dealt with separately.

Speaking for the New York merchants, the *New York Express*, at least temporarily, was filled with despair, but the editors of the *National Intelligencer* and the *Republic*, who had supported both Taylor and Fillmore, were certain that the compromise would now become a reality. Thomas Ritchie at the *Union* had not supported and would not support Fillmore, but Ritchie, too, was optimistic, even while condemning those who had slain the omnibus bill. Also, a large number of the country's local editors quoted by the *Intelligencer* continued to cite the collapse of the omnibus bill as a necessary step toward compromise. Most of them had also supported the steps recommended by Zachary Taylor. The editors of the *Albany Evening Journal* and of the *Charleston Mercury* were delighted for very different reasons. Weed's paper felt that the collapse of the omnibus bill "vindicates Gen. TAYLOR'S wisdom in recommending a simple, easy and right course." To the *Mercury*, the omnibus had been "a cheat, a charlatan's device for hiding the diseases of the body politic momentarily, and claiming the reward of curing them . . . a measure which Mr. Foote says means that the South may carry their slaves into all the territories and Mr. Clay says leaves them no right to settle a foot of the whole."[20]

The omnibus bill had never had a chance, but while Clay soon departed for a well-deserved seaside vacation, the young Illinois senator Stephen A. Douglas, as chairman of the Committee on Territories, took up the measures one by one. He and Pearce quickly framed a new Texas boundary bill that gave Texas 33,333 more square miles than the original omnibus bill had provided but relocated the boundary to give Texas the unoccupied present panhandle area, while leaving New Mexico all of its occupied territory. For sacrificing something that had never been part of Texas anyhow, the Lone Star State would be offered a compensation of $10 million.[21]

As the *Union* and other newspapers continued to call for Southern support for Texas while warning that federal opposition to Texas would lead to a civil war, Millard Fillmore and Daniel Webster were also busy. On 6 August, Fillmore sent both houses of Congress a special message that included the letter of complaint written to Taylor by the Texas governor on 14 June, Taylor's own reply to the governor, and an appeal to Congress to settle the issue. Webster had written the original drafts, but the final result was a joint production. Fillmore's position was clear, and it was virtually the same as that of his predecessor:

> If the laws of the United States are opposed or obstructed in any State or Territory by combinations too powerful to be suppressed by the judicial or civil authorities, . . . it is the duty of the President either to call out the militia or to employ the military and naval force of the United States or to do both if in his judgment the exigency of the occasion shall so require. . . . If Texas militia, therefore, march into any one of the other States or into any territory of the United States, there to execute or enforce any law of Texas, they become at that moment trespassers; they are no longer under the protection of any lawful authority, and are to be regarded merely as intruders; and if within such State or Territory they obstruct any law of the United States, whether by power of arms or mere power of numbers . . . the President of the United States is bound to obey the solemn injunction of the Constitution and exercise the high powers vested in him by that instrument and by the acts of Congress.

His letter to the governor of Texas, Fillmore added, included his reasons for believing "that New Mexico is now a Territory of the United States, with the same extent and the same boundaries which belonged to it while in the actual possession of the Republic of Mexico, and before the late war." The fifth article of the Treaty of Guadalupe Hidalgo established the boundary, and the ninth article guaranteed federal protection for all Mexicans living within those boundaries. If the boundary was in doubt, the doubt could "only be removed by some act of Congress . . . or by some appropriate mode of legal adjudication." Meanwhile, if disturbances or collisions should occur, it was "absolutely incumbent on the executive government, however painful the duty, to take care that the laws be faithfully maintained; and he [the president] can regard only the actual state of things as it existed at the date of the treaty. . . . In other words, all must be now regarded as New Mexico which was possessed and occupied by New Mexico by citizens of Mexico at the date of the treaty until a definite line of boundary shall be established by competent authority." And finally, Congress was already as capable of deciding upon the proper boundary as it would be after the report of any commissioners. If the Texas claim appeared to Congress to be "well founded in whole or in part," it was "in the competency of Congress to offer her an indemnity for the surrender of that claim." In this case, surrounded "by many cogent considerations, all calling for amicable adjustment and immediate settlement, the Government of the United States would be justified . . . in allowing an indemnity to Texas, not unreasonable or extravagant, but fair, liberal, and awarded in a just spirit of accommodation."[22]

With the Texas–New Mexico issue forced to stand on its own merits, with 750 more federal troops ordered to New Mexico, with the new president firmly committed to federal resistance against any invasion by Texas, and with their full claims obviously unrealizable in Congress, the Texans quietly accepted the offer made by Douglas and Pearce. Only two days after Fillmore's message and appeal and after a significant amendment, the bill passed by a vote of 30 to 20. The amendment provided that no more than $5 million in stock could be issued until the creditors of Texas who were holding bonds and other certificates for which duties were specifically pledged should "first file at the Treasury of the United States releases of all claims against the United States for an account of said bonds or certificates." This meant that all obligations of the federal government to Texas or its creditors incurred when the Texas customs were transferred to the United States would be canceled in full. It also meant that the profits of the bondholders were very much in the minds of the senators when they passed the bill. The amendment passed by 35 to 12, with the Texans opposed. On the final passage of the bill, the slaveholding states were divided evenly, 12 to 12, while Northern senators voted 18 to 8 in its favor.[23]

In the end, the Unionist sentiments of the Texas senators had prevailed over their ambitions for Texas. On 9 August, Sam Houston, replying to an attack by the *Southern Press* (Washington, D.C.), proclaimed that anyone who would conspire against the American Union was "more culpable . . . than Benedict Arnold . . . when Arnold committed his treason, we were but trying an experiment, whereas we are now in full fruition of blessings and glories." Current disunionists, therefore, were "below Arnold in the scale of infamy . . . let it be understood that I would rather not be, than be without a country; and without union we can have no country and no home." Houston later announced that as soon as the session had ended, he would immediately go to Texas and urge the legislature to approve the settlement.[24]

The many historians who have attributed the compromise to Millard Fillmore's pro-Southern sympathies and stressed the differences between Fillmore and Taylor obviously have paid but little attention to the angry Southern editorials and speeches answering Fillmore's threat to defend New Mexico by force. The *Union*, after its months of praising Clay and the omnibus bill, never recognized any significant difference between the policies of Taylor and those of Fillmore. "Where was the necessity," asked Ritchie, "of entering into a dissertation of the duties of the President, or on the claims and conduct of Texas? Why should the sword, at such a critical and exciting moment as this, be brandished with something like a menace over a State?" The *Union*, of course, had been shaking an iron fist at New Mexico for months, but to Ritchie, the president's threat of resistance was a blow against compromise and peace. Fillmore and Webster, he wrote in a three-column editorial defending the claims of Texas, had two purposes: one to "menace Texas with the power of the federal government, and the other to claim for the President the authority to call out the militia, and to use the army and navy of the United States (*without the sanction of Congress, although that body is now in session*) in order to repel any attempt of Texas to vindicate her territorial claim from the violent usurpation committed under the auspices of the United States troops at Santa Fe." When, however, the settlement actually passed with indemnification for Texas, Ritchie quickly decided that the settlement had saved the country from a civil war.[25]

To Alexander H. Stephens, Fillmore's policy was both unconstitutional and dangerous. Although he was commander in chief of the armed services, the president could not lawfully use the military to enforce a treaty unless empowered to do so by Congress. In 1833, said Stephens, President Jackson, with a much better case against South Carolina, had nonetheless asked the Congress to pass a force bill. By keeping Texas out of New Mexico, Fillmore was unlawfully deciding the boundary in favor of New Mexico, when, according to law, he should be on the side of Texas. If the United States fired on Texas, Stephens warned, "the freemen from the Delaware to the Rio Grande" would "rally to the rescue."[26]

The *Charleston Mercury* charged that Fillmore was "preparing to help a rebellion put down a state" because Texas was "not a Free Soil State." Even after the bill had been passed, the *Mercury* continued to insist that while Texas spirit in the Senate was low, it remained high in Texas, where the people would never "sell their birthright for a paltry $10,000,000."[27]

Defending Fillmore's message but denouncing the settlement, Thaddeus Stevens of Pennsylvania attacked his fellow Northerners with bitter sarcasm. Southern gentlemen, he said, had a mistaken impression of Northern character, although he would admit that Northern senators had "shown all the usual symptoms of cowardice." Northerners, however, had not given Texas $10 million and fifty thousand acres from cowardice, because, after all, they were descended from "the men of Bunker's Hill, of Lexington, of Bennington, of Saratoga, and of Brandywine." The real motive was benevolence. "So copious is the milk of human kindness in Northern breasts, that it overflows, runs down upon the sinews and nerves, and moistens and relaxes them, so that at the loud voice of mimic treason, and imaginary gleamings of Southern bayonets, our frames become convulsed and our knees smite together. This is not cowardice, but benevolence!—the love of peace."[28]

In contrast, the *National Intelligencer* rejoiced at the settlement of the most difficult of the problems and gave full credit to the administration of Zachary Taylor: "The history of that administration remains to be written, and when written, it will show that scarcely was one ever surrounded with more difficulties, or ever, in spite of a storm of calumny, more successfully overcame them."[29]

Also contradicting the view of Fillmore as a pro-Southern president, the antislavery editor Horace Greeley, who had criticized Taylor throughout for being too gentle with Texas on the New Mexican issue, offered extravagant praise for Fillmore's message of support for New Mexico. "This day will be rendered memorable in our country's annals by the transmission of a Message from President FILLMORE to Congress and an accompanying Letter from Secretary Webster to Gov. Bell of Texas. . . . lovers of freedom and justice will heartily approve."[30]

In the Senate, when Douglas reintroduced his earlier bill for the admission of California, Foote and Turney again tried to split the state at 36° 30', and the usual angry Southern speeches against the constitutionality of admitting California without its having to go through a territorial stage were repeated. The atmosphere, however, had relaxed considerably. During Foote's harangue, Andrew Pickens Butler yawned ostentatiously. "I perceive," said Foote, "that my friend from South Carolina seems to suffer under my speech." "I was not thinking about your speech at all," replied Butler, amid a roar of laughter.[31]

On 13 August, California was admitted by a vote of 34 to 18. Six slave-state senators voted for the admission of the enormous new free state. For the handful of slaves already in California, however, slavery was actually legal for several years after 1850, and California's senators and representatives voted with the South on almost every issue until 1861. Its delegates would support the Southern extremist position at the Democratic National Convention of 1860.

The fugitive-slave bill, destined in practice to be the most troublesome part of the compromise, went to its third reading on 23 August by a vote of 27 to 12 and passed by a voice vote three days later. The actual roll call on 23 August was not officially recorded anywhere, and obviously some 21 senators had declined to vote or were absent, while others were not anxious to have their votes made public.[32]

During the fugitive-slave debate a New York abolitionist named William L. Chaplin tried to leave Washington with two slaves belonging to Alexander H. Stephens and Robert Toombs concealed in a carriage. The runaways were intercepted by police and a civilian posse near what is now Silver Spring, Maryland, and according to the police, the runaways fired eleven shots at their captors. Several persons, including Chaplin and both slaves, were wounded, but Toombs's slave escaped. A Chaplin Fund Committee, promptly formed to raise money for Chaplin's defense, insisted that he had been unarmed and that the police had perpetrated all the violence.

The group expected Chaplin's legal expenses to total $20,000.[33] This masterly bit of timing probably helped the supporters of the bill.

The most controversial measures had passed the Senate, but their approval by the House was not a foregone conclusion. The *Washington Union*, having inaccurately identified Zachary Taylor as an enemy of compromise, now tried to do the same for Millard Fillmore by charging that once California had been admitted and the Texas boundary had been settled, the president would abandon the South and support the Wilmot Proviso for New Mexico and Utah. This, of course, was nonsense. Fillmore's sentiments were stated clearly in a private letter on 20 August 1850:

> I have strong hopes that the several bills which have passed the Senate, may pass the House and that harmony may again be restored to our beloved, but distracted country. This is the height of my ambition. I ask no prolongation of my present term. I occupy the position, by the suffrage of my fellow citizens, and the inscrutable will of Heaven. I never sought it. I do not seek its prolongation. But my only desire is to discharge my duty. To act for the good of the whole country; to know nothing but the United States; "one and indivisible," and their prosperity and harmony. Let my friends aid me in accomplishing this, and I ask no more. They may divide the accruing honors among themselves.[34]

In the House of Representatives, the chief barrier to compromise and the most obvious threat to peace was the Texas boundary issue. Ironically, a major force working to get the measure passed also provided its opponents with a trenchant argument. On the one hand, the House floor and galleries were literally overrun by Texas bondholders and their lobbyists urging congressmen to support the bill. In response, its opponents were arguing that the taxpayers should not have to give Texas and the speculators $10 million for something that did not belong to Texas anyway. Despite exhaustive research, Holman Hamilton could never show that any congressman or senator, except for one Texan who owned a small amount of bonds, had profited directly from any vote cast. This, of course, does not mean that unrecorded transactions did not take place, and Hamilton did find that some relatives and friends of specific lawmakers were involved. One ardent opponent of compromise in any form, Senator Robert W. Barnwell of South Carolina, was convinced that the "ten millions of money to be paid to the Texas creditors carried the day . . . this whole difficulty about the boundary of Texas was gotten up by Hamilton, Thompson, & Clay[,] the Texas Senators &

others interested in bonds of Texas. I can not else account for the whole proceeding." Beverley Tucker, a professor of law at William and Mary College, denounced the conduct of James Hamilton as "disgraceful" and believed that "ten millions to Texas were introduced into the scheme to supply a fund for bribing Southern men both in and out of Congress." Tucker claimed that he knew one man who had received $10,000 for "his mere *forbearance* to exert his influence against the measure."[35]

Whether or not financial incentives affected a significant number of votes, every congressman must have been aware of the vast ground swell of public support for the compromise from every state except South Carolina. The Washington and New York Whig newspapers filled their columns with editorials of support from almost every southern as well as northern and western city. Any congressman who hoped to be reelected could have found ample reason to support what the Senate had accomplished.

The final result, however, came only after some strange events. Die-hard opponents protested either that Texas and the South were being robbed or that Texas was being bribed to accept an expansion of slave territory to which it had no legal right. The *Union* continued to allege that Southerners expected Fillmore to abandon them to the Wilmot Proviso once he had got the Texas and California issues settled. Apparently to offset this fear, Linn Boyd of Kentucky on 28 August offered an amendment combining the Texas boundary settlement with the bill organizing the New Mexico territory with no action on slavery. Howell Cobb used all of his considerable talents as Speaker to keep the measure before the House, instead of allowing it to go back to a committee. Boyd defended his proposition vigorously. He was "astonished at the patience with which our constituents have borne our procrastination. I think we have talked enough—in God's name let us act." If the questions proved insoluble, every member should "resign his commission into the hands of the people" and let them "send here Representatives better disposed to do their duty and save the Union." Getting the bill passed, however, required more than eloquence.[36]

On 4 September a move to refer Boyd's bill to the Committee of the Whole passed, and his effort appeared to be dead. Then a move for reconsideration produced a tie, which the Speaker converted into a victory of 104 to 103. Then, by 103 to 101, the House rejected another effort to return the bill to committee. Shortly afterward, however, Boyd's amendment combining the Texas boundary issue with noninterference with slavery in New Mexico was rejected, and the House voted 126 to 60 against engrossing the Texas–New Mexico boundary bill alone. Bond lobbyists like W. W. Corcoran were optimistic, however, and the conclusion that some of the 126 were waiting to be rewarded for changing their votes is difficult to escape. Many Southerners, however, had already voted for Boyd's "little omnibus" and may just have been waiting for the two measures to be recombined. Some undoubtedly had taken seriously the *Union*'s warning that Fillmore would promote the Wilmot Proviso for New Mexico once the Texas boundary had been settled. Reportedly, Fillmore met with a number of congressmen, and he has occasionally been credited with having used the official patronage to sway votes, although his biographer, Robert Rayback, is silent on this question. The president may have influenced more votes by denying the *Union*'s charges and by promising to support the entire Senate package. Persuasiveness had always been one of Fillmore's major talents, both as a lawyer and as a legislator. Although following the events almost by the hour, the editors of the *National Intelligencer* confessed that they were "mystified" by the entire procedure, and 127 years later the scene still remains somewhat murky.[37]

However it may have been accomplished, success came on 6 September. With the floor, galleries, and lobbies filled with spectators and bond lobbyists, the House reconsidered its earlier votes and set the stage for a final vote on Boyd's "little omnibus bill." First, however, an angry Ohio representative demanded that the Speaker order all Texas-bond lobbyists off the floor and into the galleries, because "they could see there as well as on the floor." The Speaker gave the order, but it was ignored, and the votes were tallied amid a scene of wild confusion. Twenty-eight congressmen who had voted against Boyd's amendment on 4 September now supported it on 6 September. When Volney E. Howard of Texas, who had for months denounced every attempt to deny Texas its full claim, voted aye, a wild burst of cheering ensued. When Speaker Cobb announced the final tally, 108 to 98 to send the bill to its third reading, which meant a final passage, the chamber exploded with cheers, stamping, whistles, and shouts. After Cobb had finally restored some semblance of order, the final vote was 108 to 97.[38]

The rest was anticlimax. On Saturday, the following day, California was admitted by the overwhelming vote of 150 to 56. Shortly afterward, Utah was accepted by the closer vote of 97 to 85, as numerous congressmen did not vote. Knowing that the other measures were certain to pass, the city of Washington, as well as the members of Congress, celebrated wildly through the weekend. Fireworks lit up the air, a salute of a hundred guns honored California and Utah, and the Marine band marched up and down Pennsylvania Avenue playing patriotic music. Foote, Cass, Cobb, Douglas, Houston, Rusk, Dickinson, Boyd, Webster, and others were serenaded in turn by huge crowds. On the following morning, almost everyone complained about illness from eating the wrong food, while the city's supply of alcoholic beverages had declined precipitately. As the word spread, the scene was repeated in many other cities.

On Monday, the Senate accepted the House's combination of Texas and New Mexico, and three days later the House passed the fugitive-slave bill by 109 to 76. On 16 September the bill banning the slave trade in the District passed the Senate and was approved on the following day by the House, 124 to 59.

As the various compromise measures cleared the Senate and the House, both the *National Intelligencer* and the *Republic* viewed the results as the natural culmination of Zachary Taylor's policies, although both praised Fillmore highly. Personal relations between the White House and the Clay-Webster Whigs had obviously improved perceptibly, but the compromise had succeeded only when Taylor's plan of dealing with the issues one at a time had been adopted. Both papers praised Fillmore for his willingness to defend New Mexico by force if necessary, and both continued to argue that Texas had no right whatever to the disputed territory, although for the sake of harmony they were willing to pay Texas the $10 million.

On 10 September, with every part of the compromise either enacted or a foregone conclusion, Allan A. Hall and the *Daily Republic* made an announcement: "The circumstances which led to the change in the editorial department of the *Republic* in May last no longer existing, the undersigned cheerfully surrenders to John O. Sargent, esq., one of its able founders, the future control of its columns." Since Taylor's death, the *Republic* had defended and praised Fillmore with the same loyalty that it had shown to Zachary Taylor, and Fillmore had obviously found no fault with its editor. The paper had also, however, remained loyal to the memory of Zachary Taylor by printing and praising the numerous speeches made in defense of Taylor by senators and congressmen who, more often than not, were also strong advocates of the compromise measures. Albert T. Burnley had continued as its proprietor throughout the controversy.

For entirely too long, historians have accepted the oversimplified and inaccurate view that Zachary Taylor endangered the Union by his capricious objections to the compromise, which finally passed only because of his timely death. Even Holman Hamilton, Taylor's most thorough biographer, accepted this interpretation, although he defended Taylor by questioning the value of the compromise and pointing out that it did not prevent the Civil War from occurring eleven years later. In fact, however, Taylor did not oppose the compromise as such; he objected only to a combination of measures designed to use California as a bargaining chip for the ambitions of Texas against New Mexico. An omnibus bill all of whose parts would be acceptable to a Senate majority was impossible, with or without the support or the opposition of the president. The compromise could succeed only if divided into single bills that the true believers on each side could support or oppose without violating their most cherished principles in dealing with a contradictory action in the same bill. Only fourteen senators and only four of the thirteen members of the omnibus committee voted for all of the compromise measures, and the "father" of the omnibus bill, Henry S. Foote, voted for only one of them.[39]

Because he wrote the separate bills and labored tirelessly to get them approved in the Senate, Stephen A. Douglas deserves the credit he has received for the successful completion of the compromise. His statement, however, that the omnibus bill, which he himself had always considered hopeless, had been destroyed by a combination of Free-Soilers, Southern disunionists, and the Taylor administration can be questioned.[40] The Taylor administration opposed the combination of the bills into an omnibus, but its reaction to an omnibus bill containing the measures written exactly as they finally passed might have been quite different. For almost three months the Congress debated a steady stream of amendments, and at no time could anyone be certain as to what the omnibus bill might contain if it ever came to a final vote—which it never did. Amendments to divide California, change the projected boundary between Texas and New Mexico, devise a method for settling the dispute, determine the process by which New Mexico might become a territory, and restrict or guarantee the autonomy of the New Mexican population were being offered almost daily until the day the omnibus bill was abandoned. The last version of the omnibus bill, just before its collapse, would have denied New Mexico a territorial government until a commission had decided the boundary, and James Pearce and those who voted with him clearly recognized what a dangerous situation this would have created. For Zachary Taylor, Millard Fillmore, or anyone else with an emotional stake in the outcome, to have given the omnibus bill blind support without knowing what it was going to be would have required an unreasonable act of faith.

Fillmore did not support the omnibus principle or the sacrifice of New Mexico any more than Taylor did. Fillmore did not change Taylor's orders to Colonel Munroe; he ordered an additional 750 soldiers to New Mexico, and he informed the Congress in no uncertain terms that he would repel an invasion by Texas with force if necessary. In the end, several unionist Southerners, including the Texans, realized that they were threatening the Union for an unattainable goal. When Pearce's amendment provided an opportunity for dividing the propositions, they retreated to a more realistic position clearly in line with public opinion in both North and South and allowed the separate bills to pass. Those who created the omnibus bill and spent the long, hot summer trying to amend it in favor of Texas deserve the title of obstructionists far more than Zachary Taylor. Millard Fillmore deserves high praise for supporting and perhaps even promoting the effort to break the omnibus bill into viable parts, and he worked diligently and effectively to help get them passed. The result would have probably been the same in any case, however, because it was the only alternative for those ready to follow public opinion and work for sectional peace. James Pearce was a strong supporter and defender of President Taylor throughout, and he would probably have taken the same action if Taylor had still been alive.

Perhaps the major contribution of both presidents to sectional peace in 1850 has often been overlooked. A civil war to defend slavery against a slaveholding president would have been impossible in 1850, and by the time of Taylor's death, the obvious public support for compromise in both sections was overwhelming. The real threat of a civil war lay in the possibility that Texas troops might attack New Mexico and thereby get into a war with the United States Army. Whether it was mere bombast or not, Southern leaders and newspapers everywhere predicted that tens of thousands of Southerners who cared nothing about the New Mexican boundary would immediately flock to the aid of Texas. Clearly, a great many Texans were eager to march against New Mexico and seek revenge for earlier humiliations as well as gain new territory. Any show of weakness or indecision by the president that could lead the Texans to believe they would be fighting only against New Mexicans might well have invited the fatal attack. Zachary Taylor, however, had minced no words. When he announced that he would defend New Mexico, in person if necessary, no one doubted it.

When Taylor died, the preparations for war continued in Texas, and Southern congressmen and senators as well as Texans hoped the new president might be less resolute. On 6 August, however, Millard Fillmore stated with equal clarity that Taylor's policy had not changed. Fillmore, too, believed that New Mexico belonged to the United States, and he was prepared to defend the area with military force. The ordering of 750 additional troops to Santa Fe left no doubt that he would be as firm as his predecessor. This, rather than any verbal support or manipulation of the patronage, was probably Millard Fillmore's greatest contribution to sectional peace in 1850. Salmon P. Chase was certain that Fillmore's strong message, coupled with the request for a Texas indemnity, had changed at least six Northern votes.[41]

Wisely from their point of view, the Texas bondholders and their lobbyists left no records of their financial dealings, if such existed, with individual members of Congress—except for Corcoran's gift to Webster. The historian who considers the compromise a noble achievement can only conclude that if unworthy efforts were indeed made, they helped achieve a worthy result. If religious, he may conclude further that the Lord really does move in mysterious ways his wonders to perform.

Was Taylor the slaveholder persuaded to take a stance inimical to the best interests of the South and his own fortunes? Did he decide that slavery was wrong in principle and should be contained for moral or philosophical reasons? Was he really influenced by William Henry Seward? Was he a traitor to his own section? Did he sacrifice the personal interests of a slaveholder for a higher patriotism—namely, the defense of the Union and the principle of self-determination for California and New Mexico? Or was Zachary Taylor and not John C. Calhoun the true defender of southern slavery and the South's right to preserve it for as long as it might be profitable or otherwise desirable? Who was the realist—Taylor or Calhoun? If the South had accepted the fact, as Taylor did, that slavery could not expand and that all such demands only served to strengthen the small antislavery movement in the North, would there have been the Emancipation Proclamation in 1863 and the Thirteenth Amendment in 1865? In 1860, Abraham Lincoln would argue that a legal containment of slavery within its existing borders would quiet Northern fears and end the Northern attack upon which Southern extremism fed. This in turn, he predicted, would bring about a peaceful situation that would give the South full control of its own future destiny. Even after the angry quarrels of the 1850s and the actual secession of seven slaveholding states, the remaining members of Congress, just before the Battle of Fort Sumter, would approve by the required two-thirds majority, a thirteenth amendment that denied Congress in perpetuity the right to tamper with Southern slavery.

The question naturally arises as to why Americans could compromise much more pressing, concrete issues in 1850 but could find no common ground in 1860–61? The answer probably lies in the question. In 1850 a specific state, specific territories, and specific laws with regard to slavery, fugitive slaves, and the slave trade were involved. Logrolling and trading were possible because concrete, clearly discernible conflicting actions would result. In 1860, no specific territories were at issue at all. In 1860 the Southern fire-eaters demanded federal protection for slavery in all territories but would have been at a loss to name a single territory where they might expect the protection to be applied. Also, in 1850 the quarrels were still limited largely to politicians and editors. The great mass of the population, North and South, had not yet become emotionally involved in the struggle. The repeal of the Missouri Compromise and the Dred Scott decision denying any federal or territorial restrictions on slavery in the territories had not yet occurred, and ordinary Northerners everywhere had as yet no reason to fear that the South was determined to spread slavery everywhere. John Brown had not yet terrified white Southerners with his threat of a war to the death between the black and the white races. Perhaps ironically, each crisis occurred in a year of great national prosperity.

Significantly enough, in the light of later interpretations arguing that economic differences caused the Civil War, the debates of 1850 involved no serious conflict over tariffs or any other economic matters. John C. Calhoun charged that Northern domination of economic policies was partially responsible for the relative Northern preponderance in population growth, but nobody else supported the claim. The Walker Tariff, passed during the Polk administration, had virtually eliminated tariffs on all products except luxuries, and it had received overwhelming Southern support. If economic policies were ultimately a point of contention severe enough to be a major cause of secession and war, few, if any, political leaders of either section thought so in 1850. Clay and Webster, the great leaders of compromise throughout the debates, were lifelong advocates of the economic policies that the South had effectively stifled with scattered support from the Northeast and the Northwest.

While most of the nation rejoiced over the Compromise of 1850, the South Carolina delegation and its favorite newspaper remained a discordant note. On 21 September 1850 "A Daughter of Carolina," writing in the *Mercury*, sounded the tocsin: "Tamely you submit to the advances of Northern aggression, and humbly kiss the hand that strikes. Be up and doing. . . . Remember you are defending your altars, your homes and your sacred honor. . . . Let your watchword be the *South and her rights*, or *do or die!*" And equally ominous were the words of "Hampstead" in the same journal five days later: "The Rubicon is passed—the Executive mandate has gone forth, degrading the South from her equality in this Union. The odious, the iniquitous measures, conceived and brought forward in the Senate by the Omnibus bill of Mr. CLAY, have been consummated, and the Southern States are now vassals in this Confederacy."[42]

12

★ ★ ★ ★ ★

THE NATION'S LEADER

"The long agony is over," wrote Fillmore to Hamilton Fish on 9 September. "I have just approved and signed bills settling the disputed boundary between Texas & New Mexico & Utah. Though these several acts are not in all respects what I would have desired, yet, I am rejoiced at their passage, and trust they will restore harmony and peace to our distracted country."[1]

Fillmore's first two months in office had indeed given him very little peace of mind. In addition to the constant political pressures, he had received several crank letters, either threatening his life or warning about threats from others. No president had been assassinated yet, although a young man had tried to shoot Andrew Jackson from three feet away. In what experts called a ballistics miracle, the pistols had misfired and thereby added to Old Hickory's supernatural legend. The idea that the chief executive needed organized protection lay in the future. Fillmore, like Taylor, walked the streets and received uninvited guests unguarded. Whether or not the threats disturbed him, he would have been foolish to ignore them entirely.

Only two days after Taylor's death, an anonymous writer felt "a most solemn duty owing to my country to acquaint you with the facts which I know for certain, that Zachary Taylor . . . died an unnatural death by poison administered to him by a secular Coadjutor of the *Jesuits*." This charge was obviously aimed at Seward, who as governor of New York had been friendly with the New York Catholic leadership. Another letter from "a rustica ofellus," urged

Fillmore to take extra precautions and asked: "How did the Union know what Gen'l T. ate at dinner? How easy was it to get into the Prest's House while the Prest. was listening to Foote's foolish & invidious speech, & poison his food?"[2]

"A True Deaf and Dumb Yankee" found a supernatural coincidence between the deaths of Harrison and Taylor and urged Fillmore to save the country by appointing Thurlow Weed to his cabinet. Fillmore probably felt that the writer had designated himself properly. On 20 July, "E Pluribus Unum" was far more sinister: "The interest of the South demands your immolation—the first step you take contrary to that interest will be your death warrant. There are vigilant eyes upon your every movement and strong unflinching hands will be extended around you. Unless your course of action be vastly different from what is expected before the 25th of September 1850 the dream of Millard Fillmore will be over. The poisoned cup— the bullet and the dagger are in readiness." A few days later, L. Jones of Louisville, Kentucky, in a long, rambling letter, insisted from divine prophecy that Fillmore must resign to save his own life and the peace of the country.[3]

On 29 July, another anonymous correspondent warned that a "Society of Constitutional Vindications composed of high respectability & determined character . . . never to exceed 40" was planning to "assassinate abolitionists and freesoilers, including Corwin, Hale, Seward, Giddings, and others." Two weeks later, still another anonymous correspondent warned that a band of Southern assassins was determined to keep California out of the Union and that Fillmore would be first on the list. Two days later, "a Friend" repeated the belief that Taylor had been poisoned and warned Fillmore to watch his food and drink carefully. One Andrew B. Smolniker, styling himself the "Apostle of the Dispensation of the Fulness of Judgement of God to Millard Fillmore," sent nine pages of prophecies and warnings "delivered in Christ's name by me," predicting that Fillmore would die in office if he signed the fugitive-slave bill. A few days later, Smolniker added another ten pages of equally pointed reasoning. Like Smolniker, "a Lady who thought better things of a New Yorker," believed that Fillmore deserved death as a punishment for having signed the fugitive-slave law, but she expected God to perform the task.[4] The Reverend John Baldwin, a Union Baptist minister from Lytleville, Illinois, saw the danger from another direction. The country was being ruled by "furriners," and he wanted "the hed of this great Republick & as a humble sirvent of the Lord" to know "thar out to be a amendment . . . thar is no furriner out to be allowed to live under the starres and Stripes of liberty without being compeled to support its Laws and Constitution."[5]

Far more time-consuming than the crank letters were the dozens of appeals that the president continued to receive from people wanting jobs, loans, or favors. Such requests, of course, are a trivial part of United States history, but they do say something about the American character of the 1850s and the attitude of the citizenry toward its leaders. Misses Juliann Simonis of Bethlehem, Pennsylvania, wanted money for a divorce. Her husband had "a Buse towordes me . . . has kept with Misses Hill, a wife of James Hill, for three years stedy," who "brought forth a child." The community had driven him out of town, but poor Juliann remained off-limits to future prospects because she couldn't afford a divorce. Josiah Meiles had written a new spelling book and, having "that affection for it that a Mother has for her first born," hoped Fillmore would write a testimonial for it. Elenor Marden, a widow, named her newborn son after Fillmore and inquired: "How can you like to give my boy money. How much do you give him?" Numerous ladies wanted jobs for their husbands or loans to help them start businesses in order to feed their starving children. Abijah and Wilford Sims wrote that while they could save the money to go to California in two years, the gold might be all gone by then. Could Fillmore make them a loan? Without specifying the crime, Judson Digges pleaded with Fillmore to pardon Digges's daughter Cordelia before she reached the penitentiary. J. R. Sprague of Mount Vernon, Ohio, felt entitled to special consideration because his wife had just produced triplets: "I thought that I would wright A few lines to you And see If the Government wood not give them sum land." His family now totaled seven children, and he was very poor. A. D. Chalmer, M. D., wanted Fillmore to support his new "Female Medical College . . . chartered by the State of Penna, for the physical improvement of *females*, so that the evils and diseases which the sex are liable to from exposure, thro' an ignorance of the delicate machinery of their systems, may be thus prevented or avoided."[6]

Fillmore apparently read his mail and often answered it personally. He assured numerous supplicants that he could not loan them money because he himself was having to borrow. On 27 July 1850 he wrote George Cottingham that unfortunately, before he had received Cottingham's application to be a porter at the White House, he had already agreed to keep the incumbent. In September 1850, Fillmore thanked Dorothea Dix for a picture of her latest mental hospital: "Wealth and power never reared such monuments to selfish pride as you had reared to the love of mankind." Her name would endure when "the Pyramids themselves shall be scattered to the winds." Two weeks later, when her bill for the relief of the insane failed to pass Congress, Fillmore expressed his deep regret and urged Miss Dix to avoid despair and keep trying.[7]

In October 1850 Fillmore asked Zachary Taylor's son-in-law Colonel Bliss to write a sketch of Taylor for a French publication and offered him all available papers, documents, and sources: "The veneration which I feel for his illustrious memory and the desire that his fame shall not suffer in Europe induced me to hope that you will undertake the task, for if you do I know it will be well done."[8]

Perhaps the best part of being president for Fillmore was the fact that he and Abigail would no longer be separated by a housing problem. Also, with his daughter, Mary Abigail, as official hostess, Fillmore was prepared to carry out his presidential social duties in proper fashion. An inventory of wines "belonging to Hon. Millard Fillmore and in the White House, July 30, 1850," included 642 bottles and 32 varieties and listed 198 quarts of champagne, 58 pints of champagne, and 110 quarts of old Pale sherry. A White House formal dinner menu on 22 August 1850, when the House debate on the Texas boundary was at its climax, included mock turtle soup, broiled rockfish with butter sauce, corn with macaroni, young ducks with brown sauce, fricassee of chicken, lamb cutlet with green peas, young pigeons with olives, croquette of chicken, larded sweetbreads with mushrooms, fillet of veal with spinach, and roast chicken with salad. Desserts included charlotte russe, blanc mange, Madeira jelly, and vanilla ice cream and were followed by fruits, coffee, and liqueurs. Six pairs of white gloves were ordered especially for the waiters. The son of a desperately poor tenant farmer had come a long way.[9]

The White House staff in 1850 consisted of twelve servants, half "colored" and half white. The top monthly salary of twenty-five dollars went to the white steward, Ignatius Ruppert. The black cook, Benjamin Quarles, and the white doorkeeper, Edward McManus, each received twenty dollars. The black coachman, waiter, fireman, hall maid, and washwoman received sixteen, twelve, ten, six, and five dollars respectively. The white housekeeper, chambermaid, and laundress received ten, seven, and six and one-half dollars each. The white messenger received fifteen dollars. Racial discrimination in the matter of wages was apparently minimal if it existed at all. The total monthly outlay for servants was $152.50.[10]

To his credit, the president had not forgotten his early days or those who had shared them. "As I can not give offices to my relatives, I have concluded to give them lands," he instructed his son

Millard. "Make a deed of all the lands I have in Saginaw Co., Michigan . . . to Calvin F. Fillmore & Olin A. Johnson. For a nominal consideration as tenants in common. . . . The same to Charles D. Fillmore for 160 acres in Arkansas."[11]

If Millard Fillmore enjoyed his official duties at all, it was probably in the role of high priest for progress and prosperity. The overwhelming popularity of the compromise apparently indicated that for most Americans during the 1850s, getting ahead economically was more important than the arguments over the extension of slavery or the recapture of fugitives. Fillmore had always believed fervently in Henry Clay's American System of tariffs, federally supported banks and internal improvements, and benevolent paternalism toward business in general; and even though most of these issues were relatively dead in 1850, the spirit of Whiggery fit perfectly with the technological and industrial progress being achieved without the assistance of the government. The new order of peace and prosperity, however temporary the peace might be, was symbolized in late 1850 by the gift to Mrs. Fillmore of a magnificent coach and team of horses by the president's New York City business friends who were grateful for the compromise that had saved their profitable business ties with the South. The outfit cost $1,500, and no one suggested any impropriety in the gift.[12]

In September 1850 Fillmore urged Congress to consider subsidizing a transcontinental railroad, and while the actual process did not begin for several more years, the idea had been firmly planted. Perhaps ironically, the most important economic measure passed during Fillmore's term was a bill, sponsored by the Democrat Stephen A. Douglas and firmly supported by Fillmore, to subsidize with land grants the building of an Illinois Central Railroad from Chicago to Mobile, Alabama. A few canals, including the extremely important Sault Ste. Marie system connecting Lake Superior with the other Great Lakes, were authorized, but no tariff or banking bills were even debated during the Taylor and Fillmore presidencies.[13]

When the Erie Railroad was completed in 1851, Fillmore and his cabinet, along with other leaders from both parties, donned top hats and formal dress suits and rode the train on its maiden voyage from New York City to Dunkirk, N.Y., on Lake Erie. Smoke drifted through the open windows and kept the passengers busy dodging hot ashes, but it was all a gala affair, dedicated to sectional peace. At numerous stops along the way, Fillmore stood on the rear platform and urged large audiences to accept the compromise, because prosperity and progress required sectional harmony. In September

1851 he helped celebrate the opening of still more railroads in New England, where he repeated the same theme. His Southern cabinet members were prominently displayed on the Erie tour, and in New England only Conrad and Stuart, his ministers from the deep South, accompanied him. As Robert Rayback has pointed out, it was like putting them on exhibition so that radical New Englanders could see that Southerners were ordinary human beings after all.[14]

In November 1851 Fillmore was the star attraction at a magnificent celebration in Newport, Rhode Island, gathered to commemorate the completion of railroads connecting Canada with Massachusetts and the Great Lakes with the Atlantic Ocean, as well as the launching of a steamship line between New England and Liverpool, England. The fireworks and the feasting exalted the America that had enabled a humble farm boy to rise from poverty to the wealth and position he loved, as well as to the power and responsibility he would happily have avoided. Like Abraham Lincoln, Millard Fillmore gloried in the nation that offered so many blessings to so many and dreamed of a future in which the curse of slavery, with the help of Providence, would somehow eventually disappear by itself. Meanwhile, disunion was to be avoided, even though obedience to the Constitution required him to enforce the fugitive-slave laws.[15]

And the new fugitive-slave law would neither go away nor stop plaguing Fillmore's conscience. He had delayed signing the bill as long as he could. He knew that the denunciations of Webster throughout the Northeast would be repeated against himself. Fillmore did not like the bill, but it was clearly a necessary part of the compromise. Indeed, it was the only thing the Southerners had gained, even though they had surrendered nothing they could have used anyhow. Ultimately, Fillmore took refuge in his oath to uphold the Constitution and the laws of Congress. The Constitution, even without the law, called for the return of fugitives, and therefore gave him but little choice. Many Northern editors, politicians, and ministers denied the constitutionality of the act because it provided no jury trial for the escapees. Attorney General Crittenden argued otherwise, however, and Fillmore ultimately signed the act without consulting the other members of his cabinet.[16]

In his annual message to Congress on 2 December 1850, Fillmore promised that the Constitution would be his guide: "The powers conferred upon the Government and their distribution to the several departments are as clearly expressed in that sacred instrument as the imperfection of human language will allow, and I deem it my first duty not to question its wisdom, add to its provisions, evade its requirements, or nullify its commands. . . . In a government like ours, in which all laws are passed by a majority of the representatives of the people, and those representatives are chosen for such short periods that any injurious or obnoxious law can very soon be repealed," resistance to the laws would appear unlikely. Those who would violate the laws should remember that "without law there can be no real practical liberty; that when law is trampled underfoot tyranny rules, whether it appears in the form of a military despotism or popular violence." As for the compromise measures, no one should have expected them to bring immediate satisfaction to "people and States heated by the exciting controversies of their representatives." They were necessary, however, "to allay asperities and animosities that were rapidly alienating one section of the country from another and destroying those fraternal sentiments which are the strongest supports of the Constitution." Fillmore regarded the compromise measures as "a final settlement of the dangerous and exciting subjects which they embraced." Obviously, "none of those measures was free from imperfections, but in their mutual dependence and connection they formed a system of compromise the most conciliatory and best for the entire country that could be obtained from conflicting sectional interests and opinions." For this reason he would recommend "adherence to the adjustment established by those measures until time and experience shall demonstrate the necessity of further legislation to guard against evasion or abuse."[17]

On the surface at least, the compromise generated enormous enthusiasm throughout the North, but there were notable exceptions in the form of well-attended meetings and demonstrations against the new fugitive-slave law. Aware of this, the Southerners were preparing for political conventions and their 1851 elections, and fire-eaters everywhere were denouncing the compromise and demanding secession. Union sentiment among Southerners was still in the majority, but any serious display of bad faith in the North could change this quickly. In particular, many Southern eyes were turned toward New York, where the apostle of the "higher law," William H. Seward, could be expected to work against popular acceptance of the compromise.

For the moment, the compromise had made Fillmore extremely popular in both sections, and if a presidential election had been held in 1851, he would have been a strong favorite. Not only were Seward's presidential hopes in limbo; he and Weed faced the likelihood of having an unfriendly president control the New York patronage for the next six years. Expecting Fillmore to act as they would have under similar circumstances, Seward and Weed were filled with despair, and Fillmore, knowing this, must have enjoyed a pardonable degree of exultation. Only a few weeks earlier, Governor Fish had expressed regret that he could not retain a friend of Vice-President Fillmore's in a state office. In similar language, Fillmore now explained that he had no authority to grant Fish's request that he appoint Richard Fenimore Cooper, a son of the famous novelist, to West Point. In practice, however, for the first three months of his presidency, Fillmore removed only one of Weed's appointees. The deepest point of Fillmore's own humiliation had been the appointment of Weed's friend Levi Allen to the collectorship of Fillmore's hometown of Buffalo, and this insult he erased immediately by discharging Allen. Otherwise, the president hoped to make peace and gain New York's formal support for the compromise. When Seward asked Fillmore to get his son's military leave extended, Fillmore was happy to answer that General Scott had already done so.[18]

Weed and Seward, however, knew that the existing Whig party would never make Seward president. It would have to be reshaped into a free-soil instrument headed by Seward, even if this should require the creation of a new party. As a first step, they would persuade the New York Whig party to repudiate the compromise. Fillmore was riding a crest of national popularity, but perhaps they could cut him down by making his position appear synonymous with support for slavery. Seward's most careful biographer, Glyndon G. Van Deusen, stressed the New Yorker's genuine moral opposition to slavery, although Van Deusen admitted that Seward's ardor sometimes varied with the political circumstances.[19] Seward's dedication to abolition and to protection of the freedmen is not borne out by his subsequent career in the cabinets of Lincoln and Andrew Johnson.

The New York Whigs had already scheduled their state nominating convention at Syracuse, and the results would be an announcement of the party's attitudes toward slavery, the South, and the compromise. New York political conventions were heavily attended and were usually raucous versions of national conventions on a slightly smaller scale. The head of the New York City delegation, Daniel Ullman, arrived with instructions from Fillmore to do everything possible to avoid any controversy with Weed and Seward and to make every effort to achieve results that would show New York's willingness to abandon antislavery agitation in favor of national harmony. William Duer, the congressman from Oswego, came from

Washington with similar direct orders from Fillmore. The convention should show that New York's Whigs did not support Seward's "higher law" doctrine.[20]

At first, the convention went well for the president's objectives. Fillmore's lieutenant, the silver-haired Francis Granger, was elected chairman. Washington Hunt, who was also supported by Fillmore, won the nomination for governor. The remaining nominations for state office were approved by both sides. Then Duer, chairman of the Committee on Resolutions, introduced a statement that New York's Whigs "acquiesced in the creation of territorial governments for New Mexico and Utah in the confident belief that these acts will result in the exclusion of slavery from the territory ceded by Mexico to the United States." The wording tactfully accepted the compromise while assuring the free-soilers that slavery had been checked. At this point, the harmony disappeared. A Sewardite offered two substitute resolutions. Because the territorial governments for New Mexico and Utah did not bar slavery but assumed that nature would do so, Congress should formally prohibit slavery in those territories "on the first indication" that slavery might be possible. Seward should receive the "thanks of the Whig Party" for representing the views of New York in the Senate.

After a long day of bitter argument, the substitute resolutions passed, and Fillmore's friends, headed by Granger, marched out of the convention. Weed had rejected Fillmore's peaceful overtures and had thrown down the gauntlet. The president's "Silver Greys," named after Granger's long hair, would have to fight.

Granger's followers included a large contingent representing New York City businessmen who were eager for both sectional peace and increased profits from their Southern trade. This group, however, was divided as to strategy. Some wanted to follow Fillmore's lead and try to regain the confidence of their Southern customers by supporting the administration. Others, including several leading merchants, wanted a new party organized around the compromise supporters in both of the existing major parties. All were united in a desire for revenge against Weed and Seward. Within a few hours, the Silver Greys reconvened and called another state convention to meet at Utica on 17 October.

Fillmore was determined to keep the New York Whig party united without endangering the compromise, and he accomplished this goal with some masterly political strokes. He discharged the postmaster at Albany, as a reminder to Weed's followers that he, not Weed, had control of their jobs. Fillmore then instructed his friends to nominate Washington Hunt again at their new convention. Others, at his behest, pleaded with the New Yorkers not to start a new party and induced some sixty wealthy merchants to donate large sums of money to the task of generating public support for the compromise.

At Utica, the convention of the Silver Greys kept the party intact by renominating Hunt, who endorsed the compromise but suggested modifications in the Fugitive Slave Act. This was acceptable to most of the delegates, but the New York merchants were still not entirely satisfied with Hunt. Ten thousand merchants signed a call for a giant union meeting at Castle Garden to approve the peace measures and work against "the further progress of political agitation in the north." Only the influence of Fillmore and his friends kept this meeting from launching a new party. One faction of the merchants printed a "Union Ticket" and filled the newspapers with appeals urging Whigs to vote for the Democratic nominee for governor instead of Hunt.

On election day, Hunt won by only 300 votes, and Horatio Seymour, the Democratic candidate, carried New York City by 962 votes. However, the Whig Union candidate for lieutenant governor had received a majority of 4,437 votes in the city. Southerners viewed this as a defeat for Sewardism, and New York's business elite happily looked forward to a profitable expansion of their Southern markets. At Castle Garden, James W. Gerard denounced the abolitionists and avowed that nature had created a barrier against slavery extension stronger than ten thousand Wilmots could draw. More than one hundred leading merchants organized themselves into the Union Safety Committee and agreed to give time, energy, and money to popularize the compromise and work for national unity. Fillmore had defeated Weed and Seward in New York, at least for the moment.[21]

The news from other parts of the country was equally encouraging for those hoping for national peace. Conventions supporting the Union in Boston and Philadelphia attracted thousands of people and passed resolutions of unity similar to those in New York. Leading Whigs and Democrats addressed great Union crowds in almost every state. The Kentucky legislature gave the dying Clay a magnificent public reception where he spoke eloquently enough to draw tears from some of his oldest and most bitter enemies. Texas accepted the new boundaries and the proffered money with remarkable tranquility. In South Carolina, extremists like Robert Barnwell Rhett and William L. Yancey delivered fire-and-brimstone appeals for secession, but only a minority listened. The Nashville convention held its second session in November, but only a few delegates came, and the proceedings attracted minimal attention. Delegates made fiery speeches to each other, but the overall impact was negligible.[22]

Seward and Weed, however, were not yet ready to surrender. If they could undermine Fillmore by stirring up sectional animosities, they would continue to do so. Fillmore's success in helping to elect Unionist candidates in New York's 1850 elections had left them wounded but still very much alive. For whatever reasons, either idealistic or cynical or both, they now demanded an immediate modification of the fugitive-slave act to eliminate the possibility that a legally free man might be returned illegally to slavery. It was a popular issue because many Northern Whigs supported the compromise on principle, even though they disliked being linked with slaveholders in support of the fugitive-slave law. Modification could enable moderate Whigs to support the compromise while still maintaining their ties with the more vocal and more dedicated opponents of slavery within the party.

Fillmore recognized all of this and privately expressed agreement that perhaps the law should be modified "to secure the free blacks from such an abuse of the object of the law, and that done we at the North have no just cause of complaint." In 1850, however, the threat to the Union came from the South, not from the North. In his annual message to Congress on 2 December 1850, therefore, Fillmore had contented himself with a suggestion that no change should be made in the law "until time and experience shall demonstrate the necessity of further legislation to guard against evasion or abuse."[23]

In New York meanwhile, Weed had reached agreements with the Democrats who controlled the state's canal board, whereby Fillmore's Silver Greys who supported the compromise would be replaced by Weed's followers in all of the canal's offices. In return, he promised that the Whig governor would be generous with the Barnburners in making other appointments. New York City's important offices, however, were still controlled by the president, and in late 1850, both Governor-elect Hunt and retiring Governor Fish wrote Fillmore eloquent appeals for party harmony and peace between Fillmore and Weed. The New York legislator Samuel P. Lyman came to Washington bearing the olive branch. He assured Fillmore and the cabinet that Weed's hostility to the administration rested entirely upon a fear that his friends would lose their jobs, particularly in the New York custom house. Hugh Maxwell and former governor John Young were Weed's foremost enemies in the custom house. If Fillmore would discharge them or have them take orders from Weed's friends Moses Grinnell and Robert B. Minturn, Weed would consider selling his newspaper. As a show of good faith, Weed's *Evening Journal* praised Fillmore's annual message to Congress.

Fillmore met Weed's overtures with equal shrewdness. He replied that he could not discharge Maxwell or Young but that he had no desire to remove anyone else from office, whether they supported Weed or himself. Fillmore would reinstate one of Weed's friends whom Maxwell had removed. Maxwell, meanwhile, was commissioned to test Weed's sincerity by offering to buy the *Evening Journal*. Praising Fillmore's message had by implication put Weed on record in support of the president's position against the immediate modification of the fugitive-slave law, and Fillmore now moved to test the editor's sincerity and, if possible, get the New York Whig party to support the law also. He instructed Assemblyman J. B. Varnum to announce that he, Varnum, would offer a legislative resolution against any immediate change in the law. At this point, all pretense ended. Weed attacked the idea and again became an open enemy.[24]

Because the resolution had no chance for passage, Fillmore's friends resolved to accomplish the same objective by getting the legislature to elect a Fillmore man to the United States Senate. The logical Whig candidate was former governor Hamilton Fish, who was subservient to Weed but wanted the Senate seat badly enough to deceive Fillmore in order to get his support. In several exchanges of letters, Fish avoided a specific endorsement of Fillmore's formula "when time and experience demonstrate the need," but he expressed full agreement with the president's interpretation of the country's need for harmony.

Meanwhile, the Union Safety Committee of New York, composed of wealthy merchants dedicated to the preservation of the compromise, demanded a statement from Fish. When Fish failed to respond, these men, assuring everyone that it was Fillmore's wish, threw their support to the Democratic incumbent, Daniel S. Dickinson. Fillmore was reluctant to oppose the compromise's strongest advocates, but he knew that he and his supporters would be blamed for the defeat of Fish and that this would leave Seward and Weed in full control of the Whig party. Fillmore therefore urged his supporters in the legislature to vote for Fish, and after more than a month of stalemate, Fish was elected by a single vote. Weed now charged that the election was a repudiation of both Fillmore and the compromise, but Fillmore published letters showing that he had supported Fish all along and that Weed was making untrue statements for strictly political objectives. At this point, Fillmore finally decided that peace was impossible and ordered a general housecleaning of Weed's friends holding federal offices.[25]

Meanwhile, just as New York was considered a Northern bellwether, all eyes in the South were on Georgia. Governor George W. P. Towns had called a state convention to meet on 10 December, but Cobb, Toombs, and Stephens spoke for the compromise in every district, while Toombs published a widely distributed pamphlet in its favor. Various radical newspapers made secession sound like a possibility, but on election day, some seventy thousand voters chose an overwhelming majority of Union delegates. The convention expressed Georgia's devotion to the Union and to the compromise, but it also added that the state would resist, to the point of secession, the abolition of slavery in the District of Columbia without the consent of the slaveholders, any abolition of slavery on federal property within a slaveholding state, any refusal to admit any state or territory because it had chosen slavery, any federal act forbidding slavery in New Mexico or Utah, and any changes in the new fugitive-slave laws.[26]

The Union victory in Georgia heightened the courage of Southern unionists everywhere, and in most places, three groups were plainly visible. The fire-eaters, led by Robert Barnwell Rhett of South Carolina, Edmund Ruffin of Virginia, William L. Yancey of Alabama, and John A. Quitman of Mississippi, denounced the compromise and demanded immediate secession. They charged that the measure denied the South any rights in California, New Mexico, and Utah and that it had robbed Texas of a vast slave territory. Abolition of the slave trade in the District of Columbia, they warned, would pave the way for the abolition of the slave trade among the states.

At the opposite pole were the ultra-Unionists, led by Clay and Henry Foote, who had decided that the compromise as it had passed was not so bad after all. If climate and soil would permit, they argued, New Mexico and Utah might yet become slave states, but in any case, Southern honor had been upheld. Merchants, wealthy planters, and the nonslaveholding Southern hill people were at the center of this group. Many of them would ultimately oppose secession and be designated as scalawags during Reconstruction.

The largest number of Southerners apparently believed that Southern rights and the Union could be reconciled, but only by mutual efforts. They would accept the compromise, but only so long as the

North also honored every part of it. The Georgia resolutions reflected their views. If the North would enforce the new fugitive-slave laws and leave slavery alone where it existed, they would stand by the Union. Otherwise, they would secede.

The significance of these events was not lost on Millard Fillmore. The Union could be kept intact, but not if he should refuse to support every part of the compromise. Also, the evidence indicated that in both the North and the South a majority of the people wanted the compromise to succeed. The only part of the compromise that actually gave the South anything was the Fugitive Slave Act, and this would be the test of Northern intentions. A great many Northerners, however, had no intention of obeying it. Webster had been denounced widely as a fallen Ichabod for voting for it. The public meetings denouncing it had been much smaller than those praising the overall compromise, but they had been just as numerous and far more emotional. The enforcement of federal law begins in the White House, where the president selects the attorney general of the United States and is responsible for his actions. Millard Fillmore would have happily surrendered this power and responsibility, but it was inescapable.

The fugitive-slave law itself contained provisions unnecessarily irritating to Northern sensibilities without actually making its enforcement any easier. Several opponents of the measure had argued that existing laws provided the same legal basis for federal action to recover runaways but contained none of the emotional firebrands of the new legislation. The recent act did not provide any jury trial for fugitives, although the Constitution provided that in suits where the value exceeded twenty dollars, a jury should make the decision. The alleged owner was required to take the fugitive to a federal commissioner, who would listen to the evidence and decide if the claim was legal. If the commissioner ruled in favor of the slaveholder, his fee was ten dollars. If he found that a mistake had been made, the fee was only five dollars. No evidence exists to indicate that any commissioner ever put someone back into slavery just to earn an extra five dollars, but the effect of this possibility upon the public mind was very serious. And finally, the marshals or deputies responsible for the arrest of a fugitive could be fined one thousand dollars if they refused to do their duty. They could summon all citizens to their aid, and any person guilty of concealing a fugitive could be fined one thousand dollars, imprisoned for six months, and assessed one thousand dollars in civil damages for every slave involved. The original bill had provided a jury trial back in the slaveholder's home district, but this principle had been defeated. This process rarely, if ever, would have brought freedom to the fugitive, but it would have at least kept the issue clearly within the bounds of the federal Constitution.[27]

Most Northerners were ready to accept the fugitive-slave law and get on with the business of economic development, expansion, and progress, but the practical aspect of the problem had to be confronted. The runaway slave seeking freedom from the control of a master, whether kind or cruel, appealed to the sensitivities of thousands of Americans for whom slavery as a Southern institution was easy to ignore. In most Northern states the free blacks suffered from many of the disabilities and discriminations that would eventually be called "Jim Crow" when later enacted into law by the so-called New South of the 1890s. Still, however, in at least a few Northern cities and towns, there were long-time black refugees who had won the respect and sympathy of white communities by their industry and exemplary behavior. Many blacks had long basked in the protection afforded by state "liberty laws," which forbade state officials to cooperate in capturing them and returning them to slavery. Now, however, federal officials would come looking for runaways, and anyone helping them would be subject to severe punishments.[28]

All over the North, religious presses joined with abolition sheets to denounce the new act as immoral, undemocratic, unchristian, and unconstitutional. People who had never seen a slave and had no wish whatever to have Afro-American fugitives living in their midst were nonetheless ready to defy a law that would prevent their helping an innocent fugitive on his way to the safety of Canada. Others were ready to expand the so-called Underground Railroad into an efficient network for getting fugitives from city to city. Ironically, while the fate of any single slave cannot be regarded as unimportant, the numbers involved did not justify the hue and cry in both sections. Also, the border states from which most of the fugitives escaped remained relatively quiet, while the deep Southern states from which an effective escape was almost impossible remained in a constant uproar. Conversely, the fury against the bill was greatest in the Northern states farthest away from the border. With a very few notable exceptions, most people in Pennsylvania and the Ohio River states obeyed the law and either helped or acquiesced in the return of fugitives, while many citizens in New England, Wisconsin, and Michigan acted as though they were being invaded daily by swarms of unscrupulous slave catchers. In a few cases, citizens of a community where a long-time resident was suddenly taken captive simply collected enough money to buy his freedom. In others, angry crowds pressured the commissioner into making an adverse ruling. A few spectacular cases stirred up intense feelings in both sections. The incidents were few in number and did not really indicate any mass resistance to the law, but both sections interpreted them as typical, whether or not the fugitive was returned to slavery, judged to be free, or simply protected from capture.[29]

Perhaps even more important, the symbolic moral condemnation of the South that was implied every time a fugitive was helped was further intensified by the well-publicized speeches, sermons, editorials, and pamphlets damning the law. Cassius M. Clay of Kentucky, the son of a slaveholder, had been converted to abolitionism at Yale when he had attended a lecture by William Lloyd Garrison. In 1850 Clay had run unsuccessfully for governor on an antislavery platform, and he now denounced the Fugitive Slave Act throughout the state. Most of the great New England literati, like Ralph Waldo Emerson, James Russell Lowell, James Greenleaf Whittier, and Henry Wadsworth Longfellow, vied for attention with ringing denunciations of their fallen idol, Daniel Webster, for having supported the act. In Massachusetts, an antislavery Democrat, George S. Boutwell, was elected governor. Robert Rantoul ran for Congress on a platform denouncing the law and was later chosen to finish the unexpired term of Webster in the Senate after the latter became secretary of state. Perhaps most significant for the future, the legislature elected Charles Sumner, the eloquent and fanatical spokesman for the "conscience" Whigs, to the open six-year term in the United States Senate.[30]

Millard Fillmore faced hard choices. He had helped promote the compromise that had produced the fugitive-slave act, and its enforcement was now his constitutional responsibility. In the case of *Prigg* v. *Pennsylvania*, the Supreme Court had already placed the responsibility for recovering fugitive slaves on the shoulders of the federal government, and the new teeth in the law of 1850 made this burden inescapable. The Constitution and the laws forbade actions by either state or local government and by individuals that would help a slave escape or hinder a master's effort to recover his property. Opposition to these restrictions was based entirely upon the higher law of man's conscience and the laws of God as seen by the individuals involved. The president, however, had sworn an oath to support the Constitution, and he was dedicated to the preservation of the Union.

In October 1850, within weeks after the act had been passed, the first challenge came. Attempting to hold a captured fugitive against a mob, a marshal in Pennsylvania tried to invoke the new law by enlisting a posse from the local citizenry. Instead, the crowd broke into the temporary jail and rescued the fugitive. Two Pennsylvania judges, Robert C. Grier and John Kane, asked the president for a general order authorizing the use of federal troops in all such crises. Fillmore was reluctant to use troops, but he recognized that anything less might prove totally ineffective. He was not concerned for the slaveholders, but he did fear that any failure to enforce the law would strengthen the Southern secessionists. He would, as he wrote Webster, "admit no right of *nullification* North or South." Crittenden and Webster were absent from Washington, but the remainder of Fillmore's cabinet agreed unanimously that he had both the power and the duty to use military force in support of civil authorities trying to enforce the law. After painful soul-searching, Fillmore instructed the marine commander at Philadelphia to assist the marshal or deputy if he was supported by a federal judge. Hoping that it would prevent rather than cause trouble, he announced that all marshals and commissioners would have the same support when needed. "God knows," he wrote Webster, "that I detest slavery, but it is an existing evil, for which we are not responsible, and we must endure it, and give it such protection as is guaranteed by the constitution, till we can get rid of it without destroying the last hope of free government in the world." He would avoid the use of military force if possible, "not doubting that there is yet patriotism enough left in every State north of Mason's and Dixon's line to maintain the supremacy of the laws; and being particularly anxious that no state should be disgraced, by being compelled to resort to the army to support the laws of the Union." He would use force only as a last resort, but if necessary, he would "bring the whole force of the government to sustain the law."[31]

Two years earlier, William and Ellen Craft had ridden trains openly from Georgia to Boston, with the light-skinned wife disguised as a young planter with a broken arm that exempted her from signing hotel registers and with her husband assuming the not-uncommon role of a dutiful slave. In October 1850 their masters, armed with the new law, sent two slave catchers to Boston to recover the Crafts. Led by Theodore Parker and Wendell Phillips, the Boston abolitionists concealed the fugitives, organized a protest meeting against the fugitive act itself, and had the Southern agents arrested for defamation of character. Webster himself went to Boston to support the marshal, and Fillmore, with no other legal alternative, announced that he would use troops, if necessary, to enforce the law. At this point, the abolitionists put the Crafts on a ship bound for England, and the crisis as a practical matter had ended. Fillmore and Webster, however, were subjected to a torrent of abuse in both sections. The owner of the Crafts demanded that Fillmore discharge the Boston marshal for dereliction of duty, but Fillmore refused. The Crafts, incidentally, remained in England until after the Civil War; they were named honorary citizens of Lancashire as a show of support for the Union by the textile workers, despite the hardships caused by the "cotton famine." After the war, the Crafts happily returned to their native Georgia.[32]

In February 1851 a slave being examined by the Boston commissioner was freed by a crowd of free blacks who stormed the courtroom and made off with the fugitive. He was later spirited safely to Canada. Theodore Parker called the rescue the "noblest deed done in Boston since the destruction of the tea in 1773," but Southerners were furious. By this time the Congress was back in session, and Henry Clay and Henry Foote were particularly indignant because the government had allowed blacks to intimidate the white authorities. The short session was consumed almost entirely by arguments over the Boston affair and the fugitive-slave law. Numerous petitions for the repeal of the law or for softening its penalties were presented, but all were quickly tabled. A few petitions for strengthening the act got referred to a committee but went no further. Seward and others complained angrily about this discrimination in favor of the proslavery petitions.[33]

South Carolina's Butler was willing for all petitions on each side of the argument to go to a committee because "you might as well attempt to put a maniac asleep by lullabies as attempt to restrain agitation on this subject." Jefferson Davis, consistent as always, was perfectly willing for Northern states to nullify the fugitive-slave laws, because he believed in every state's right to nullify any law that it considered unconstitutional. While Seward denied that he was an agitator, John Hale of New Hampshire gloried in the title because "the first great agitator" was Jesus, the son of God and the founder of Christianity. In reply, Henry S. Foote saw "little of the true spirit of agitation in his noble sermon on the Mount; but a placid dignity, a gentle and effective persuasiveness, which one of your fierce and murdering agitators would find it difficult either to understand or to imitate." Hale continued by further identifying as agitators those who had overthrown kings in Europe and those among the American founding fathers who had started the Revolution. Unable to counter this thrust directly, Foote retreated a few thousand years to denounce the first agitator, Satan in the Garden of Eden, and to quote John Milton at length to show the ultimate fate of Satan. As others joined the discussion, Hale insisted that Satan was a seducer, rather than an agitator, and that the result of Satan's efforts was the enslavement of Adam and Eve and of all mankind in general. After several senators had finished parading their Biblical and Miltonian erudition, the petition in question was tabled.[34]

It was Henry Clay's final Senate session, and the old Kentuckian returned once more to an idea that he had first espoused some thirty years earlier. He agreed with Northern critics of the cruel foreign slave trade, and he advocated more help to British ships trying to suppress it, but he insisted that the only real solution to this problem and every other point at issue between the North and the South was colonization. Slaves and free blacks alike, according to Clay, should be returned to Africa, where they could be happy. This, in turn, would remove the real barrier between the North and the South. Suppressing the African slave trade by sending the slaves in the return direction was a novel solution, but Clay defended it eloquently and was supported by several others. Ultimately, both houses of Congress passed a bill providing funds for the "Relief of the American Colonization Society." The barbs in these debates were often punctuated by laughter, and the speeches lacked the menacing threats of the preceding session. Clearly, however, the slavery controversy was still alive and would need only another significant concrete issue to revive it.[35]

Millard Fillmore would prevent such an issue if he could. Under the caption "Noble Conduct of Mr. Fillmore," Henry Foote later wrote that after he had conferred with Henry Clay on the Boston episode, Clay had sent Foote to the White House to speak for both of them. Fillmore, he remembered, unhesitatingly assured Foote that he would "enforce the laws of the land at all hazards, and put down, with the whole power of the government, if need be, any illicit or violent attempt to counteract or overturn them." At Fillmore's suggestion, Foote also called upon Webster, who offered equally strong assurances.[36]

The president soon got more chances to put his brave words into action. Just before the elections of 1851, Edward and Dickerson Gorsuch—a slave owner and his son from Maryland—along with a local constable and a few others, went to a farm near Lancaster,

Pennsylvania, to recover a slave. A large group of free blacks, armed with guns and clubs, gathered to protect the fugitive. Two Quakers from the community pleaded with the whites to avoid a violent collision, and even the son begged his father to abandon the project, at least temporarily. The whites were outnumbered by at least fifty to ten, and the blacks were urging them to leave, but the elder Gorsuch opened fire. When the blacks responded in kind, Gorsuch was killed instantly, and his son was wounded, while the others fled to a safe spot already occupied by the constable before the firing had begun. Most of the state's newspapers denounced the killing of Gorsuch, and the two Quakers, along with some forty blacks, were arrested and charged with high treason for having levied war against the government of the United States. Perhaps fortunately for the Southern moderates and Unionists running for office, the defendants were still in jail on election day. Ultimately, however, with Thaddeus Stevens as one of the four defense attorneys, everyone charged was acquitted. The affair, however, caused the defeat of the antislavery governor, who before the event had been an overwhelming favorite for reelection. As before, Fillmore was able to give public support to the law without accomplishing the return of the slave or slaves in question.[37]

All of these events, of course, coincided with the Southern legislative and gubernatorial elections of 1851. Recognizing the popularity of the compromise in most of the slaveholding states, the fire-eaters targeted South Carolina, Mississippi, Alabama, and Georgia for their strongest efforts in the fall elections of 1851. As a result, in each of these states the old Whig-versus-Democrat rivalry gave way to a new alignment pitting the Southern-rights supporters against the Union party, with the older parties internally divided on this issue.

In South Carolina the state legislature, which was elected by a propertied franchise, cast the state's electoral vote for president. Because this had always denied the general population any participation in the country's most important national experience, the state's lack of emotional attachment to the Union was not surprising. South Carolina's aristocratic leaders, most of them Huguenots, Scotch-Irish, and Scotch Calvinists, were accustomed to ruling the state in their own way.

South Carolina had been one of the wealthiest, most independent, and least democratic colonies, and the transition to statehood had changed the political atmosphere but little. Its cotton and rice fields had been depleted by constant cultivation, however, and the competition of the new states to the west had brought a chronic decline in the area's formerly dominant economic position. In 1832 the Carolinians had blamed their troubles on the tariff and had threatened to secede unless their right to nullify the tariff should be recognized. The awesome threat of military force, led by the iron-willed Andrew Jackson, and a face-saving tariff reduction that for the first few years was more apparent than real led the Carolinians to declare a victory and abandon nullification, but their alienation from the Union had deepened. In 1846 the Walker Tariff had removed most of their grounds for complaint, but their statesmen, led by Calhoun, had continued to talk as if the long-since-abandoned 1828 Tariff of Abominations were still in effect. Alone among the states, South Carolina in 1850 was imbued with a self-contained national spirit and patriotism that extended no further than the Mason and Dixon line, if, indeed, it went beyond the state boundary itself.

Calhoun had reflected this feeling while doing much to shape it. He had denounced the Declaration of Independence and had insisted that the ancient Greek democracy, which enabled the intelligent and patriotic to rule while slaves did all the menial work, was the only true basis for any workable republic. Frustrated in his attempts to become president, Calhoun had developed a paranoid fixation against the North; had converted his own disappointments into dangers to the South; had ignored the Southern control of the White House, Senate, and Supreme Court; and had spent his final years trying to promote a Southern move for independence. The Mexican War and the acquisition of vast new territories over and beyond the new slave state of Texas had provided his final opportunity. The litany of Northern oppressions enumerated in his final address were largely imaginary, but his fellow South Carolinians, looking for simple answers to their state's economic decline, reading Charleston newspapers, and listening only to their idol, accepted them as gospel truth. For the nonslaveholding whites who might have responded more reasonably to more rational arguments, there was always the terrifying fact that they were heavily outnumbered by the black population. When Calhoun predicted that an abolition would occur and would be followed by race war and their own enslavement by the victorious blacks, he found anxious listeners.

Most South Carolinians, however, were not foolish enough to think they could survive as a single independent state. Between those ready to secede alone and the few ready to stand by the Union at all costs was a majority hoping for secession but willing to risk it only if other states were willing to join them. As a tiny independent nation, they argued, the state would suffer greatly reduced trade and an immediate flood of Carolina bank notes from other states, demanding immediate payment in specie. Equally important, as an independent nation, South Carolina would be subject to the American law forbidding the importation of slaves, and the state could no longer sell its ever-growing excess of slaves to owners in other states.

In October 1851 South Carolinians elected delegates to their state convention. For whatever reasons, the Unionists and the cooperationists won a majority vote of 25,045 to 17,710. The Unionists, led by Benjamin F. Perry, Francis Lieber, William J. Grayson, and Joel R. Poinsett, had fought hard, but the victory against unilateral secession came largely from the efforts of those ready to secede whenever they could persuade other states to join them.[38]

The cooperationist victory in South Carolina paralleled the election for governor in Mississippi. The fire-eating governor John A. Quitman hoped to be reelected despite or perhaps because of his involvement in the López filibustering expedition against Cuba. He had been indicted and taken to New Orleans for trial in a federal court, but the prosecutor had dismissed the case, and Quitman had returned to Mississippi for a hero's welcome. The Democratic convention actually preferred Jefferson Davis, but Quitman contested the choice, and Davis withdrew. Henry S. Foote was the Union candidate, and, as might have been expected, a formal public debate between Foote and Quitman ended with a fistfight on the platform. When the Union ticket won by a vote of 28,402 to 21,241 in the election to the convention, Quitman withdrew in favor of Davis. Davis agreed with the state's Democratic platform, which rejected the compromise but considered secession inexpedient. He had just been elected to a new six-year term in the Senate, however, and he accepted Foote's challenge at a considerable sacrifice. Foote won by only a thousand votes, 28,738 to 27,729, but it was still a Union victory.[39]

The results were similar in Georgia and Alabama. Running as a Constitutional Unionist, Howell Cobb was elected governor by a margin of more than eighteen thousand votes. The new legislature was three-fourths Unionist, and it elected Toombs to the Senate. Unionists also won three of the five congressional elections. In Alabama, Yancey's extremist group did not even nominate a candidate for governor. Whig papers everywhere supported Unionist candidates, and Unionists won five of the seven seats in Congress.[40]

In each of the prominent fugitive-slave cases in which he could not escape responsibility, Fillmore had spoken and acted decisively in support of the law. With the Southern Unionists and moderates fighting for their political lives, he could see no alternative. The abolitionists complained bitterly, but Southern voters choosing from among secessionists, moderates, and Unionists watched and applauded. Even when the fugitives had eluded the federal authorities, the Southerners could not fault Fillmore's intentions, and the effects of this on the Southern elections were clearly discernible. Despite clear evidence to the contrary, the *Washington Union* and its Democratic satellites in the South spent the summer and fall of 1851 insisting that Fillmore had joined Seward and Weed in opposition to the South. The Whig party, it proclaimed, was the party of free-soilism and abolition, and the president was its spokesman. Many of the Unionist candidates did have direct ties with Fillmore and would have been gravely weakened without his open support for the fugitive-slave law.[41]

While he was ready to obey the Constitution's guarantees to the South and soothe ruffled feelings where he could, however, Fillmore was not prepared to tolerate any serious moves toward disunion. When the second Nashville Convention was about to meet in November 1850, the angry editorials and speeches of would-be secessionists kept the president in a state of constant concern. James L. Petigru of Charleston, South Carolina, reported to Fillmore that the radicals were planning to seize the federal forts at Charleston as the first step toward secession. The United States attorney and other federal officers in South Carolina resigned, and Fillmore had great difficulty in replacing them. For weeks, the state had no United States attorney until Petigru was finally persuaded to take the job. Fillmore reacted by including General Scott in cabinet meetings designed to plan future contingency policies in case an insurrection should occur. On Scott's advice, Fillmore strengthened the Charleston forts and stationed additional troops in both South and North Carolina. When the governor of South Carolina demanded an explanation, Fillmore replied that it was his duty as commander in chief of the armed forces to station troops wherever he thought it would serve the public interest and that he owed no explanation to the governor of South Carolina. Whether or not this contributed significantly to the victory of those who would secede only in cooperation with others cannot be determined, but Fillmore's attitude and intentions were clear and unmistakable.[42]

In September 1851, after the death of Supreme Court Justice Levi Woodbury, Fillmore again demonstrated his independence of any Southern connections. After consulting Webster, Fillmore quickly appointed Benjamin R. Curtis, a noted Boston attorney and scholar, to fill the post. In 1857, when the Court in the Dred Scott decision ruled that neither the federal government nor a territorial government could bar slavery from any territory, Curtis wrote a vigorous dissent and resigned from the Court.

Secession had been defeated, and Unionism had triumphed, but the Whig party was nevertheless in deep trouble. Sewardites and other ostensibly anti-Southern Whigs in the North might be in the minority, but they could garner Southern headlines with speeches attacking the South and slavery. Southern Whigs might share the Northern Whigs' economic and political principles, but remaining in the same party with them was rapidly becoming impossible. The realignment of Unionists, conditional Unionists, secessionists, and conditional secessionists had destroyed the sentimental ties that had done much to hold the Whig party together. The decline in importance of the traditional economic conflicts between the parties had also contributed to the process. And finally, Clay, the Kentucky slaveholder, and Webster, the Boston compromiser, were passing off the stage, and no one of equal reputation in the Whig party stood ready to symbolize and defend the mutual respect the sections owed each other. If the Whigs in 1852 should prove unable to find a presidential candidate with a strong base in each section, the party would be doomed.

13

★ ★ ★ ★ ★

MANIFEST DESTINY—
WITH LIMITS

Since the earliest days of the republic, a few visionaries had predicted that United States trade, influence, and enlightenment would ultimately spread to China and India, and by 1850 a dream that had caused men to tap their foreheads was becoming closer to reality. Since the turn of the century, Yankee traders and whalers had operated in Chinese waters, and merchants had eyed the Celestial Empire as a potentially vast source of profit. Much closer was the archipelago known as the Sandwich Islands, which would soon be called Hawaii. Safe harbors, ample food and water, and beautiful native women had long attracted sailors to the fledgling town of Honolulu, and New England missionaries were soon on the way to save souls and protect the native girls from the sins of the flesh. The furs of the northwestern Pacific coast had already helped create the dynasty of John Jacob Astor, and the great Pacific harbors of Puget Sound, San Francisco, Los Angeles, and San Diego had been part of the Manifest Destiny that had triggered the Mexican War.

Until 1842 the Chinese had restricted trade to the single city of Canton during a specified part of the year, but various British, American, Portuguese, French, and Spanish traders had used this opportunity to introduce opium to the Chinese and garner high profits from the trade. The British had tried unsuccessfully to persuade the Chinese to exchange diplomatic recognition and adopt normal (as defined by the British) relations with the outside world. In 1842, however, an unusual Chinese viceroy refused the usual bribes and destroyed twenty thousand chests of British opium. Britain declared war, destroyed a small Chinese fleet, and dictated a peace treaty that opened six more cities and imposed recognition and extraterritoriality on the Chinese. The United States criticized the British for such blatant imperialism and promptly demanded the same concessions. Profiting from this piggyback diplomacy, United States traders built scores of new ships, including the magnificent Yankee clippers, for the trade and soon convinced the British that their erstwhile stepchildren were worthy competitors indeed.[1]

All of this was the background for Zachary Taylor's efforts to begin the construction of an isthmian canal and for the British insistence upon holding the Atlantic Ocean end of the San Juan River for the benefit of the downtrodden Mosquito Indians. Taylor's treaty had eased the tensions with the British temporarily, but whether the British would agree to the United States interpretation that the treaty was a pledge to abandon control of the area remained to be seen.

Meanwhile, the great clipper *Sea Witch* had cut 60 days off the usual 159 days taken by ships sailing from New York to San Francisco around Cape Horn. Designed for speed, with great length and a narrow beam, the *Sea Witch* and the fleet of imitators that followed her for a few years almost overwhelmed their British competitors. A still greater advance, however, was near at hand. Paddle-wheel steamships had already taken over the bulk of the coastal and river trade, and steam propulsion awaited only the development of the screw propeller before it would prove eminently superior on the ocean also. All of this meant that coaling stations around the world would become vital points of international competition. It also meant that either a canal or a railroad across Mexico or Central America was becoming a vital necessity.

Whereas Zachary Taylor had had the able and vigorous, even if occasionally intoxicated, John Clayton to offer advice and represent his views in the give-and-take of foreign relations, Daniel Webster gradually became for Millard Fillmore little more than a prestigious figurehead. Although relatively vigorous at first, Webster ultimately became weakened by advancing age and various chronic ailments and spent more and more time at his Marshfield estate in Massachusetts. Fillmore encouraged this and never at any time suggested that the old man resign. This meant, however, that in 1852 Fillmore himself had to take a more active personal role in determining foreign policy.

The three most likely routes from ocean to ocean were located in Panama, the Isthmus of Tehuantepec in Mexico, and Nicaragua.

An earlier treaty with New Granada (Colombia) had provided a United States company with permission to build a railroad across Panama. The Polk administration, when negotiating for peace with Mexico, had tried unsuccessfully to buy transit rights across the Isthmus of Tehuantepec, but this route was always inferior to the other two possibilities. Also, the British showed no interest in interfering with the American company that was busily laying tracks across Panama. The Treaty of New Granada had specified that the route would be neutral and open to the use of all. In December 1851 Fillmore could report with obvious satisfaction that this project was going full speed ahead and that mail and passengers would soon be using the route.[2]

In dealing with the British on Nicaragua, Fillmore followed the example set by Taylor. Fillmore's goals were to convince the British that American objectives there did not threaten British interests and to persuade them to give up their control of San Juan voluntarily. At one point, Lord Palmerston suggested that Britain might withdraw after ceding San Juan to Costa Rica, but Fillmore and Webster immediately saw this as a way for Britain to abandon a weak claim to San Juan while allowing Costa Rica to block the building of a canal. Before the argument could heat up, however, Nicaragua and Costa Rica went to war over their disputed boundary, and a group of Nicaraguan superpatriots used the conflict as a means for overthrowing the government that had granted the canal-route concession to the United States. For months all was chaos in Nicaragua, which enabled the British to reiterate the necessity for their presence in San Juan.

Then, in November 1851, the captain of the American steamship *Prometheus* refused to pay $123 in port dues claimed by the authorities in San Juan. When he tried to leave the harbor, the British warship *Express* pursued, fired a shot that forced the American ship to heave to, and forced him to pay the money. Amid angry public outcries in the United States, Secretary of State Webster informed Lord Palmerston that no protectorate over the Mosquitos could justify the collection of port dues by a British warship, and Fillmore ordered a United States warship to the scene.

From London, Lord Granville, the new foreign minister, very sensibly disavowed the action of his consul in San Juan, and the crisis ended. This led to negotiations that ended in April 1852 with the signing of a convention by the United States, Britain, Costa Rica, and Nicaragua. It was an excellent settlement from the United States point of view, but the Nicaraguan revolutionaries repudiated the work of their minister to the United States and refused to ratify the treaty. Various subsequent filibustering activities would weaken the trust established by Taylor between the United States and Britain.[3]

The route across the Isthmus of Tehuantepec in Mexico was too long for a canal, but it was much closer to United States ports than Nicaragua or Panama were, and it offered excellent conditions of topography and climate for a railroad. United States promoters had begun to plan this feat as early as 1842. Antonio López de Santa Anna, president of Mexico, had granted another Mexican, Don José de Garay, a sixty-year monopoly of any transit over the route. Garay was to receive all the land for ten leagues on each side of the proposed 100-mile roadway. For this million-acre gift, however, Garay had to begin construction by July 1844. Revolutions and the Mexican War made that deadline an impossible goal, but Santa Anna granted a one-year extension, and the later dictator Mariano de Salas ultimately extended the concession until 1848, even though it had legally lapsed in 1846.

Garay, meanwhile, shrewdly sold his charter to foreign investors, and his title was ultimately owned by an American, Peter A. Hargous, who in turn sold two-thirds of his property to a group of New Orleans businessmen headed by Judah P. Benjamin. In July 1850 the New Orleans group dispatched American engineers to survey the route. Believing in the work itself and in their government's duty to promote it, Fillmore and Webster ordered Robert Letcher, the United States minister to Mexico, to negotiate a treaty that would give the builders almost unlimited authority over the future road. The Mexicans insisted upon joint responsibility for maintaining order and peace in the area, but in January 1851 Letcher and the president of Mexico signed a treaty that also recognized the validity of Garay's original grant. This meant that the United States company would receive a million acres of Mexican land. Remembering the loss of half their total area in a war only three years earlier, the Mexican congress invalidated the grant on the grounds that it had expired in 1846 and that the decree of Salas had been the work of a usurper. The United States engineers were forcibly prevented from completing the survey.

Judah P. Benjamin, who later became secretary of state and secretary of war for the Confederacy, demanded action from his fellow Whig in the White House. The United States should protect the railroad's interests with force if necessary. Fillmore refused. Benjamin then threatened that the railroad company itself would send five hundred armed men to resist any attempt to drive them off, and a collision between them and Mexican authorities would start a war. His company had invested $100,000, and it must be protected. Fillmore did not flinch. He considered the Tehuantepec railroad an important "national enterprise," and he would urge Mexico to accept the treaty, but he would not threaten Mexico with war just to satisfy "the cupidity of any private company."[4]

Ultimately, the Mexican government offered to grant a right of way to Americans if it could be done at less cost to Mexico than the Garay grants. At the urging of Webster and Fillmore, Hargous and Benjamin tried to get the new contract, but in 1853 the Mexicans awarded it to Col. A. G. Sloo, a New Orleans rival of Hargous and Benjamin. Fillmore promptly had Roscoe Conkling, who had replaced Letcher, negotiate a new treaty giving the United States the right to protect the company in the construction and use of the road. Unfortunately, however, the continuing legal squabbles between the rival companies delayed and ultimately precluded any construction, and Conkling's treaty arrived in Washington after Franklin Pierce had succeeded Fillmore. Pierce did not even present the treaty to the Senate for ratification.[5]

If Fillmore could not shorten the distance to the Pacific, he was nonetheless ready to promote American interests in the Orient. An ideal stopping place en route to the East was Hawaii, where American traders, whalers, and entrepreneurs had already secured a strong influence. Under pressure from various foreigners, the ruling family of Hawaii had promulgated a rather democratic western-style constitution in 1840, and in 1843 the United States, with Webster as Tyler's secretary of state, had recognized the islands' independence. Others had followed suit, but the United States had emerged as the primary advocate of both independence and equality of opportunity for the foreigners of every nation in exploiting the area's considerable resources. In 1843, however, when the British and the French signed an agreement binding themselves not to annex the islands, the United States government applauded but declined to join. In 1849 Napoleon III repudiated the action of his predecessors and seized Honolulu, but in the face of United States and British protests, he withdrew.

A continuing suspicion of France coincided with the American dream of Manifest Destiny that had been fulfilled only temporarily by the Mexican War and its conquests. With naval officers and various editors suggesting that it was time for the United States "to shake the tree in order to bring the luscious fruit readily into our lap," Millard Fillmore again looked ahead to the possible consequences of a premature action. The Hawaiian king, Kamehameha III, urged on by United States citizens close to his throne, actually suggested a secret annexation that would be honored only if the rumors of a French takeover should be true. The United States commissioner, Luther Severance, who had helped to promote the idea, sent the proposal to Washington with great enthusiasm. Webster, however, advised against anything secret or underhanded. If the king wanted to make a public offer, it would be considered, but secret machinations must be avoided.

Meanwhile, in 1851, Napoleon tried another approach. His commissioner presented King Kamehameha III with a list of demands that would make the islands in effect a French protectorate. Webster and Fillmore, however, informed Napoleon in plain language that the United States would tolerate no action that would threaten Hawaii's independence. If anyone were to annex Hawaii, it would be the United States. With far more serious and more important challenges holding his attention in other parts of the world, Napoleon rescinded the demands. Hawaii would remain independent until the United States had more time and fewer crises elsewhere.[6]

Beyond Hawaii, meanwhile, lay China, and on the way to China, in an ideal location ideal for a stopping place and coaling station, was the hermit kingdom of Japan. In the late sixteenth and early seventeenth centuries, the ruling shogunate had come to power after a period of bloody civil wars in which various foreigners, including Christian missionaries, had been involved. Having already achieved power and stability, the Tokugawa shoguns in the 1620s and 1630s had decreed that henceforth no foreigners could enter and no Japanese could go outside a fifteen-mile limit. All Japanese Christians were required to recant or face death, and some forty thousand converts chose the fatal alternative. Only on the tiny island of Deshima did the Japanese maintain a small window to the outside world. There, Dutch merchants were allowed to trade on a limited basis but only after observing a rite that involved trampling on a crucifix. Since 1792, various ships from European and American nations had tried unsuccessfully to penetrate the bamboo curtain, but the Japanese had been adamant.[7]

The British success in China during the 1840s and 1850s stirred up new hopes that the same results could be achieved with Japan. The United States had followed piggyback diplomacy in China, with the British doing the work, taking the risks, and incurring the odium for oppressive imperialism. With regard to Japan, however, Millard

Fillmore decided that the United States would be the prime mover. This, presumably, would give the United States an initial edge in negotiations for whatever trade and other advantages might be derived from Japan, and it would show the world that the young democracy was indeed a world power. Fillmore, Webster, and Webster's successor, Edward Everett, probably hoped also that a diplomatic success of such importance might create a sense of national achievement in both North and South and thereby help allay the sectional hostilities.

Beginning in December 1850, Fillmore's Japan project slowly took shape. The first choice for commander was Commodore John H. Aulick, who had been instrumental in persuading Webster and the president to undertake the project. The pretext for the expedition would be the return of some shipwrecked Japanese sailors who had been rescued by an American ship and brought to San Francisco. Through a misunderstanding, however, Aulick was replaced by Commodore Matthew C. Perry, and after Webster's death, the final plans were made by the new secretary of state, Edward Everett.

Perry was a superb choice. Large, magisterial, and dignified, he created the kind of dramatic atmosphere needed for a mission to a nation still in the toils of feudalism. His orders were difficult. He was to convince the Japanese that the incursion of Americans into Japan was inevitable and that they should abandon their position of hostility. He was to remember, however, that his mission was "necessarily of a pacific character," and he should use force only in self-defense. The Japanese were "proud and vindictive," and he was to be "courteous and conciliatory" but "firm and decided." He was to "submit with patience and forbearance to acts of discourtesy . . . by a people unfamiliar with our ways," but he was to allow no insults. His one consolation: "Any error of judgment" on his part would be viewed with "indulgence" by his superiors in Washington.

Ultimately, Perry set sail with four powerful ships carrying two years of provisions; gifts, including one hundred gallons of Kentucky bourbon whiskey, wines, two telegraph transmitters with several hundred feet of wire, a quarter-scale railroad with 370 feet of track, four volumes of Audubon's *Birds of America*; and an excellent interpreter. Eight months later, Perry delivered Fillmore's letter assuring the Japanese emperor, his "Great and Good Friend," that Perry and the United States wanted only "friendship, commerce, a supply of coal, and protection for our shipwrecked people." In closing, Fillmore added, "May the Almighty have your imperial majesty in His great and holy keeping." The successful conclusion of Perry's mission would occur during the following administration, but for better or for worse, the combination of military threat and peaceful assurances that opened Japan was conceived, planned, organized, and staffed by Daniel Webster, Millard Fillmore, and Edward Everett.[8]

Fillmore, like Taylor, was an aggressive defender of United States rights and a promoter of United States advantages wherever feasible, but neither man believed in taking advantage of another nation's weakness or in following any policy that could not be morally defended.

Less than twenty miles off the bone-dry coast of Peru lay the equally arid, barren, and uninhabited Lobos Islands. Through the centuries, millions of birds had found them a suitable resting place and had filled and covered them with a manure known as guano. In the early nineteenth century, enterprising explorers had discovered that the guano was a magnificent fertilizer, and soon the ships of various countries were hauling it away to sell at five pounds a ton. The islands were barely outside the usual line defined by international precedent as the coastal limit of Peru, but during the 1830s the Peruvian government claimed them. In 1850 a new revolutionary government in Peru announced that it would attack any ship that came to get the guano.

Meanwhile, a group of American traders and shipowners, headed by one A. G. Benson, had organized a corporation that planned to send a hundred ships to Peru and haul away thousands of tons of guano. The group, which included some of Fillmore's wealthy political friends, asked Secretary of State Webster for naval support, and Webster gave the necessary orders. Benson and his group would have "full and complete protection."

At this point the Peruvian minister protested, and Fillmore for the first time confronted the problem. Webster was at Marshfield, and Fillmore knew nothing about the orders that had been given to the navy. After studying the situation and learning that the British had also accepted the claim of Peru, Fillmore reversed his secretaries of state and the navy. If Americans removed guano without the consent of Peru, they would do so at their own risk. Benson's fleet, meanwhile, had sailed. When Benson learned of Fillmore's decision, he and his friends deluged the president with letters of protest. Learning for the first time of Webster's promise, Fillmore took sharp issue with him, and Webster admitted that he had blundered. The protests and pressures continued, but Fillmore stood firm. He would not use the navy, even if the group asked the government for indemnities because of Webster's promise. Benson finally proposed that

Peru permit the first flotilla to load without paying Peru's price. Then, if Fillmore insisted upon honoring Peru's claim, the United States government would pay Peru because it had encouraged the expedition. The Peruvian minister agreed, because the source of the payment was irrelevant. Benson came to Washington with a delegation of Fillmore's political supporters from the New York business community. Either the government would pay, or Fillmore would face the angry opposition of the New York merchants and a swarm of private compensation bills in Congress that might cost the government an equal amount after severe political conflicts. The pressure was too great. Fillmore agreed to pay for the guano taken by the ships already en route, but he had made it clear that Peru owned the deposits and that the company would henceforth have to pay for them. Perhaps most important, Fillmore had refused to bully a weaker neighbor.[9]

Far more troublesome were the continuing United States filibustering efforts to take Cuba. The possibility that Spain might emancipate Cuba's slaves or that the latter might stage a bloody revolt on the same scale as that of Haiti in 1798 was constantly proclaimed by the Southern radicals. Obviously, they argued, such an event in Cuba would inspire a general revolt of American slaves also. If, however, Americans could annex the island, slavery could be expanded rather than curtailed. Such a large fertile area only ninety miles from Florida should become an asset instead of a mortal danger. Actually, only a few of the advocates of annexation had thought carefully about the various possibilities inherent in annexing a system of slavery that was quite different from that in the United States and that, indeed, was in the process of being overturned. Free blacks and mestizos outnumbered the slaves in Cuba, and they were not a population the Southern planters would have welcomed.

Zachary Taylor had sorely disappointed his fellow slaveholders by helping to foil the first two expeditions of Narciso López, but the latter was not discouraged. Again López managed to recruit and arm some four hundred young adventurers and to acquire another small steamer. A few of his men were Cuban exiles and Hungarian refugees, but most of them were aristocratic young American Southerners, including the nephew of Attorney General Crittenden. Fillmore was aware of these preparations, and he ordered the customs and naval officials in New Orleans to do everything possible to stop López. Fillmore also issued a public proclamation that any volunteers would be violating United States laws as well as risking the wrath of the Spaniards and would have no hope for United States protection.

With their usual slackness, however, the New Orleans authorities allowed López and his four-hundred-man army to sail for Cuba on the morning of 3 August 1851. Eight days later they landed in Cuba at Playtas, some 120 miles from Havana. As before, they were disappointed when no popular uprising occurred to greet them. The main force marched inland, while others remained behind to unload and transport supplies. When the rear guard tried to join the main force, Spanish troops intercepted and defeated them in a fierce battle. Colonel Crittenden and some fifty others managed to launch some boats, but the Spanish coast guard captured them. Within three days they were tried by a military court and executed by firing squad. A few days later, López and the others were also captured. Some were killed in the fighting. López was hanged in Havana's public square. Some 160 others were taken to Spain for penal servitude in the mines.

The execution of Crittenden and the other Americans shocked the American public, even in the North, and if Fillmore had wanted a war for Cuba, he probably could have found enough support to launch it. A mob in New Orleans sacked the premises of a Spanish-language newspaper and broke into the office of the Spanish consul, where they destroyed property, defaced pictures of the Spanish queen, and shredded a Spanish flag. The terrified consul fled to Havana. Webster and Fillmore risked a storm of criticism with their response. Webster apologized to the Spanish government for these "disgraceful acts," and he promised a salute for the Spanish flag and proper treatment for any consul who should be sent to New Orleans. As a result of this conciliatory action, the administration was able to persuade Spain to release the 160 Americans imprisoned in Spain. And while Webster explained to the Spanish that the United States did not have the same responsibility toward Spanish private citizens that it did toward the consul, Congress, after Spain had released the prisoners, voted $25,000 to compensate the victims of the New Orleans riot. It was a statesmanlike ending to what could have been a serious crisis, and Fillmore and Webster deserve high marks. Perhaps unfortunately, however, the efforts of Taylor and Fillmore to stop the filibustering expeditions were extremely unpopular in the South and played a role in the dissolution of the Whig party and the election of the Democrat Franklin Pierce in 1852.[10]

On the other hand, the filibustering attempts encouraged the British and the French to offer protection to Spain. French and British ships patrolled off Cuba, but when Spain asked the two nations to guarantee its sovereignty over the island, the British were unwilling, unless Spain would liberalize the Cuban government and repress the slave trade. Finally, in 1852 the British and French offered to sign a treaty with the United States, pledging that all three would respect Spain's ownership of Cuba. Knowing that this would be another weapon against Whig efforts to retain the White House, Fillmore and Secretary of State Everett gave private assurances against any interference in Cuba, but they postponed the question of a treaty until after the presidential election.

Pierce's landslide victory in 1852 seemed to indicate that Americans wanted Cuba, and Fillmore and Everett were unwilling to create a future barrier. In a long letter to the British and the French, Everett announced that the United States would not sign the treaty guaranteeing Spanish ownership of Cuba. The president, he wrote, did not covet Cuba, but anyone who looked at a map and realized the proximity of Cuba to the United States could see that it was an American question, quite remote from the interests of Europe. The United States could not disable itself permanently from making an acquisition that might occur "in the natural order of things." Indeed, fixing the status of Cuba by a permanent treaty would be like trying to dam up the Gulf Stream. Cuba commanded the approach to the Gulf of Mexico, which bordered on five states; it barred the entrance to the Mississippi River; and it was at the doorway of American routes to California across the isthmus. If an island like Cuba "guarded the entrance to the Thames or the Seine, and the United States should propose a convention like this to England and France," they would certainly feel "that the disability assumed by ourselves was far less serious than that which we asked them to assume." Fillmore himself told the British and French ministers that "this question would fall like a bomb" in the midst of the presidential election and would reopen the North-South conflict.[11]

In his final annual message to Congress, however, Fillmore reiterated his objections to any forcible seizure of Cuba. If voluntarily ceded by Spain, it would be "a most desirable annexation," but under existing circumstances, its incorporation would be "a most hazardous measure." The Cubans were a different "national stock, speaking a different language," and its acquisition "might revive those conflicts of opinion between the different sections of the country,which lately shook the Union to its center." Less than two years later, the antics of Pierre Soulé, as United States minister to Spain, and the Ostend Manifesto recommending an American conquest of Cuba to preserve slavery would stir up a wave of sectional anger, just as Fillmore had feared. The same events also strengthened the determination of Spain to hold Cuba rather than sell or surrrender it for any price.[12]

Fillmore did all that he could to stop the filibustering, but he could not ignore the presence of British and French warships in the area. In addition to searching for American filibusters, the British were authorized by the Webster-Ashburton Treaty of 1842 to join with the United States in repressing the foreign slave trade. The United States contributed little if anything to this effort, but the British relentlessly pursued suspected slavers with considerable success. Unfortunately, this was a complicated process, because slave ships of different nationalities usually had a United States flag ready to run up the mast whenever a British man-of-war came near. The possibility that innocent American traders might be stopped and searched was always present, and the United States had sworn to prevent this violation of American honor even before the War of 1812. Fillmore and Navy Secretary Conrad protested and warned, and soon United States warships had joined the fleets encircling Cuba.[13]

Amid the ensuing tension, George Law, a vociferous and aggressive trader and ship-line owner from New York, deliberately tried to precipitate a crisis. The purser on his ship *Crescent City* was a spy for a Cuban revolutionary group in New York that had published articles condemning Spanish policies in Cuba. The angry authorities in Havana announced that none of Law's ships would be allowed in the harbor unless he discharged the purser. Law protested the Cuban action to Webster, who advised Law to comply and fire the purser. Law, however, kept the purser and threatened to defy the Spanish and force them to fire on his ship. This, he believed, would compel Fillmore to choose between using military force against the Spanish or facing the condemnation of an American public that was infuriated by a blow to national honor and was in the mood to annex Cuba anyhow.

With Webster at the point of death, Fillmore handled this crisis himself. He ordered the New York port authorities to prevent the *Crescent City* from sailing, and he publicly denounced all efforts of private citizens to make war on a friendly nation. Law wisely discharged the purser, while Fillmore agreed to try to negotiate the controversy with the Spanish.[14]

And finally, interspersed among the president's other cares and irritations was the continuation of Hungary's efforts to win its independence from Austria. Despite his statements of support for Hungary, Taylor had been denounced as the leader of the "Austrian party" by those who advocated but probably would not have voted for aid to Hungary. Taylor had been ready to recognize Hungary as an independent nation until the Austrian-Russian combination had snuffed out the rebellion, and he had publicly condemned Austria in March 1850, when he gave the Senate the correspondence with his special envoy to Budapest, A. Dudley Mann.

On 2 October 1850 Webster received from J. G. Hulsemann, the Austrian chargé in Washington, an angry note accusing the United States of wanting the "downfall of the Austrian monarchy" and expressing the wish in offensive language. Secretary Webster answered that the American people were the world's primary "representatives of purely popular principles of government. . . . They could not, if they would, conceal their character, their condition, their destiny." The United States would not interfere with European governments, but it was bound to wish success to any people "contending for popular constitutions and national independence." If Austria threatened, the American people would "take their chances and abide their destiny." The United States covered "one of the richest and most fertile" areas of the globe, while the Austrian empire was just "a patch on the earth's surface."[15]

The Congress, with sectional animosities momentarily shelved, applauded almost unanimously, instructed Fillmore to get the Hungarian hero Lajos Kossuth released from his Turkish prison, and invited Kossuth to visit America. The United States minister to Turkey interceded, won Kossuth's freedom from a Turkish government eager to be rid of him, and put him aboard the USS *Mississippi* bound for New York.

When Kossuth stepped off the gangplank, a multitude of New Yorkers greeted him with frenzied applause. Forts and warships in the harbor fired salutes, while Hungarian and United States flags were everywhere. On the surface at least, the possibility that public opinion might demand intervention in the cause of Hungary appeared quite imminent. William H. Seward, always ready to ride the crest of popular enthusiasm, took the "Noble Magyar" in tow, while Democrats like Stephen A. Douglas and free-soiler Jacksonians like the slaveholding Francis Preston Blair vied for Kossuth's attention. Blair invited Kossuth to deliver the major address at the annual Democratic dinner commemorating the Battle of New Orleans, and his daughter Lizzie, along with a host of other ladies, was thrilled by the great rebel's dynamic presence. Kossuth's words, appearance, and delivery left his listeners singing paeans for days. Blair's friend Thomas Hart Benton, however, feared that hotheads might get the United States actually involved and took a dim view of the whole matter.[16]

At the White House, Millard Fillmore agreed with Benton. He and Webster were resolved to treat Kossuth "with respect" but to "give him no encouragement that the established policy of the country will be in any degree departed from." Seward and Democratic Senator James Shields of Illinois brought Kossuth to the State Department, where he requested an introduction to the president. When Webster communicated the request, Fillmore answered: "If he desires simply an introduction, I will see him, but if he wants to make a speech to me, I most respectfully decline to see him." Assured that Kossuth had promised to refrain from oratory, Fillmore agreed to an audience the next day. Later the same evening, Kossuth and his suite consumed great quantities of food and wine at the expense of Congress and did considerable damage to the furniture at Brown's hotel. Seward roused the Hungarian hopes further with his typical brand of exaggerated rhetoric.[17]

At the White House on the following day, Kossuth broke his promise by making a long speech and presenting a long list of specific requests for aid. Fillmore replied that as an individual, he sympathized with Kossuth's "brave struggle," but as president, he would have to continue to follow the principles originally laid down by Washington. No practical assistance would be forthcoming.

At Blair's Jackson Hall banquet on the following evening, Webster competed with Seward for the support of Kossuth's American following. Americans, he announced, would "rejoice to see our American model upon the lower Danube and on the mountains of Hungary." His toast: "Hungarian Independence, Hungarian control of her own destinies; and Hungary as a distinct nationality among the nations of Europe."[18]

Whatever the popular response would have been if Fillmore had called for aid to Hungary, the path Fillmore did follow was entirely acceptable to an American public always ready to enjoy popular enthusiasms briefly and just as quickly to tire of them. During Kossuth's tours in the South and the West, excited crowds gave him loud acclaim but no practical encouragement, although he did manage to raise some money in New England. In the end, Kossuth County, the largest in Iowa, would be his only permanent American memorial.[19]

The "Hungarian craze" had a final chapter early in the following administration. When Kossuth departed for Europe, his colleague Martin Koszta remained behind to become a United States citizen. In 1853, while traveling in Turkey, Koszta was seized and imprisoned on an Austrian ship. Before the ship could sail for Austria, however, a United States warship commanded by Capt. David Ingraham trained her guns on the Austrians and demanded Koszta's release. Believing the threat, the Austrians turned their captive over to the French consul. The Austrian government demanded that Ingraham be censured and that Koszta be returned but the Pierce administration ruled that because Koszta had taken the first steps toward naturalization, he was entitled to full United States protection. Eventually Koszta returned to United States and the Democrats thereby gained added political support among America's immigrant voters.[20]

Like Taylor, Millard Fillmore deserves high praise for his leadership as a maker of foreign policy. His decisions and actions were clear and unequivocal and were marked by imagination, moderation, and firmness. He followed his own judgments with but little regard for public or political pressures, although he did allow Everett to soften his Cuban policy with some harmless rhetoric. Webster, before he was overtaken by illness, and Everett, after Webster's death, were able secretaries of state, but the president was the final arbiter and accepted full responsibility. In appointing Webster, Fillmore, unlike some presidents, did not hesitate to give the top cabinet post to a man whose national reputation far exceeded his own. Everett, a brilliant scholar, was an equally wise choice. Fillmore worked closely with both of them, participated fully in the making of virtually every decision, and did not hesitate to countermand Webster over the incident with Peru.

14

★ ★ ★ ★ ★

THE DEATH OF A PARTY

Both major political parties faced the election of 1852 in a state of confusion, even though the country itself was infinitely calmer than it had been in 1848. Wealthy Northern businessmen everywhere were attracted by the Democratic party's apparent willingness to appease the South. In the spring of 1851 the *Boston Courier* advocated a boycott of all storekeepers, physicians, lawyers, and clergymen who opposed the fugitive-slave law. A Webster supporter defeated Charles Sumner for Congress by an overwhelming margin in Webster's former district, and the Massachusetts legislature defeated a motion of censure against Webster. Sumner, however, was later sent to the Senate by a coalition of Democrats and "conscience" Whigs in the Massachusetts legislature. The Union Safety Committee, which had been established by New York merchants as a pro-Fillmore group against Weed and Seward, sent speakers and pamphlets into rural areas to preach the gospel of sectional peace.[1]

During the spring and summer of 1852 the Congress met in an atmosphere of good will between the sections, but it accomplished little. From the speeches, a stranger might have concluded that war between the United States and Austria might actually be imminent and that those unwilling to fight for the freedom of Hungary were betraying the best ideals of the United States. Fillmore, in both 1851 and 1852, recommended higher tariffs and complained that the ad valorem system of collection at the point of embarkation was giving rise to frauds and chicanery of various sorts. In December 1850, however, he also reported that the government's total receipts for the past fiscal year had been $47,421,748.90, while the total expenditures were only $43,002,168.90. In December 1851 the corresponding figures were $52,312,979.87 for receipts and $48,005,878.68 for expenditures. The estimated receipts for the next fiscal year totaled $51,800,000.00, as opposed to only $42,892,299.10 for expenses. With money piling up in the national treasury, tariffs or any other additional taxes were difficult to justify. The Congress ignored the whole subject, except for a brief but unsuccessful effort to impose a duty on iron used by the railroads. [2]

With the Treasury in such a flourishing condition, various efforts to attain subsidies for railroads were debated at length, but only a land subsidy to Missouri passed. The most attention was given to a bill for subsidizing two railroads to California, but it was finally defeated on 30 August by a vote of 31 to 21, with a mixture of Northern and Southern votes on each side. The continuing effort to get a canal between Lakes Michigan and Superior at the Falls of St. Mary's was the most important internal-improvement effort to enjoy any success. Likewise, a homestead bill was also briefly debated before being voted down. With gold pouring in from California, with new industries being created almost daily, with farm prices high in both North and South, and with railroads being constructed everywhere in both sections without governmental aid, prosperity and economic issues were not a serious factor as the parties squared off for the coming presidential election.[3]

Perhaps most important, the House overwhelmingly passed a resolution that the Compromise of 1850 was a final settlement. Horace Greeley's *New York Tribune* admitted that the election of an opponent of the fugitive-slave law would be impossible. The question rarely emerged during the entire 1852 congressional session. On 11 February, when the Congress approved a resolution from the New Jersey legislature endorsing every part of the compromise, Joshua R. Giddings protested and delivered a speech against the fugitive-slave law. Congressman Edward Stanly answered Giddings briefly, but the rather witty exchange provoked more laughter than tension. On 27 July, Charles Sumner introduced a bill for the repeal of the fugitive-slave law, but he could speak only briefly for it on the following day because the Senate voted 32 to 10 against considering it.[4]

The slavery issue, however, was far from dead. Inspired by the Fugitive Slave Act and its immediate aftermath, Harriet Beecher Stowe published *Uncle Tom's Cabin* in March 1852, and by election day its content and its status as an international best seller helped make

Southerners determined to oppose anyone even slightly tainted by criticism of slavery. The validity or the factual errors involved in Stowe's story, setting, and dialogue are not part of this study. Suffice it to say, even though there were good and bad masters in the story, readers were left with images that identified the institution and its practitioners with total evil. And perhaps the content of the book itself was even less important to the South than its commercial success in the North. The success of the book, like the speeches of Seward and other radicals, the harsh criticisms of the abolitionist minority, and the Southern failure to get equal rights for slavery beyond Texas, was a moral condemnation that sensitive Southern souls found difficult to tolerate.

The goal of the Democratic party's leadership in 1852 was to unite the Free-Soil Democrats of the North and the States' Rights Democrats of the South behind a candidate acceptable to the moderates in both sections who had supported the Compromise of 1850. Andrew Jackson Donelson, Old Hickory's nephew and a staunch Unionist, replaced Thomas Ritchie as editor of the party's chief newspaper, the *Washington Union,* and the major aspirants for the presidency were all Union men. Lewis Cass had advocated popular sovereignty as the party's standard bearer in 1848 and had supported the compromise in the Senate. Stephen A. Douglas was the final author of the separate compromise measures, and Sam Houston's flexibility toward the most extreme claims of Texas had helped end the omnibus effort and achieve the settlement with New Mexico. James Buchanan was the Southern favorite—a bachelor whose Southern friends were his emotional substitute for the wife and children he lacked. William L. Marcy, as secretary of war for Polk, represented the anti-free-soil faction in New York. William O. Butler, the Mexican War general from Kentucky, had been the party's vice-presidential candidate in 1848.

For several months, Douglas appeared to be the odds-on favorite. He was young and dynamic, and he had much appeal to younger voters everywhere. His rhetoric favoring revolutionary movements in Europe created much excitement, while he carefully avoided making practical proposals that would require any American sacrifices. Unfortunately for Douglas, he allowed a journalist named George Sanders to become his primary booster, and Sanders made so many vicious attacks on the elder statesmen among the aspirants that the friends of all the other candidates were soon united against Douglas. Douglas was a gregarious individual who enjoyed being surrounded by all types of people, and this made it easier for his opponents to charge that he wanted the office only for the favors that he could then grant to his faithful army of sycophants and thieves. The senator's drinking habits produced the classic comment that while his habits were loose, he was often tight.

The apparent decline in Douglas's chances left Buchanan the favorite because of his overwhelming Southern support, but in the North outside Pennsylvania, he had many enemies. Among them was the former Jacksonian editor Francis P. Blair, who denounced Buchanan far and wide as the worst possible candidate. Marcy had been an able secretary of war, but the political wars among Democrats in New York had almost equaled those of the Whigs, and his chances for the ultimate victory were slight. Out on the fringes was a handful of delegates who liked Franklin Pierce, the Mexican War brigadier general who had served in both the House and the Senate. In January, Pierce had admitted in a speech that he disliked the Fugitive Slave Act and thought it inhumane, but he had later effectively repudiated the statement with a declaration that the compromise measures must be sustained.

The Democrats met at Baltimore on 1 June and began balloting three days later, after passing a rule requiring a two-thirds vote for nomination. With 192 votes necessary for a nomination, the first forty-seven roll calls were fruitless. Cass reached 116 on the first; Buchanan, 104 on the twenty-second; and Cass, 133 on the thirty-third, as delegates shifted to oppose the front runner in each case. The Southerners could not select the candidate, but the two-thirds rule gave them a veto, and many of them distrusted the doctrine of popular sovereignty espoused by Cass and Douglas. At a caucus, Pennsylvania and five Southern states supporting Buchanan agreed that they would try to prove to the adherents of the lesser candidates that the latter's men had no chance and thereby recruit them for Buchanan. Three states would stay with Buchanan, while the others would experiment with other men. Unfortunately for Buchanan, on the forty-seventh ballot, they swung to Franklin Pierce, and a sudden snowball developed. On the forty-ninth wearying ballot, the exhausted delegates nominated Pierce. The candidate and his wife were enjoying a leisurely ride when a friend galloped up with the good news. Mrs. Pierce fainted and fell out of the carriage.[5]

The qualities that would make Pierce a catastrophically weak president made him a magnificent presidential candidate. He was an empty page upon which each faction of Democrats could draw its own self-image. Southerners ranging from strong Unionists to fire-eaters were delighted. Thomas Hart Benton, who had recently been defeated for senator in Missouri, was ready to labor wholeheartedly for Pierce's election. Francis P. Blair, a Free-Soil leader in 1848, compiled and distributed speech material for Pierce's supporters and wrote a blistering pamphlet attacking Gen. Winfield Scott, the Whig candidate for president, which Blair did not sign because of his friendship with Scott's daughter. The bitter New York enemies William H. Marcy and John Van Buren each thought Pierce a splendid choice. So did John's father, the 1848 Free-Soil candidate for president. On 13 July, Pierce received letters from the radical Virginian John Letcher and David Wilmot, the original author of the antislavery proviso. Each was certain that Pierce echoed his sentiments on the subject of slavery.[6]

In retrospect, the only Whig candidate with any chance to win was the man already in the White House. The winner must carry the South, and while Pierce was widely acclaimed as a pro-Southern candidate, no one really knew this for certain, while Fillmore could point to a consistent record of supporting the compromise and trying to enforce the Fugitive Slave Act.

Millard Fillmore, however, did not really want another term. He enjoyed the affluence, the acclaim, the comfort, and the satisfaction of having achieved his country's highest honor, but he had no thirst for power. He felt no great vindictiveness toward his enemies and had no real taste for unpleasant responsibilities and difficult choices that pitted his personal feelings against political exigencies. He later remembered that he had resolved not to seek reelection almost as soon as he actually had become president. He did not shrink from responsibilities, however, and no fair judge would call him a weakling. He served throughout his term with complete dedication and considerable ability, but by December 7, 1851, his mind was made up. On that date he confided to his long-time adherent, the Buffalo editor Thomas Foote, that he would not be a candidate to succeed himself.

All available evidence indicates that this was an honest decision and not an effort to court a draft. Fillmore was not given to idle words. Interior Secretary Stuart later remembered a conversation in which several cabinet members agreed fully with Crittenden's remark that in the three years of their association, none of them had ever heard Fillmore "utter a foolish or unmeaning word, in all that time." Even the frantic and deceptive efforts of Weed and Seward to cut Fillmore down had not inspired an effort to defeat them in 1852. Fillmore's control over the federal patronage could have guaranteed him a renomination if he had manipulated it to that end, but he had used this power to his own advantage only in selected cases when he was trying to gain support in New York for the 1850 compromise. The port collectors in both Boston and Philadelphia worked for the interests of Seward and Weed, but both remained undisturbed because neither directly threatened Fillmore's principles. Weed's editorials charging Fillmore with using the patronage to get himself reelected angered Fillmore, but he realized that a premature denial would only weaken his administration. As early as March 1851, however, Fillmore directed his friend Dr. Thomas Foote, who was coeditor of the pro-Fillmore paper that Foote had established in Albany, to begin spreading rumors that Fillmore would not run for reelection. By this time, however, Fillmore was the almost unanimous choice of the Southern Whigs, and no one really believed the rumors.[7]

Southern Whigs quite correctly realized that Fillmore was the only Whig who could be elected. His support for the Fugitive Slave Act had been directed toward keeping the Southern fire-eaters from winning the elections of 1851, but it had also given him a status in the South enjoyed by no other Whig hopeful. In the North also, those Whigs who applauded the compromise far outnumbered the higher-law adherents of Seward. Messages of support and editorials advocating his reelection blossomed everywhere.[8]

Thurlow Weed surrendered, temporarily at least. He advised his friends to allow the compromise Whigs to pick the party's candidate and then took a ship for Europe. William H. Seward, however, ignored his mentor's advice. The only two candidates other than Fillmore who were being considered were Webster and Gen. Winfield Scott. Most people did not realize the desperate condition of Webster's health, and he himself did not admit it. He could hardly walk, but his will and his lifetime ambition to be president were as strong as ever. The Whigs' only two previous victories had occurred with a famous general as the candidate, and Scott, despite his pomposity, filled this role. Eager to defeat Fillmore, Seward in early 1851 threw his support to Scott. Meanwhile, Webster's friends organized a committee to support their favorite. In late fall 1851, Fillmore assured Webster's friends that the old man was Fillmore's own choice.[9]

The possibility that Winfield Scott could be nominated with the support of the one Whig most anathema to the South meant that the Whig party was on the edge of destruction. The party could survive the nomination of almost any reasonable candidate who had supported the compromise, but the choice of someone tainted by an intimate association with Seward would drive out the Southerners and leave the Northern remnant in the hands of the Free-Soilers.

It is easy to criticize Fillmore for not immediately putting the salvation of his party and the interests of the country ahead of his own personal feelings, but the crushing burdens of the office on a truly conscientious man had taken their toll even in a short time. The White House of 1852 had no appeal for anyone without a genuine taste for combat. During the 1850s, furthermore, the president did not have a huge building full of people researching national problems and advising a staff that was authorized either to tell the president what to say and do or present him with a very narrow range of alternatives. No one budgeted the president's time or decided which issues he would consider or what information he would receive on a given day, and no one tried to protect him from his own mistakes. In one day, Fillmore might deal with the slavery quarrels and the threats to the Union, the threats of Texas against New Mexico, crank letters threatening his life, violations of a fugitive-slave law that he deplored but felt obligated to enforce, dozens of requests for jobs or favors, crises with the British over Central America, a railroad company's threat to start a war with Mexico, attempts by the French or the British to seize Hawaii, a secret offer by Hawaii to join the United States, Southern filibustering efforts against Cuba, and the project to enhance trade with China by forcibly opening up the islands of Japan. The constant pressures of the job had contributed to the early death of James K. Polk and the death in office of Zachary Taylor. Between Andrew Jackson (1829–37) and Theodore Roosevelt (1901–9) only Ulysses S. Grant managed to actually serve out two consecutive terms, and Grant's administration was badly marred by serious negligence. Admittedly, however, the assassinations of three presidents contributed to this phenomenon. Like Polk and Taylor, Fillmore was totally conscientious, did not shrink from responsibility, and did not consider his personal popularity when making decisions. Some of these decisions involved serious inner conflicts. For him the burdens far outweighed any pleasure derived from the prestige, power, and perquisites of the office. For those who believe that the preservation of the Whig party would have served the American national interest, Fillmore's weariness of the presidency in 1852 was both understandable and highly regrettable.

Also, of course, the danger to the party was not as obvious to Fillmore in 1851 and early 1852 as it is to the historian today. Fillmore had always admired Daniel Webster and felt that the old man deserved a final effort for the prize that he had craved so long. The godlike Daniel's health failed badly during the late summer of 1852, but for a time he served Fillmore well. Driven in part by wishful thinking, the president continued until too late to hope that Webster's nomination was the best solution. Webster's support for the compromise and for the fugitive-slave law as secretary of state had given him a new popularity in the South, and despite the condemnation of the Free-Soilers, he still retained a powerful Northern following. A strong and healthy Webster might have won the nomination with Fillmore's help, and he would have had an excellent chance for election. Even a strong showing and a close election might have saved the party, regardless of the final result.

Fillmore's decision filled the party faithful with despair. From friends everywhere came pleas for a reconsideration. Scott actually supported the compromise, but his ties with Seward would render Scott anathema to the South, and Webster's age and health were irrevocable barriers. A severe defeat would destroy the Whigs as a national party and force a new realignment based upon attitudes toward slavery extension. The reelection of Fillmore was the party's only real hope, unless some other leader could keep the party conservative enough on slavery to continue to hold its Southern membership. The New York business leaders who had always urged cooperation with the South and had abjured the "higher law" recognized this fact, and their Union Safety Committee openly sought an alliance with the "National Democrats." Webster, too, recognized both the danger and the opportunity and saw himself as the "great national man" anointed to lead a new combination of Old Whigs and moderate Northern Democrats.[10]

In Philadelphia, meanwhile, various nativist elements were coalescing into a single party. The secret society the Order of the Star Spangled Banner was working closely with the older Native American party, which now was calling itself the American Democratic party. This group supported the Webster-Fillmore Whig faction in Philadelphia and hoped to become the new national party that would replace the Old Whigs.[11]

Fillmore, however, rejected the idea of new parties and clung to a faith that the Whig party could survive, even though he was unwilling to become the only standard bearer with a chance to save it. He asked his New York friends to obstruct the Whig-Democratic combination efforts of the Union Safety Committee, but this group illustrated the conservatism of New York City by winning most of the 1851 city elections. To the Union Safety Committee, a victory over the hated Sewardites was more important than preserving the Whig party. Fillmore quickly had the word spread that he had supported

the whole ticket and not just the candidates of the Safety Committee. His friends still talked of uniting with the Hunker Democrats,
but Fillmore continued to resist. He did begin to doubt his policy in
late 1851, however, when the Whigs suffered serious election losses
in every Northern state. This did not threaten the compromise or
the Union because Northern Democrats were more devoted to these
causes than were the Northern Whigs, but it did widen the gap still
further between Northern and Southern Whigs.

On 7 December 1851, Fillmore's friend Dr. Foote labored long
and hard to convince Fillmore that sectional peace required the preservation of the Whig party and that only Fillmore himself could
accomplish this goal. Fillmore finally yielded and again postponed
any formal announcement of his retirement. He retained the right to
withdraw at any time he might feel that his name could not be used
to advantage, but for the time being, the "National" Whigs could
continue to use him as their rallying point.

As 1852 dawned, letters urging Fillmore to run for a second
term deluged the White House, and newspapers representing every
faction joined the cry. In March the dying Henry Clay rallied long
enough to issue a ringing plea for his party to nominate and elect
Fillmore. Fillmore had "administered the Executive Government with
signal success and ability." He had "been tried and found true, faithful, honest, and conscientious." His competitors, one in the field,
the other in the cabinet, were good men, but neither had actually
been tried.[12]

Simultaneously, however, the Seward Whigs attacked their own
president with malicious lies and half-truths. Fillmore's attempts to
enforce the Fugitive Slave Law, they said and wrote, were the acts of
a traitor who had sacrificed friends and principles for the sole purpose of gaining reelection. They charged that he had once been as
aggressive against slavery as Giddings and Hale and even more so
than Seward, but he had now abandoned every sacred principle for
the hope of reelection.[13]

Both the support and the attacks made Fillmore's withdrawal
increasingly difficult. Webster was running a poor third, and Scott's
candidacy with Seward's endorsement would destroy the Whig party
in the South. George Babcock, Fillmore's man in Buffalo and Albany,
spoke accurately when he observed that the Sewardites really hoped
to see a Southerner elected who would oppose Northern economic
interests and antislavery feelings and thereby unite the North behind
a sectional candidate, obviously Seward, in 1856. Equally true, if
Fillmore abandoned the field to Seward in 1852, the latter's follow-

ers would control the convention and could force the Southerners out with an obnoxious platform.

Fillmore thus found himself the only barrier to Seward's plans, but he was still reluctant to be a candidate. Various friends, however, assured him that no other Whig could carry New York, Pennsylvania, or Ohio and that his own chances were problematical without disharmony among the Democrats. In late May, however, the Democrats united behind the largely unknown Franklin Pierce, who had managed to be all things to all people among the otherwise badly divided Democrats.

For Fillmore, it was a painful situation. If he won the nomination, he would probably lose the election. If he withdrew, the Sewardites would command the convention and drive out the National Whigs, both Northern and Southern. In 1856 a sectional party would be ready to nominate Seward. Believing, as Fillmore did, that a sectional party would be the first step toward disunion, he finally decided to become a candidate and risk the probable humiliation.[14]

Baltimore was boiling hot in June 1852, and the heat did nothing to enliven the Whig convention. Even the abundant liquor on hand could not penetrate the funereal atmosphere. Seward arrived a week early to direct the delegates supporting Scott. Webster remained in Washington, and the hopelessness of his cause was clear. Fillmore's friends arrived without instructions, but they were prepared either to nominate the president or to foil the enemies of sectional peace. Rumors circulated that Babcock had been authorized to withdraw Fillmore's name at the propitious moment, and no one could either confirm or deny it. Fillmore's strength came from New York City, Iowa, and the solid South. Scott was strong in the Middle West and the north-central areas. Webster had New England except for Maine. Fillmore's long vacillation, plus the uncertainties and rumors, as well as his failure to wield the patronage in his favor, had cost him a great many delegates.

Before the convention formally opened at noon on 16 June, the Southern delegates caucused and unanimously adopted a platform declaring the compromise to be the final settlement. After two days of bitter debate, caucusing, and back-room discussions, punctuated by all kinds of parliamentary delays, the convention accepted a platform that unequivocally endorsed the compromise measures, including the Fugitive Slave Act.

Having accomplished this basic objective, Fillmore asked that his delegates be transferred, if possible, to Webster. If the Sewardites won the nomination, they would still have to run on a compromise platform. The Democrats had also endorsed the compromise; if they won, the compromise would remain intact, and the Seward forces could be blamed for the defeat.

Fillmore's friends, however, refused to obey. The thrill of victory appeared possible, and they would not abandon it. On Friday evening 18 June, the balloting began, with 147 votes necessary for a nomination. On the first round, Fillmore had 133 votes to 131 for Scott and 29 for Webster. Fillmore had received all but one Southern vote. After six more long-drawn-out votes, the result remained essentially the same. Fillmore and Webster had a clear-cut majority between them. Webster could have nominated Fillmore, but his stubborn New England friends insisted that the transfer should come from Fillmore.[15]

Babcock did indeed hold a letter from Fillmore withdrawing from the race, but it was to be read only when Babcock should think it proper. "You will consider only the cause in which we are engaged," Fillmore had written. "I ask nothing for myself. . . . You will . . . guard against any premature act or disclosure which might embarrass my friends . . . while . . . you will not suffer my name to be dragged into a contest for a nomination which I have never sought, [and] do not now seek." Babcock did not recognize any such moment.[16]

On Saturday 19 June, after thirty-one ballots had been taken, a delegate moved that if no candidate had a majority on the fiftieth ballot, the nomination should go to the highest vote getter. This motion was defeated. After ballot number forty-six, the exhausted and angry delegates adjourned until the following Monday. Over the weekend, various conferences showed that the transfer of Fillmore's entire vote to Webster was impossible. Southerners were being influenced by Scott's promise to honor the platform and by the party's record of winning only when led by a military hero. Fillmore's friend John Barney hurried to Washington and pleaded with Webster to withdraw in favor of Fillmore. Webster, however, was stubborn in the face of his humiliation. He would wait and hope "for a decent vote that I may retire without disgrace." Barney replied: "It is a fearful responsibility you are about to assume of defeating the *true* Whig party by delaying action."[17]

Meanwhile in Baltimore, Fillmore's supporters offered those of Webster a fair proposition. If Webster could get his total up to 40, the Fillmore managers would deliver to Webster the 107 he would need for the nomination. If Webster could not get the 40 after another ballot or two, his votes would go to Fillmore.

On Sunday, groups went to Washington to see both Webster and Fillmore. The president readily agreed to the offer that had been made. Webster remained adamant until Monday morning and then finally came to his senses. He informed Fillmore that he had sent a letter to Baltimore to end the controversy, and he expected Fillmore to be nominated by one o'clock.

It was too late, however. Webster failed to gain the votes needed according to Fillmore's offer, but the transfer to Fillmore never occurred. On the forty-eighth ballot, two Fillmore votes from Missouri switched to Scott, and the Webster delegates, New Englanders after all, switched to Scott instead of Fillmore. On the fifty-third ballot, the nomination finally went to Scott.

Fillmore received the news with no sadness. Webster was distraught over the result and assured Fillmore over and over that he had not given preference to Scott. Fillmore knew this, and did his best to ease Webster's conscience. When Webster offered to resign, Fillmore would not hear of it.[18]

It was a hopeless nomination. A Southern Whig conference in Washington resolved not to vote for Scott under any circumstances. The members threatened to condemn Secretary of the Navy Conrad for having accepted the vice-presidential nomination, but they finally settled for an expression of regret that the North Carolinian was connected with Scott. Scott had lost the South because of his connection with Seward, but New England was equally unhappy. National Whigs in the North and virtually all Whigs in the South considered themselves to be without a party. For ordinary voters everywhere, "Old Fuss and Feathers" lacked the personal appeal of "Old Rough and Ready." Also, Scott's bumbling and unsuccessful efforts to attract the foreign vote only served to alienate the Nativists. In November, Scott carried only Massachusetts, Vermont, Kentucky, and Tennessee, and the Whig party as a truly national organization was dead. Franklin Pierce stood ready to become president.[19] Democrats everywhere rejoiced, but only the ultra-Southerners in the party would remain happy for long.

It was the Whig party's final appearance in a national election. Some have believed that the weakening or blurring of the traditional economic differences that had separated the two major parties was the primary factor in the demise of the Whig party and the resulting collapse of the existing two-party system. It can also be argued, however, that while the controversies over the tariff, currency and banking, internal improvements, and land distribution had been dulled by the booming progress and prosperity and had been temporarily overshadowed during the period 1848–1850 by the slavery issue, they were by no means dead. It can also be argued that the repeal of the Missouri Compromise in 1854 rather than the election of 1852 was the lethal blow to the Whig party. The Whigs suffered a crushing defeat in 1852 because they nominated a candidate who was unacceptable to the South and, as a result, was also unpalatable to great numbers of normally Whig businessmen who wanted to maintain their peaceful and profitable relations with the South. With a different candidate like Fillmore, the Whigs might have done far better. Despite his handicaps, Scott received almost 44 percent of the popular vote, and Pierce won the election with less than 51 percent. Also, the many-sided image of the Democratic candidate attracted voters of every conflicting opinion. American voters have always been fickle and mercurial, however, and their political parties have often recovered quickly after devastating losses. The existing two-party system might have survived both the fugitive-slave law and the prosperity that eased the traditional party rivalries, but it could not survive both the nomination of an inept candidate perceived as an enemy by the South and the 1854 threat of slavery expansion into a vast territory hitherto reserved for freedom by mutual agreement between the sections.

Fillmore's lame-duck final four months were relatively serene. Members of Congress avoided even the mention of slavery, and a new era of good feeling appeared possible. Fillmore tried to appoint his most loyal friends to high office, but several were denied confirmation by the ungrateful opposition of Senator Hamilton Fish. He did get Postmaster General Hall appointed to a New York judgeship, and Graham, who had resigned to run for vice-president, was replaced by the very able John P. Kennedy of Baltimore. Webster died in October, but Fillmore had for several months been making all of the foreign-policy decisions anyhow. Webster's close friend, the brilliant orator Edward Everett, became secretary of state in time to render excellent service on several matters.[20]

A final message to Congress had to be written, and with no real crises threatening, Fillmore could have contented himself with a few genial banalities. The slavery question was still pressing, however, and the president was at first determined to make a final contribution to the slavery-extension argument. Despite his feelings against the institution, he had made important concessions to its practitioners for the sake of sectional peace, and his conscience and his hopes for a favorable verdict on his administration from future historians were important motives. He therefore prepared a long disquisition on slavery extension which his cabinet at first approved and then persuaded him to omit from the message.

Fillmore's unpublished message is important for any evaluation comparing him with his immediate successors. It clearly shows that his abandonment of the Wilmot Proviso and his reluctant support of the Fugitive Slave Act followed a painful inner struggle in which he decided that the salvation of the Union and the prevention of a civil war were goals that transcended his conscience on the immediate slavery questions. From the perspective of the late twentieth century, Fillmore's essay expresses the kind of racism that a great many Americans have quite properly come to abhor. From the vantage point of a mid-nineteenth-century politician trying to grapple with the problem of reconciling slavery with an idealistic democratic ideology, it appears far more reasonable. During the recent 1850 debates, Thomas Hart Benton had pleaded against extending the institution because the aspect of racial conflict made it an incurable evil once it had become established. Fillmore developed the same theme. Sooner or later, he predicted gloomily, the terrible race war in San Domingo would be reenacted in America unless something could be done to prevent it. Antislavery agitation would never stop; indeed, it would be renewed every time a new state applied for admission. The South would never accept a coerced emancipation, nor would it voluntarily free its slaves if they were to remain in the South as freedmen; and Northerners would not welcome them either. Whether they be free or slave, the presence of blacks would ultimately produce a civil war. The only remedy, therefore, was colonization in either Africa or the West Indies. Congress should encourage Southerners to free their slaves by offering to remove them to other areas. It was hoped that this might be accomplished at the rate of some one hundred thousand slaves annually. The resulting labor shortage could be relieved by new immigration from Asia. This solution for abolishing slavery, Fillmore concluded, would take many years, but it was the only way to eliminate the evil without violence and bloodshed.[21] If the recommendation was impossible and appears insensitive by twentieth-century standards, it was at least a recognition that slavery was a national problem, to be solved by the Congress, with both the North and the South sharing in the effort and the expense. Abraham Lincoln would urge the same solution at the time of his Emancipation Proclamation.

In the final message that Fillmore actually sent to Congress, he emphasized the peace and prosperity that could be seen everywhere, and he expressed humble gratitude:

Besides affording to our own citizens a degree of prosperity of which on so large a scale I know of no other instance, our country is annually offering a refuge and a home to multitudes, altogether without example, from the Old World. . . . We must all consider it a great distinction and privilege to have been chosen by the people to bear a part in the administration of such a Government. Called by an unexpected dispensation to its highest trust at a season of embarrassment and alarm, I entered upon its arduous duties with extreme diffidence. I claim only to have discharged them to the best of a humble ability, with a single eye to the public good, and it is with devout gratitude in retiring from office that I leave the country in a state of peace and prosperity.[22]

In late February 1853 the Fillmores shipped most of their belongings to Buffalo and made arrangements to spend a few days at Willard's Hotel before leaving for an extended tour of the South. On a cold, snowy, windy 4 March, they left the White House for the inauguration of Franklin Pierce. Fillmore was happy to lay down the burdens of the presidency, and he was gratified when Pierce, in his Inaugural Address, took a pledge to uphold the Compromise of 1850 in every way.

The retiring president's satisfaction, however, and his anticipation of a happy journey through the South and back to Buffalo were soon shattered. Standing in the cold wind and slush of a melting snow, Abigail Fillmore developed a severe cold that quickly turned into pneumonia. For the next three weeks, her husband and children remained at her bedside while the best doctors applied the only remedies they knew. On 30 March she died, leaving her loved ones in a state of overwhelming sorrow. She had been the inspiration of Fillmore's youth and had shared his life, thoughts, challenges, problems, and triumphs for twenty-seven years, and his grief was almost uncontrollable. Sadly, the family returned to Buffalo to bury her and to seek a new anchor for their lives.[23]

The Fillmores were not alone in their sorrow. Only eleven days before the inauguration, President-elect Pierce, his wife, and his eleven-year-old son were riding on a train that jumped the track and went hurtling down a steep embankment. The son was killed instantly before his parents' eyes, and Mrs. Pierce never fully regained her sanity. The fourth of March 1853 would not be remembered as a happy day by the two men who had planned to enjoy it most.

15

★ ★ ★ ★ ★

THE AFTERMATH

If Abigail had lived and if the Fillmores had followed their original plans, the president's historical reputation might have been quite
different. Unfortunately, from the historian's viewpoint, however,
he suffered and brooded silently for a year and then returned to the
political wars.

In 1853–54, Stephen A. Douglas tore the scab of compromise
off the wounds inflicted upon Northern and Southern sensibilities
by the debates of 1850. He introduced a bill for creating the territories of Kansas and Nebraska, and ignoring the fact that the slavery
issue there had been settled for thirty-four years by the Missouri
Compromise, he called for popular sovereignty and the repeal of the
compromise. Douglas was certain that the area would become free
regardless, and he thought most Northerners would agree with him
and ignore the implications of his bill. For tens of thousands of
Northerners, however, the repeal of the sacred compromise was a
Southern attempt to steal everything from the Mississippi River to
the Pacific for slavery, and the ultimate result was a new Republican
party, composed of dissident northwestern Democrats and antislavery
Whigs, held together only by their common opposition to slavery
extension.

The national Whigs, exemplified by Fillmore, could survive as
a party, or so it seemed, only by joining with another new political
phenomenon, the Native American party, built upon ideological opposition to further mass immigration from Europe. This organization

broadcast all manner of scurrilous and false attacks upon Catholicism and Catholics and demanded that limitations be put on the citizenship of all such immigrants. The newcomers were often desperately poor when they arrived and required charitable assistance. Also, the Irish drank their share of whiskey and were somewhat prone to fighting, while the Germans liked their beer and Beethoven on Sunday as well as on any other day. The most important basis for the party was the harsh competition for jobs between the older American ethnic groups and the newcomers as well as the ancient Protestant bias against Catholicism in general. Also, several states did allow immigrants to vote prior to the attainment of citizenship, and many Whigs were convinced that the immigrant voters herded to the polls by unscrupulous Democrats had cost them the elections of 1844 and 1852.[1] Others, like Fillmore, John J. Crittenden, John Bell of Tennessee, and Willie Mangum and William Graham of North Carolina, as well as a few Democrats like Andrew Jackson Donelson, convinced themselves that the American, or "Know-Nothing," party had a program that might reunite North and South against common enemies. Unable to abide either the Republicans or the Southern Democrats, these men saw no other alternative.[2]

Their hopes were roused by the elections of 1854, in which the Know-Nothings carried Massachusetts and Delaware and shared a victory with the old-line Unionist Whigs in Pennsylvania. The party elected a total of seventeen congressmen, and it won every state office in Massachusetts except two. It almost carried Virginia, Georgia, Alabama, Mississippi, and Louisiana, and it did elect several officials in Texas. In Louisiana and the other southern states east of the Mississippi, the Know-Nothings ran only sixteen thousand votes behind their opponents. They also made a very strong showing in New York against the Weed-Seward Whigs, who would soon become Republicans.

Fillmore personally may have been driven to a resumption of political activity by the sudden death in July 1854 of twenty-two-year-old Mary Abigail, his favorite daughter. She had served as his hostess in Washington, and he adored her. For the second time in sixteen months he was utterly devastated. With both his wife and his daughter gone, Fillmore may have sought a necessary distraction by immersing himself again in politics.

On New Year's Day 1855, Fillmore wrote to an old friend who was a leader in Philadelphia's Native American party. Fillmore knew that the letter would be published and that it might gain him the party's presidential nomination. In effect he announced that he would oppose "the corrupting influence which the contest for the foreign vote is exciting upon our elections." Both parties, in "bargaining for the foreigners' ballots," were "corrupting the ballot box—that great palladium of our liberty—into an unmeaning mockery. . . . Where is the true-hearted American whose cheek does not tingle with shame . . . to see our highest and most courted foreign missions filled by men of foreign birth to the exclusion of the native born?" Nevertheless, he added, Europe's oppressed should be given asylum and equal protection of the law. Constitutional liberty could best be preserved, however, by restricting officeholding to those who had been "reared in a free country." Washington himself, said Fillmore, had seen the dangers of foreign influences and had warned against them. Soon afterward, Fillmore took the prescribed oaths and joined the Order of the Star Spangled Banner.[3]

In March 1855 Fillmore boarded a ship for Europe and spent a year visiting England, Ireland, France, Italy, Egypt, Turkey, and Prussia. Everywhere, people were charmed by his easygoing but impeccable manners. He had a friendly audience with the pope. Reportedly, Queen Victoria thought him the handsomest man she had ever seen. Oxford University offered him an honorary doctorate, but the former president graciously refused the honor: "I had not the advantage of a classical education, and no man should, in my judgment, accept a degree he cannot read." In Paris, Fillmore rescued an old enemy, Horace Greeley, from jail by paying a debt for which the erratic editor had been incarcerated.[4]

During Fillmore's absence, the Know-Nothing party nominated him for president, and his arrival back in New York Harbor was greeted by several thousand well-wishers, a display of fireworks, and a fifty-gun salute. The other alternatives in 1856 were the pro-Southern Democrat James Buchanan and the entirely northern Republican candidate, John C. Frémont, who would receive no Southern votes. Many Southerners warned that a Frémont victory would bring an immediate secession, and a great many people took the threat seriously. Many who detested Buchanan, like Frémont's own father-in-law, Thomas Hart Benton, supported Buchanan as the best hope to avoid the election of a purely Northern candidate and the danger of secession and civil war.

Fillmore saw himself as the best hope for sectional peace among the three. In twenty-seven public speeches, he ignored the antiforeign and anti-Catholic sentiments of his party and dwelt upon the terrible sectional conflict that would follow the election of Frémont. "As an American," he told one audience, "I have no hostility to foreigners. . . . Having witnessed their deplorable condition in the old country, God forbid I should add to their sufferings by refusing them an asylum in this."[5] The Buchanan adherents, not Fillmore, accused Frémont of Catholicism because he and Jessie Benton had been married by a Catholic priest. John and Jessie were both Protestants, but in the course of their elopement when she was only seventeen, they had been unable to find a Protestant minister brave enough to risk her father's wrath by marrying them.

In the end, many who had once supported Fillmore voted for Buchanan because they recognized the hopelessness of the Know-Nothing cause and considered Frémont the ultimate danger. Fillmore carried only Maryland, but he gained a respectable 21.53 percent of the total vote, while Buchanan won with 39.00 percent. Fillmore's identification with the Know-Nothings looks far worse to twentieth-century liberal historians than it did to his contemporaries, and his motives were far more enlightened than was the ideological basis of the party. The Know-Nothing movement deserves condemnation, but Fillmore's candidacy should not affect judgments as to the effectiveness of his presidency.

The election of 1856 was Fillmore's last venture into national politics, although he was only fifty-six years old. He married a wealthy and childless fifty-two-year-old widow and settled into a comfortable life as Buffalo's leading citizen. He and his new wife bought a huge mansion and entertained lavishly. They generously supported almost every conceivable cause. Charities, public education, museums, Buffalo's Fine Arts Academy, the incipient University of Buffalo, libraries, the YMCA, the Historical Society, the Buffalo General Hospital, the Orphan Asylum, the Society for the Prevention of Cruelty to Animals, and the Natural Sciences Society were just some of the activities that profited from their talents, time, and money.

When secession came, Fillmore supported the cause of the Union wholeheartedly, although he voted for McClellan in 1864. He enjoyed watching the formerly ostensible radicals Weed and Seward suddenly become all-out supporters of his own conservative policies. Before the war, Weed and Seward proposed the strengthening of the Fugitive Slave Act, the modification of the states' personal-liberty laws, and the abandonment of the Wilmot Proviso. As secretary of state, Seward went behind Lincoln's back and tried to give Fort Sumter to the South without a struggle.

Four days after the Battle of Fort Sumter, Fillmore organized a giant Union demonstration. Before a huge crowd, he called for volunteers and pledged five hundred dollars for the support of their families. He organized and led the "Union Continentals," a military corps of men who were too old to enlist but who supposedly were ready to act in a local emergency. By all accounts, this group did much to encourage enlistments among the younger men. They led parades and marched as funeral escorts. The Fillmores helped organize a fair that raised $25,000 for the war effort.

When the war ended, Fillmore continued in his happy role of a leading senior citizen, representing the city on ceremonial occasions and promoting its interests whenever possible. On 13 February 1874, he suffered a stroke, and on 8 March he died. His statue still graces the square in front of the Buffalo City Hall.[6]

16

★ ★ ★ ★ ★

IN RETROSPECT

No two presidents have been more victimized by history than Zachary Taylor and Millard Fillmore. Virtually every poll of historians who have been asked to rate presidents has placed them near the bottom, and Fillmore has become the subject of a humorous cult based upon the assumption that he is "America's most forgettable president."

Taylor, of course, has suffered from the fact that he was president for only sixteen months. Also, for the elitist historians of the nineteenth century, it was easy to treat him with the same disdain accorded to the earlier general-president, Andrew Jackson. Taylor had little formal education, spent most of his rough life on military frontiers, and lacked previous political experience. Even the affectionate sobriquet given him by soldiers and the voters was a derogatory label. How could such a person possibly be a successful president? Jackson's reputation recovered and blossomed during the Progressive movement and New Deal periods, but Taylor, after all, had been a Whig. Unlike Jackson, Taylor had fought no crusade against an all-powerful United States Bank, and he could not be identified with the expanded suffrage and political egalitarianism that came to be called Jacksonian Democracy. Taylor, unlike Jackson, could not be mistakenly identified as an incipient Progressive or an early New Dealer, nor could he stir up the historical controversies these views generated. Charles A. and Mary R. Beard wrote a lengthy history of the United States, in which they mentioned Taylor only as a Mexican War general and ignored Fillmore entirely.

If Northern historians found it easy to stress the mediocrity of a slaveholder, Southerners were equally unwilling to forgive a heretic—a slaveholder who hobnobbed with abolitionists and opposed Southern territorial ambitions. However, when the so-called revisionists of the late 1930s and the 1940s began stressing the ideals of moderation and peace and suggested that perhaps the Civil War might have been avoided, Zachary Taylor should have been one of their heroes. He looked beyond his own immediate interests as a large slaveholder, recognized that slavery could not be expanded, and tried to check unrealistic Southern demands that could only multiply Northern opposition to the institution itself. Instead, however, most revisionists made the compromise efforts of 1850 the centerpiece of his administration and accepted the accusation of Taylor's enemies, led by the Democratic *Washington Union*, that he was an obstacle to its achievement. Supporters of the omnibus bill like James Pearce, Jacob Miller, John Bell, and others defended him against the charge, and the editors of the *Republic* and the *National Intelligencer* insisted throughout that Taylor would support any compromise that did not give New Mexico to Texas. Their views, however, somehow escaped serious consideration by historians, including Taylor's friendly biographers.

The exciting spectacle of the aged Henry Clay making his last stand for the glorious Union against the opposition of a jealous president was too dramatic to be marred by the fact that it was only half true. The equally inspiring but tragic figure of the dying John C. Calhoun expounding his final defense of the South obscured the realism of Taylor's views on how best to preserve slavery. The fact that combining the compromise measures into an omnibus bill actually delayed the compromise for several months and allowed the danger of a military clash between Texas and New Mexico to become ever more imminent was ignored. A few did give belated credit to Stephen A. Douglas for guiding the separate bills through the Senate, but virtually no one pointed out that this was the process Taylor had advocated all along. The sudden removal of Taylor—by Providence, the Almighty, fate, or America's usual good luck—just in time to enable Clay, Douglas, and Fillmore to save the Union was another illusion too exciting to bear a closer examination. Daniel Webster was the first to suggest that only Taylor's death had prevented a civil war, but Webster was hardly a disinterested witness. He was trying desperately to prove to New Englanders that his support for the fugitive-slave law was necessary to prevent a war, and as secretary of state, he had written the first draft of Fillmore's message dealing with Texas and New Mexico.

In fact, however, Fillmore's view of the Texas boundary dispute was identical to that of Taylor, although Fillmore did not threaten to defend New Mexico in person. Obviously, Fillmore was on a more friendly personal basis with Clay, Foote, and the other supporters of the omnibus bill, but he cooperated fully with Senator James Pearce and the others who broke the bill into separate pieces. Pearce, whose actions were responsible for the separation process, was throughout the debates a strong supporter and defender of Zachary Taylor, and Pearce would probably have followed the same course if Taylor had lived. Fillmore's powerful and well-argued reaffirmation of Taylor's support for New Mexico was very effective, but it did no more than expound a policy already in place. With either Taylor or Fillmore in the White House, the Texans and their Southern supporters had to recognize that they could not take New Mexico without a military clash with the United States. Fortunately, the two Texas senators were devoted to the Union and were not ready to promote an actual war with either Taylor or Fillmore. Regardless of who was president, the Texas bondholders would have been present with their various blandishments to help persuade senators and congressmen to preserve a viable New Mexico in return for the $10 million award to Texas. In 1850 the Southern people were not ready to secede against a president who owned 145 slaves, and the overwhelming evidence of mass public support in both sections for a compromise would probably have dictated the passage of compromise measures not significantly different from those that were enacted. And finally, there is no reason to believe that Taylor would have vetoed any such acts. Even before Taylor's death, the radical Southern convention at Nashville had died with only a mild whimper, and only a formal passage of the Wilmot Proviso, which an overwhelming majority in Congress opposed, or a war between Texas and New Mexico could have revived it.

Those who believe that the war should have been postponed as long as possible in the hope that changing circumstances might have made it unnecessary should consider Taylor's death a calamity, rather than a blessing. If he had survived and presided over a compromise, which seems very likely, he would certainly have been renominated and very probably reelected. His personal popularity was still high everywhere, and Southerners would have had to feel secure with a president who had just invested heavily in another slave-worked plantation. In 1852 the solid South plus the states won by Scott plus almost any combination of two other Northern states in which Pierce's majority was close would have been enough to reelect the president. A Whig victory or even a strong showing in the South in 1852 would have preserved the party for at least another election. Certainly, with Taylor in the White House, there would have been no repeal of the Missouri Compromise or a "Bleeding Kansas" to induce a great many Northern Democrats to coalesce with the rudderless Northern Whigs into a new, entirely northern Republican party. In 1852 the Free-Soil party received less than 5 percent of the total presidential vote, but with the Northern Whigs forced to choose between Republicans and Know-Nothings and with the life-giving blood transfusion provided by the conflict in Kansas, the Republicans had become a major party by 1856.

As for Fillmore, even those who have given him high marks for supporting the compromise have done so almost grudgingly, probably because of his Know-Nothing candidacy in 1856. They have also usually implied inaccurately that his administration was a sharp turn away from that of Taylor. Fillmore's first important contribution to the compromise came when he worked to bring about what Taylor had advocated all along—a separation of the omnibus bill into separate bills. His second and equally vital action was his announcement that like Taylor he would defend New Mexico with military force if necessary. True, he combined this announcement with a plea for compensation to Texas, but an indemnity for the Texans if they should lose part of their territorial claim had been a certainty throughout the debates. Reputable historians have attributed the passage of the compromise to Fillmore's strong pro-Southern sentiments, but only his usually unsuccessful efforts to enforce the fugitive-slave law can be cited as evidence that he was pro-Southern. The *Daily Union*, its Southern satellites, and numerous Southern leaders certainly did not consider Fillmore a friend during the debates. Ironically, throughout 1851 and 1852 the *Union* constantly denounced Fillmore as a partner with Seward and Weed in the cause of abolition and free-soilism. Simultaneously, Weed's *Albany Evening Journal* was accusing Fillmore of truckling to the South and betraying the North in exchange for Southern support for his reelection.

Fillmore was, in fact, a conscientious president faced by a painful conflict between his personal conscience and his constitutional oath to enforce the laws of Congress and preserve the Union. He chose to honor his oath and thereby helped the Southern moderates to maintain control of their section for a few more years. By this decision he also gained an inaccurate historical reputation for being pro-Southern—a sentiment that ultimately came to be portrayed as his primary motive for having supported the compromise.

Daniel Webster correctly described Fillmore as "a good-tempered, cautious, intelligent man, with whom it is pleasant to transact business. He is very diligent, and what he does not know he quickly learns." Fillmore had other attractive personal virtues which may have been political weaknesses. He was modest, extremely unselfish, and devoid of ambition for personal aggrandizement. He did not value the prestige, power, and perquisites of the presidency enough to want four more years of heavy responsibilities, even though on the surface it looked as though he had come through the tunnel into daylight. With Taylor gone, his own renomination was vitally important to the future of his party and the nation, but he was at first too modest to recognize this. Instead of using the power of his office and his early popularity to court delegates and guarantee a quick nomination, he tried to escape the burdens and reward the still-eager ambitions of Daniel Webster. He could have and should have sought renomination vigorously to thwart the nomination of Scott, the ambitions of Seward, and the collapse of the Whig party.

There are those, of course, who believe that because the Civil War was inevitable, men like Taylor, Fillmore, Clay, Webster, Benton, Foote, Bell, and others who sought to avoid it should not be admired. In this view, those like John C. Calhoun and Thaddeus Stevens were the true realists, and the war, presumably, should have come sooner. And furthermore, they argue, those who take high moral ground and defend their principles to the death, if necessary, serve mankind better in the long run than do the temporizers and the compromisers. Because slavery could have been ended only by war, the quicker the event occurred, the better. Because the South could feel secure only as an independent nation, its leaders should have been equally eager to make the effort. This approach ignores the fact that the would-be peacemakers of the 1850s did not know that war was inevitable. As an analysis of the American situation in 1850, this viewpoint may be entirely accurate and justifiable. One must hope, however, that it does not become the philosophy of those destined to determine the issues of peace and war among the superpowers of the late twentieth century.

Modern presidents are often rated in terms of public charisma and their ability to influence Congress, although most historians praise the "imperial presidency" only when they agree with its results. In 1850, however, with no radio or television, charisma was created primarily by deeds that lent themselves to a favorable press. Whether Zachary Taylor mumbled, as his enemies charged, or spoke clearly, as his friends insisted, very few people ever heard him speak or saw him personally. However, when both parties still thought he might be their candidate, the newspapers turned his military victories against heavy odds and his well-earned sobriquet Old Rough and Ready into a heroic public image that transcended most issues. If circumstances had required the use of force to suppress any serious threat of disunion, he would have had overwhelming public support—in many parts of the South as well as the North. Trying to dominate Congress, however, was a practice that the Whig party had been condemning since the alleged "reign" of Andrew Jackson. Perhaps ironically, Old Hickory's reputation as a strong president had resulted from his vetoes after only minimal support for his policies in Congress. Taylor's friends denied that he was trying to influence Congress at all, and whether even an experienced spoilsman could have used the patronage effectively to gain support for such bitterly contested policies is doubtful. The administration's effort, if such it was, to win Northern support for California statehood and against a formal Wilmot Proviso by giving the New York patronage to Seward seemed logical, but its impact upon Southern moderates was a political disaster.

Fillmore, by all accounts, was more eloquent than Taylor, but he lacked the general's heroic image and consequent public charisma. Having served as a congressman and as vice-president, however, Fillmore knew more members personally, understood the workings of the system better, and was more ready to stroke sensitive egos. The mere fact that he was known to be an enemy of Seward was enough to make Southerners more friendly, and he apparently did use personal relations and make a few patronage promises when the compromise measures were in their final stages. In all likelihood, however, his most important contribution to the compromise was his firmness in dealing with Texas. If there had been no fugitive-slave controversy, Fillmore might well be remembered as the ideal spokesman for an optimistic age of scientific, technological, economic, and social progress. If at the peak of his popularity, when Americans everywhere were celebrating the compromise, he had announced his availability for reelection and had made an all-out effort to achieve such a result, American history and Fillmore's own reputation might have been quite different.

While neither Taylor nor Fillmore had an opportunity to achieve greatness, both were, in fact, superior presidents when rated by the standards most Americans would accept as important. They studied the issues, they reached independent conclusions that were always reasonable and often wise, they based decisions upon their views of the common good, they acted decisively and vigorously, they did not shun any responsibility, they were totally honest in both words and deeds, they kept no secrets, they followed and defended the Constitution and the laws of Congress faithfully, and they were morally above reproach.

Both Taylor and Fillmore advocated and tried to promote policies that were certain to prevent the expansion of slavery into the new areas acquired from Mexico. Taylor's willingness to cultivate personal friendships with outspoken opponents of slavery indicated an unusual breadth of vision. Some modern historians have lamented the fact that the defenders and opponents of slavery could not establish the kind of peaceful dialogue that might have led eventually to a cooperative effort against the institution. There is no evidence that Taylor was looking ahead to the demise of slavery, but he respected the views of its opponents, and he tried to promote personal tolerance and understanding between the opposing groups.

Both presidents were attacked viciously and unfairly by partisan enemies and newspapers in both the North and the South, but neither allowed personal considerations to affect his policies. Each in his own way played a vital role in leading the country safely through a serious crisis, and Fillmore retired at a moment of restored harmony and immense prosperity. Both men exercised an admirable combination of aggressiveness, restraint, and imagination in advancing and protecting American interests abroad. Each deserves a far better historical reputation than he has received.

NOTES

CHAPTER 1
PROGRESS AND PARADOX

1. Allan Nevins, in *Ordeal of the Union*, 2 vols. (New York: Scribner's, 1947), 1:34–112, offers a vivid account of America at midcentury; see also Robert Sobel, *Machines and Morality: The 1850s* (New York: Thomas Y. Crowell Co., 1973).

2. United States Bureau of the Census, *The Statistical History of the United States from Colonial Times to the Present* (New York: Basic Books, 1978), pp. 239, 590, 593, 600, 602, 606, 865, 899, henceforth cited as *Statistical History*.

3. Ibid., p. 959.

4. Ibid., pp. 512, 518; John T. Schlebecker, *Whereby We Thrive: A History of American Farming* (Ames: Iowa State University Press, 1975), pp. 97–129.

5. *Statistical History*, p. 732; *Congressional Globe*, 30th Cong., 2d sess., 1848/49, pp. 470–74; Elbert B. Smith, *Magnificent Missourian: The Life of Thomas Hart Benton* (Philadelphia: J. B. Lippincott Co., 1958), pp. 253–56; George Fort Milton, *The Eve of Conflict: Stephen A. Douglas and the Needless War* (Boston, Mass.: Houghton Mifflin, 1934), pp. 99–101.

6. *Statistical History*, pp. 750–51; Nevins, *Ordeal of the Union*, 2:214–41.

7. *Statistical History*, p. 790.

8. Ibid., p. 805.

9. This spirit is brilliantly portrayed by John Ward in *Andrew Jackson: Symbol for an Age* (New York: Oxford University Press, 1955).

10. Henry G. Goode and James D. Teller, *A History of Western Education* (New York: Macmillan, 1969), pp. 431–65; Sidney L. Jackson, *America's Struggle for Free Schools* (Washington, D.C.: American Council on Public Affairs, 1941); *Statistical History*, p. 370.

11. The dates of origin are from *The World Almanac* (New York: Newspaper Enterprise Association, Inc., 1984 edition), pp. 165–89. Some of them probably had very humble beginnings as of their own published dates of origin.

12. The generalizations are based upon extensive research in newspapers.

13. Alice F. Tyler, *Freedom's Ferment: Phases of American Social History to 1860* (Minneapolis: University of Minnesota Press, 1944); Nevins, *Ordeal of the Union*, 1:113–49.

14. Stanley Elkins, *Slavery: A Problem in American Institutional and Intellectual Life* (Chicago: University of Chicago Press, 1959), pp. 193–222; Leon F. Litwack, *North of Slavery: The Negro in the Free States* (Chicago: University of Chicago Press, 1961); Nevins, *Ordeal of the Union*, 1:498-535; Avery Craven, *Coming of the Civil War* (New York: Scribner's Sons, 1942), pp. 117–50.

15. William S. Jenkins, *Pro-Slavery Thought in the Old South* (Gloucester, Mass.: P. Smith, 1960); George Fitzhugh, *Sociology for the South; or, The Failure of Free Society*, and *Cannibals All; or, Slaves without Masters* (both Richmond, Va.: A. Morris, 1854 and 1857); Craven, *Coming of the Civil War*, pp. 151–74; Nevins, *Ordeal of the Union*, 1:494–98.

16. Tyler, *Freedom's Ferment*, pp. 25–67, 108–95.

17. See note 15 above.

18. Cf. John R. McKivigan, *The War against Proslavery Religion: Abolitionism and the Northern Churches, 1830–1865* (Ithaca, N.Y.: Cornell University Press, 1984).

CHAPTER 2
THE PRICE OF CONQUEST

1. Reprinted in Avery Craven, Walter Johnson, and F. Roger Dunn, *A Documentary History of the American People* (Boston: Ginn & Co., 1951), pp. 376–80.

2. *Congressional Globe*, 30th Cong., 1st sess., 1847/48, p. 1074; also pp. 804–5, and 30th Cong., 1st sess., 1847–48 app., pp. 684–86.

3. Frederick Douglass, *The Life and Times of Frederick Douglass, Written by Himself* (Hartford, Conn.: Park Publishing Co., 1881), pp. 406–7; Ralph Morrow, "The Proslavery Argument Revisited," *Mississippi Valley Historical Review* 48 (June 1961): 70–94; Charles Sellers, "The Tragic Southerner," in Sellers, ed., *The Southerner as American* (Chapel Hill: University of North Carolina Press, 1960); Elbert B. Smith, *The Presidency*

of *James Buchanan* (Lawrence: University Press of Kansas, 1975), pp. 129–42; Bertram Wyatt-Brown, *Honor and Violence in the Old South* (New York: Oxford University Press, 1986), pp. 25–62; the entire book supports this viewpoint.

4. James K. Polk, *The Diary of James K. Polk during His Presidency, 1845 to 1849*, ed. Milo M. Quaife, 4 vols. (Chicago: A. C. McClurg & Co., 1910), 2:406–8, 418; Elbert B. Smith, *Magnificent Missourian: The Life of Thomas Hart Benton* (Philadelphia: J. B. Lippincott Co., 1958), pp. 253–56.

5. Allan Nevins, *Ordeal of the Union*, 2 vols. (New York: Scribner's, 1947), 1:202–9.

6. Holman Hamilton, *Zachary Taylor, Soldier in the White House* (Indianapolis, Ind.: Bobbs-Merrill Co., 1951), pp. 86–97; Robert Rayback, *Millard Fillmore* (Buffalo, N.Y.: Henry Steward, Inc., for the Buffalo Historical Society, 1959), pp. 181–91; cf. Glyndon Van Deusen, *Thurlow Weed, Wizard of the Lobby* (New York: Da Capo Press, 1969; reprint of Little, Brown & Co.'s 1947 edition), pp. 156–64.

CHAPTER 3
OLD ROUGH AND READY

1. For details of Taylor's ancestry and earlier life I have relied upon Brainerd Dyer, *Zachary Taylor* (Baton Rouge: Louisiana State University Press, 1946, hereafter cited as Dyer, *Taylor*); Holman Hamilton, *Zachary Taylor, Soldier of the Republic* (Indianapolis, Ind.: Bobbs-Merrill Co., 1941), henceforth referred to as Hamilton, *Taylor*, vol. 1; and K. Jack Bauer, *Zachary Taylor* (Baton Rouge: Louisiana State University Press, 1985), henceforth cited as Bauer, *Taylor*. Of these, Hamilton is much more detailed, while Bauer is generally the most critical.

2. Holman Hamilton, *Zachary Taylor, Soldier in the White House* (Indianapolis, Ind.: Bobbs-Merrill Co., 1951), pp. 30–37; henceforth cited as Hamilton, *Taylor*, vol. 2.

3. Taylor to Thomas Jesup, 4 Dec. 1832, Taylor Papers, Library of Congress, henceforth cited as LC; Hamilton, *Taylor*, 1:135.

4. Taylor to Thomas Jesup, 18 June 1821, Taylor Papers.

5. Bauer, *Taylor*, p. 54; in pp. 29–74, Bauer skillfully traces Taylor's earlier military career.

6. Ibid., pp. 69–70; Hamilton, *Taylor*, 1:101–9.

7. Bauer, *Taylor*, pp. 75–95; Hamilton, *Taylor*, 1:122–41.

8. Taylor to Jesup, 4 Dec. 1837, Taylor Papers; Dyer, *Taylor*, pp. 117–18.

9. Joseph P. Taylor to Zachary Taylor, 31 Jan. 1838, forwarded to Jesup with a request that Romeo be taken care of; Taylor to Jesup, 13 and 14 Feb., 20 Mar., and 26 Apr. 1838, Taylor Papers; for further examples of Taylor's fairness to the Indians see Hamilton, *Taylor*, 1:136, and Bauer,

Taylor, p. 86.

10. Taylor to Maj. Ethan A. Hitchcock, 19 May 1841, Taylor Papers; Dyer, *Taylor*, p. 130.

11. Bauer, *Taylor*, pp. 96–97, 103; Dyer, *Taylor*, pp. 409–10.

12. Dyer, *Taylor*, pp. 133–39; Hamilton, *Taylor*, 1:147–53; Bauer, *Taylor*, pp. 99–100.

13. Taylor to Jefferson Davis, 24 June 1847, Taylor Papers.

14. James K. Polk, *The Diary of James K. Polk during His Presidency, 1845 to 1849*, ed. Milo M. Quaife, 4 vols. (Chicago: A. C. McClurg & Co., 1910), 1:386–90.

15. Hamilton, *Taylor*, 1:181–90; Bauer, *Taylor*, pp. 117–65; Dyer, *Taylor*, pp. 165–85.

16. Dyer, *Taylor*, p. 192; Hamilton, *Taylor*, 1:173; Bauer, *Taylor*, p. 165.

17. Bauer, *Taylor*, pp. 162–63; Bauer is a better military historian than I am, and I may be unduly sympathetic to a general who took a short-term view against sacrificing manpower.

18. Hamilton, *Taylor*, 1:166.

19. Bauer, *Taylor*, pp. 166–85; Hamilton, *Taylor*, 1:191–216.

20. Taylor to Dr. R. C. Wood, 2 Nov. 1847, in *Letters of Zachary Taylor from the Battlefields of the Mexican War*, ed. William H. Samson (Rochester, N.Y.: Genesee Press, 1908, in Rare Book Room, LC), p. 148; Bauer, *Taylor*, p. 193.

21. Hamilton, *Taylor*, 1:231–42; Bauer, *Taylor*, pp. 186–207.

22. Taylor to Wood, 20 Mar. and 4 Apr. 1847, *Letters*, pp. 90–91, 93–96.

23. Taylor to Wood, 4 Apr. 1847, *Letters*, p. 96.

24. Taylor to Wood, 30 May 1847, *Letters*, pp. 102–3.

25. Taylor to Wood, 30 May 1847, *Letters*, pp. 101–3.

26. Taylor to Jefferson Davis, 20 June 1847, Taylor Papers.

27. Taylor to Wood, 20 July 1847, *Letters*, pp. 116–19.

28. Taylor to Davis, 16 Aug. 1847, Taylor Papers.

29. Taylor to Wood, 19 and 27 Oct. 1847, *Letters*, pp. 141–47.

30. Taylor to Wood, 27 Sept. 1847, *Letters*, pp. 131–37.

31. Taylor to Wood, 18 Feb. 1848, *Letters*, pp. 152–55; see also Hamilton, *Taylor*, 2:43–50; and Bauer, *Taylor*, pp. 226–31.

32. Hamilton, *Taylor*, 2:76–81, letter in full, pp. 79–81; Bauer, *Taylor*, p. 233.

33. Taylor to R. T. Allison (his nephew), 25 June 1848, *Letters*, pp. 160–64.

34. Hamilton, *Taylor*, 2:121–25; Bauer, *Taylor*, p. 243; Robert Rayback, *Millard Fillmore* (Buffalo, N.Y.: Henry Steward, Inc., for the Buffalo Historical Society, 1959), pp. 190–91.

35. Taylor to Wood, 10 Dec. 1848, *Letters*, pp. 167–69.

CHAPTER 4
THE ACHIEVER

1. For this sketch of Fillmore's earlier life and achievements I have relied almost entirely upon Robert Rayback's thoroughly documented biography *Millard Fillmore: Biography of a President* (Buffalo, N.Y.: Henry Steward, Inc., for the Buffalo Historical Society, 1959), pp. 1–191, and upon Frank Severance, ed., *Millard Fillmore Papers*, 2 vols., vols. 10 and 11 of Publications of the Buffalo Historical Society (Buffalo, N.Y., 1907).

2. Rayback, *Millard Fillmore*, pp. 189–91; Holman Hamilton, *Zachary Taylor, Soldier in the White House* (Indianapolis, Ind.: Bobbs-Merrill Co., 1941), pp. 115–26; K. Jack Bauer, *Zachary Taylor* (Baton Rouge: Louisiana State University Press, 1985), p. 253; Glyndon Van Deusen, *Thurlow Weed, Wizard of the Lobby* (New York: Da Capo Press, 1969; reprint of 1947 edition), p. 163.

3. Rayback, *Millard Fillmore*, pp. 165–89.
I have given Fillmore's career before 1848 much less space than that of Taylor because it was more clear-cut and less controversial, as was his career as president. The bare facts of Fillmore's spectacular rise from dire poverty to great professional, political, and administrative success demonstrate the high intelligence and political skills that one always hopes to find in a president. Taylor, however, has often been downgraded for his lack of political experience, while his military exploits have rarely been attributed to intelligence or to any other intellectual quality usually associated with the presidency. In my view, Taylor's character, insights, attitudes, and military experience did in fact equip him well for the presidency in 1848, and I have therefore discussed them in much more detail as evidence to support this argument.

CHAPTER 5
THE ADMINISTRATION

1. James K. Polk, *The Diary of James K. Polk during His Presidency, 1845 to 1849*, ed. Milo M. Quaife, 4 vols. (Chicago: A. C. McClurg & Co., 1910), 4:184, 375–76.

2. Ibid., pp. 374–76.

3. James D. Richardson, comp., *A Compilation of the Messages and Papers of the Presidents, 1789–1897*, vol. 5 (Washington, D.C.: Government Printing Office, 1900), pp. 4–6.

4. Alexander H. Stephens to John J. Crittenden, 6 Feb. 1849, Ulrich B. Phillips, ed., "The Correspondence of Robert Toombs, Alexander H. Stephens, and Howell Cobb," *Annual Report of the American Historical Association for the Year 1911* (Washington, D.C., 1913), 2:146, henceforth cited as *AHA*, 1911.

5. Mary W. Williams, "John M. Clayton," in Samuel F. Bemis and Robert H. Ferrell, eds., *American Secretaries of State*, 20 vols. (New York: Cooper Square Publishers, 1963); Holman Hamilton, *Zachary Taylor, Soldier in the White House* (Indianapolis, Ind.: Bobbs-Merrill Co., 1951), pp. 162-68 (hereafter cited as Hamilton, *Taylor*, vol. 2), offers valuable sketches of each cabinet member.

6. Holman Hamilton, *Zachary Taylor, Soldier of the Republic* (Indianapolis, Ind.: Bobbs-Merrill Co., 1941), p. 163, hereafter cited as Hamilton, *Taylor*, vol. 1; K. Jack Bauer, *Zachary Taylor* (Baton Rouge: Louisiana State University Press, 1985), p. 260, hereafter cited as Bauer, *Taylor*; Allen Johnson and Dumas Malone, eds., *Dictionary of American Biography*, 10 vols. (New York: Charles Scribner's Sons, 1930-35, updated to 1959), 6:548-49, henceforth cited as *DAB*.

7. *DAB*, 3:237-38.

8. *DAB*, 2:520.

9. Harold D. Langley, "William Ballard Preston," in Paolo E. Coletta, Robert G. Albion, and K. Jack Bauer, eds., *American Secretaries of the Navy*, 2 vols. (Annapolis, Md.: Naval Institute Press, 1980), 1:243-44.

10. *DAB*, 2:300; Hamilton, *Taylor*, 2:165; Bauer, *Taylor*, p. 262. Bauer writes that Collamer disliked patronage politics, but according to Hamilton he was "as proscriptive as Ewing," though "less vigorous."

11. Bernard Steiner, *The Life of Reverdy Johnson* (Baltimore, Md.: Norman, Remington Co., 1914); *DAB*, 5:112-14.

12. Henry Clay to Daniel Ullman, 16 Sept. 1848, *The Private Correspondence of Henry Clay*, ed. Calvin Colton (New York: A. S. Barnes Co., 1857), pp. 576-77; Stephens to Crittenden, 6 Feb. 1849, *AHA*, 1911, p. 146.

13. Taylor to Davis, 11 Sept. 1849, cited by Hamilton in *Taylor*, 1:237-38.

14. Mrs. Chapman Coleman, *The Life of John J. Crittenden*, 2 vols. (Philadelphia: J. B. Lippincott Co., 1871), 1:346; this is a printed collection of letters to and from Crittenden, rather than a biography.

15. Elbert B. Smith, *Francis Preston Blair* (New York: Free Press, 1980), pp. 45-61.

16. Hamilton, *Taylor*, 1:170-71.

17. Ibid., pp. 172, 324.

18. Crittenden to Brown, 3 and 26 July 1849, in Coleman, *Life of John J. Crittenden*, 1:343, 346-47.

19. Generalizations from well-known facts about Seward's life from any Seward biography; cf. Glyndon Van Deusen, *William Henry Seward* (New York: Oxford University Press, 1967); Hamilton, *Taylor*, 1:168-70; Robert Rayback, *Millard Fillmore: Biography of a President* (Buffalo: Henry Steward, Inc., for the Buffalo Historical Society, 1959), pp. 194-96.

20. Rayback, *Millard Fillmore*, pp. 200-206; Hamilton, *Taylor*, 2:168-69; Bauer, *Taylor*, pp. 263-64.

21. Joseph P. Taylor to Zachary Taylor, 8 Sept. 1847, Taylor Papers.

22. Chase to Charles Sumner, 13 Apr. 1850, in Edward G. Bourne et al., eds., "Diary and Correspondence of Salmon P. Chase," *Annual Report of the American Historical Association for the Year 1902*, vol. 2 (Washington, D.C.: Government Printing Office, 1903), pp. 207–8.

23. Some examples are Martin Van Buren, Amos Kendall, and Francis P. Blair, for Andrew Jackson; Abraham Lincoln, with the help of the Blairs and others; and James Farley, for Franklin Roosevelt.

24. Michael F. Holt, *The Political Crisis of the 1850s* (New York: W. W. Norton & Co., 1978), pp. 74–76.

25. Taylor to Davis, 11 Sept. 1849, cited by Hamilton, *Taylor*, 2:238.

26. Hamilton, *Taylor*, 2:203–17.

27. Ibid., pp. 171–72, 236–38.

CHAPTER 6
THE STATESMAN

1. Holman Hamilton, *Zachary Taylor, Soldier in the White House* (Indianapolis, Ind.: Bobbs-Merrill Co., 1951), pp. 299–300, hereafter cited as Hamilton, *Taylor*, vol. 2; *Congressional Globe*, 31st Cong., 1st sess., 1849/50, vol. 21, pp. 200–205, 257–61.

2. *Senate Executive Documents*, 31st Cong., 1st sess., no. 1, pp. 93–94, 117, 119–22, 125–26, 132–33, 136; Hamilton, *Taylor*, 2:183–85.

3. *Senate Executive Documents*, 31st Cong., 1st sess., no. 1, pp. 108, 115, 138–42, 149–52; *Washington Union*, 11 and 25 Sept. 1849; Hamilton, *Taylor*, 2:185–86.

4. Henry Blumenthal, *France and the United States* (Chapel Hill: University of North Carolina Press, 1970), p. 219; Hamilton, *Taylor*, 2:187–90; K. Jack Bauer, *Zachary Taylor* (Baton Rouge: Louisiana State University Press, 1985), pp. 275–77, hereafter cited as Bauer, *Taylor*; *Washington Union*, 23 Sept. 1849; *Washington Republic*, 19 Mar. 1850.

5. Holman Hamilton, *Zachary Taylor, Soldier of the Republic* (Indianapolis, Ind.: Bobbs-Merrill Co., 1941), pp. 190–91, hereafter cited as Hamilton, *Taylor*, vol. 1; Bauer, *Taylor*, pp. 277–78.

6. Hamilton, *Taylor*, 1:191.

7. Oscar T. Barck, Jr., and Nelson M. Blake, *The United States in Its World Relations* (New York: McGraw-Hill, 1960), pp. 256–57; Hamilton, *Taylor*, 1:191–92; Bauer, *Taylor*, p. 287.

8. Lady Jane Franklin to Zachary Taylor, 4 Apr. 1849 and John M. Clayton to Lady Franklin, cited in various newspapers and in Bauer, *Taylor*, p. 277; James D. Richardson, comp., *A Compilation of the Messages and Papers of the Presidents, 1789–1897*, vol. 5 (Washington, D. C.: Government Printing Office, 1900), pp. 25–29; Hamilton, *Taylor*, 1:329, 353.

9. Dana G. Munroe, *The Latin American Republics* (New York: Appleton Century-Crofts, 1960), pp. 155–65, 404–11; J. Fred Rippy, *Latin America* (Ann Arbor: University of Michigan Press, 1958), pp. 43–45, 219–24.

10. Thomas A. Bailey, *A Diplomatic History of the American People*, 10th ed. (Englewood Cliffs, N.J.: Prentice-Hall, 1980), pp. 272–76, concluded that the treaty was "something of a triumph for American Diplomacy." Cf. Barck and Blake, *United States in Its World Relations*, pp. 232–38; Hamilton, *Taylor*, 2:192–98, 357–67; Bauer, *Taylor*, pp. 281–86; Richard Van Alstyne, "British Diplomacy and the Clayton-Bulwer Treaty," *Journal of Modern History* 11 (1939).

11. Hamilton, *Taylor*, 1:196.

12. Ibid., p. 360.

13. Ibid., p. 362.

14. Ibid., p. 364.

15. Ibid., pp. 364–65.

16. Ibid., pp. 365–67; Bauer, *Taylor*, pp. 285, 287; Barck and Blake, *United States in Its World Relations*, pp. 237–38.

17. Richardson, *Messages and Papers of the Presidents*, 5:19–24, whole message; Hamilton, *Taylor*, 2:198–99, 202, 356–57; Barck and Blake, *United States in Its World Relations*, p. 221.

18. Quoted by Hamilton, *Taylor*, 1:199.

19. *Senate Executive Documents*, 31st Cong., 1st sess., 1849–50, no. 57, pp. 4–8, 67–69; Barck and Blake, *United States in Its World Relations*, pp. 242–44; Hamilton, *Taylor*, 1:199–201, 224–25, 368–71; Bauer, *Taylor*, pp. 278–81; Richardson, *Messages and Papers of the Presidents*, 5:7–8, 11–12; Bailey, *Diplomatic History*, pp. 285–91.

CHAPTER 7
THE CRISIS

1. Richard C. Crallé, ed., *Reports and Public Letters of John C. Calhoun*, 6 vols. (New York: D. Appleton & Co., 1864), 6:285–313.

2. Howell Cobb to Mrs. Cobb, 8 Feb. 1849, cited by Avery Craven in *Coming of the Civil War* (New York: Scribner's Sons, 1942), p. 244, see also p. 243; Robert Toombs to John J. Crittenden, 3 Jan. 1849, in Ulrich B. Phillips, ed., "The Correspondence of Robert Toombs, Alexander H. Stephens, and Howell Cobb," *Annual Report of the American Historical Association for the Year 1911* (Washington, D.C., 1913), pp. 139–40.

3. Elbert B. Smith, *Magnificent Missourian: The Life of Thomas Hart Benton* (Philadelphia: J. B. Lippincott Co., 1958), pp. 248–49.

4. Craven, *Coming of the Civil War*, pp. 244–45.

5. Allan Nevins, *Ordeal of the Union*, 2 vols. (New York: Scribner's, 1947), 1:240–44.

6. James D. Richardson, comp., *A Compilation of Messages and Papers of the Presidents, 1789–1897*, vol. 5 (Washington, D. C.: Government Printing Office, 1900), pp. 7–8; Holman Hamilton, *Zachary Taylor, Soldier in the White House* (Indianapolis, Ind.: Bobbs-Merrill Co., 1951), p. 255, pp. 224–28 for entire tour, hereafter cited as Hamilton, *Taylor*, vol. 2.

7. *Republic*, reprinted in *Lexington* (Mo.) *Observer and Reporter*, 4 Aug. 1849.

8. Benton to the people of California and New Mexico, 27 Aug. 1848, *Niles Register* 74 (1848): 244–45; Smith, *Magnificent Missourian*, p. 245.

9. William C. Binkley, "The Question of Texas Jurisdiction in New Mexico under the United States, 1848–1850," *Southwestern Historical Quarterly* 26 (1920/21): 1–38; F. S. Donnell, "When Texas Owned New Mexico to the Rio Grande," *New Mexico Historical Review* 8 (1933): 65–75; Loomis N. Gannaway, "New Mexico and the Sectional Controversy, 1846–1861," *New Mexico Historical Review* 18 (1943): 113–47, 205–46, 325–48.

10. Nevins, *Ordeal of the Union*, 1:383–84.

11. *Congressional Globe*, 31st Cong., 1st sess., 1849/50, vol. 21, pp. 44, 51–59; Hamilton, *Taylor*, 2:261.

12. Richardson, *Messages and Papers of the Presidents*, 5:9–24; quotations on pp. 16, 18, 19, 20, 23, 24.

13. *Republic*, 3 Jan. 1850.

14. Richardson, *Messages and Papers of the Presidents*, 5:26–29.

15. Ibid., pp. 29–30.

16. Thurlow Weed Barnes, *Memoirs of Thurlow Weed* (Boston, Mass.: Houghton Mifflin Co., 1884), pp. 176–78; Hamilton, *Taylor*, 2:300–301.

17. *New York Herald*, 13 and 23 June, 17 and 21 Aug. 1876, contains the various letters of Stephens, Weed, Toombs, Clingman, and Hamlin, debating over what Taylor actually said. I am indebted to Mark J. Stegmaier for calling my attention to these exchanges.

18. *Congressional Globe*, 21:2–12, 15–22; Hamilton, *Taylor*, 2:243–53; Nevins, *Ordeal of the Union*, 1:251–53; Craven, *Coming of the Civil War*, pp. 247–49.

19. *Congressional Globe*, 21:22–39, 41–44, 51, 61–67; Holman Hamilton, *Zachary Taylor, Soldier of the Republic* (Indianapolis, Ind.: Bobbs-Merrill Co., 1951), pp. 250–52, hereafter cited as Hamilton, *Taylor*, vol. 1; Craven, *Coming of the Civil War*, pp. 247–48.

20. *Congressional Globe*, 21:27–28; Craven, *Coming of the Civil War*, p. 248.

21. Holman Hamilton, *Prologue to Conflict: The Crisis and Compromise of 1850* (Lexington: University of Kentucky Press, 1964), pp. 32–33.

22. *Congressional Globe*, 21:165–66.

23. Ibid., pp. 166–71; Oliver Dyer, *Great Senators of the United States Fifty Years Ago* (New York: Robert Bonner's Sons, 1889), pp. 128, 139, 278; Grace Greenwood (Sarah J. Lippincott), *Greenwood Leaves* (Boston,

Mass.: Ticknor, Reed, & Fields, 1852), pp. 302–3, 316; cf. Henry S. Foote, *Casket of Reminiscences* (Washington, D.C.: Chronicle Publishing Co., 1880), pp. 78–82; Smith, *Magnificent Missourian*, pp. 262–63.

24. Smith, *Magnificent Missourian*, pp. 187–205, 213–14, 234–60.

25. Holman Hamilton, "Texas Bonds and Northern Profits: A Study in Compromise, Investment, and Lobby Influence," *Mississippi Valley Historical Review* 43 (1957): 579–94; see also Hamilton, *Prologue to Conflict*, pp. 20, 124–32.

26. *Congressional Globe*, 21:244–47.

27. *Daily Union*, 22 Jan., 6 and 7 Feb. 1850; *Congressional Globe*, 21:247–52.

28. Foote, *Casket of Reminiscences*, pp. 78–82.

29. *Congressional Globe*, 21:451–55, quotation on p. 455.

30. My view that Calhoun's speech was unrealistic is not shared by everyone; cf. Craven, *Coming of the Civil War*, pp. 252–55.

31. *Congressional Globe*, 21:463–64; *Republic*, 12 Mar. 1850; Nevins, *Ordeal of the Union*, 1:283–85; Craven, *Coming of the Civil War*, pp. 261–64; Benton's letter to *Jefferson Enquirer* (Jefferson City, Mo.), 8 Mar. 1850.

32. *Congressional Globe*, 21:640–44; Craven, *Coming of the Civil War*, pp. 255–56; Nevins, *Ordeal of the Union*, 1:286–93; Hamilton, *Prologue to Conflict*, pp. 76–83; for differing analyses of the speech. The *Congressional Globe* did not record Calhoun's remarks, but they were remembered by witnesses: see Peter Harvey, *Reminiscences and Anecdotes of Daniel Webster* (Boston, Mass.: Little, Brown & Co., 1882), pp. 218–20; Claude M. Fuess, *Daniel Webster*, 2 vols. (Boston, Mass.: Little, Brown & Co., 1930), 2:213–14; and Richard N. Current, *Daniel Webster and the Rise of National Conservatism* (Boston, Mass.: Little, Brown & Co., 1955), p. 167.

33. Hamilton, *Prologue to Conflict*, p. 81.

34. Hamilton, *Taylor*, 2:313.

35. John Wentworth, *Congressional Reminiscences* (Chicago: Fergus Co., 1882), pp. 23–24; Craven, *Coming of the Civil War*, pp. 258–59.

36. *Congressional Globe*, 31st Cong., 1st sess., 1848/49, vol. 22 (app.), pp. 202–11; *The Collected Works of Abraham Lincoln*, ed. Roy P. Basler, 9 vols. (New Brunswick, N.J.: Rutgers University Press, 1953), 3:547–48.

37. *Congressional Globe*, 22:260–69.

38. *Republic*, 15 Mar. 1850; Hamilton, *Taylor*, 1:316–19, 321–23; Glyndon Van Deusen, *William Henry Seward* (New York: Oxford University Press, 1965), pp. 122–28.

39. Quoted from Hamilton, *Taylor*, 1:297; see also pp. 294–98.

40. Ibid., pp. 341–42.

41. Ibid., p. 386.

CHAPTER 8
AN UNDESERVED ALBATROSS:
THE GALPHIN DILEMMA

1. The issue is thoroughly researched by William P. Brandon in "The Galphin Claim," *Georgia Historical Quarterly* 15 (1931): 114–41; it is also presented in much detail in *National Intelligencer*, 24 May 1850.

2. *Congressional Globe*, 31st Cong., 1st sess., 1849/50, vol. 22 (app.), pp. 546–49; Brandon, "The Galphin Claim," p. 117.

3. Brandon, "The Galphin Claim," pp. 126–29, quoting directly from *Congress, Executive Documents*, 31st Cong., 2d sess., 1850/51, no. 55.

4. Holman Hamilton, *Zachary Taylor, Soldier in the White House* (Indianapolis, Ind.: Bobbs-Merrill Co., 1951), pp. 345–47, hereafter cited as Hamilton, *Taylor*, vol. 2.

5. Ibid., p. 347.

6. *Congressional Globe*, 22:546–51, 554, 895–96; ibid., 31st Cong., 1st sess., 1849/50, vol. 21, pp. 1027, 1353–54; Brandon, "The Galphin Claim," pp. 134–40; Hamilton, *Taylor*, 2:346–52.

7. *National Intelligencer*, 24 May 1850; Hamilton, *Taylor*, 2:353.

8. Samuel Eliot Morison, *The Oxford History of the American People* (New York: Oxford University Press, 1965), p. 573.

9. Hamilton, *Taylor*, 2:352–53.

10. *Autobiography of Thurlow Weed*, ed. Harriet A. Weed (Boston, Mass.: Houghton Mifflin, 1883), pp. 590–92; Hamilton, *Taylor*, 2:355; Glyndon Van Deusen, *Thurlow Weed, Wizard of the Lobby* (New York: Da Capo Press, 1969; reprint of 1947 edition), pp. 177–78.

CHAPTER 9
THE OMNIBUS BILL

1. *Congressional Globe*, 31st Cong., 1st sess., 1849/50, vol. 21, p. 712.

2. Robert Toombs to John J. Crittenden, 22 Jan. 1849, in Ulrich B. Phillips, ed., "The Correspondence of Robert Toombs, Alexander H. Stephens, and Howell Cobb," *Annual Report of the American Historical Association for the Year 1911* (Washington, D. C., 1913), vol. 2, p. 141, henceforth cited as *AHA*, 1911. Aside from Butler's testimony, the course of the debates presents strong circumstantial evidence that this was the purpose for combining the various measures into a single bill. The objection that California might be admitted without any concessions to the South could have easily been met, as it ultimately was, by passing the Texas–New Mexico measures first.

3. *Congressional Globe*, 21:365.

4. Ibid., pp. 365–68.

5. Ibid., p. 368.

6. Ibid., pp. 395, 371–73, 395–98.

7. Ibid., pp. 400–404.

8. Holman Hamilton, *Prologue to Conflict: The Crisis and Compromise of 1850* (Lexington: University of Kentucky Press, 1964), pp. 121–22.

9. *Union*, 6 Feb. 1850; Henry S. Foote, *Casket of Reminiscences*, (Washington, D.C.: Chronicle Publishing Co., 1880), pp. 24–27; Cleo Hearon, *Mississippi and the Compromise of 1850* (reprinted from Publications of the Mississippi Historical Society, vol. 14, 1913), pp. 112–14.

10. *Union*, 1, 2, 3, and 4 Dec. 1849; 2, 6, 19, and 22 Jan. 1850.

11. Ibid., 29 and 30 Jan. 1850.

12. Ibid., 6, 7, and 16 Feb., 19 Mar., and 7 Apr. 1850. Almost any issue could be cited in support of my generalizations.

13. *Richmond* (Va.) *Enquirer*, 4 and 15 Feb. 1850, for choice examples of opposition rhetoric.

14. *Charleston* (S.C.) *Mercury*, 15 May 1850.

15. *Congressional Globe*, 21:517–21, 640–42, 708–9.

16. Ibid., pp. 365, 709; George Fort Milton, *The Eve of Conflict: Stephen A. Douglas and the Needless War* (Boston, Mass.: Houghton Mifflin, 1934), pp. 58–59, 65–68.

17. *Congressional Globe*, 21:656–62, quotations on pp. 657, 660.

18. Ibid., pp. 602–4.

19. Ibid., pp. 762–64; *Daily Union*, 19 Apr. 1850; John Wentworth, *Congressional Reminiscences* (Chicago: Fergus Co., 1882), p. 48; Allan Nevins, *Ordeal of the Union*, 2 vols. (New York: Scribner's, 1947), 1:310; Elbert B. Smith, *Magnificent Missourian: The Life of Thomas Hart Benton* (Philadelphia: J. B. Lippincott Co., 1958), pp. 271–72.

20. *Congresssional Globe*, 21:1480–81.

21. Ibid., pp. 944–48; *Mercury*, 15 May 1850.

22. *Congressional Globe*, 21:948–56, 1003.

23. Ibid., pp. 1134–36, 1142–44.

24. Holman Hamilton, *Zachary Taylor: Soldier in the White House* (Indianapolis, Ind.: Bobbs-Merrill Co., 1951), pp. 324–25, 233–34, hereafter cited as Hamilton, *Taylor*, vol. 2; *Republic*, 14 and 20 May 1850.

25. *Congressional Globe*, 31st Cong., 1st sess., 1849/50, vol. 22 (app.), pp. 612–16. Note that the appendix for the 1849/50 session is vol. 22.

26. *Republic*, 27 May 1850; cf. Hamilton, *Taylor*, 2:335–38.

27. Hamilton, *Taylor*, 2:333–35; Robert Rayback, *Millard Fillmore: Biography of a President* (Buffalo, N.Y.: Henry Steward, Inc., for the Buffalo Historical Society, 1959), pp. 231–32; K. Jack Bauer, *Zachary Taylor* (Baton Rouge: Louisiana State University Press, 1985), pp. 306–9, hereafter cited as Bauer, *Taylor*; Brainerd Dyer, *Zachary Taylor* (Baton Rouge: Louisiana State University Press, 1946), p. 383, hereafter cited as Dyer, *Taylor*. Historians who have shared or echoed the view that Taylor opposed a compromise include Allan Nevins, John Garraty, Avery Craven, Ray Bil-

lington, Edward Channing, John B. McMaster, Samuel Morison, Arthur Schlesinger, John D. Hicks, and Michael Holt, among many others. James Schouler, however, thought Taylor's plan was "simple, sagacious, and eminently moderate" (*History of the United States* [New York: Dodd, Meade & Co., 1894], vol. 5, pp. 154-59). Hicks believed that if Taylor had lived, his "capacity for decisive action might have preserved the Union, even without the compromise measures of 1850, some of which he would doubtless have refused to sign" (*The Federal Union* [Cambridge, Mass.: Houghton Mifflin, 1957], p. 492). When I disagree with them, my trepidation is equaled only by my conviction.

28. Bauer, *Taylor*, p. 308; Michael F. Holt, *The Political Crisis of the 1850s* (New York: W. W. Norton & Co., 1978), pp. 72-80; Toombs to John J. Crittenden, 25 Apr. 1850, in Mrs. Chapman Coleman, *The Life of John J. Crittenden*, 2 vols. (Philadelphia: J. B. Lippincott Co., 1871), 1:364-66.

29. *National Daily Intelligencer*, 23, 24, 25, 26, and 29 Jan., 4, 9, 11, 16, 21, 23, 25, 26, 27, and 28 Feb., 11 Mar. 1850.

30. Ibid., 30 Apr. 1850.

31. Ibid., 18 May 1850.

32. Ibid., 24 June 1850.

33. *Republic*, 14 May 1850.

34. Ibid., 6, 9, and 10 May 1850.

35. Quoted by Hamilton, *Taylor*, 2:353. Hamilton attributed the resignations entirely to the differences between Taylor and Clay and felt that the editors' efforts to minimize these differences did not represent the true feelings of Taylor; see pp. 324-25, 332-34, 337.

36. *Daily Union*, 24 May 1850; *Republic*, 24 and 27 May 1850.

37. *Congressional Globe*, 21:1154-65.

38. Ibid., 22:789-800, 815-18, 852-59.

39. Hamilton, *Prologue to Conflict*, pp. 98-99; *Congressional Globe*, 21:1134, 1145-46, and 22:902, 911.

40. Hamilton, *Prologue to Conflict*, pp. 99-101; *Congressional Globe*, 21:1110, 1123, 1148, 1151, 1167, 1173-78, 1182-1201; Stevens's speech, p. 1218.

41. *Congressional Globe*, 21:1219.

42. Ibid., 22:676-84, for the entire speech.

43. Ibid., p. 681.

44. Ibid., 22:1565, 1574, 1579-80.

45. William C. Binkley, "The Question of Texas Jurisdiction in New Mexico under the United States, 1848-1850," *Southwestern Historical Quarterly* 26 (1920/21): 8-9; Senate Executive Document no. 74, *Congressional Documents*, 31st Cong., 1st sess., 1849/50, no. 562, p. 2.

46. Binkley, "The Question of Texas Jurisdiction in New Mexico," pp. 24-35; Hamilton, *Taylor*, 2:374-76.

47. James D. Richardson, comp., *A Compilation of the Messages and*

Papers of the Presidents, 1789–1897, vol. 5 (Washington, D. C.: Government Printing Office, 1900), pp. 47–48.

48. Dyer, *Taylor*, pp. 387–88; Hamilton, *Taylor*, 2:383.

49. *Congressional Globe*, 21:1319–21; *Republic*, 2 July 1850.

50. *Congressional Globe*, 22:1007.

51. Ibid., 22:1088–92, 1094–95.

52. *Charleston Mercury*, 1, 3, and 4 July 1850.

53. *Union*, 2 July 1850.

54. Hamilton, *Taylor*, 2:380.

55. Ibid., pp. 379, 382; Myrta A. Avary, ed., *Reminiscences of Alexander H. Stephens* (New York: Doubleday, Page & Co., 1910), pp. 26–27.

56. *National Intelligencer*, 6 July 1850.

57. Ibid., 12 July 1850; Hamilton, *Taylor*, 2:387–89.

58. Henry S. Foote, *War of the Rebellion; or, Scylla and Charybdis* (New York: Harpers, 1866), p. 149; Hamilton, *Prologue to Conflict*, p. 106.

59. Hamilton, *Taylor*, 2:388–93. Samuel Eliot Morison, *Oxford History of the American People* (New York: Oxford University Press, 1965), p. 573, also believed that Taylor's medical treatments did him more damage than the original ailment, but I also reached this conclusion independently.

60. Hamilton, *Taylor*, 2:392–98; and numerous press reports.

61. *Daily Union*, 7 and 10 July 1850.

62. *New York Tribune*, 10 July 1850. For examples of fluctuation see 23, 24, 26, 28, and 31 Jan., 9 Mar., 19 and 29 Apr., 13, 14, and 28 May, 3 and 29 June 1850.

63. *Charleston Mercury*, 11 July 1850.

CHAPTER 10
THE NEW PRESIDENT

1. Hiram Ketchum to Fillmore, 14 Mar. 1850, Millard Fillmore Papers, Buffalo Historical Society; *Albany Express*, 16 May 1849.

2. Mrs. Reed to Fillmore, 7 and 18 June 1849; Robert Beale to Charles W. Delevan, 15 June 1849, Fillmore Papers.

3. Fillmore to Abigail, 1, 5, and 7 Apr. 1850, Fillmore Papers.

4. Susannah Hamilton to Fillmore, 8 Feb. 1849, and Fillmore to Mrs. Hamilton, 31 July 1849, Fillmore Papers.

5. Priest to Fillmore, 4 Apr. 1850; Morse to Fillmore, 23 Feb. 1850; Cottingham to Fillmore—all in Fillmore Papers.

6. Todd to Fillmore, 10 Apr. 1850; Fillmore to Todd, 21 Apr. 1850, Fillmore Papers. Todd had worked very hard for Taylor's nomination and election, but for some reason he did not regain the post he wanted.

7. Jewett to Fillmore, 7 Apr. 1850; G. W. Hosher to Fillmore, 12 Apr. 1850; numerous letters to Miss Dix—all in Fillmore Papers; see also Charles M. Snyder, ed., *The Lady and the President: The Letters of Dorothea Dix and Millard Fillmore* (Lexington: University of Kentucky Press, 1975).

8. Henry to Fillmore, 23 June 1849 and 9 May 1850, concerning Smithsonian finances, and several other letters in Fillmore Papers.

9. Fillmore to Joseph Boughton, 24 July 1849; N. K. Hall to Fillmore, 27 July 1849; P. J. Wagner to Fillmore, 30 July 1849; Lothrop Cooke to Fillmore, 30 July 1849; other similar letters—all in Fillmore Papers; Robert Rayback, *Millard Fillmore: Biography of a President* (Buffalo, N.Y.: Henry Steward, Inc., for the Buffalo Historical Society, 1959), pp. 211–13; John T. Bush to Fillmore, 24 June 1849, Fillmore Papers.

10. Rayback, *Millard Fillmore*, p. 212.

11. Fillmore to Edward Everett, 11 July 1849, Fillmore Papers.

12. *Congressional Globe*, 31st Cong., 1st sess., 1849/50, vol. 21, pp. 631–32, for both Fillmore's report and Foote's response.

13. Rayback, *Millard Fillmore*, p. 214.

14. Ibid., pp. 225–28.

15. Ibid., p. 237; Fillmore to James Brooks, 24 May 1852, in Frank Severance, ed., *Millard Fillmore Papers*, 2 vols., vols. 10 and 11 of Publications of the Buffalo Historical Society (Buffalo, N.Y., 1907), 2:321–22.

16. Fish to Fillmore, 21 June 1850, Fillmore Papers.

17. Rayback, *Millard Fillmore*, pp. 255–56; Allan Nevins, *Ordeal of the Union*, 2 vols. (New York: Scribner's, 1947), 1:336–37.

18. Scott to Colonel Munroe, 5 Aug. 1850, cited by William C. Binkley in "The Question of Texas Jurisdiction in New Mexico under the United States, 1848–50," *Southwestern Historical Quarterly* 26 (1920/21): 32–33. In a speech at Louisville, Kentucky, on 15 Mar. 1854, Fillmore recalled that he had "ordered a portion of the army and munitions of war to the frontier of Texas. . . . The army was put in motion, and then, and not till then, did Congress act upon the subject" (Severance, *Millard Fillmore Papers*, 1:432).

CHAPTER 11
THE COMPROMISE

1. *Charleston (S.C.) Mercury*, 18 Sept. 1850.

2. Grace Greenwood (Sarah J. Lippincott), *Greenwood Leaves* (Boston, Mass.: Ticknor, Reed, & Fields, 1852), p. 304.

3. *Congressional Globe*, 31st Cong., 1st sess., 1849/50, vol. 21, pp. 1380–83; ibid., 31st Cong., 1st sess., vol. 22 (app.), pp. 1261–66.

4. Ibid., 22:1389–94.

5. Ibid., pp. 1246–52.

6. Ibid., p. 1413; the entire speech is on pp. 1405–14.

7. For entire debates, 24–31 July 1850, see *Congressional Globe*, 21:1448,

1456–57, 1481–82, 1490–91; and 22:1420–85; Holman Hamilton, *Prologue to Conflict: The Crisis and Compromise of 1850* (Lexington: University of Kentucky Press, 1965), pp. 108–17.

8. *Congressional Globe,* 22:1449–56; *New York Express,* 6 Aug. 1850.

9. *Congressional Globe,* 22:1470–72.

10. Robert Rayback, *Millard Fillmore: Biography of a President* (Buffalo, N.Y.: Henry Steward, Inc., for the Buffalo Historical Society, 1959), pp. 249–50. Rayback cites Bernard Steiner, "Some Letters from the Letters of James Alfred Pearce," *Maryland Historical Magazine* 16 (1921): 332, in evidence, but nothing on this page or in several following articles supports the story. The above title actually applies to pages 150–78. See also Steiner, "James Alfred Pearce," *Maryland Historical Magazine* 16:319–39; 17 (1922): 33–47, 177–90, 269–83, 348–63; 18 (1923): 38–52, 134–50, 257–73, 341–57; 19 (1924): 13–28, 162–79. These continuing sketches of Pearce and quotations from his letters are neither chronological nor well organized and must be read in full to get a comprehensive picture of Pearce in 1850.

11. *Congressional Globe,* 22:1025–29.

12. Ibid., 22:1473–88, for 31 July proceedings; cf. Hamilton, *Prologue to Conflict,* pp. 109–17.

13. *Congressional Globe,* 22:1473.

14. Ibid., p. 1474.

15. Ibid., p. 1475.

16. Ibid., pp. 1476–78.

17. Elizabeth Blair Lee to Samuel Phillips Lee, 1 Aug. 1850, Blair-Lee Papers, Princeton University, Princeton, N.J.

18. *New York Express,* 2 Aug. 1830; Allan Nevins, *Ordeal of the Union,* 2 vols. (New York: Scribner's, 1947), 1:340.

19. Hamilton, *Prologue to Conflict,* pp. 111–13.

20. *New York Express,* 1 and 2 Aug. 1850; *National Intelligencer,* 2 and 3 Aug. 1850; *Republic,* 1 and 2 Aug. 1850; *Daily Union,* 11, 12, 23, and 30 July, 1 and 4 Aug. 1850; *Albany* (N.Y.) *Evening Journal,* 2 Aug. 1850; *Charleston Mercury,* 2 Aug. 1850.

21. George F. Milton, *The Eve of Conflict: Stephen A. Douglas and the Needless War* (Boston, Mass.: Houghton Mifflin, 1934), pp. 74–75.

22. Webster to Fillmore, 30 July, 3 and 6 Aug. 1850, Fillmore Papers, Buffalo Historical Society; James D. Richardson, comp., *A Compilation of the Messages and Papers of the Presidents, 1789–1897,* vol. 5 (Washington, D.C.: Government Printing Office, 1900), pp. 67–73. Rayback, *Millard Fillmore,* p. 251, cites only the part of the message that asks Congress to set the boundary. He omits most of the important segments, which I have quoted and which drew by far the most attention.

23. *Congressional Globe,* 21:1540–45, 1551–52, 1554–56, and 22:1517, 1561–81; Hamilton, *Prologue to Conflict,* pp. 136–38.

24. *Congressional Globe,* 22:1241–44.

25. *Daily Union,* 7, 9, and 10 Aug. 1850.

26. *Congressional Globe*, 22:1081–84.

27. *Charleston Mercury*, 10 and 20 Aug. 1850.

28. *Congressional Globe*, 22:1107–9; *National Intelligencer*, 14 Aug. 1850.

29. *National Intelligencer*, 13 Aug. 1850.

30. *New York Daily Tribune*, 6 and 8 Aug. 1850.

31. *Congressional Globe*, 22:1615; *New York Express*, 6 Aug. 1850; Hamilton, *Prologue to Conflict*, p. 140.

32. Hamilton, *Prologue to Conflict*, pp. 140–41.

33. *Republic*, 10 and 22 Aug. 1850.

34. *Daily Union*, 17, 18, 21, 24, 27, and 31 Aug. and 3 Sept. 1850. The *National Intelligencer*, 20 Aug. 1850, denied the charge. Fillmore letters are in Fillmore Papers.

35. Hamilton, *Prologue to Conflict*, p. 129; for full treatment of the bond issue, see pp. 118–32.

36. *Congressional Globe*, 21:1682–87, 1695–1704; Hamilton, *Prologue to Conflict*, pp. 155–56.

37. *Congressional Globe*, 21:1727, 1736–38, 1746–50; Hamilton, *Prologue to Conflict*, pp. 157–58; *National Intelligencer*, 6 and 7 Sept. 1850.

38. *Congressional Globe*, 21:1762–64; Hamilton, *Prologue to Conflict*, pp. 158–59.

39. Hamilton, *Prologue to Conflict*, pp. 141–42, 161–64, for analysis of the voting, but not for my generalizations.

40. Douglas to Charles H. Lanphier and George Walker, 3 Aug. 1850, quoted by Hamilton, *Prologue to Conflict*, pp. 146–47.

41. Chase to E. S. Hamlin, 14 Aug. 1850, in Edward G. Bourne et al., eds., "Diary and Correspondence of Salmon P. Chase," *Annual Report of the American Historical Association for the Year 1902*, vol. 2 (Washington, D.C.: Government Printing Office, 1903), p. 217.

42. *Charleston Mercury*, 21 and 26 Sept. 1850.

CHAPTER 12
THE NATION'S LEADER

1. Fillmore Papers, Buffalo Historical Society.

2. Letters of 11 July 1850, and undated, no. 580, ibid.

3. Letters of 15 and 20 July 1850, ibid.

4. Letters of 29 July, 12 and 14 Aug., and 5 Sept. 1850, as well as other similar letters in Fillmore Papers.

5. Letter of 30 July 1850, ibid.

6. These letters and others like them in Fillmore Papers.

7. Fillmore to Dorothea Dix, 15, 22, and 27 Sept. 1850, ibid.

8. Fillmore to Bliss, 7 Oct. 1850, ibid.

9. List and menu, ibid.

10. Ibid.

11. Fillmore to Millard Fillmore, Jr., 31 July 1850, ibid.

12. Robert Rayback, *Millard Fillmore: Biography of a President* (Buffalo: Henry Steward, Inc., for the Buffalo Historical Society, 1959), pp. 291–92.

13. Ibid., p. 294; George Fort Milton, *The Eve of Conflict: Stephen A. Douglas and the Needless War* (Boston, Mass.: Houghton Mifflin, 1934), pp. 9–11.

14. Rayback, *Millard Fillmore*, pp. 289–90.

15. Ibid., pp. 293–94.

16. Ibid., pp. 252–53; Mrs. Chapman Coleman, *The Life of John J. Crittenden*, 2 vols. (Philadelphia: J. B. Lippincott Co., 1871), 1:377.

17. James D. Richardson, comp., *A Compilation of the Messages and Papers of the Presidents, 1789–1897*, vol. 5 (Washington, D.C.: Government Printing Office, 1900), pp. 80, 93.

18. Fish to Fillmore, 21 June and 17 Sept. 1850; Fillmore to Fish, 20 Sept. 1850; Fillmore to Seward, 20 July 1850—all in Fillmore Papers; Rayback, *Millard Fillmore*, pp. 256–57.

19. Glyndon Van Deusen, *William Henry Seward* (New York: Oxford University Press, 1967), pp. 65–67, 93–95, 102–4, 122–24, 140. After all of his rhetoric, Seward in 1852 voted against Charles Sumner's move to repeal the fugitive-slave law.

20. Ullman to Fillmore, 21 and 24 Sept. and 5 Oct. 1850; Fillmore to Ullman, 22 Sept. and 3 Oct. 1850, Fillmore Papers; Rayback, *Millard Fillmore*, pp. 258–59; Van Deusen, *William Henry Seward*, pp. 134–36.

21. Rayback, *Millard Fillmore*, pp. 259–67.

22. Allan Nevins, *Ordeal of the Union*, 2 vols. (New York: Scribner's, 1947), 1:345–50; Avery Craven, *Coming of the Civil War* (New York: Scribner's Sons, 1942), pp. 259–64.

23. Fillmore to Webster, 23 Oct. 1850, Fillmore Papers; Rayback, *Millard Fillmore*, p. 277; Richardson, *Messages and Papers of the Presidents*, 5:93.

24. Rayback, *Millard Fillmore*, pp. 278–81.

25. Ibid., pp. 279–84; cf. Nevins, *Ordeal of the Union*, 1:395–96.

26. Nevins, *Ordeal of the Union*, 1:354–56; David Potter, *The Impending Crisis*, completed and edited by Don E. Fehrenbacher (New York: Harper & Row, 1976), pp. 125–28. The resolutions are given verbatim in Richard M. Johnston and William H. Browne, *Life of Alexander H. Stephens* (Philadelphia: J. B. Lippincott Co., 1878), pp. 259–60.

27. *U.S. Statutes at Large*, vol. 9 (1845–51), pp. 462–65.

28. William Still, *The Underground Railroad* (reprint, New York: Arno Press, 1968), catalogs many such cases; cf. Craven, *Coming of the Civil War*, pp. 309–12; Nevins, *Ordeal of the Union*, 1:382–83.

29. Nevins, *Ordeal of the Union* 1:383–84.

30. Ibid., pp. 390–91.

31. Rayback, *Millard Fillmore*, pp. 270-71.

32. Ibid., pp. 272-73; Still, *Underground Railroad*, pp. 368-77.

33. Craven, *Coming of the Civil War*, pp. 309-10; *Congressional Globe*, 31st Cong., 2d sess., 1850/51, vol. 23, pp. 491, 573-79, 595-99, 660-61, 675.

34. *Congressional Globe*, 23:575, 576-79.

35. Ibid., pp. 307-8, 597-99, 811.

36. Henry S. Foote, *Casket of Reminiscences* (Washington, D.C.: Chronicle Publishing Co., 1880), pp. 162-65.

37. Alexander K. McClure, *Recollections of Half A Century* (Salem, Mass.: Salem Press Co., 1902), pp. 18-23, tells this story in great detail and calls it the first battle of the Civil War.

38. Nevins, *Ordeal of the Union*, 1:358-61, 362-64, 370-71; Rollin G. Osterweis, *Romanticism and Nationalism in the Old South* (New Haven, Conn.: Yale University Press, 1949), pp. 132-54.

39. Nevins, *Ordeal of the Union*, 1:372-74.

40. Ibid., pp. 374-75; Potter, *Impending Crisis*, pp. 125-30.

41. After approving the compromise on 6 October, the *Union* announced that the heroes of the struggle were Lewis Cass and Daniel S. Dickinson, while Fillmore "in defiance of right and of justice had sanctioned the illegal proceedings of Gen. Taylor's cabinet."

42. Rayback, *Millard Fillmore*, pp. 274-75.

CHAPTER 13

MANIFEST DESTINY—WITH LIMITS

1. Meribeth E. Cameron et al., *China, Japan, and the Powers* (New York: Ronald Press, 1952), pp. 163-79; Harold M. Vinacke, *A History of the Far East in Modern Times* (New York: Appleton-Century-Crofts, Inc., 1950), pp. 29-52.

2. James D. Richardson, comp., *A Compilation of the Messages and Papers of the Presidents, 1789-1897*, vol. 5 (Washington, D.C.: Government Printing Office, 1900), p. 121; Robert Rayback, *Millard Fillmore: Biography of a President* (Buffalo: Henry Steward, Inc., for the Buffalo Historical Society, 1959), p. 296; Robert R. Russel, *Improvement of Communication with the Pacific Coast as an Issue in American Politics, 1783-1864* (Cedar Rapids, Iowa: Torch Press, 1948), pp. 54-61.

3. Rayback, *Millard Fillmore*, pp. 302-5; Russel, *Improvement of Communication with the Pacific Coast*, pp. 73-85; Richardson, *Messages and Papers of the Presidents*, 5:155-56.

4. Fillmore to Webster, 19 July 1851, cited by Rayback in *Millard Fillmore*, p. 306, see also pp. 305-9; Russel, *Improvement of Communication with the Pacific Coast*, pp. 86-94.

5. Russel, *Improvement of Communication with the Pacific Coast*, pp.

93-94.

6. Rayback, *Millard Fillmore*, pp. 310-12; Richardson, *Messages and Papers of the Presidents*, 5:120, 159; R. W. Alstyne, "Great Britain and the United States and Hawaiian Independence, 1850-55," *Pacific Historical Review* 4 (1935): 15-16.

7. Cameron et al., *China, Japan, and the Powers*, pp. 114-17.

8. Rayback, *Millard Fillmore*, pp. 313-17; Thomas A. Bailey, *A Diplomatic History of the American People*, 10th ed. (Englewood Cliffs, N.J.: Prentice-Hall, 1980), pp. 309-11; Cameron et al., *China, Japan, and the Powers*, pp. 192-99.

9. Rayback, *Millard Fillmore*, pp. 319-21; Richardson, *Messages and Papers of the Presidents*, 5:167; Maurice G. Baxter, *Daniel Webster and the Union* (Cambridge, Mass.: Belknap Press of Harvard University Press, 1984), p. 473.

10. Rayback, *Millard Fillmore*, pp. 321-27; Richardson, *Messages and Papers of the Presidents*, 5:111-15, 165-66; Bailey, *Diplomatic History*, pp. 289-91; Oscar T. Barck, Jr., and Nelson M. Blake, *The United States in Its World Relations* (New York: McGraw-Hill, 1960), pp. 242-44; Thomas G. Paterson et al., *American Foreign Policy*, 2 vols. (Lexington, Mass.: D. C. Heath & Co., 1983), 1:130-33.

11. Paterson et al., *American Foreign Policy*, p. 133-34; Bailey, *Diplomatic History*, p. 291; Barck and Blake, *United States in Its World Relations*, p. 244; Paterson thinks Everett was "hunting larks with an elephant rifle."

12. Richardson, *Messages and Papers of the Presidents*, 5:165-66; Rayback, *Millard Fillmore*, pp. 326-27.

13. Richardson, *Messages and Papers of the Presidents*, 5:117; Rayback, *Millard Fillmore*, p. 324; Barck and Blake, *United States in Its World Relations*, pp. 261-62.

14. Richardson, *Messages and Papers of the Presidents*, 5:165; Rayback, *Millard Fillmore*, pp. 324-25; Basil Rauch, "American Interest in Cuba," in William A. Williams, ed., *The Shaping of American Diplomacy* (Chicago: Rand McNally & Co., 1964), pp. 265-66.

15. Daniel Webster, *Writings and Speeches of Daniel Webster*, 18 vols. (Boston, Mass.: Little, Brown & Co., 1903), 10:165; Rayback, *Millard Fillmore*, pp. 328-29; Baxter, *Daniel Webster and the Union*, pp. 464-67.

16. Glyndon Van Deusen, *William Henry Seward* (New York: Oxford University Press, 1967), pp. 139-40; Elbert B. Smith, *Francis Preston Blair* (New York: Free Press, 1980), p. 209.

17. Rayback, *Millard Fillmore*, pp. 330-31; Benjamin Perley Poore, *Perley's Reminiscences of Sixty Years in the National Metropolis*, 2 vols. (Washington, D.C., 1886), 2:405.

18. Rayback, *Millard Fillmore*, p. 331; Webster, *Writings and Speeches*, 13:452.

19. Bailey, *Diplomatic History*, pp. 271-72. The 1851/52 session of

Congress spent an enormous amount of time debating the Kossuth issue. Perhaps it was a healthy diversion. See *Congressional Globe*, 32d Cong., 1st sess., vol. 24.

20. Bailey, *Diplomatic History*, p. 271; Barck and Blake, *United States in Its World Relations*, pp. 222-23.

CHAPTER 14
THE DEATH OF A PARTY

1. Allan Nevins, *Ordeal of the Union*, 2 vols. (New York: Scribner's, 1947), 1:391-94, 400-402.

2. *Congressional Globe*, 32d Cong., 1st sess., 1851/52, vol. 24. The Kossuth citations are too numerous for mention; James D. Richardson, comp., *A Compilation of the Messages and Papers of the Presidents*, vol. 5 (Washington, D.C.: Government Printing Office, 1900), pp. 83-85, 122-26.

3. *Congressional Globe*, 24:21, 272, 577, 878, 941, 1187, 1460, 1793, 2100, 2232, 2438, 2466, 2468. The dearth of serious achievement is indicated by the index.

4. Ibid., 24:531-35, 1934-38.

5. For the entire 1852 campaign see Roy Nichols and Jeannette Nichols, "The 1852 Election," in *History of American Presidential Elections*, ed. Arthur M. Schlesinger, Jr., 10 vols. (New York: Chelsea House, 1971), 2:921-1002; Nevins, *Ordeal of the Union*, 2:16-23; David Potter, *The Impending Crisis*, completed and edited by Don E. Fehrenbacher (New York: Harper & Row, 1976), p. 142.

6. Nevins, *Ordeal of the Union*, 2:32-33; Elbert B. Smith, *Francis Preston Blair* (New York: Free Press, 1980), pp. 210-11; Potter, *Impending Crisis*, p. 142.

7. Robert Rayback, *Millard Fillmore: Biography of a President* (Buffalo: Henry Steward, Inc., for the Buffalo Historical Society, 1959), pp. 334-35.

8. Ibid., pp. 336-39; Maurice G. Baxter, *Daniel Webster and the Union* (Cambridge, Mass.: Belknap Press of Harvard University Press, 1984), pp. 484-90.

9. Rayback, *Millard Fillmore*, p. 341; Glyndon Van Deusen, *William Henry Seward* (New York: Oxford University Press, 1967), pp. 141-42, denied that Seward actually supported Scott, but this was certainly the universally held impression in the South.

10. Rayback, *Millard Fillmore*, pp. 341-43; Baxter, *Daniel Webster and the Union*, pp. 488-90; Nevins, *Ordeal of the Union*, 2:25-26.

11. Ray A. Billington, *The Protestant Crusade, 1800-1860* (New York: Reinhart & Co., 1952 edition), pp. 380-81; Rayback, *Millard Fillmore*, pp. 343-45.

12. *National Intelligencer*, 24 Mar. 1852; Rayback, *Millard Fillmore*,

pp. 350–51.

13. Rayback, *Millard Fillmore*, p. 352.

14. Ibid., pp. 352–54.

15. Ibid., pp. 354–58; Baxter, *Daniel Webster and the Union*, pp. 489–92.

16. Rayback, *Millard Fillmore*, p. 358.

17. Ibid., pp. 359–60.

18. Ibid., pp. 360–61; Baxter, *Daniel Webster and the Union*, pp. 491–92.

19. Rayback, *Millard Fillmore*, pp. 362–63; Glyndon Van Deusen, *Thurlow Weed, Wizard of the Lobby* (New York: Da Capo Press, 1969; reprint of 1947 edition), pp. 191–92; Potter, *Impending Crisis*, pp. 233–38; Michael F. Holt, *The Political Crisis of the 1850s* (New York: W. W. Norton & Co., 1978), pp. 96–99, 118–23; Van Deusen, *William Henry Seward*, pp. 142–44; Nevins, *Ordeal of the Union*, 2:33–38.

20. Rayback, *Millard Fillmore*, pp. 367–68.

21. Ibid., pp. 368–69.

22. Richardson, *Messages and Papers of the Presidents*, 5:163–82.

23. Rayback, *Millard Fillmore*, pp. 372–74.

CHAPTER 15
THE AFTERMATH

1. Ray A. Billington, *The Protestant Crusade, 1800–1860* (New York: Reinhart & Co., 1952 edition), pp. 193–211, 262–80, 322–430, for entire Know Nothing story.

2. Ibid., pp. 393–94, describes this motive but names no names.

3. Robert Rayback, *Millard Fillmore: Biography of a President* (Buffalo: Henry Steward, Inc., for the Buffalo Historical Society, 1959), pp. 390–96.

4. Ibid., p. 399.

5. Ibid., pp. 403–14, quotation on p. 407.

6. Ibid., pp. 415–45.

BIBLIOGRAPHICAL ESSAY

The technological and economic progress of the 1840s and the 1850s has been well catalogued in books like Thomas C. Cochrane and Thomas B. Brewer, eds., *Views of American Economic Growth* (New York: McGraw-Hill, 1966); Gilbert C. Fite and Jim E. Reese, *An Economic History of the United States* (Boston: Houghton Mifflin Co., 1965); Robert Sobel, *Machines and Morality: The 1850s* (New York: Thomas Y. Crowell Co., 1973); Allan Nevins, *Ordeal of the Union*, vol. 1 (New York: Scribner's, 1947); and any number of American-history textbooks. My own figures came from the invaluable United States Bureau of the Census, *The Statistical History of the United States from Colonial Times to the Present* (New York: Basic Books, 1978). Other background books that contribute to an understanding of the United States that elected Taylor and Fillmore include John Ward, *Andrew Jackson: Symbol for an Age* (New York: Oxford University Press, 1955); Edward Pessen, *Jacksonian America: Society, Personality, and Politics* (Homewood, Ill.: Dorsey Press, 1969); Arthur M. Schlesinger, Jr., *The Age of Jackson* (Boston: Little, Brown & Co., 1949); Henry G. Goode and James D. Teller, *A History of Western Education* (New York: Macmillan, 1969); Lawrence A. Cremin, *American Education: The National Experience* (New York: Harper & Row, 1980); Alice F. Tyler, *Freedom's Ferment: Phases of American Social History to 1860* (Minneapolis: University of Minnesota Press, 1944); William S. Jenkins, *Pro-Slavery Thought in the Old South* (Gloucester, Mass.: P. Smith, 1960); George Fitzhugh, *Sociology for the South; or, The Failure of Free Society*, and *Cannibals All; or, Slaves without Masters* (both Richmond, Va.: A. Morris, 1854 and 1857); Leon F. Litwack, *North of Slavery: The Negro in the Free States* (Chicago: University of Chicago Press, 1961); Winthrop Jordan,

White over Black (Chapel Hill: University of North Carolina Press, 1968); Bertram Wyatt-Brown, *Honor and Violence in the Old South* (New York: Oxford University Press, 1986); Charles Sellers, ed., *The Southerner as American* (Chapel Hill: University of North Carolina Press, 1960); Frederick Jackson Turner, *The Frontier in American History* and *The Significance of Sections in American History* (New York: Henry Holt & Co., 1920 and 1932); Stanley Elkins, *Slavery: A Problem in American Institutional and Intellectual Life* (Chicago: University of Chicago Press, 1959); Ray A. Billington, *The Protestant Crusade, 1800–1860* (New York: Reinhart & Co., 1952 edition); Ralph Gabriel, *The Course of American Democratic Thought* (New York: Ronald Press, 1956); Vernon L. Parrington, *Main Currents in American Thought*, vol. 2 (New York: Harcourt, Brace & World, 1958 edition); and Merle Curti, *The Growth of American Thought* (New York: Harper & Row, 1964 edition); to name only a few.

Most of Zachary Taylor's personal papers were apparently destroyed by the Union army during the Civil War, but the few remaining ones are highly revealing. His *Letters of Zachary Taylor from the Battlefields of the Mexican War*, edited by William H. Samson at Rochester, New York, in 1908, and his letters at the Library of Congress, comprising two rolls of microfilm that are easily attainable, are our only sizable collections. The modern biographies of Taylor by Brainerd Dyer, *Zachary Taylor* (Baton Rouge: Louisiana State University Press, 1946); Holman Hamilton, *Zachary Taylor, Soldier of the Republic* and *Zachary Taylor, Soldier in the White House* (Indianapolis, Ind.: Bobbs-Merrill Co., 1941 and 1951); and K. Jack Bauer, *Zachary Taylor* (Baton Rouge: Louisiana State University Press, 1985) are excellent books, although I disagree with their portrayals of Taylor's role in the sectional conflict of 1850. Dyer is highly anecdotal; Hamilton is most detailed but occasionally confusing because of his entirely chronological organization; and Bauer is best on Taylor's military career and is more critical. Dyer attributed Taylor's disagreements with Clay to Taylor's jealousy; Hamilton found Taylor's objections to the compromise wise because the agreements did not prevent the later Civil War; Bauer believed that Taylor had deliberately abandoned his Southern allies because the Northern Whigs were more numerous.

Fillmore, on the other hand, left a large collection of papers but has received only one full biography. In 1907 Frank Severance edited two volumes of *Millard Fillmore Papers*, Buffalo Historical Society Publications, vols. 10 and 11, but the original collection has been much expanded and microfilmed. Robert Rayback, *Millard Fillmore: Biography of a President* (Buffalo, N.Y.: Buffalo Historical Society, 1959), did a superb job of following Fillmore through the maze of New York partisan politics and proved the high abilities and qualities of the man. Again, however, I have disagreements about 1850. The sketches of Taylor and Fillmore by Norman Graebner in Henry F. Graff, *The Presidents* (New York: Charles Scribner & Sons, 1984), are also well worth reading. The brief work by Benson Lee

Grayson, *The Unknown President: The Administration of Millard Fillmore* (Washington, D.C.: University Press of America, 1981), contains inaccuracies but offers some sound conclusions, particularly his emphasis upon the significance of Fillmore's strong stand against the Texas threat to New Mexico.

My interpretation of the relationship of Taylor and Fillmore to the sectional struggle comes primarily from the actual debates, speeches, and parliamentary maneuvering recorded in the *Congressional Globe* (Washington, D.C.: Rives & Blair) for the Thirtieth, Thirty-first, and Thirty-second Congresses, 1848–53; from selected newspapers that wielded great influence among other papers, as well as on the general public; from a number of highly relevant letters written by and about the two men; and from their public messages. The *Washington Daily Union* and its echo, the *Richmond* (Va.) *Enquirer*, presented a viciously unfavorable view of both presidents that has retained a long-time influence. Ironically, Thurlow Weed's praise for Taylor and his condemnation of Fillmore in his Albany, New York, *Evening Journal* helped create a false image of both men. The more logical portrayals of Taylor and Fillmore by the *National Intelligencer* (Washington, D.C.), the *Republic* (Washington, D.C.), and the *New York Tribune* have received less attention. The *New York Courier and Enquirer* and the *New York Express* also contradict the usual stereotypes. The *New York Evening Post* condemned both presidents for truckling to the South. The *Charleston* (S.C.) *Mercury* and its satellites, meanwhile, found no integrity, justice, or sanity anywhere among those unwilling to force slavery upon all of the new territories. The *New York Herald* for 13 and 23 June, and 17 and 21 August 1876 contains a vivid argument among Weed, Stephens, Clingman, Toombs, and Hamlin over whether or not Taylor threatened to hang the two Georgians in 1850.

The abundant published correspondence and other contemporary writings of the period include Richard K. Crallé, ed., *Reports and Public Letters of John C. Calhoun*, 6 vols. (New York: D. Appleton, 1864); J. Franklin Jameson, ed., "Correspondence of John C. Calhoun," *Annual Report of the American Historical Association*, 1899, vol. 2; Robert P. Brooks and Chauncey S. Boucher, eds., "Correspondence Addressed to John C. Calhoun, 1837–1849," *Annual Report of the American Historical Association*, 1929; James T. McIntosh, ed., *The Papers of Jefferson Davis* (Baton Rouge: Louisiana State University Press, 1981); *The Diary of James K. Polk during His Presidency, 1845 to 1849*, ed. Milo M. Quaife, 4 vols. (Chicago: A. C. McClurg & Co., 1910); *The Private Correspondence of Henry Clay*, ed. Calvin Colton (New York: A. S. Barnes Co., 1855); Edward G. Bourne et al., eds., "Diary and Correspondence of Salmon P. Chase," *Annual Report of the American Historical Association for the Year 1902*, vol. 2; Ulrich B. Phillips, ed., "The Correspondence of Robert Toombs, Alexander H. Stephens, and Howell Cobb," *Annual Report of the American Historical Association for the Year 1911*, vol. 2; Mrs. Chapman Coleman, *The Life of John J. Crittenden*, 2 vols. (Philadelphia: J. B. Lippincott Co., 1871); Daniel

Webster, *Writings and Speeches of Daniel Webster*, 18 vols. (Boston, Mass.: Little, Brown & Co., 1903); Bernard Steiner, "Some Letters from the Letters of James Alfred Pearce," *Maryland Historical Magazine*, vol. 16 (1921), and "James Alfred Pearce," ibid., vols. 16–19 (1921–24); Charles M. Snyder, ed., *The Lady and the President: The Letters of Dorothea Dix and Millard Fillmore* (Lexington: University of Kentucky Press, 1975); and James D. Richardson, comp., *A Compilation of the Messages and Papers of the Presidents, 1789–1897*, vol. 5 (Washington, D.C.: Government Printing Office, 1900).

In his *Thirty Years View*, vol. 2 (New York: D. Appleton Co., 1856), Thomas Hart Benton defended himself and Zachary Taylor against the charge of having been opposed to compromise. Other valuable memoirs include Henry S. Foote, *Casket of Reminiscences* (Washington, D.C.: Chronicle Publishing Co., 1880); *Autobiography of Thurlow Weed*, ed. Harriet A. Weed (Boston, Mass.: Houghton Mifflin Co., 1884); Thurlow Weed Barnes, *Memoirs of Thurlow Weed* (Boston, Mass: Houghton Mifflin Co., 1884); *William H. Seward: An Autobiography*, ed. Frederick W. Seward (New York: Derby & Miller, 1891); John Wentworth, *Congressional Reminiscences* (Chicago: Fergus Co., 1882); *Reminiscences of Alexander H. Stephens*, ed. Myrta A. Avary (New York: Doubleday, Page & Co., 1910), deals primarily with Stephens's brief imprisonment but contains some relevant pages; Nathan Sargent, *Public Men and Events*, 2 vols. (Philadelphia: J. B. Lippincott Co., 1875); *The Diary of Philip Hone*, ed. Bayard Tuckerman (New York: Dodd, Mead & Co., 1910); Benjamin Perley Poore, *Perley's Reminiscences of Sixty Years in the National Metropolis*, 2 vols. (Philadelphia: Hubbard Brothers, and New York: W. A. Houghton, 1886); Alexander K. McClure, *Recollections of Half a Century* (Salem, Mass.: Salem Press Co., 1902); Oliver Dyer, *Great Senators of the United States Fifty Years Ago* (New York: Robert Bonner's Sons, 1889); Grace Greenwood (Sarah J. Lippincott), *Greenwood Leaves* (Boston, Mass.: Ticknor, Reed, & Fields, 1852); E. L. Magoon, *Living Orators in America* (New York: Baker & Scribner, 1850); Horace Greeley, *Recollections of a Busy Life* (New York: J. B. Ford & Co., 1868); and Varina Davis, *Jefferson Davis*, vol. 1 (New York: Belford Co., 1890).

The many biographies that help illuminate the period include Glyndon Van Deusen's prodigious output: *The Life of Henry Clay* (Boston: Little, Brown & Co., 1937), *Thurlow Weed, Wizard of the Lobby* (Boston, Mass.: Little, Brown & Co., 1947; reprint Da Capo Press, 1969), *Horace Greeley: Nineteenth Century Crusader* (Philadelphia: University of Pennsylvania Press, 1953), and *William Henry Seward* (New York: Oxford University Press, 1967). John C. Calhoun has been treated very generously by Charles M. Wiltse, *John C. Calhoun*, 3 vols. (Indianapolis, Ind.: Bobbs-Merrill Co., 1944, 1949, and 1951), and by Margaret L. Coit, *John C. Calhoun: An American Portrait* (Boston, Mass.: Little, Brown & Co., 1950). Much more critical, and in my view more accurate, is Gerald M. Capers, *John C.*

Calhoun: Opportunist (Gainesville: University of Florida Press, 1960). Thomas Hart Benton's modern biographers are William N. Chambers, *Old Bullion Benton: Senator from the New West* (Boston: Little, Brown & Co., 1956), and Elbert B. Smith, *Magnificent Missourian: The Life of Thomas Hart Benton* (Philadelphia: J. B. Lippincott Co., 1958). Chambers portrays Benton as a free-soiler, while I point out Benton's vigorous campaigning in 1848 for Cass in New York and argue that Benton considered the free-soilers to be unnecessary threats to sectional peace. The Webster and Clay biographies are numerous and usually favorable. Claude M. Fuess, *Daniel Webster*, 2 vols. (Boston, Mass.: Little, Brown & Co., 1930), and Maurice G. Baxter, *Daniel Webster and the Union* (Cambridge, Mass.: Belknap Press of Harvard University Press, 1984), are devotees, while Richard Current, *Daniel Webster and the Rise of National Conservatism* (Boston, Mass.: Little, Brown & Co., 1955), and Norman D. Brown, *Daniel Webster and the Politics of Availability* (Athens: University of Georgia Press, 1969), are somewhat more critical. In addition to the work of Van Deusen, Clay has been eulogized by George Poage, *Henry Clay and the Whig Party* (Chapel Hill: University of North Carolina Press, 1936), and by Clement Eaton, *Henry Clay and the Art of American Politics* (Boston, Mass.: Little, Brown & Co., 1957), to name only two. Other biographies that are relevant to the Taylor-Fillmore presidencies include Clement Eaton, *Jefferson Davis* (New York: Free Press, 1977); Charles H. Ambler, *Thomas Ritchie: A Study in Virginia Politics* (Richmond, Va.: Bell Book & Stationery Co., 1913); Elbert B. Smith, *Francis Preston Blair* (New York: Free Press, 1980); Richard M. Johnston and William H. Brown, *Life of Alexander H. Stephens* (Philadelphia: J. B. Lippincott Co., 1878), which contains many of Stephens's letters verbatim; Rudolph R. Von Abele, *Alexander H. Stephens* (New York: A. A. Knopf, 1946); Ulrich B. Phillips, *The Life of Robert Toombs* (New York: B. Franklin Co., 1968; reprint of 1913 edition); Albert Kirwan, *John J. Crittenden* (Lexington: University of Kentucky Press, 1962); Richard H. Sewell, *John Hale and the Politics of Abolition* (Cambridge, Mass.: Harvard University Press, 1965); Richard Current, *Old Thad Stevens* (Madison: University of Wisconsin Press, 1942); Fawn Brodie, *Thad Stevens, Scourge of the South* (New York: Norton Press, 1959); George Fort Milton, *The Eve of Conflict: Stephen A. Douglas and the Needless War* (Boston, Mass.: Houghton Mifflin, 1934); Robert W. Johannsen, *Stephen A. Douglas* (New York: Oxford University Press, 1973); Bernard Steiner, *The Life of Reverdy Johnson* (Baltimore, Md.: Norman Remington Co., 1914); and Don E. Fehrenbacher, *Chicago Giant: A Biography of Long John Wentworth* (Madison, Wis.: American History Research Center, 1957). For quick reference to those who are not blessed with a handy biography, the *Dictionary of American Biography*, edited originally by Allen Johnson and Dumas Malone (New York: Charles Scribner's Sons, 1930–35, or later editions), is essential. Secretaries of state and secretaries of the navy may also be found in Samuel F. Bemis and Robert H. Ferrell, eds., *American Secretaries of State*

(New York: Cooper Square Publishers, 1963); and Paolo E. Coletta et al., eds., *American Secretaries of the Navy* (Annapolis, Md.: Naval Institute Press, 1980).

Books that deal with Taylor and Fillmore within the context of the coming of the Civil War are countless. Holman Hamilton's *Prologue to Conflict: The Crisis and Compromise of 1850* (Lexington: University of Kentucky Press, 1964) is a masterly study. While I analyzed a number of voting patterns for myself, I also depended heavily upon Hamilton's extensive calculations of who voted how on the various amendments. Allan Nevins's *Ordeal of the Union*, 2 vols., and *The Emergence of Lincoln*, 2 vols. (New York: Charles Scribner's Sons, 1947, 1950), are rich in detail, immensely readable, and sound in the author's stress upon racial prejudice and fears, but Nevins depends entirely too much upon the *Washington Daily Union* when dealing with the 1850 crisis. Avery Craven, in *Coming of the Civil War* (New York: Charles Scribner's Sons, 1942), was a pioneer in developing the so-called revisionist thesis that the Civil War resulted from human weaknesses and errors and might have been avoided. David Potter, *The Impending Crisis*, completed and edited by Don E. Fehrenbacher (New York: Harper & Row, 1976), offers many profound insights. Michael F. Holt, *The Political Crisis of the 1850s* (New York: W. W. Norton & Co., 1978; 1983 paperback edition), develops new ideas concerning the realignment of the major political parties on a sectional basis. I agree with everything except his belief that Zachary Taylor played a conscious role in the process. William L. Barney, *The Road to Secession: A New Perspective on the Old South* (New York: Praeger, 1972), argues that the Southern demand for equal rights in the territories stemmed from fears of social disintegration because of the excessive concentration of slaves in various areas. I would find the argument more persuasive if most of the Southern fire-eaters had not also advocated the reopening of the African slave trade. Eugene Genovese, *The Political Economy of Slavery* (New York: Pantheon Books, 1961), believes that slavery had to expand or die and that the planters had to expand it or lose their ruling-class status in Southern society. I find the evidence that many Southerners thought in these terms both sparse and unconvincing. Other related books well worth reading include Don E. Fehrenbacher, *The South and Three Sectional Crises* (Baton Rouge: Louisiana State University Press, 1980); William R. Brock, *Conflict and Transformation: The United States, 1844-1877* (New York: Penguin Books, 1975); George T. McJimsey, *The Dividing and Reuniting of America: 1848-1877* (Arlington Heights, Ill.: Forum Press, 1981); David Lindsey, *Americans in Conflict: The Civil War and Reconstruction* (Boston, Mass.: Houghton Mifflin, 1973); and James M. McPherson, *Ordeal by Fire: The Civil War and Reconstruction* (New York: A. A. Knopf, 1981). The elections of 1848 and 1852 are discussed thoroughly in Arthur M. Schlesinger, Jr., ed., *History of American Presidential Elections*, 4 vols. (New York: Chelsea House, 1971). For those who wish exposure to many differing interpretations, both old and new, there are excellent anthologies, such as Charles Crowe, ed., *The Age of Civil War and Reconstruction* (Homewood, Ill.: Dorsey Press, 1966 and 1975; I prefer the 1966 edition); Edwin Rozwenc, *The Causes of the American Civil War* (Lexington, Mass.: D. C. Heath & Co., 1972); Hans Trefousse, *The Civil War: Institutional Failure or Human Blunder* (Malibar, Fla.: Krieger Press, 1971).

Invaluable articles related to Taylor and Fillmore include William C. Binkley, "The Question of Texas Jurisdiction in New Mexico under the United States, 1848–1850," *Southwestern Historical Quarterly* 26 (1920/21); F. S. Donnell, "When Texas Owned New Mexico to the Rio Grande," *New Mexico Historical Review* 8 (1933); Loomis N. Gannaway, "New Mexico and the Sectional Controversy, 1846–1861," *New Mexico Historical Review* 18 (1943); William P. Brandon, "The Galphin Claim," *Georgia Historical Quarterly* 15 (1931); Richard Van Alstyne, "British Diplomacy and the Clayton-Bulwer Treaty," *Journal of Modern History* 11 (1939), and "Great Britain and the United States and Hawaiian Independence, 1850–55," *Pacific Historical Review* 4 (1935); Holman Hamilton, "Texas Bonds and Northern Profits: A Study in Compromise, Investment, and Lobby Influence," *Mississippi Valley Historical Review* 43 (1957); E. Merton Coulter, "The Downfall of the Whig Party," *Kentucky Historical Society Press* 22 (1924); and J. B. Lackey, "A Neglected Aspect of Isthmian Diplomacy," *American Historical Review* 41 (1936).

Books that contribute to an understanding of the Taylor and Fillmore foreign policies include Thomas A. Bailey, *A Diplomatic History of the American People*, 10th ed. (Englewood Cliffs, N.J.: Prentice-Hall, 1980); Oscar T. Barck, Jr., and Nelson M. Blake, *The United States in Its World Relations* (New York: McGraw-Hill, 1960); Armin Rappaport, *A History of American Diplomacy* (New York: Macmillan Co., 1975); Thomas G. Paterson et al., *American Foreign Policy*, vol. 1 (Lexington, Mass.: D. C. Heath & Co., 1983); William A. Williams, ed., *The Shaping of American Diplomacy*, vol. 1 (Chicago: Rand McNally & Co., 1964); Frederick Merk, *Manifest Destiny and Mission in America* (New York: Vintage Edition, 1966); Henry Blumenthal, *France and the United States* (Chapel Hill: University of North Carolina Press, 1970); J. Fred Rippy, *Latin America* (Ann Arbor: University of Michigan Press, 1958); Meribeth E. Cameron et al., *China, Japan, and the Powers* (New York: Ronald Press, 1952); Hosea B. Morse and Harley F. MacNair, *Far Eastern International Relations* (Boston, Mass.: Houghton Mifflin, 1931); Harold M. Vinacke, *A History of the Far East in Modern Times* (New York: Appleton-Century-Crofts, 1950); R. S. Kuykendall, *The Hawaiian Kingdom, 1778–1854* (Honolulu: University of Hawaii Press, 1938); and Robert R. Russel, *Improvement of Communication with the Pacific Coast as an Issue in American Politics, 1783–1864* (Cedar Rapids, Iowa: Torch Press, 1948). The last is particularly valuable on Central American relations.

To colleagues whose worthy books I have neglected I apologize.

INDEX